LICENSE TO DEAL

Investor's Blueprint for Dubai Real Estate

By

Moiz Rajkotwala

With contributions from

Hajra Jaafar

July 2025 Edition

Copyright & Disclaimer

License to Deal:
Investor's Blueprint for Dubai Real Estate

First Edition, July 2025

ISBN 978-1-9192565-1-1

Published by Regent & Co. UK

www.regentandco.uk

Author: Moiz Rajkotwala with contribution by Hajra Jaafar (Women and Real Estate – Investing with Confidence)

Cover and book design: Batul Saboowala / Point One Four

The information contained in this book is based on sources believed to be reliable and accurate at the time of publication. It is intended for educational purposes only and does not constitute legal, financial, or investment advice. The author and publisher disclaim any liability arising directly or indirectly from the use of the material contained in this publication. Readers are encouraged to consult appropriate professionals before making any investment decisions.

Dedication

To my mom, for your consistent presence, unwavering support, and endless belief in me.

To my life partner, Sumaiyah, for being by my side and having my back.

To my daughter, Naqiyah, for inspiring me to be better every day as I watch you soar and excel in everything you do. My software solutions for data analysis mentioned in this book are a direct outcome of you challenging me to code on my own, and this book is a direct outcome of you asking me to make a book out of the License to Deal course.

Acknowledgments

This book is the culmination of a journey supported by many. My heartfelt thanks go to all who, in their unique ways, made it possible.

To my brothers, Murtaza and Aziz, and my sister-in-law, Rehana, and my wonderful nieces, Asma and Munira, for your steadfast support and encouragement.

To Batul, designer par excellence, who has been with me for the past eight years through thick and thin. Your input and tireless effort are an inseparable part of this work.

To my exceptional team - Caroline, Rehana, Anisha, Fajar, Mamta, Jyotshna, Sayali, Prachi, and many others over time, whose support, insightful questions, and dedication have strengthened this book. Your ability to provide investors with patient, day-in and day-out solutions continues to inspire me to strive for better.

To my friend and co-writer, Hajra Jaafar. In the short time we have known each other, you have become my sounding board and a constant source of inspiration through your endless efforts to help others.

To my dear friends, Preeti, Khadeeja, Bindi, Tasneem, and Seemant, for your friendship and encouragement.

To Sanjay Pathak and Ali Barbhaya, my mentors and best friends. I have learned so much from you both and continue to turn to you whenever I need guidance. To Ali and Murtaza, my friends and partners who made Leap Ventures a reality.

To my BNI family, especially the BNI Evergreen chapter members. Each of you has helped me in many ways. A special thanks to Zen, collaborating with you to create a course was the spark that brought this book to life.

To all the investors, partners, and clients who have become friends. Your trust and support have deepened my understanding of this market.

Finally, to you, dear reader, I look forward to welcoming you into this extended family through the pages of this book, and I hope we can create many wins together.

Table of Contents

Important Disclaimer: The Ever-Evolving Dubai Real Estate Market

All legal, factual, pricing, and procedural details contained within this book are accurate to the best of my knowledge as of July 2025.

This book is designed to be your **"License to Deal,"** which is your comprehensive training, not your final legal document. It is your permission to engage with Dubai's property market from a position of strategic strength.

However, the real estate landscape in Dubai is a dynamic and forward-thinking environment. New laws, regulations, and processes are continuously being implemented to enhance market transparency and investor protection. As such, information presented here is intended as a foundational guide and strategic framework, not as definitive legal or financial advice for any specific transaction.

Before you proceed with any actual real estate deal, it is imperative that you conduct your own independent research and seek counsel from qualified professionals. Always verify all information with:

- **Government Authorities:** Such as the Dubai Land Department (DLD) and the Real Estate Regulatory Agency (RERA).
- **Developers:** For the latest project and payment plan details.
- **Qualified Brokers and Legal Experts:** For specific advice tailored to your situation.

Your **"License to Deal"** empowers you with the knowledge to navigate the market with confidence, but for the final destination, always confirm your route with a current map.

Bibliography Introduction

This book blends the most current market realities of Dubai with globally recognised investment principles, adapted to the emirate's unique regulatory, economic, and cultural environment. The research behind this work draws from official UAE government sources, leading market data platforms, authoritative consultancy reports, and respected international investment literature. Each strategy, framework, and case study presented here is grounded in verified information as of July 2025, ensuring relevance to today's market while providing timeless principles that apply across economic cycles. Where global concepts have been referenced, they have been reinterpreted through the lens of Dubai's property laws, market structure, and investor behaviours, resulting in a resource that is both locally specific and globally informed.

Foreword

In almost every area of life, whether it is mastering a skill or improving our well-being, we naturally seek training. From driving to swimming or even running, we strive to learn, practise, and sometimes get certified to gain essential knowledge. Yet, when faced with life-altering investment decisions that shape our future, many of us still rely on hearsay, instinct, or impulse.

This contradiction is striking. I firmly believe that we are stewards of the money that belongs to our future selves and our families. This responsibility demands care and a commitment to equipping ourselves with the proper knowledge and tools. This book, ***License to Deal,*** is designed to offer just that. It is your comprehensive guide to making informed decisions, regardless of your background or reasons for entering Dubai's real estate market. Whether you are investing for the first time, looking for a family home, expanding your portfolio, developing a project, or venturing into new sectors as a business owner, this book is for you.

My commitment to this principle was shaped by adversity. Seventeen years ago, as a young father and working professional, I made my first property investment in Dubai. The developer disappeared, and I lost everything. That experience occurred during the 2008 downturn, before today's escrow protections were in place. It cost me more than money. It compelled me to understand this market thoroughly, from residential apartments and commercial towers to villa plots and institutional transactions.

Since then, I have had the privilege of advising a wide range of clients, including first-time buyers, multinational developers, and global brands from the United Kingdom, India, Turkey, Russia, Morocco, and beyond. This book is the result of that journey. It contains practical insights, frameworks, and tools to help you avoid common mistakes and invest with confidence.

Think of this book as a hands-on guide. It is here to walk with you, not speak at you. You will find checklists, reflection prompts, and real-world case studies to support every step of your journey.

If you need personal guidance, help with analysing complex deals, or simply a sounding board for your strategy, I invite you to connect. Scan the QR code below to access my contact details and explore how I can support your success.

Moiz Rajkotwala

Founder & CEO,
Leap Ventures Real Estate

YOUR FOUR-PART

INVESTMENT JOURNEY

Before we dive into the details, it is important to see the big picture of your investment journey. This book is structured into four distinct parts, each building on the last to take you from preparation to execution, growth, and advanced strategies. Think of it as your roadmap, a clear sequence that ensures you never jump ahead without mastering the stage before it. Whether you are starting out or refining an existing portfolio, these stages will help you move with confidence, avoid costly mistakes, and stay focused on the results that matter.

PART 1

Defining the Opportunity – Preparation Phase

Laying the foundation for long-term success by shaping your mindset, understanding why Dubai is a strong investment market, identifying where to look, learning how to analyse opportunities, and knowing when to act.

PART 2

The Buying Blueprint – Execution Phase

Step-by-step guidance through the buying process, from due diligence and legal structures to taking handover of your property with confidence and security.

PART 3

Maximising Returns – Growth Phase

Strategies to generate consistent income and long-term value through both long-term leasing and short-term rentals, with practical tools for pricing, marketing, and management.

PART 4

Strategic Exits and Advanced Strategies – Expansion Phase

Going beyond the basics with advanced strategies for scaling your portfolio, exploring innovative investment approaches, and mastering strategic exits. This section also highlights the growing role of women in real estate, offering tailored insights, case studies, and resources to inspire and equip female investors to lead with confidence in Dubai's market.

Keppel

PART 1

Defining the Opportunity

Building Your Unshakeable Foundation for Success – The Preparation Phase

01

So, you are ready to enter the world of Dubai real estate. Perhaps it is a long-held dream, or maybe the opportunities this city presents have caught your attention. Whatever has brought you here, remember this: your journey is about far more than buying a property. It is about making informed, strategic decisions that align with your personal goals and the unique rhythm of this evolving market.

Part 1: **Defining the Opportunity** is the preparation phase of your investment journey. This is where you replace guesswork with a structured, evidence-based approach, ensuring that every step you take is deliberate and aligned with long-term success.

The most profitable investments are made long before any contract is signed. That is why, before we explore buying, leasing, or flipping, we will work through a sequence that moves from big-picture thinking to precise, data-backed execution.

In this part, you will:

How to Think
Learn to think like a professional investor by building the C.D.R.C. pillars (Clarity, Discipline, Resilience, and Strategic Choice) and applying the L.E.A.D. approach (Long Game, Embrace Calculated Risk, Adapt, Drive Value). Define SMART investment goals that guide every decision (Chapter 1).

Why to Invest
Understand why Dubai offers exceptional opportunity by examining its policy framework, safety, demographics, and economic engines. See how these drivers support growth, stability, and global capital inflows (Chapter 2).

Where to Look: Macro View
Discover how Dubai's long-term vision, urban planning, and mega-projects shape its real estate landscape. Learn the core, emerging, and peripheral zones concept, and understand why Dubai functions as a magnet for wealth, talent, and innovation (Chapter 3).

When to Act
Recognise the patterns in real estate cycles and learn how to time your entry and exit using inflection indicators such as transaction momentum, yield compression, and policy catalysts (Chapter 4).

How to Quantify
Master the essential real estate math that turns raw numbers into clear investment decisions. From ROI to cash-on-cash returns, align the right financial metrics with your strategy (Chapter 5).

What to Invest In
Compare residential and commercial property types, weigh off-plan versus ready investments, and understand legal structures such as freehold, leasehold, and usufruct (Chapter 6).

How to Validate
Conduct rigorous research and due diligence for both off-plan and secondary market properties, using structured frameworks to evaluate developers, projects, and communities (Chapter 7).

By the time you complete Part 1, you will have a complete, evidence-based investment blueprint, knowing exactly how to think, why Dubai deserves your capital, where to look, when to move, what to invest in, and how to validate every decision.

This clarity will give you the confidence and competitive edge to act decisively as you move into **Part 2: From Plan to Purchase**, where strategy becomes execution.

CHAPTER 1

The Dubai Real Estate Mindset: Clarity, Discipline, and Goals

> An investment in knowledge pays the best interest.
>
> **Benjamin Franklin**

Imagine standing at the edge of Dubai's incredible skyline, cranes reaching high, towers shimmering, the city constantly in motion. Every day here truly brings new opportunities. Before any property search, contract negotiation, or investment calculation, there is a more critical starting point: how you think, and what shapes your decisions

This chapter is all about hitting the reset button on your mindset. It lays the crucial groundwork for that fundamental shift, focusing on building the mental habits and discipline that genuinely set serious investors apart from those simply chasing the next shiny deal. You will discover how to cultivate clarity, resilience, and the right kind of curiosity. These are invaluable traits that transform casual interest into genuine confidence, and a first deal into a robust, growing portfolio. This overview will guide you through mindfully reflecting on your goals and defining the investor mindset that will serve you well.

In this market, your mindset is arguably your most powerful asset. It will dictate how you react to market swings, how you analyse potential deals, and crucially, whether you adhere to your strategy when emotions threaten to take over. Dubai's market is wonderfully dynamic, and sometimes, yes, a little unpredictable. But it's those who invest with clear intention and unwavering resilience who truly thrive.

1.1. The Real Estate Investor Mindset Defined

Thinking like a savvy investor isn't just about crunching numbers; it's about maintaining clarity, discipline, and staying firmly rooted in logic over emotion. Successful investors don't drift; they set crystal-clear goals, follow a well-defined strategy, and base their decisions on solid data rather than fleeting trends or hype. This precise mindset empowers you to navigate market volatility, steer clear of impulsive decisions, and consistently keep your focus on long-term outcomes. It also demands a commitment to continuous learning, enabling you to adapt gracefully to new regulations, market cycles, and emerging opportunities.

Below, you'll find the four core pillars that define a winning investor mindset, each supported by key habits that consistently separate seasoned professionals from casual speculators:

- **Confidence through Clarity:** Start by being clear about your goal. Are you looking for capital growth, passive income, or simply spreading risk across a few assets? Your "why" should guide every property decision you make. And here's something most people overlook — are you investing, or are you planning to live in the property? That one choice changes everything about how you think, what you buy, and how you measure success.
- **Discipline in Execution:** Consistently follow your investment strategy, even when the market is noisy or full of hype. Stick to your due diligence process before every deal. Actively avoid impulsive buying that's driven by fleeting emotions, a sense of urgency, or peer pressure.
- **Resilience Under Volatility:** Remain calm and composed during market dips, policy shifts, or unexpected delayed handovers. Always focus on the long-term value of your investment rather than getting caught up in short-term fluctuations. Build both financial and mental buffers to handle any uncertainty with genuine confidence.
- **Curiosity for Continuous Learning:** Keep yourself in the loop. Follow changes in laws, notice how developers behave, and watch which areas are picking up. Study every deal you can — yours or someone else's — and figure out what worked and what didn't. The more you learn, the sharper you get. That curiosity is what keeps you ahead of the game.

To help these core pillars stick in your mind, think of them with the mnemonic: **C.D.R.C. - Clarity, Discipline, Resilience, and Curiosity.**

You can also visualise these pillars as your **Investor's Compass**, guiding your journey through Dubai's real estate landscape:

- **Confidence through Clarity:** This is your **North Star** – clearly defining your ultimate destination and what success truly looks like for you.
- **Discipline in Execution:** This is the **Unwavering Needle** – consistently pointing you towards your planned route, ensuring you stick to your strategy even when external forces try to pull you off course.
- **Resilience Under Volatility:** This is the **Durable Casing** – protecting your compass (and your mindset) from the storms, unexpected detours, and bumps you'll encounter along the investment journey.

- **Curiosity for Continuous Learning:** This is the Ever-Updating Map – constantly seeking new information to refine your route, discover unexplored terrains, and adapt to changing conditions. Your commitment to learning empowers you to make the most **Strategic Choices**.

DID YOU KNOW

Dubai's real estate sector has undergone multiple distinct cycles, including recoveries and corrections. This makes the **C.D.R.C. mindset (Clarity, Discipline, Resilience, and Curiosity)** essential, allowing investors to thrive by adapting to every market phase rather than just reacting to it.

INVESTOR INSIGHT

"Every dirham you invest must work for you. If it doesn't generate income or appreciate, it's a purchase, not an investment."

Mindset Check-in:

- Have I clearly defined my core "why" for investing in Dubai?
- Am I committed to following my strategy, even if it feels counterintuitive sometimes?
- How do I typically react to market news? Can I maintain calm during fluctuations?
- What's one new thing I've learned about the Dubai market this week, helping me make better choices?
- Is this decision grounded in absolute numbers, or am I just going with my gut feelings?

The Investor Mindset is Rooted in Four Pillars

C — Clarity of Purpose

Knowing your "why" and defining clear objectives (e.g., capital growth, passing income, tax optimization).

D — Discipline in Execution

Following a repeatable investment strategy regardless of market noise

C — Curiosity for Continuous Learning

Proactively staying informed on market trends, regulatory updates, and new investment strategies to adapt and grow.

R — Resilience Under Volatility

Remaining composed during downturns or regulatory changes.

1.2. SMART Investment Goals

As you begin to shape your real estate strategy, one of the very first and most impactful mindset shifts I recommend is setting SMART goals. This robust framework, **S**pecific, **M**easurable, **A**chievable, **R**elevant, and **T**ime-Bound, is far more than just a motivational acronym. It's a practical, actionable tool that brings invaluable structure and razor-sharp focus to your decisions.

Whether your ultimate goal is to achieve AED 100,000 in annual rental income or to reach financial independence by a specific age, SMART goals translate those broad intentions into clear, actionable steps. This proven methodology was initially developed by consultant George T. Doran in 1981, and it has genuinely stood the test of time. Companies like Google and Microsoft use it for a reason: it undeniably brings clarity, accountability, and forward momentum.

As a real estate investor, this framework will empower you to cut through distractions, stay perfectly aligned with your long-term objectives, and make decisions consistently based on sound logic rather than impulsive emotion. It sharpens your planning, significantly reduces risk, and dramatically increases your chances of achieving real, tangible success.

Let's look at an example to make this concrete:

Bad Goal:

"I want to make money from Dubai real estate." (Too vague, no clear path).

SMART Goal:

"I will acquire a 1-bedroom apartment in Jumeirah Village Circle (JVC) with a target net rental income of AED 60,000 per year by Q4 2026, aiming for capital appreciation of 15% within 5 years of purchase."

ACTIVITY EXAMPLE

Turning "I want to make rental income" into a SMART Investment Goal

Most new investors begin with a broad intention like:

"I want to buy property in Dubai to earn rental income."

But to make that goal truly useful, we need to break it down and build it from the ground up. Here's how to go from vague ambition to a SMART investment goal and how to back it up with actual research.

This SMART goal defines exactly what you want, how you'll track progress (net rental income, capital appreciation), is achievable within market realities, relevant to financial growth, and has a clear deadline.

SPECIFIC

Define exactly what you want. For example, "I want to earn AED 60,000 in net rental income per year."

ACHIEVABLE

Align your goal with your resources and market realities.

TIME-BOUND

Set a clear deadline. "Within 3 years of purchase" gives you focus.

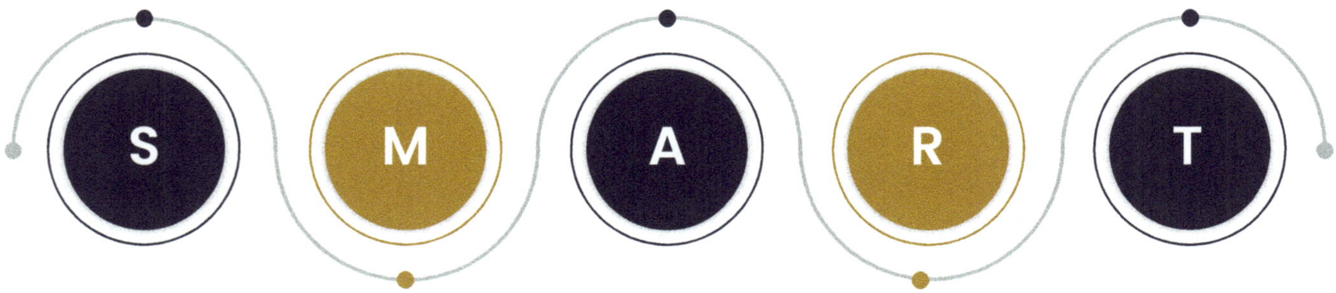

MEASURABLE

Track your progress. Use metrics like yield percentage, cash flow or ROI.

RELEVANT

Make sure your goal matches your life priorities—whether that's financial freedom, legacy planning, or something else.

Step 1: Start with What You Can Invest

Ask yourself:

- How much capital can I commit ***today*** for down payment, fees, and closing costs?
- Will I take a mortgage, or do I plan to pay in cash or on an off-plan payment plan?
- How much more can I allocate over the next one to two years, if needed?

Example Response:

I can invest AED 250,000 upfront. I am open to taking a mortgage for up to AED 700,000 more, or consider a post-handover payment plan for an off-plan property.

Step 2: Narrow Down Realistic Property Options

Now use your budget range to filter areas and property types that fit.

Research Tools:

- Look up ready and off-plan listings on Bayut, Property Finder, or DXBInteract.
- Filter for 1-bedroom apartments priced between AED 700,000 and AED 900,000.
- Focus on areas known for solid rental demand: JVC, Arjan, Dubai Hills, Business Bay, etc.

Example Response:

In this range, I found strong rental potential in JVC and Dubai Hills. Yields are around 7–8% gross for well-maintained 1-beds.

Step 3: Estimate Net Rental Income and ROI

Now model the numbers based on current rents and costs.

Example:

- Purchase Price: AED 850,000
- Estimated Annual Rent: AED 72,000
- Service Charges + Vacancy: AED 12,000
- Net Income: AED 60,000
- Net ROI: 7.05%

Step 4: Now Apply SMART Criteria

With this information, we now have what we need to convert the goal into a structured format.

Original Goal (Too vague):
"I want to make rental income."

SMART Goal (Refined):
"I will purchase a one-bedroom apartment in JVC by Q4 2025, priced up to AED 850,000, with a net rental income target of AED 60,000 annually and a minimum net ROI of 7 per cent in the first year."

1.3. Additional Mindset Strategies for Expert Investors

While the core pillars lay a strong foundation, experienced investors cultivate additional layers to their mindset, transforming them from good to truly exceptional. These insights go beyond the basics, equipping you for deeper strategy and more robust performance.

To help remember these advanced mindset strategies, think of the mnemonic: **L.E.A.D. - Long Game, Embrace Calculated Risk, Adapt and Learn, Drive Value.**

1.3.1. Embracing the "Long Game" Beyond Resilience

Beyond simply enduring market fluctuations, expert investors proactively embrace the **"Long Game" mindset.** This isn't just about waiting; it's a deep, strategic commitment to patience, knowing that the most significant wealth in real estate is built consistently over decades, not just a few quarters. They hold an unwavering belief in the power of compounding returns and actively ride out multiple market cycles, deliberately treating short-term volatility as noise rather than signals for panic. This mindset transforms market challenges from obstacles into opportunities to accumulate quality assets.

1.3.2. Calculated Risk-Taking: Beyond Avoiding Pitfalls

While discipline in execution is vital for avoiding mistakes, expert investors also master the art of **calculated risk-taking.** They understand that genuinely lucrative opportunities often reside beyond obvious, "safe" choices. This involves not just identifying potential risks to mitigate, but critically quantifying, understanding, and then making informed decisions to take *smart, deliberate risks* that align perfectly with their desired return profile. It's a proactive approach to embracing opportunity, rather than a passive retreat from anything that isn't guaranteed.

1.3.3. Adaptability and Learning from *All* Outcomes

"Curiosity for Continuous Learning" is broadened by an expert's deep commitment to adaptability, seeing every single outcome, especially setbacks or unexpected challenges, as a profound learning opportunity. This isn't just about staying current with market news; it's about dissecting *why* things went well or why they didn't, and then immediately integrating those lessons to refine future strategies. This fosters a continuous cycle of improvement, driven by real-world feedback rather than theoretical knowledge alone.

1.3.4. The Value Creation Mindset

Finally, sophisticated investors adopt a proactive **value-creation mindset**. Instead of merely chasing properties expected to appreciate passively, they actively seek opportunities to *manufacture* equity. This can be through astute acquisition strategies, efficient property management that boosts net yield, targeted renovations, or by identifying and serving previously underserved market niches. They don't just wait for the market to give them returns; they actively work to build them.

Consider these L.E.A.D. strategies as part of **The Master Investor's Playbook** – your guide to playing chess, not checkers, in real estate:

- **Long Game:** This is your *Strategic Opening Move* – understanding that the real power in your portfolio is in patiently setting up your long-term play, letting time and compounding do their heavy lifting.
- **Embrace Calculated Risk:** This is your *Calculated Gambit* – knowing when and how to make a bold, informed move that creates an advantage, rather than simply avoiding any perceived danger.
- **Adapt & Learn:** These are your *Real-Time Adjustments* – constantly analysing the "board" (market conditions) and adapting your tactics based on new information, rather than rigidly sticking to a plan that's no longer working.
- **Drive Value:** This is your *Winning Strategy* – actively shaping your investment's outcome by seeking opportunities to enhance its worth, rather than passively waiting for the market to dictate your returns.

Long Game

(Power of Patience)

- Build positions with the future in mind.
- Let time + compounding quietly multiply your returns.
- Avoid the lure of short-term noise.

L

Embrace Calculated Risk

(The Bold Gambit)

- Take measured risks when odds are in your favor.
- Use research to turn uncertainty into opportunity.
- Seize moments others hesitate on.

E

Drive Value

(Your Winning Strategy)

- Actively improve your asset's value (renovations, repositioning, better tenant mix).
- Don't just wait for the market – make the market work for you.
- Stack multiple value levers for compounded impact

D

A

Adapt & Learn

(Real Time Adjustments)

- Monitor market "signals" like a chess master reads the board.
- Pivot quickly when conditions shift.
- Replace stubbornness with smart adaptability.

The Expert's Edge Challenge:

- Reflect on a past investment (or even a personal decision). Did you approach it with a "Long Game" perspective?
- Can you identify a time when taking a "calculated risk" might have yielded a better outcome?
- How quickly do you adapt your plans when new information emerges?
- Beyond just price appreciation, how can you actively "Drive Value" in your next real estate venture?

1.4. Time Horizon and Strategic Fit

Your investment timeline and carefully defined exit strategy should always shape *what* and *where* you choose to buy. Whether you're considering the potential of off-plan opportunities or exploring ready properties in the resale market, your time horizon serves as your fundamental compass.

For many first-time investors, residential real estate often presents itself as the most accessible and, frankly, the most forgiving entry point into the market. But please, don't mistake simplicity for passivity. What truly sets successful investors apart is not just *what* they buy, but *how* they think about that very purchase. This book is specifically designed to train you to think far beyond glossy brochures and fleeting buzzwords, and instead, to develop a clear, data-backed strategy for every single decision you make. We'll delve deeply into the different property types and how to analyse market cycles, time your entry, and plan your exit strategy *before* you even commit to a purchase in the upcoming chapters.

This introductory understanding of time horizon will guide your initial strategic choices, which we will elaborate on with specific examples of communities and property types in later sections of this book, particularly in Chapter 4 (Market Dynamics) and Chapter 6 (Property Types).

Chapter Summary

Chapter 1, **"The Dubai Real Estate Mindset: Clarity, Discipline, and Goals,"** establishes a core truth for success. Your mindset is your most powerful asset and ultimate determinant of your success. It moves beyond merely seeking properties to cultivating a deliberate investor's perspective.

The chapter outlines four essential pillars of this mindset, easily remembered as **C.D.R.C. – Clarity, Discipline, Resilience, and Curiosity: Confidence through Clarity** (knowing your precise "why"), **Discipline in Execution** (unwavering adherence to your strategy), **Resilience Under Volatility** (maintaining calm through market shifts), and **Curiosity for Continuous Learning** (constantly adapting and growing, leading to strategic choices). I have compared these pillars to an **Investor's Compass**, providing an unfailing guide for every decision and action.

Furthermore, you've been equipped with the power of **SMART (Specific, Measurable, Achievable, Relevant, Time-Bound) Goals**, providing a practical framework to translate broad aspirations into concrete, actionable investment objectives, as vividly demonstrated by a clear, Dubai-specific example.

The chapter then delves into **Additional Mindset Strategies for Expert Investors**, a robust set of advanced principles encapsulated by the mnemonic **L.E.A.D. - Long Game, Embrace Calculated Risk, Adapt & Learn, Drive Value**. These strategies, forming **The Master Investor's Playbook**, highlight the vital importance of a proactive long-term vision, embracing calculated risks, continuous adaptability to all outcomes, and a deliberate, value-creation mindset.

By practising and inculcating these mindsets into your investment approach, you are not just participating; you are empowering yourself to come out ahead consistently. This robust foundation in self-awareness and disciplined thinking is your winning edge, enabling you to navigate the property market with clarity, resilience, and purpose, and unlock your true investment potential.

YOUR JOURNEY
NAVIGATOR

Part 1: Defining the Opportunity

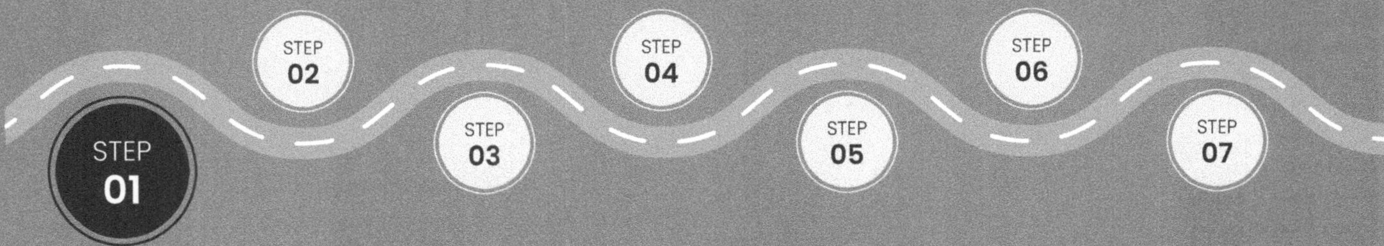

Recap

You have just completed **Chapter 1: The Investor Mindset**, which established the *how to think* foundation for your property journey. In this chapter, you built the C.D.R.C. pillars (Clarity, Discipline, Resilience, and Curiosity), applied the L.E.A.D. approach (Long Game, Embrace Calculated Risk, Adapt, and Learn, Drive Value), and defined SMART goals to guide every decision you make.

Next Chapter Preview

We now move into the *why Dubai* stage. **Chapter 2: Dubai's Blueprint: Policy, People, and Economic Drivers** reveals the structural forces that make Dubai a compelling investment destination. You will see how the city's policy framework, demographic profile, and diverse economic engines create sustained opportunity for investors.

You Will Learn

- ☑ The policy and regulatory framework shaping Dubai's property market.
- ☑ Demographic shifts driving demand across asset classes.
- ☑ The economic sectors fuelling growth and stability.
- ☑ How to align these long-term drivers with your investment strategy.

Link to Framework

This chapter deepens your C.D.R.C. mindset by building confidence through data-backed market understanding, and strengthens your L.E.A.D. approach by showing how to adapt and drive value using long-term growth forces.

Purpose / Big Picture Link

This is the *Why* stage of your investment journey. Understanding why Dubai offers opportunity ensures that every *where*, *when*, and *how* decision you make later in the book is grounded in evidence rather than assumption.

CHAPTER 2

Dubai's Blueprint: Policy, People, and Economic Drivers

> Understanding Dubai's real estate market is like learning a language: the better you speak it, the richer the conversations and opportunities become.

Congratulations on establishing your investor mindset in Chapter 1 – that's your essential compass for this journey. Now, it's time to gain an understanding of the terrain itself. Real estate success isn't just about the bricks and mortar, or the square footage; it's about understanding the context. And in Dubai, context truly is everything. This is a city where global migration trends, proactive government policies, evolving investor sentiment, and sophisticated developer behaviour all intersect to shape the value of every single property intricately.

Dubai isn't just another fast-growing city. It operates as a semi-sovereign emirate within a federal framework, meaning it's governed by its distinct legal system, planning authorities, and investment regulations. This unique structure gives Dubai a significant edge: the ability to move quickly, adapt policies faster than many other markets, and consistently stay ahead of global cycles.

In this chapter, we will break down the underlying structure that powerfully drives Dubai's real estate engine. We'll examine the fundamental forces; the policies that enable growth, the people who drive demand, and the economic engines that fuel development. This chapter is how you piece together the foundational puzzle pieces of *why* the market moves as it does, enabling you to act strategically in your investor journey. The dynamic aspects of market movements and investment timing will be the dedicated focus of Chapter 4.

2.1. What Makes Dubai's Market Tick: From Policy to People

To make genuinely strategic decisions in the Dubai real estate market, you need first to grasp its core operating system. This section unpacks the fundamental forces that actively shape the market. By understanding these, you'll gain clarity on why certain areas perform differently and how broad trends impact your specific investment. This isn't just theory; it's the foundation for informed action in your portfolio.

2.1.1. Dubai: A Global People Magnet

I define a thriving city as a "people magnet"—a place where individuals genuinely want to live, work, and play. The more a location successfully attracts people, the more it naturally grows and evolves into a vibrant urban centre. By this very definition, Dubai undeniably stands out as one of the world's strongest magnets. With its remarkably safe and inclusive lifestyle and planned environment, Dubai consistently continues to attract people from every corner of the globe. This remarkable magnetism truly is the essence of its charm.

Top ROI, Moderate Risk: Dubai's Unique Position in Global Real Estate

To truly grasp how Dubai positions itself on the global stage, we turn to reputable analyses such as the UBS Global Real Estate Bubble Index 2024. This annual report assesses the housing market conditions of 25 major cities worldwide, evaluating both the risk of a housing bubble and the potential investment returns. While many markets grapple with inflated prices and often deliver poor returns, Dubai stands out in a remarkably unique way. It consistently offers one of the highest rental yields, a critical Return on Investment (ROI) metric, while maintaining only a moderate risk rating.

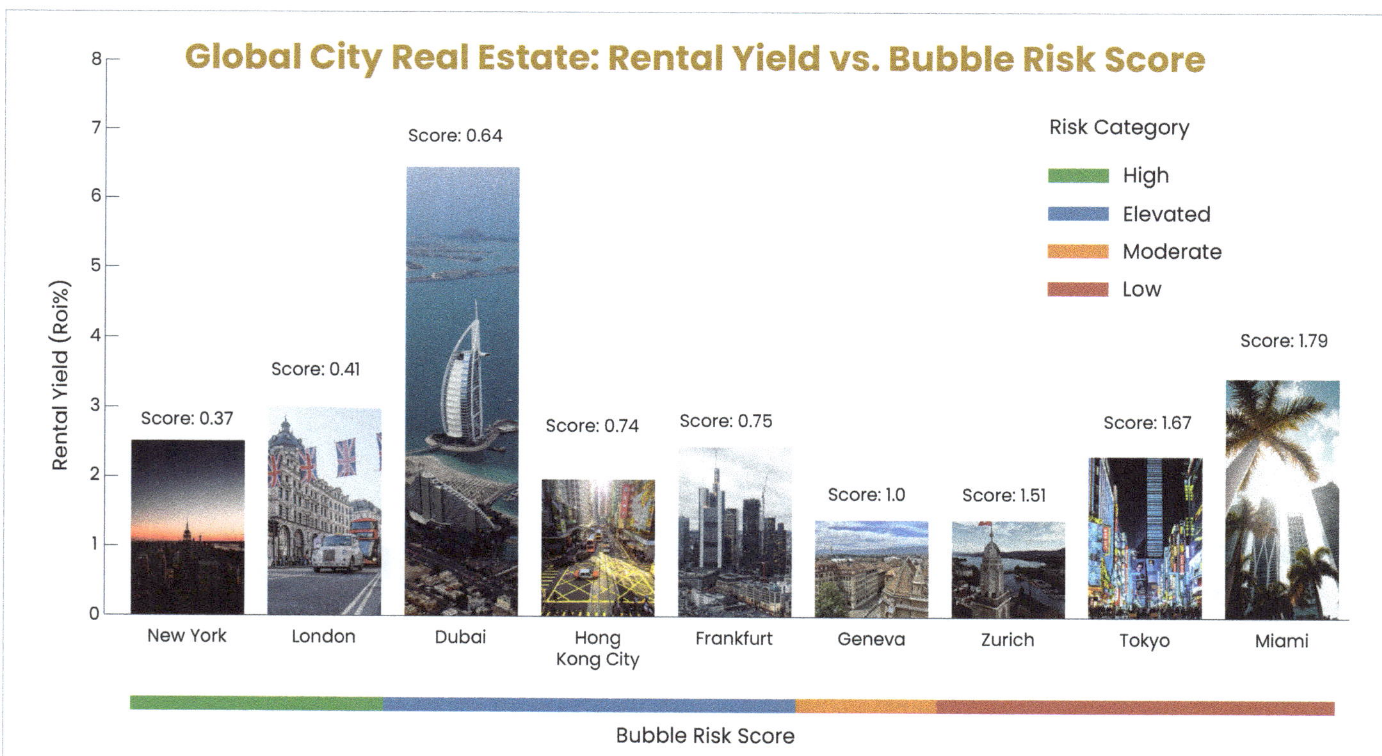

Table 2.1: Dubai's ROI vs. Bubble Risk in UBS Global Real Estate Bubble Index 2024

City	Bubble Risk Score	Risk Category	Rental Yield (ROI)	UBS Commentary
Dubai	0.64	Moderate	6-7%	Highest price & rent growth; strong fundamentals; speculative caution
Zurich	1.51	High	~1-2%	Price-to-rent ratio is very high; yields are compressed
Tokyo	1.67	High	~2.4%	High valuations, fuelled by low interest and currency weakness
Geneva	1.00	Elevated	~1-2%	High rents, but prices outpacing income
Hong Kong	0.74	Moderate	~2%	Rental growth lagging; affordability crisis
Frankfurt	0.75	Moderate	~2-3%	Recent corrections: stabilising rents
Miami	1.79	High	~3-4%	Luxury-driven; insurance and climate risks noted
London	0.41	Low	~3%	Rent growth, but affordability stretched
New York	0.37	Low	~2-3%	Stable but low ROI; price plateau

2.1.2. Safety as a Foundation for Growth

One of the most powerful, yet often understated, reasons people consistently choose to live, work, and invest in Dubai is its comprehensive safety, in every sense of the word. Dubai provides remarkable economic stability through its stable currency, investor-friendly regulations, and a highly predictable business environment. Even amidst global disruptions, it has consistently proven to be a reliable safe harbour for both capital and entrepreneurship.

Then there's personal safety. Dubai consistently ranks among the safest cities in the world in terms of crime rates, public order, and law enforcement efficiency. People genuinely feel safe walking the streets at night, and families can raise children with peace of mind. That exceptional level of daily security is a rarity in most global cities, and residents deeply value it.

Health and lifestyle safety form another crucial pillar. Clean infrastructure, world-class healthcare, and government-backed wellness initiatives all contribute significantly to a high quality of life. Convenience is seamlessly woven into the city's very DNA, whether it's effortless access to essential services, consistently reliable utilities, or streamlined digital platforms.

Importantly, women's safety in Dubai is a standout feature. Women here live, work, and truly thrive with freedom, dignity, and robust protection. Whether you're an executive, an entrepreneur, or a parent, Dubai consistently offers an environment where safety isn't just a promise, it's a policy-backed reality. This comprehensive safety net represents one of Dubai's most compelling value propositions. It's why people commit not merely to visit, but to build a future here.

2.2. The UAE: Structure, Size, and Demographics

To truly grasp Dubai's real estate laws and its unique investor environment, you first need to understand the fundamental structure of the UAE.

Formed in 1971, the United Arab Emirates is a robust federation comprising seven emirates: Abu Dhabi, Dubai, Sharjah, Ajman, Umm Al Quwain, Ras Al Khaimah, and Fujairah. Each emirate is led by its ruler, yet they collectively operate under a unifying federal constitution. This framework seamlessly unites them on critical national issues such as defence, foreign policy, and education. At the very top sits the Federal Supreme Council, comprising all seven rulers, with the presidency traditionally held by the ruler of Abu Dhabi.

What truly sets the UAE apart, and why it holds such significance for you as an investor, is the remarkable degree of autonomy each emirate retains. While the federal government establishes broad national policies, each emirate primarily operates independently in matters about its economy, courts, and specific regulations. For investors, this translates into Dubai operating with significant independence. Dubai has its distinct real estate laws, planning authorities, bespoke visa programmes, and unique development strategies—all administered by institutions such as the Dubai Land Department (DLD) and the Real Estate Regulatory Agency (RERA). This dual system provides a powerful combination of both political stability and policy agility. Dubai can move swiftly, consistently launching innovative initiatives like freehold zones, digital title deeds, and the enticing Golden Visa schemes to attract global investors actively

Table 2.2: UAE at a Glance - The Seven Emirates.

Emirate	Capital City	Notable Characteristic
Abu Dhabi	Abu Dhabi City	Largest by landmass; federal capital
Dubai	Dubai	Commercial and financial hub
Sharjah	Sharjah	Cultural capital of the UAE
Ajman	Ajman	Smallest in size
Umm Al Quwain	UAQ	Quiet, low-density emirate
Ras Al Khaimah	RAK	Industrial base, tourism potential%
Fujairah	Fujairah	The only emirate with a coastline on the east

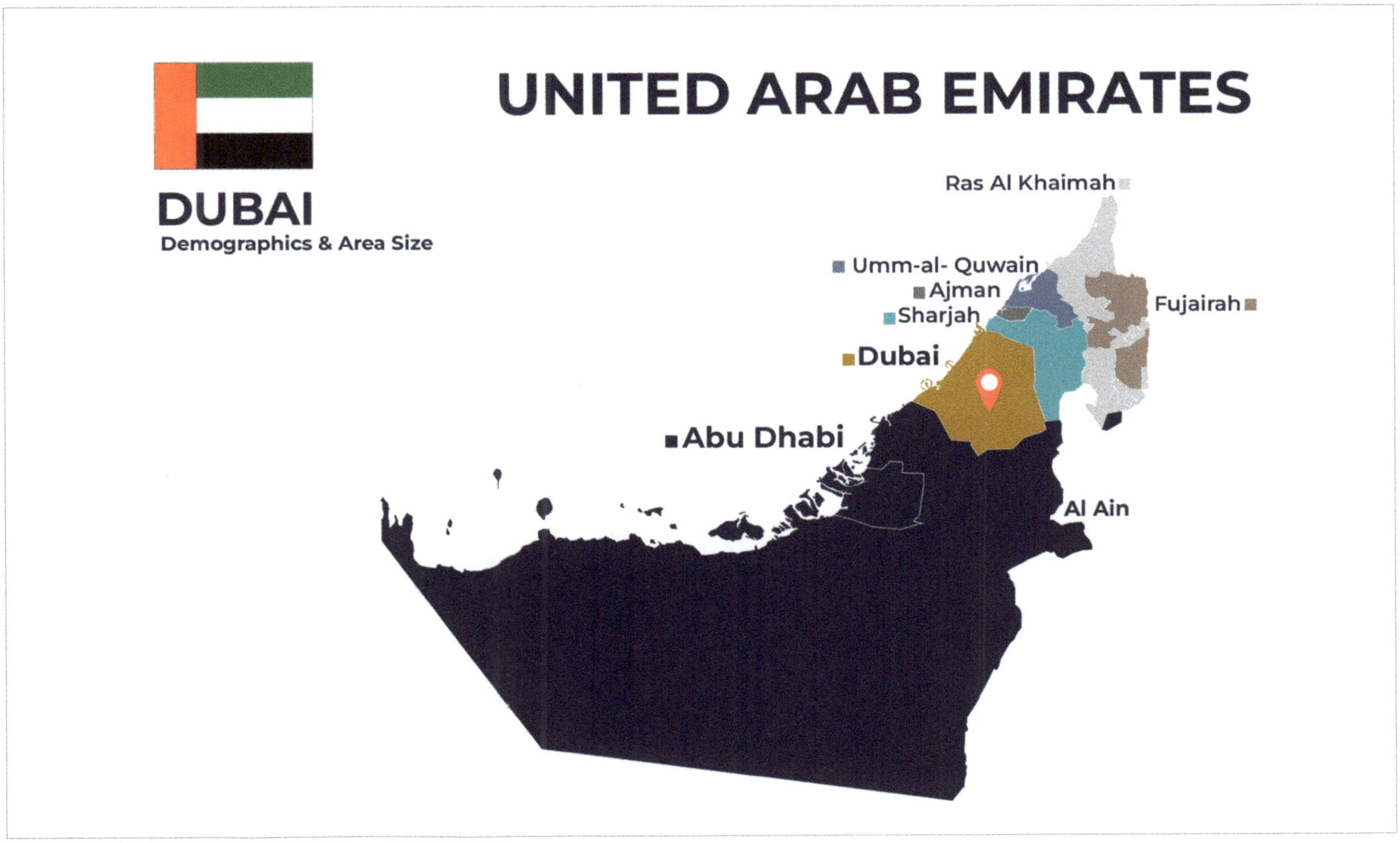
UNITED ARAB EMIRATES
DUBAI
Demographics & Area Size
Ras Al Khaimah
Umm-al- Quwain
Ajman
Sharjah
Fujairah
Dubai
Abu Dhabi
Al Ain

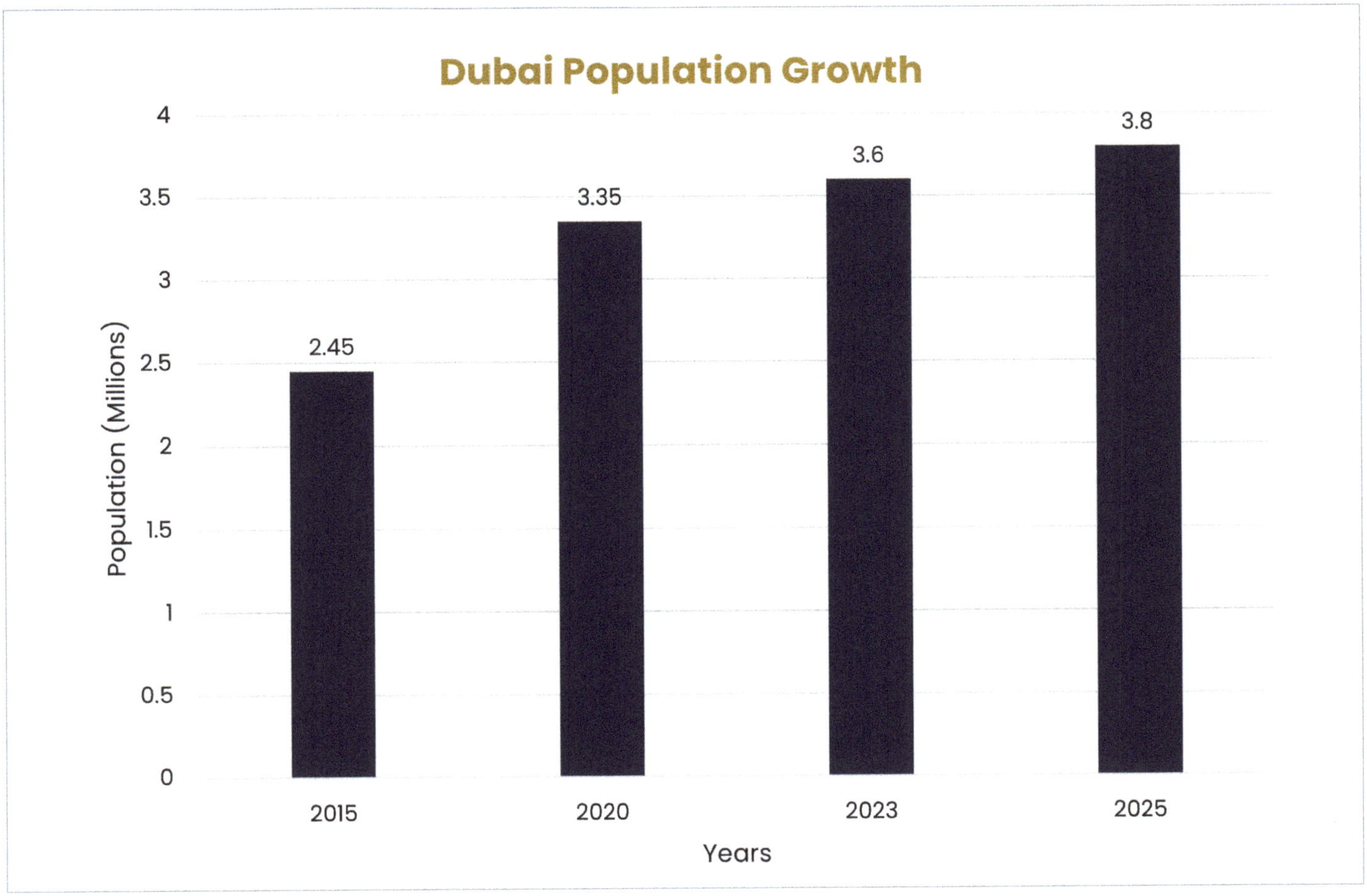
Dubai Population Growth
Population (Millions)
4
3.5
3
2.5
2
1.5
1
0.5
0
2.45
3.35
3.6
3.8
2015
2020
2023
2025
Years

2.3. Dubai in Context: History

Dubai's extraordinary rise didn't begin with its towering skyscrapers. It humbly started as a small fishing and pearl-diving settlement in the early 1800s. Its natural harbour nestled along Dubai Creek provided an early, inherent trade advantage, drawing merchants from far-flung regions like India, Persia, and East Africa. Over time, it steadily grew into a bustling trading post, characterised by its openness, commercial savviness, and a well-earned reputation for policies that actively favoured business, long before the discovery of oil even entered the picture.

The pivotal shift, a true game-changer, arrived in 1971, when Dubai joined forces with six other emirates to form the United Arab Emirates officially. This strategic union provided Dubai with the critical security of federal governance while crucially preserving its cherished autonomy to shape its economic future. Dubai, without hesitation, seized that profound opportunity.

Under the visionary leadership of His Highness Sheikh Mohammed bin Rashid Al Maktoum, the revered Ruler of Dubai and the Vice President and Prime Minister of the UAE, the emirate has majestically transformed into a formidable global powerhouse in finance, tourism, logistics, and real estate. Ambitious planning, forward-thinking policy, and a relentless, unwavering focus on flawless execution have collectively made it one of the most investor-responsive cities anywhere on the planet.

INVESTOR INSIGHT

Dubai's autonomy is not just political—it's economic. The emirate possesses the distinct authority to regulate its real estate framework, urban planning, and residency programmes. This remarkable agility grants Dubai a significant edge, enabling it to adapt swiftly and consistently attract global capital

2.3.1. How the UAE and Dubai Govern Together

The Federal Supreme Council, comprising the rulers of all seven emirates, governs the UAE. The President of the UAE (traditionally the ruler of Abu Dhabi) and the Vice President and Prime Minister (traditionally the ruler of Dubai) jointly lead national policy and strategically guide federal-level strategy.

Dubai's autonomy empowers it to manage its economy and determine its unique development path adeptly. Simultaneously, it works in close and continuous coordination with the federal government on crucial matters such as visa policy, extensive infrastructure development, and national security. This collaborative model, federal unity synergised with profound local flexibility, creates an exceptionally stable and remarkably investor-friendly environment. It is a fundamental element that continuously attracts international capital and fosters long-term confidence within the UAE's burgeoning real estate sector.

Figure 2.1: Land Mass Comparison of the UAE and Its Emirates

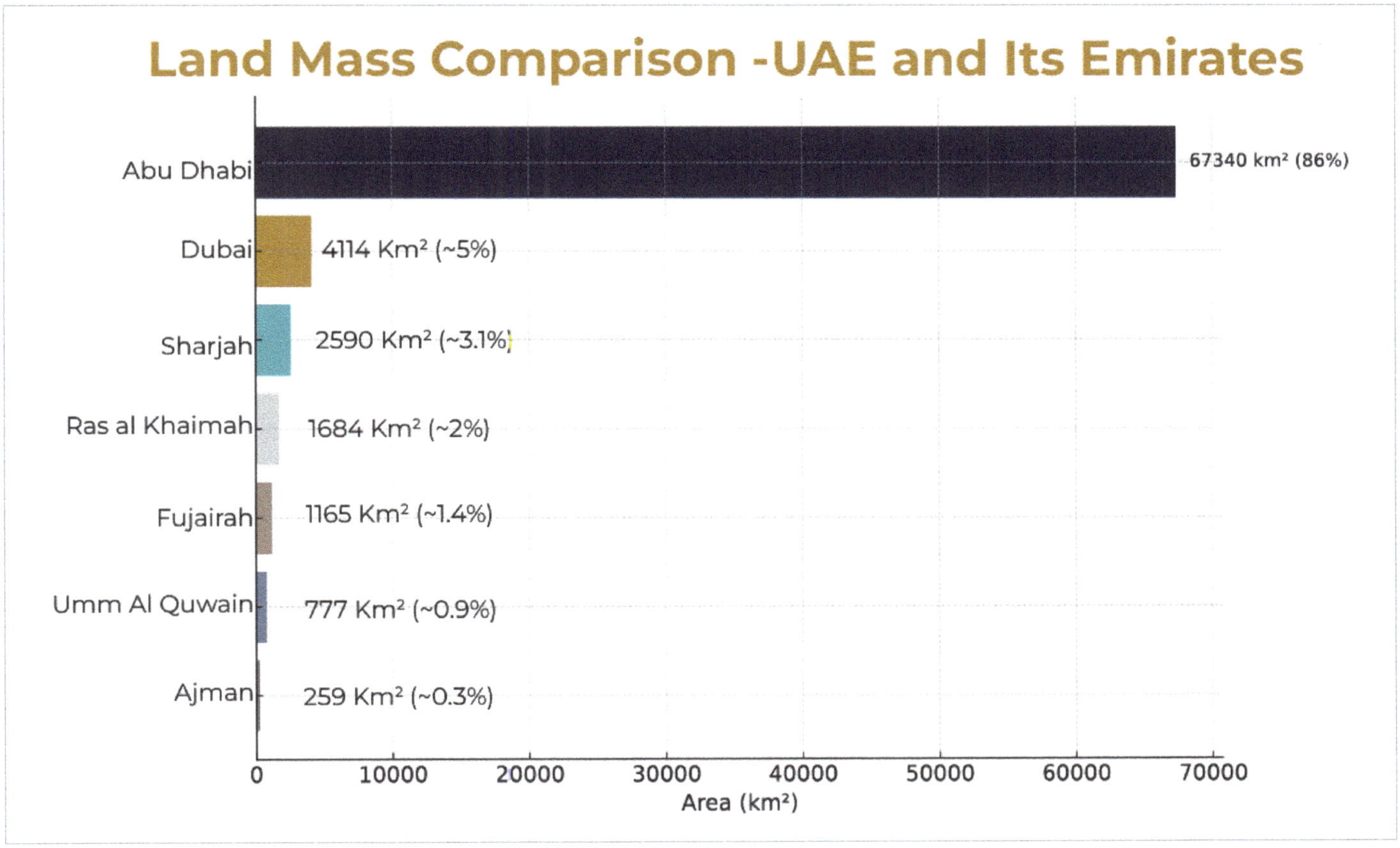

Dubai's economy is now less than 1% reliant on oil. Unlike many of its regional peers, Dubai made an early and intentional shift towards trade, tourism, aviation, logistics, and real estate. As an investor, understanding this shift is crucial: you're stepping into a diversified, globally connected economy, far less vulnerable to oil price shocks and better positioned for long-term stability. This non-oil foundation is one of Dubai's most substantial economic advantages.

INVESTOR INSIGHT

Dubai's unique blend of federal stability and local policy agility means the government can swiftly implement investor-friendly reforms and infrastructure projects. This proactive governance significantly de-risks long-term investments by ensuring consistent support for economic growth and real estate development.

2.3.2. Demographics: UAE and Dubai

Dubai isn't just a city; it's a global crossroads. With over 200 nationalities and a population that's approximately 90% expatriate, it stands as one of the most international urban centres in the world. Indians alone account for over 40% of residents, followed by large communities from Pakistan, Bangladesh, the Philippines, Egypt, and a strong presence of Western professionals. This diverse makeup is no accident; it's the result of deliberate policies, economic openness, flexible labour rules, and long-term visa incentives that attract a mix of professionals, entrepreneurs, and investors from around the world.

Who Lives in Dubai and Why It Matters

Dubai's population is young, mobile, and highly driven by opportunities. It's made up of job seekers, business owners, remote workers, and long-term residents, many of whom rent, invest, and contribute to the economy. As a real estate investor, understanding this intricate mix is essential. Housing demand isn't just about size or location; it directly follows the lifestyles and income levels of this highly segmented expatriate population.

Table 2.3: Dubai's Population by Nationality/Region - Yr. End 2023 Estimate

Nationality / Region	Approx. Population	% of Total (2023 est.)
Emiratis	292,400	8.0%
Indians	1,060,000	29.0%
Pakistanis	475,000	13.0%
Bangladeshis	256,000	7.0%
Filipinos	241,000	6.6%
Egyptians	219,000	6.0%
Sri Lankans	131,000	3.6%
Britons	110,000	3.0%
Nepalese	102,000	2.8%
Iranians	88,000	2.4%
Chinese	73,000	2.0%
Other Arab Nations	292,000	8.0%
Other Asians	146,000	4.0%
Other Westerners	110,000	3.0%
Africans	36,000	1.0%
Total (rounded)	**3,655,000**	**100%**

Investor Wow Points:

- 92% of Dubai's population is expatriate, making it one of the most foreigner-friendly real estate markets globally.
- Indians form over 40% of the population—a vital statistic for tailoring product offerings, pricing strategies, and payment plans.
- Population growth averages 3-5% annually, with notable spikes during key events (e.g., Expo 2020 or changes in visa policy).
- Demand is highly segmented: South Asian renters often prefer mid-market clusters; Western expats typically lean towards premium, low-density communities.

2.3.3. Why This Data Matters

Dubai's population is structurally distinct from that of most cities. With a real estate market driven more by tenants than owner-occupiers, demand spans a wide range of property types and price points. Between 2020 and 2024, over 500,000 new residents moved in, largely thanks to flexible visa reforms like the 10-year Golden Visa, retirement residency, and freelance permits. The government aims to grow the population to 7.8 million by 2040, with 5.8 million projected to reside in urban areas. These aren't just abstract numbers; they represent real, diverse housing demand.

From blue-collar workers needing affordable studios, to executives seeking four-bedroom villas, to tech startups leasing Grade-A office space, the common thread is clear: Dubai's population is economically active, highly mobile, and fundamentally housing-dependent. For you as an investor, this translates into steady, multi-layered demand, whether you're considering a studio in Jumeirah Village Circle (JVC) or a warehouse in Dubai South.

Table 2.4: Dubai's Demographic Drivers and Real Estate Implications

Demographic Factor	Key Insight	Real Estate Impact
Expat (92%) Population	The vast majority of residents are non-citizens	High structural demand for rental housing across all asset classes
Indian (29.0%) Community	Largest nationality group	Drives demand for family apartments and investment properties in emerging corridors
Population Growth	Over 500,000+ new residents added between 2020 and 2024	Leads to consistent uptake of inventory, especially in affordable and mid-market segments
Golden Visa & Visa Reforms	Introduction of 10-year Golden Visa, retirement visa, and freelance visa schemes	Fuels a rise in long-term residency, significantly boosting owner-occupier and upgrader demand
Urbanisation Vision 2040	The population is expected to reach 7.8 million by 2040	Necessitates the expansion of master communities and drives infrastructure demand in outer zones
Cultural & Income Segmentation	Diverse tenant profiles ranging from labourers to CEOs	Requires a multi-tiered investment strategy: from studios to villas, and logistics to office spaces
Mobile, Youthful Workforce	High mobility and job churn among mid-level professionals	Creates strong prospects for short- to mid-term rental models, including co-living formats
Startup and Tech Ecosystem	Surge in startup licenses and freelancers post-COVID	Leads to growing demand for flexible office spaces and stimulates live-work communities

2.4. The Economic Engine Behind Dubai Real Estate

While demographics define *who* is demanding property, Dubai's robust economic system defines *why* that demand is sustainable. This section delves into the foundational economic drivers that keep the real estate market thriving.

Why It Matters

Dubai's real estate market is driven not only by buildings but also by a dynamic economic system firmly rooted in trade, tourism, significant capital inflows, and exceptional policy foresight. To accurately predict where value will genuinely grow, you need to understand what consistently drives demand deeply. That deep understanding is what gives you a critical edge and helps you move before the general crowd does.

1. **Trade and Global Connectivity - Dubai's Commercial DNA**

Dubai has long been a global hub for trade. Long before its iconic skyline took shape, it thrived on pearls, gold, textiles, and re-exports. Today, that powerful legacy continues through:

- Jebel Ali Port (run by DP World) is one of the world's busiest shipping hubs.
- Dubai International Airport is recognised as the world's busiest for international passengers.
- Over 40 free zones, including prominent ones like DIFC, DMCC, and Dubai South, all offering 100% foreign ownership.
- Global access to over 2.5 billion people across Asia, Africa, and Europe.

INVESTOR INSIGHT

Trade consistently drives job creation, fosters migration, and necessitates infrastructure development, all of which directly feed real estate demand. Areas like Dubai South, JAFZA, and Business Bay are strategically positioned for significant long-term value appreciation.

2. GDP Growth and Economic Resilience

Dubai's economy is built for endurance. With multiple substantial and diversified sectors, including real estate, logistics, tourism, finance, technology, and clean energy, it remains remarkably resilient even amidst global disruptions.

- The 2024 GDP forecast projects approximately 3.8% growth.
- The non-oil GDP share now stands at over 75%.
- A stable AED/USD exchange rate, consistently pegged at 3.6725, provides strong reassurance to foreign investors.
- It benefits from robust global capital flows originating from both developed and emerging markets.

INVESTOR INSIGHT

Consistent economic growth directly translates into higher incomes for residents, which in turn means more tenants seeking quality housing, stronger demand from businesses for commercial spaces, and ultimately, real estate assets that work harder for you.

3. Tourism and Short-Term Rental Demand

Dubai continues its remarkable evolution as a premier global lifestyle and events destination:

- A record 17.1 million tourists visited in 2023, with projections aiming for over 20 million by 2025.
- This fuels strong short-term rental demand in key areas such as Downtown, Dubai Marina, Palm Jumeirah, and Business Bay.
- Dubai is actively shaping vibrant live-work-play communities across the city.

INVESTOR INSIGHT

Short-term rentals can offer significantly high yields, particularly in well-located, furnished units or branded residences. Savvy investors learn to leverage tourism cycles to time their entry and maximise their returns.

4. Global Capital Inflows and Safe-Haven Status

Dubai consistently offers what discerning investors globally seek: stability, abundant opportunity, and remarkable efficiency.

- It boasts no property tax, no capital gains tax, and no inheritance tax.
- Golden Visa programmes actively attract high-net-worth individuals and encourage long-term capital commitment.
- There's growing investment originating from India, China, Russia, various European nations, and across Africa.

INVESTOR INSIGHT

In uncertain global times, capital instinctively seeks safety. Dubai consistently provides that much-needed security, coupled with significant upside potential.

5. Key Economic Metrics at a Glance

These key economic indicators provide a snapshot of Dubai's robust performance, essential for your overall investment thesis.

Table 2.5: Key Economic Metrics at a Glance

Metric	2022	2023	2024	2025 (proj.)
GDP Growth (%)	4.40%	3.50%	3.80%	4.20%
Tourist Arrivals (M)	14.4	17.1	18.5	20+
Inflation Rate (%)	3.40%	2.90%	2.70%	2.50%
AED/USD Exchange Rate	3.6725	3.6725	3.6725	3.6725
Non-Oil GDP Share	71%	74%	75%+	76%+

Table 2.6: Economic Drivers and Real Estate Impacts

Driver	Key Insight	Real Estate Impact
Population Growth	Over 3.6M residents, 92% expats	Sustained rental demand across all segments
GDP Resilience	Diversified, stable economy	Long-term income and demand growth
Tourism Magnetis m	20M+ visitors expected by 2025	Boosts short-term rental returns and branded residences
Capital Inflows	Tax-free, politically stable, globally open	Ensures capital preservation with yield and asset appreciation

INVESTOR TAKEAWAY

If you genuinely want to succeed in real estate, don't just analyse the property itself; examine the entire system that inherently makes it valuable. In Dubai, that powerful system is intricately built on global trade, remarkable economic resilience, predictable tourism cycles, and a strong magnetism for international capital. Each of these pillars consistently supports housing demand, commercial space uptake, and robust long-term investment returns. Use them as your strategic map.

Apply Now:

- Actively track fast-growing zones, such as Dubai South, Dubai Island, Arjan, and Dubai Land, for early-stage appreciation potential.
- Use prevailing tourism patterns to guide your short-term rental strategy intelligently.
- Pay close attention to government announcements and major infrastructure rollouts, new metro lines, and free zone expansions, which often signal tomorrow's hot spots for investment.

2.5. Government Policies and Regulatory Foundations

Policy frameworks are the invisible architects of market trust and stability. Understanding them ensures your investment is not just about opportunity but also about protection.

> **INVESTOR INSIGHT**
>
> "The best investors don't just ask 'what can I buy?' they ask 'what protects my investment?'."

A Clear Policy Framework That Supports Investors

Dubai's real estate sector operates within a defined legal and regulatory structure. This robust framework has continuously evolved to provide investors with greater clarity, consistency, and confidence in their decisions. For anyone entering the market, whether purchasing a single apartment or building a larger portfolio, it's incredibly helpful to understand how the system is built and where specific responsibilities lie.

Several key government entities play a central and indispensable role in managing and regulating real estate activity across Dubai. Each one serves a distinct function and collectively contributes significantly to the overall transparency and integrity of the market. Knowing how to effectively interact with them and strategically utilise their readily available tools is an integral part of being a well-prepared and confident investor..

The Core Institutions and Systems

- **Dubai Land Department (DLD):** The DLD is the primary government authority responsible for overseeing all property transactions. It handles title deed registration, ownership transfers, and ensures that projects comply with legal requirements such as escrow account funding and developer approvals.
- **Real Estate Regulatory Agency (RERA):** RERA functions as the regulatory arm of the DLD. It monitors developers, licenses brokers, approves new project launches, and governs Owners' Associations. Its crucial role is to ensure that all market activity strictly adheres to established rules and that both buyers and sellers operate within clear guidelines.

Digital Platforms That Support Compliance

Over the years, both the DLD and RERA have progressively introduced advanced digital tools that significantly simplify many aspects of the property transaction process. These include:

- **Oqood:** This platform is specifically used to register off-plan properties and monitor their construction progress.
- **Ejari:** This system standardises and officially records tenancy contracts, providing legal protection.

- **Trakheesi:** This platform issues permits for property listings and verifies broker licenses, ensuring legitimacy.
- **Mollak:** This system brings enhanced transparency to service charges and monitors Owners' Association budgets.

These comprehensive digital systems empower investors to verify crucial information, minimise potential misunderstandings, and engage more directly and confidently with key aspects of their valuable investments.

Table 2.7: Dubai Real Estate Governance Landscape

Platform /Authority	Purpose & Function
Dubai Land Department (DLD)	Registers property, issues title deeds, regulates escrows, and oversees legal frameworks
RERA	Regulates developers, brokers, and Owners' Association (OA) entities; ensures compliance and project oversight
Oqood	Tracks off-plan registrations and Sale and Purchase Agreement (SPA) approvals
Ejari	Digitally registers rental contracts; provides legal protections for landlords and tenants
Mollak	Monitors and approves Owners' Association budgets and service charges
Trakheesi	Verifies property advertisements, broker licenses, and listing legitimacy

Chapter Summary

Chapter 2, "Dubai's Blueprint: Policy, People, and Economic Drivers," provides a comprehensive understanding of the intricate context that governs Dubai's real estate market. It moves beyond superficial observations to dissect the fundamental forces at play, equipping you with the knowledge to make strategic investment decisions.

The chapter begins by highlighting Dubai's unique position as a global magnet, underpinned by remarkable safety and robust economic stability. It then delves into the UAE's federal structure, emphasising Dubai's crucial autonomy in shaping its distinct real estate laws and initiatives, a key factor for understanding its policy agility.

You've explored Dubai's dynamic demographics, a population primarily composed of economically active expatriates, which generates consistent and diverse housing demand. We then examined the formidable economic engines behind this demand, including global trade connectivity, resilient GDP growth, burgeoning tourism, and significant capital inflows, all contributing to the market's stability.

Finally, the chapter presented the crucial Government Policies and Regulatory Foundations, detailing the roles of key institutions like the DLD and RERA, and the digital platforms that ensure transparency and protection for investors.

By grasping the intricate interplay of Dubai's policies, people, and economic drivers, you gain an invaluable blueprint. This knowledge is your foundation for strategically navigating this thriving market and consistently making confident investment decisions that align with your long-term goals.

Key Takeaways:

- **Understand the Federal-Local Duality:** Dubai sets its own rules for real estate while benefiting from the UAE-wide stability.
- **Demographics Drive Demand:** The city's expat-heavy population ensures consistent rental demand and investor interest.
- **Regulation Strengthens Confidence:** Institutions like RERA, DLD, and escrow laws provide a structural framework for investor safety.
- **Economic Diversification is Key:** Dubai's non-oil economy, driven by trade, tourism, and capital, underpins long-term market stability.

OUR JOURNEY
NAVIGATOR

Part 1: Defining the Opportunity

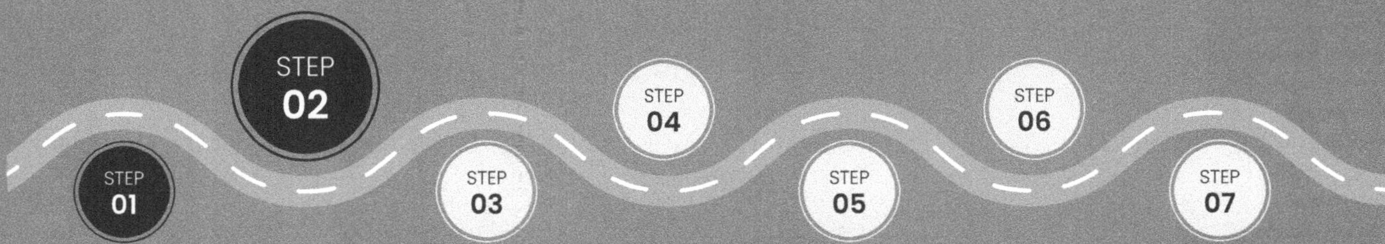

Recap

You have just completed **Chapter 2: Dubai's Blueprint: Policy, People, and Economic Drivers**, where you examined the rules, population trends, and economic engines that shape Dubai's property market. This chapter gave you the evidence behind *why* Dubai offers opportunity, grounding your strategy in facts rather than assumptions.

Next Chapter Preview

We now move into the *where* stage. **Chapter 3: The Dubai Property Map: Core, Emerging, and Peripheral Zones** introduces a strategic view of the city's geography, showing how different districts contribute to opportunity. You will also explore the "Dubai as a Magnet" concept, which explains how infrastructure, amenities, and economic hubs pull demand into specific locations.

You Will Learn

- ☑ The three investment zones: Core, Emerging, and Peripheral, and their characteristics.
- ☑ How infrastructure and lifestyle amenities create pull factors for buyers and tenants.
- ☑ The link between zone classification and expected rental yields or capital growth.
- ☑ How to align your property search with your long-term investment objectives.

Link to Framework

This chapter builds on your C.D.R.C. mindset by strengthening clarity, helping you know exactly where to focus. It enhances your L.E.A.D. approach by linking long-term strategy to physical location, enabling more adaptable and value-driven decisions.

Purpose / Big Picture Link

This is the "Where" stage of your investment journey. Understanding the city's zones and the forces that draw people into them ensures that every when and how decision you make later is targeted to the most promising areas for your goals.

CHAPTER 3

Dubai's Vision in Action: Urban Planning and Mega-Projects

> They say the sky is the limit. We say: the sky is only the beginning.
>
> **— Sheikh Mohammed bin Rashid Al Maktoum.**

Picture yourself atop the Burj Khalifa, gazing out over a city that, not so long ago, was little more than coastline and desert. Today, that same view reveals a global metropolis defined by cutting-edge skylines, planned, self-contained communities, and thriving economic zones. This extraordinary transformation wasn't due to luck; it was built on unwavering vision, planning, and a relentless drive to become a true world capital for business, tourism, and innovation.

In this chapter, we pivot from the macro-level blueprint to one of the most critical drivers of real estate success: location. But in Dubai, location isn't just about a postcode; it's about strategically positioning yourself in precise alignment with the city's long-term, visionary plans. When I guide clients through the Dubai market, I don't treat it as a single, uniform landscape. Instead, I show them how to break it down into distinct zones—Core, Emerging, and Peripheral—each possessing unique characteristics, investment timelines, and expected market behaviour. This approach helps us identify where genuine value currently exists, and, more importantly, where it is most likely to emerge in the future.

While future chapters will delve into the granular, on-the-ground details of specific communities, road access, and amenities, this chapter's focus is on strategically mapping Dubai's growth blueprint and understanding its future direction.

The real opportunity often comes when we successfully match these zones to Dubai's overarching urban vision. From the ambitious Dubai 2040 Urban Master Plan to the powerful D33 Economic Agenda, every major policy initiative is fundamentally geared towards one core objective: sustainable, strategic growth. These plans are far more than just political slogans; they are powerful investment signals. They tell us where critical infrastructure is heading, where future populations will concentrate, and where significant capital is being actively directed. Whether you're investing in ultra-luxury waterfront properties, innovative new-age sustainable communities, or logistics hubs in strategic corridors, aligning your portfolio with the city's future plans consistently gives you a decisive edge. That's the mindset we'll adopt as we analyse Dubai by zones and look beyond the present to see where long-term value is truly being built. This chapter delves into the institutions, mega-projects, and policy blueprints that will actively shape the next decade. You'll gain clarity on why global investors continue to double down on Dubai and how you can effectively identify the signals they're following.

INVESTOR INSIGHT

"Ride the policy wave, not the hype. Every time Dubai launches a visionary plan, it builds the necessary infrastructure to make it a reality. Savvy investors align with that momentum."

3.1. Dubai's Long-Term Vision and Strategic Zoning

To navigate Dubai's real estate market effectively, you need more than just a property search; you need a spatial investment strategy. That's why I use a simple but powerful framework to analyse the city: segmenting it into Core, Emerging, and Peripheral zones. Each of these zones represents a distinct stage of urban maturity and market behaviour. Core zones are established, high-demand districts with strong liquidity. Emerging zones offer significant upside tied to upcoming infrastructure and demographic growth. Peripheral zones are long-horizon plays that often depend heavily on future policy changes or the realisation of major mega-projects.

INVESTOR INSIGHT

Ability to find buyers for your property in case you want to sell it, i.e. Liquidity, is a key aspect in my differentiating different locations into zones. Core Zones are the ones with the highest liquidity, Emerging are at mid-level liquidity, and Peripheral are long-term game and would generally have a more extended wait period if you want to sell.

This structured approach helps investors move past superficial comparisons and delve into the underlying drivers of value. Whether you're primarily focused on rental income, aiming for capital appreciation, or exploring development potential, understanding where a location sits within the broader urban matrix is key. Ultimately, location is one of the most strategic decisions you'll make. The more you can define that location within Dubai's evolving real estate ecosystem, the more effectively you can shape your portfolio's performance.

3.1.1. Core Zones: Liquidity, Stability, and Prestige

These are Dubai's mature, high-demand areas that typically attract institutional buyers, committed end-users, and long-term investors.

- **Examples:** Downtown Dubai, Business Bay, Dubai Marina, DIFC. Please note that there are some low-value Core Zones, such as Discovery Gardens, which are already developed and stable; however, they lack a premium and prestige component. Also, well-developed Villa Zones and gated communities like Emirates Living (Emirates Hills, The Springs, The Meadows, The Greens, The Lakes) and Jumeira Islands, Golf Estates, Arabian Ranches 1 & 2 are considered core zones as well.
- **Investor Profile:** Conservative to moderate risk-takers primarily focused on wealth preservation and high liquidity.
- **Market Traits:** Generally exhibit lower rental yields, but compensate with high transaction volumes and robust price stability. These zones tend to recover quickly after market downturns.
- **Common Strategy:** Ideal for buying low-volatility assets with strong resale demand. Perfect for investors seeking capital protection coupled with modest, consistent appreciation.

CORE ZONES

The Conservative Capital Protector

Traits:

→ Prioritizes stability and brand equity

→ Prefers low-risk, high-liquidity assets

→ Often high-net-worth or institution-

Assets:

→ Branded Apartments
→ Premium Offices
→ Waterfront Units

Strategy:

→ Buy-hold, wealth parking, resale within market cycles

Risk Tolerance:

→ Low

ROI Expectation:

→ 4–6% annually

Time Horizon:

→ Short-to-mid (2–5 years)

Core Zones

Index
1. Downtown Dubai
2. Business Bay
3. DIFC
4. Jumeirah
5. Dubai Marina
6. Palm Jumeirah
7. City Walk
8. Barsha Heights (Tecom)
9. JLT, Jumeirah Park, Jumeirah Island
10. Emirates Living
11. Arabian Ranches 1 & 2
12. Al Barsha 1
01
02
03
04
05
06
07
08
09
10
11
12
13
Sharjah
Dubai
Deira

3.1.2. Emerging Zones: Value Appreciation Plays

These areas are actively in the growth phase, still undergoing development but demonstrating substantial infrastructure progress and rising community appeal.

- **Examples:** JVC (Jumeirah Village Circle), Arjan, Al Furjan, Jadaf.
- **Investor Profile:** Moderate risk-takers aiming for medium-term capital gains and above-average rental yields.
- **Market Traits:** Typically exhibit more price fluctuation, ongoing construction activity, and a steadily rising rental base. Younger investors and first-time buyers often target these zones. They are also portfolio targets for investors who are well secured in their Core Zone properties and are looking for higher calculated upside.
- **Common Strategy:** Best to enter during early-to-mid development cycles. Diligently monitor delivery timelines and supply metrics. Plan exits within a 3–5 year horizon to maximise appreciation.

EMERGING ZONES

The Strategic Yield Hunter

Traits:

→ Seeks value before it's fully priced in

→ Responds to infrastructure and supply curves

→ Agile and data-driven

Assets:

→ Off-plan Units
→ Mid-market Townhouses
→ Yield-focused Buildings

Strategy:

→ Early entry, rental + capital gain mix, exit at maturity

Risk Tolerance:

→ Moderate

ROI Expectation:

→ 6-9% annually

Time Horizon:

→ Mid (3–5 years)

Emerging Zones

Index

- 1. Jumeirah Village Circle (JVC)
- 2. Arjan
- 3. Dubai Hills Estate
- 4. MBR City
- 5. Al Furjan
- 6. Majan
- 7. Meydan
- 8. Jumeirah Village Triangle (JVT)
- 9. Dubai Creek Harbour
- 10. Emirates Garden City
- 11. Al Jaddaf
- 12. Maritime City
- 13. Sports City
- 14. Dubai Silicon Oasis (DSO)
- 15. Dubai Investment Park (DIP)
- 16. Town Square
- 17. Motor City
- 18. Studio City
- 19. Dubai Iland
- 20. IMPZ

3.1.3. Peripheral Zones: High-Risk, Long-Horizon Bets

These zones are located on the urban edge and often rely heavily on future infrastructure or policy developments to unlock their actual value.

- **Examples:** Dubai South, Remraam, DIP (Dubai Investment Park), the Area between DIC and Shk Zayed Road, All Developing communities off E611 towards Al Qudra, right up to Al Ain Road and Emaar Valley, Jebel Ali Hills, and the Jebel Ali side of Shk Zayed Road.
- **Investor Profile:** More aggressive investors, land-bankers, or those with a genuinely long investment horizon.
- **Market Traits:** Characterised by low current demand and limited liquidity, but offer the potential for outsized returns if macroeconomic conditions align favourably.
- **Common Strategy:** Focus on acquiring plots or low-entry units. There are constantly villa, townhouse or mixed-use communities being announced in these locations. They are good long-term entry points, especially in Off Plan. Position yourself early in areas with confirmed future infrastructure or significant economic drivers. Patience is key, as cycles here typically take longer to play out fully.

PERIPHERAL ZONES

The Patient Visionary

Traits:

- Willing to wait for infrastructure alignment
- Believes in exponential return curves
- Takes macro-policy into account

Assets:

- Plots
- Warehouses
- Affordable Units Near New Corridors

Strategy:

- Long-term capital growth, strategic land bank, repositioning

Risk Tolerance:

- High

ROI Expectation:

- 10–15%+ IRR

Time Horizon:

- Long (5–10+ years)

Peripheral Zones

Final Word: Use Zones to De-Risk Your Strategy

Every investor possesses a different risk appetite and return expectation. Your chosen zoning strategy should directly reflect that. Knowing *where* to invest is frequently more important than knowing what to invest in. Understanding which Zone you are investing in can really help your L.E.A.D. strategy and can balance your portfolio between stable & liquid assets and high-yield long-term investments.

I would highly recommend starting any investment analysis by doing your S.M.A.R.T. introspection and, based on the timeline and outcomes, deciding the zone which works for you before diving into the opportunities present within that zone. It will give you clarity on where to invest, as well as what opportunities to look for.

Start with Dubai Vision and Policy to guide your long-term investment outlook, identify your zone, then move on to the confluence of infrastructure and other development attributes to determine the location you want to invest in. You will notice in this book that I have been careful not to focus on or push any particular area or opportunity. I believe that finding areas of opportunity is dependent on your goals. However, if you came to me with your goals, we would use them to identify the zone where you should invest as a beginning point.

3.2. The Skyline That Defines Ambition

Dubai's skyline is a living, breathing statement of its intent. At an astonishing 828 metres, the Burj Khalifa remains the tallest building in the world, a record it has proudly held since 2010. But the city's vertical dominance doesn't stop there. With an impressive 18 supertall towers (each over 300 metres), Dubai significantly outpaces every other city on the planet. This isn't just engineering prowess; it's a profound statement of identity.

Iconic projects like One Za'abeel, featuring the world's longest occupied skybridge, the marvel of the man-made Palm Jumeirah, and the upcoming Dubai Creek Tower, designed to push architectural boundaries even further, represent more than mere skyline milestones. They are bold, unwavering expressions of a city that fundamentally refuses to stand still. Dubai doesn't build incrementally; it builds exponentially. Every new landmark is an integral part of a broader, cohesive strategy: to firmly position the city as a future capital, where ambition, imagination, and world-class infrastructure move in perfect lockstep.

Dubai by the Numbers – What Makes It a Global Investment Magnet

- **Tallest Building:** Burj Khalifa - 828 metres (world record)
- **Supertall Buildings:** 18 towers over 300m
- **Tourism Contribution:** 12% of UAE GDP
- **Greenfield FDI Projects (2024):** 1,117 (#1 globally, 4th consecutive year)
- **IMD Smart City Index (2025):** Ranked 4th globally
- **TripAdvisor Travellers' Choice:** #1 global destination (2022-2024)
- **Millionaire Migration:** #1 destination globally, 130,500+ millionaires reside in Dubai
- **Golden Visa:** 10-year residency for investors, professionals, and creators.

3.3. Global Outperforming Companies and Institutions

World-class institutions power Dubai's economic engine. Emirates, consistently ranked among the world's most profitable airlines, and DP World, a global leader in logistics and port operations, both serve as powerful benchmarks for operational excellence. Their continuous growth directly reinforces demand for commercial real estate, expansive logistics zones, and high-grade office space, firmly cementing Dubai's position as a global hub for business and trade. These institutions don't merely contribute to GDP; they actively shape entire investment corridors.

Case Study Corner: DIFC - Financial Core, Real Estate Magnet

The Dubai International Financial Centre (DIFC) has rapidly emerged as the leading financial hub for the Middle East, Africa, and South Asia (MEASA) region, attracting a wave of global asset managers, hedge funds, family offices, and fintech firms. As of 2024, DIFC-based institutions collectively manage over USD 700 billion in assets, with more than USD 1.2 trillion held through family office structures and private wealth platforms operating within the zone.

This concentration of capital has transformed DIFC into more than just a business district; it has become a magnet for high-income professionals, C-suite executives, and global entrepreneurs who increasingly choose to base both their companies and their families in Dubai. The lifestyle preferences of these individuals are shaping the urban landscape: luxury residential towers in Downtown, Business Bay, and City Walk, as well as villa communities in Meydan, MBR City, Sobha Hartland, and Dubai Creek Harbour, are witnessing sustained demand and appreciation.

In effect, DIFC's success as a financial powerhouse is directly powering Dubai's upscale real estate market. These high-net-worth residents demand premium living spaces, branded residences, and short-term executive rentals, setting a new standard for what it means to "live where you work" in one of the world's most dynamic global cities.

Case Study Corner: Dubai Internet City & Media City - Innovation Districts Driving Lifestyle and Residential Demand

Dubai Internet City (DIC) and Dubai Media City (DMC) form the cornerstone of Dubai's Innovation and Creative Economy Corridor. Together, they host regional headquarters for global tech giants such as Google, Microsoft, Oracle, and SAP, as well as leading media powerhouses like CNN, BBC, MBC Group, and Thomson Reuters. This dynamic ecosystem attracts a high concentration of digital professionals, creative talent, tech entrepreneurs, and media executives, all seeking connectivity, infrastructure, and lifestyle benefits.

DIC and DMC are fully developed free zones with world-class commercial spaces, stable regulatory frameworks, and thriving support ecosystems (including accelerators, co-working hubs, and academic partnerships). As a result, office space occupancy remains consistently above 90%, with limited new supply, reinforcing rental stability and investor interest in commercial assets.

The demand ripple effect extends well beyond the office towers. Nearby residential communities such as:

- **The Greens and The Views** – known for mid-rise, community-focused living.
- **Barsha Heights (Tecom)** – offering mixed-use, affordable rental options.
- **Dubai Marina and JLT** – preferred for premium waterfront apartments and executive lifestyle choices.

...have all seen sustained **rental yields of 6–7%**, low vacancy rates, and consistent resale demand. These zones cater directly to the lifestyle and convenience needs of knowledge economy professionals.

INVESTOR INSIGHT

Where tech and media talent congregate, residential demand follows. The clustering effect of innovation ecosystems like DIC and DMC creates a resilient and high-demand rental market in all surrounding communities.

Case Study Corner: JAFZA & DP World – Trade Titans Fueling Real Estate Growth

Jebel Ali Free Zone (JAFZA), anchored by the globally strategic Jebel Ali Port and operated by DP World, is the logistics and trade backbone of Dubai's non-oil economy. With over 9,500 companies from 130+ countries, JAFZA contributes an estimated 23.9% of Dubai's GDP and handles more than 33% of the UAE's non-oil exports. DP World itself manages a global portfolio of 90+ ports and terminals across 69 countries, placing Dubai at the centre of global logistics and maritime trade.

The post-pandemic surge in e-commerce, regional manufacturing, and third-party logistics (3PL) has only accelerated demand for industrial real estate. JAFZA and surrounding areas have seen a notable uptick in warehousing, cold storage, and freight-forwarding facilities, with institutional investors and logistics funds actively acquiring or developing new assets.

This logistics boom has directly impacted the real estate market in several key ways:

- **Warehouse & Industrial Asset Demand:** Freehold industrial plots and warehouse units in JAFZA, Dubai Industrial City, and DIP offer net yields of 6–8%, with high occupancy and multi-year lease stability, especially in built-to-suit logistics parks.
- **Workforce Housing & Staff Accommodation:** The surrounding zones, including DIP, Jebel Ali Village, and Al Furjan, have seen steady demand for affordable residential rentals from blue-collar and mid-income workers employed across port, logistics, and manufacturing sectors.
- **Developer & Investor Opportunities:** Strategic land parcels and pre-leased warehouse clusters are increasingly sought after by real estate funds, REITs, and JV developers, looking to tap into the strong fundamentals of the logistics sector.

INVESTOR INSIGHT

JAFZA is not just a trade hub; it's a real estate demand engine. As global trade flows increasingly pass through Dubai, the need for logistics infrastructure, industrial land, and surrounding residential stock will continue to expand.

3.4. Dubai 2040 Urban Master Plan: The Blueprint Behind Tomorrow's Real Estate Boom

> Cities that plan decades ahead win the long game.
> Dubai is not just growing, it's evolving with purpose.

A Vision Beyond Skylines. The Dubai 2040 Urban Master Plan, unveiled in 2021, is a strategic shift in how the city plans to grow over the next two decades. With targets that balance economic expansion, sustainability, and livability, the plan redefines Dubai's urban future..

At its core, the 2040 plan envisions:

- A population surge from ~3.7 million to between 5.8 and 7.8 million residents.
- A fundamental pivot from horizontal sprawl to high-quality, compact, livable communities.
- Integrated planning for green spaces, transport, jobs, and housing—all within 20-minute proximity.

What This Means: 70–100% Population Growth in 15 Years:

This projected growth isn't abstract. It translates into millions of new residents, each needing:

- A place to live
- Schools, healthcare, retail
- Mobility access
- Leisure and green spaces

If Dubai reaches even the midpoint of its 2040 population target—say, 6.5 million—that's nearly 3 million new residents.

Assuming an average household size of 2.5 to 3.0 persons, this means:

Dubai will need between 1 million and 1.2 million new housing units over the next 15 years.

This is double the current housing stock.

Housing Demand: How It Will Shift

Dubai has historically been a city of superlatives and ambitious launches. But the 2040 plan changes the focus from speculative overbuilding to data-backed urban development aligned with population growth, job creation, and community wellness.

Key Housing Trends the Plan Reinforces:

- **Core zones** (Downtown, Business Bay, Marina) will densify with premium vertical communities.
- **Emerging areas** (JVC, Arjan, Dubai Hills, Expo City, Sobha Hartland) will scale mid- to high-income housing on a large scale.
- **Peripheral zones** (Dubai South, DIP, DLRC) will see institutional and workforce-driven housing clusters.
- **Villa communities** like MBR City, Meydan, Dubailand, along the Al Ain Corridor, along E66 and new waterfront communities will cater to upper-middle-class families and remote professionals.

Investor Insight: See the Future Firsthand

Explore the Official Master Plan:
Visit dubai2040.ae/en – the official Dubai government website outlining the full
Dubai 2040 Urban Master Plan.

What Investors Should Pay Attention To

The Dubai 2040 plan isn't just for urban planners; it's a playbook for long-term property investors. Here's how to interpret it:

Table 3.1:

What the Plan Says	What Investors Should Do
Population doubling	Focus on **supply gaps** and mid-tier housing stock
+105% green spaces	Bet on **master-planned communities** with integrated parks
55% transit proximity	Invest near **Metro, RTA, and arterial corridors**
Decentralization	Target **secondary hubs** like Expo City, DSO, and Dubai Hills
Global hub positioning	Expect **premium tenant demand** in financial and tech zones

Investor Wow Points

- Dubai's housing stock must double by 2040 to keep pace with expected growth.
- The shift toward livability and walkability makes mixed-use communities extremely attractive.
- Greenfield areas with strong infrastructure, like Dubai South, DSO, and Dubailand, are positioned for high absorption and ROI.
- Decentralised nodes like Expo City and DIFC satellite zones will create new centres of premium demand.
- With visa reforms and tax clarity, Dubai remains a long-term magnet for talent and capital.

3.5. D33 Economic Agenda – Doubling Dubai's Economy by 2033

Launched in January 2023, the D33 Economic Agenda sets the tone for a transformative decade: a plan to double the size of Dubai's economy by 2033, targeting a cumulative output of AED 32 trillion (USD 8.7 trillion). It outlines 100 transformational initiatives designed not only to accelerate trade and investment, but to reshape Dubai's urban and real estate landscape. This is not merely policy; it is a detailed, investable map of future opportunity.

Key Economic Ambitions

- Top 4 Global Financial Hubs by 2033
- AED 25.6 trillion in cumulative foreign trade
- AED 650 billion in new foreign direct investment
- 400+ global cities connected via trade and logistics partnerships

D33 places particular focus on four engines of growth: logistics, tourism, finance, and the digital economy. Each sector is spatially anchored to specific zones across Dubai, creating a geographic investment thesis rooted in urban strategy.

Logistics

- AED 10T targeted trade volume (DP World + JAFZA)
- JAFZA 23.8% of Dubai's total FDI
- Peripheral growth zones: Jebel Ali industrial, DIP, Dubai South, Jebel Ali Hills
- High-Yield plays in warehousing, logistics parks, workforce housing

Tourism

- Goal: 40M hotel guests annually by 2031
- Core & coastal hotspots: Downtown, Jumeirah, Marina, JBR, Palm Jumeirah
- Emerging entrants: Dubai Creek Harbour, Dubai maritime City
- Demand drivers: branded residences, luxury hotel apartments, waterfront living

Finance

- DIFC doubling in size, creating tens of thousands of high-value jobs.
- USD 700B assets under management; 1,800+firms
- Core real estate winners: Downtown, Business Bay, Jumeirah, City Walk
- Emerging premium zones: Meydan, MBR City, Sobha Hartland, Creek Harbour.

Digital

- Goal: 30 unicorns by 2033
- Innovation clusters: Dubai internet City, Media City, Dubai Silicon Oasis.
- Product demand: flexible offices, mid-high end apartments, live-work-play ecosystems
- Emerging mixed-use hubs: Hessa corridor, Dubai Land, Al Ain Road Corridor

Finance and Capital – DIFC and the Core Investment Spine

At the heart of D33 is the Dubai International Financial Centre (DIFC), set to double in size, adding tens of thousands of high-value jobs across fintech, private equity, asset management, and family offices. As of 2024, DIFC manages over USD 700 billion in assets, with over 1,800 registered firms, including 50+ family offices tied to USD 1.2 trillion in global wealth.

This capital influx directly fuels real estate demand in Core zones like:

- **Downtown Dubai:** Luxury residences, branded apartments, and executive rentals
- **Business Bay:** Grade A offices, short-term rentals, co-living formats
- **Jumeirah and City Walk:** Lifestyle-led waterfront and low-density upscale options

Moreover, this financial gravity spills into Emerging luxury enclaves like Meydan, MBR City, Sobha Hartland, and Creek Harbour, where international executives and investors are acquiring villas and waterfront apartments designed for premium living within 15–20 minutes of the DIFC.

Trade & Logistics – Dubai South, JAFZA, and Peripheral Growth Corridors

DP World and Jebel Ali Free Zone (JAFZA) are pivotal to Dubai's non-oil trade ambitions under D33, collectively driving over AED 10 trillion in targeted trade volume. JAFZA alone contributes over 23.8% of Dubai's total FDI, positioning it as a logistics nucleus.

The real estate impact is clear in the Peripheral zones:

- **Jebel Ali Industrial Area & DIP:** Industrial plots, warehouses, and staff housing see 6–9% net yields
- **Dubai South:** Rapidly urbanising with off-plan mid-market units, logistics parks, and Expo-driven mixed-use development
- **Jebel Ali Hills:** High-end 10,000 sq ft villa community, poised for residential and commercial spillover from industrial and port-linked growth

Investors focused on logistics, warehousing, or workforce accommodation will find compelling opportunities across these Peripheral expansion zones, especially with new infrastructure and airport logistics corridors being built in tandem.

Tourism & Hospitality – Supercharged Core and Coastal Clusters

D33's ambitious aim to host 40 million hotel guests annually by 2031 unlocks significant potential in Dubai's tourism corridors. Emirates Airlines will play a pivotal role in enabling this scale, directly supporting demand for branded residences, luxury hotel apartments, and tourism-led residential clusters.

Core and coastal zones most impacted include:

- **Downtown Dubai and Jumeirah:** High-end short-term rentals, branded luxury
- **Dubai Marina & JBR:** Strong rental yields and waterfront appreciation
- **Palm Jumeirah:** Ultra-luxury apartments and resort-residences
- Emerging zones like Dubai Creek Harbour and Dubai Maritime City are rapidly entering this narrative with marina-facing towers and premium hospitality formats.

Tech & Innovation – Digital Economy Zones in Transition

Dubai aims to launch 30 unicorns and expand its digital infrastructure massively. This puts a spotlight on innovation clusters like:

- **Dubai Internet City and Media City:** Anchored by Google, Microsoft, and regional unicorns
- **Dubai Silicon Oasis:** Expanding with R&D, deeptech, and co-working hubs

These Emerging zones are witnessing strong demand for:

- Flexible office formats and commercial plots
- Mid-to-high-end apartments for tech professionals
- Live-work-play ecosystems such as Hessa Corridor, Dubai Land, and the Al Ain Road corridor

As talent density increases in these areas, rental demand and developer appetite are following closely, particularly in mixed-use communities that integrate residential, co-working, and lifestyle infrastructure.

Investor Insight: Follow the Capital, Map the Zones

The D33 Agenda does more than make promises; it signals capital concentration, job creation, and geographic focal points for real estate growth.

- **Core Zones (Downtown, DIFC, Marina):** Look for stable luxury yields, capital appreciation, and premium retail + hospitality opportunities
- **Emerging Zones (Meydan, DSO, Hessa Corridor, Internet City):** These are your mid-term alpha zones, where infrastructure is catching up to demand
- **Peripheral Zones (Jebel Ali Hills, DIP, Dubai South outskirts, Al Ain Road and Qudra Corridor):** Strong ROI in logistics, industrial, and affordable housing tied to workforce and port expansion

Final Word: D33 as a Real Estate Investment Compass

This agenda gives investors not just sectoral clarity, but a location-based strategy. From the vertical towers of DIFC to the logistic sprawl of Dubai South, every dirham of growth is tied to physical demand for real estate, residential, commercial, industrial, or hospitality.

Savvy investors will treat D33 like a real estate playbook, identifying the right entry points based on zone maturity, job growth, and capital flows:

3.6. Digital Innovation and Tokenisation - Real Estate in the Blockchain Era

Forget simply ***waiting*** for the future, Dubai is building it, piece by piece. And guess what? You're invited to invest in it. As this city pushes to lead the world in digital governance and investment, it's completely transforming the way real estate is transacted. The launch of the region's first fully licensed tokenised property isn't just tech talk; it's a clear signal of how global money will flow into property here for years to come..

A New Model of Ownership and Access

At its heart, tokenisation means you can own a piece of Dubai real estate without buying the whole unit. Imagine buying shares in a high-value property, but instead of paper, your ownership is secured by super-secure digital tokens on a blockchain. This isn't just tech talk; it means a much lower entry point for you, and faster, more transparent deals for everyone involved. It also means a more democratised market with a lower entry point, opening up the market for millions of global investors.

Forget slow, costly paperwork. Thanks to smart contracts, what once took weeks can now happen in minutes, with full audit trails and less risk of fraud. This isn't a future dream it's happening now in Dubai, with real properties and strong regulatory oversight. It's truly setting a global standard for how we invest.

We'll dive much deeper into the exciting world of real estate tokenisation, including how to buy and sell these digital shares, in Chapter 16: Smart Real Estate – From REITs to AI-Powered Investing.

Dubai's Blockchain Strategy 2030 envisions the emirate becoming the world's first fully blockchain-powered government, integrating these systems into legal frameworks, mortgage approvals, rental registries, and even urban planning. For real estate investors, this translates to greater legal certainty, lower transaction friction, and future-proofed asset structures.

As the digital infrastructure matures, we will likely see:

- Increased transaction volume as fractional and cross-border deals proliferate
- Emergence of new investor classes: tech-savvy millennials, crypto-holders, and institutions diversifying beyond equities
- Institutional-grade real estate platforms, where entire developments may be tokenised and traded like shares

From Real Estate to Real-Time Investment

Just as Dubai redefined retail through malls and hospitality through luxury, it is now redefining real estate investment through programmable ownership. Imagine a world where a villa, an office floor, or a branded residence can be listed, purchased, and settled globally in real-time, using blockchain. That world is now being built in Dubai.

And unlike some global jurisdictions where innovation outruns regulation, Dubai has taken a "regulate-first" approach, ensuring investor protection, KYC compliance, and market integrity are never compromised. This positions the city as not just a leader in tokenisation, but as a safe gateway for global real estate capital.

Innovation Insight

- **Global First:** Dubai is the first in the MENA region to launch a regulated tokenised real estate platform, enabling secure fractional ownership.
- **Smart Contracts:** Real estate deals can be closed in minutes using blockchain logic, cutting out delays and human error.
- **Inclusive Investing:** International investors from retail to institutional can now enter Dubai's real estate market with lower capital outlays.
- **FDI Catalyst:** Tech-backed transparency and accessibility are converting interest into inflows, drawing newer, younger, and more global capital sources.

Investor Takeaway: Dubai is Building the Infrastructure for the Next Trillion

Investing in Dubai real estate is no longer just about bricks and location; it's about systems, platforms, and access. Tokenisation, smart contracts, and government-backed digital frameworks are transforming the city into a next-generation property marketplace. For investors who want not only appreciation but also liquidity, compliance, and innovation-readiness, this is the time to pay close attention.

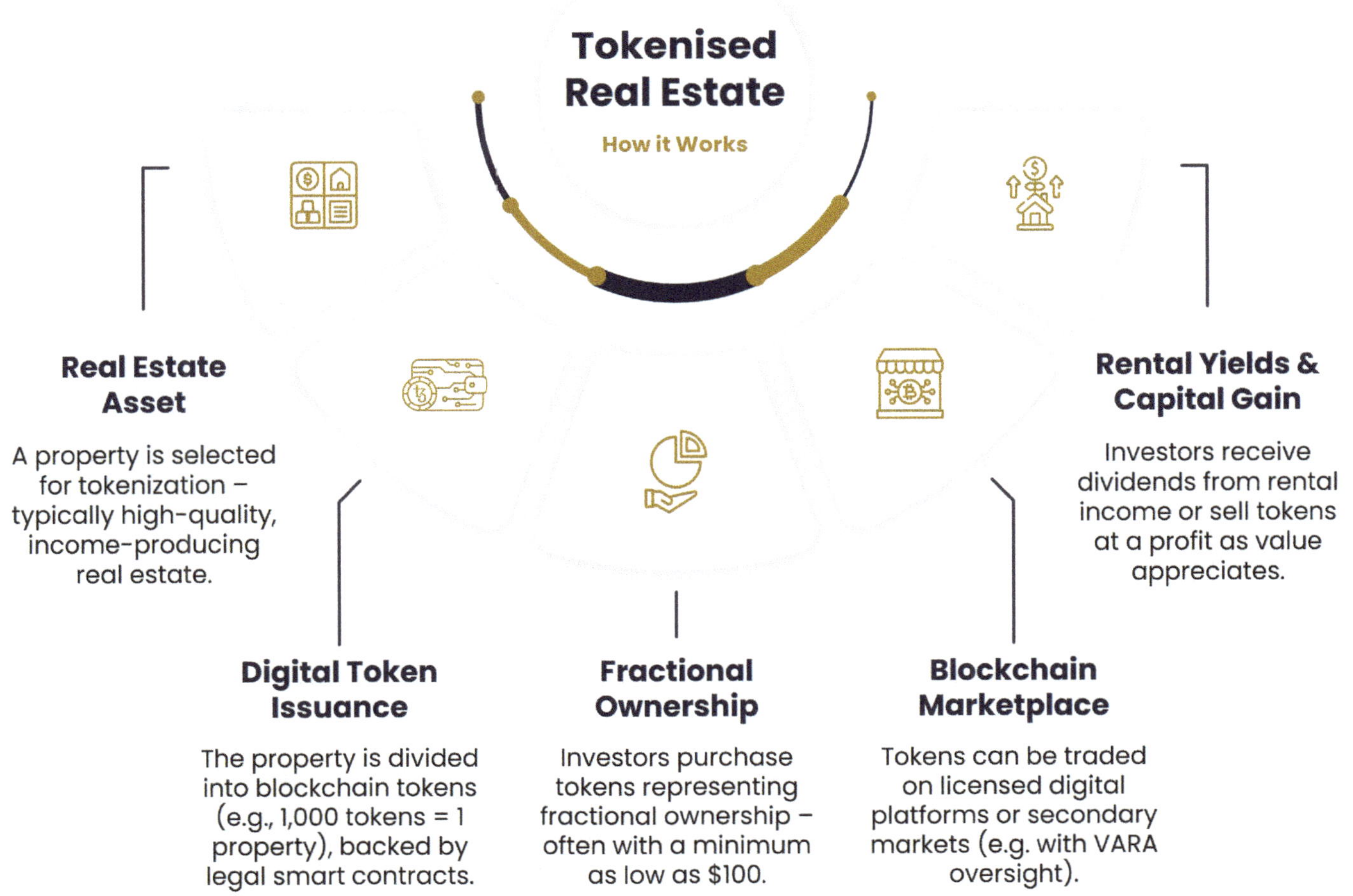

3.7. Sustainability - The New Standard for Long-Term Value

Thinking "green" isn't just a nice idea anymore; it's becoming a core part of how the city grows. It's built into its big plans, like aiming for clean energy by 2050. You can see this happening everywhere, from massive solar projects to new buildings that *must* follow strict green codes, and even entire communities designed for low-carbon living.

For you, the investor, this isn't just about doing the right thing. It's a smart move for your portfolio. Properties built with sustainability in mind often come with lower running costs and naturally appeal more to a growing number of tenants and big investors who care about responsible living. As Dubai keeps moving forward, being "green compliant" will simply be the norm. So, investing in sustainable properties today is really about future-proofing your assets for tomorrow's market.

What to Look For: Your Green Property Checklist

When you're assessing a property's long-term appeal, understanding its green features can make a big difference. Look for certifications like:

- **LEED Certification:** This is an international stamp of approval for a building's energy and water efficiency.
- **Al Sa'fat (Dubai Municipality):** This is Dubai's own official green building rating, and it's been mandatory for all new constructions since 2020.
- **Estidama Pearl Rating:** While originally from Abu Dhabi, this rating is often applied to larger communities across the UAE, assessing their sustainability in terms of resource use.

These aren't just badges; they're indicators of a property designed for efficiency and long-term appeal in a city that's committed to a greener future.

Case Study Corner: LEED-Certified Towers in DIFC

When ICD Brookfield Place launched in 2019, it entered the market at a premium. With LEED Platinum certification, advanced energy systems, and a focus on environmental design, it came with higher upfront costs compared to conventional towers. Some investors hesitated. But those who backed it early were rewarded.

The Result:

- **High Occupancy:** Global firms such as EY and UBS have moved in, drawn by ESG compliance and wellness standards.
- **Rental Premium:** The tower consistently achieved rents 15-20% higher than those of nearby non-certified office spaces.
- **Lower Operating Costs:** Smart energy and water systems reduced utility overheads by up to 40%, significantly improving net yield.
- **Exit Advantage:** As ESG demand surged, the asset naturally attracted institutional buyers seeking sustainable, future-ready properties.

INVESTOR TAKEAWAY

Paying more upfront for a sustainable, certified asset can unlock more substantial long-term returns. In Dubai, where ESG standards are gaining ground, green buildings are increasingly outperforming.

3.8. Dubai: A Magnet for Global Wealth and Talent

Have you ever wondered why so many millionaires and top professionals are choosing Dubai? It's not by chance. This city has become a powerhouse, attracting an incredible influx of wealth and talent. Just look at the numbers: between 2014 and 2024, Dubai's millionaire population more than doubled, and in 2025 alone, we expect nearly 10,000 new millionaires to call it home, far more than global giants like Singapore or London.

So, what's drawing them in? It's a powerful combination of advantages:

- **Zero Tax:** No income tax, no capital gains tax. Every dirham you earn, you keep.
- **Stability:** A politically stable and globally neutral environment.
- **World-Class Living:** Top-tier infrastructure and a lifestyle that's hard to beat.
- **Golden Visas:** Long-term residency options for investors, entrepreneurs, and professionals.
- **Business-Friendly:** A legal and financial system designed to make doing business easy.

For you, the real estate investor, this trend is a massive signal. It directly translates into a booming demand for:

- **Luxury Homes:** Think stunning villas in Emirates Hills or beachfront properties on Palm Jumeirah.
- **Premium Apartments:** High-end penthouses in areas like DIFC and Dubai Marina.
- **Top-Tier Commercial Spaces:** Offices perfect for family wealth firms.

This continuous inflow of high-net-worth individuals, including those with over $100 million, consistently pushes prices higher in Dubai's most exclusive communities. It's not just about capital appreciation; it also ensures strong liquidity when it's time to sell.

INVESTOR TAKEAWAY

Dubai is no longer a speculative play; it's a global capital of capital. The steady inflow of wealth genuinely underpins long-term price stability, sustained buyer demand, and robust investor confidence across premium real estate segments.

3.9. Events & Tourism: The Unseen Engine Driving Real Estate

Dubai has evolved into a global hub for events, tourism, and international media, solidly cementing its position as a premier real estate and hospitality market. In 2024, the city welcomed a record 17 plus million international visitors, with projections aiming for 20 plus million by 2025. This impressive growth follows the massive success of Expo 2020, which attracted over 24 million visitors and generated more than 94,000 jobs annually through its legacy site, Expo City Dubai.

Now rebranded as a future-facing smart district, Expo City is home to the Dubai Exhibition Centre (DEC) and is set to host over 600 events annually, ranging from global trade shows to vibrant cultural festivals, generating consistent year-round demand for hotels, residences, offices, and retail.

Dubai's event calendar is packed with global fixtures:

- **GITEX, Gulfood, Dubai Airshow, Dubai World Cup** - consistently drawing tens of thousands of international visitors
- **Coca-Cola Arena** - a 17,000-seat venue for concerts, sports, and entertainment
- **Global Village** - a seasonal mega-attraction hosting over 40,000 daily visitors

These events consistently produce predictable, cyclical spikes in hotel occupancy, short-term rentals, and retail sales, particularly in areas such as Downtown, Business Bay, Dubai Marina, and Expo City.

INVESTOR INSIGHT

Dubai's event ecosystem isn't seasonal hype, it's structural. With world-class venues and a growing tourism portfolio, the city creates recurring demand across hospitality, mixed-use, and short-term rental assets. For investors, it serves as a reliable engine for generating yield and liquidity.

3.10. Infrastructure That Moves Markets: Dubai Metro and Airports

Infrastructure is the backbone of urban growth, directly influencing property values and accessibility. Dubai's commitment to world-class transport is a prime example of this.

3.10.1. Dubai Metro Expansion - Investing Ahead of the Curve

The Dubai Metro, launched in 2009, marked a significant milestone in the city's development. As the first urban rail system in the Arabian Peninsula, it began with the Red Line, spanning Sheikh Zayed Road from Rashidiya to Jebel Ali, linking key business and residential hubs including Burj Khalifa, Dubai Mall, World Trade Centre, and Dubai Marina. The Green Line, which opened in 2011, extended coverage into heritage districts such as Deira, Bur Dubai, and Dubai Healthcare City.

With sleek, driverless trains and fully climate-controlled stations, the Metro quickly became a symbol of futuristic, efficient urban infrastructure.

Real Estate Impact: From its earliest days, the Metro reshaped real estate values. Properties located within easy walking distance of stations consistently commanded premiums of 10-25%, particularly in mixed-use zones such as Business Bay, JLT, and Dubai Marina. Commercial buildings situated near stations experienced increased foot traffic, stronger tenant demand, and ultimately, higher rental yields.

Route 2020, an extension launched ahead of Expo 2020, connected Al Furjan, Discovery Gardens, and Expo City Dubai, effectively opening up entirely new growth corridors. Investors who strategically targeted these previously underdeveloped zones saw significant upside as the supporting infrastructure came online.

Today, with over 200 million annual riders, the Dubai Metro is not just a transport system; it's a powerful development blueprint. Each new line and station consistently signals a fresh wave of opportunity for capital appreciation, rental growth, and urban regeneration.

INVESTOR TAKEAWAY

Follow the tracks. Metro expansion has consistently created significant price surges in adjacent areas. For investors, proximity to current or future stations should be a core factor in asset selection, particularly when evaluating off-plan and value zones.

STRATEGY TIP

Metro proximity is more than a lifestyle feature; it's a price multiplier. Tracking future station maps can help identify the next wave of high-performing investment zones. You can visit https://gis.dda.gov.ae/DIS/ to see how future metro lines are planned, including the future blueprint of the Brown, Pink, and Gold lines.

Dubai's Metro system is currently undergoing significant expansion to keep pace with the emirate's rapid urban growth. The upcoming Blue Line, which stretches 30 kilometres and features 14 new stations, is scheduled to launch by 2029. It will strategically connect key districts, including International City, Dubai Creek Harbour, Dubai Festival City, and Dubai Silicon Oasis, while integrating seamlessly with the existing Red and Green Lines. Looking further ahead, Dubai plans to more than double its total metro stations from 55 to over 130 by 2040. These extensive additions will link emerging economic zones, such as Dubai South, Expo City, and Academic City, enabling broader access to public transportation and significantly reducing car dependency.

Investor Advantage:

For real estate investors, the implications are clear:

- Properties near upcoming metro stations typically experience capital appreciation of 15-25% within 2-3 years of completion.
- Rental demand is consistently strengthening in well-connected districts, particularly among young professionals and commuters.
- The city's strong push toward transit-oriented development means infrastructure will continue to drive long-term real estate value.

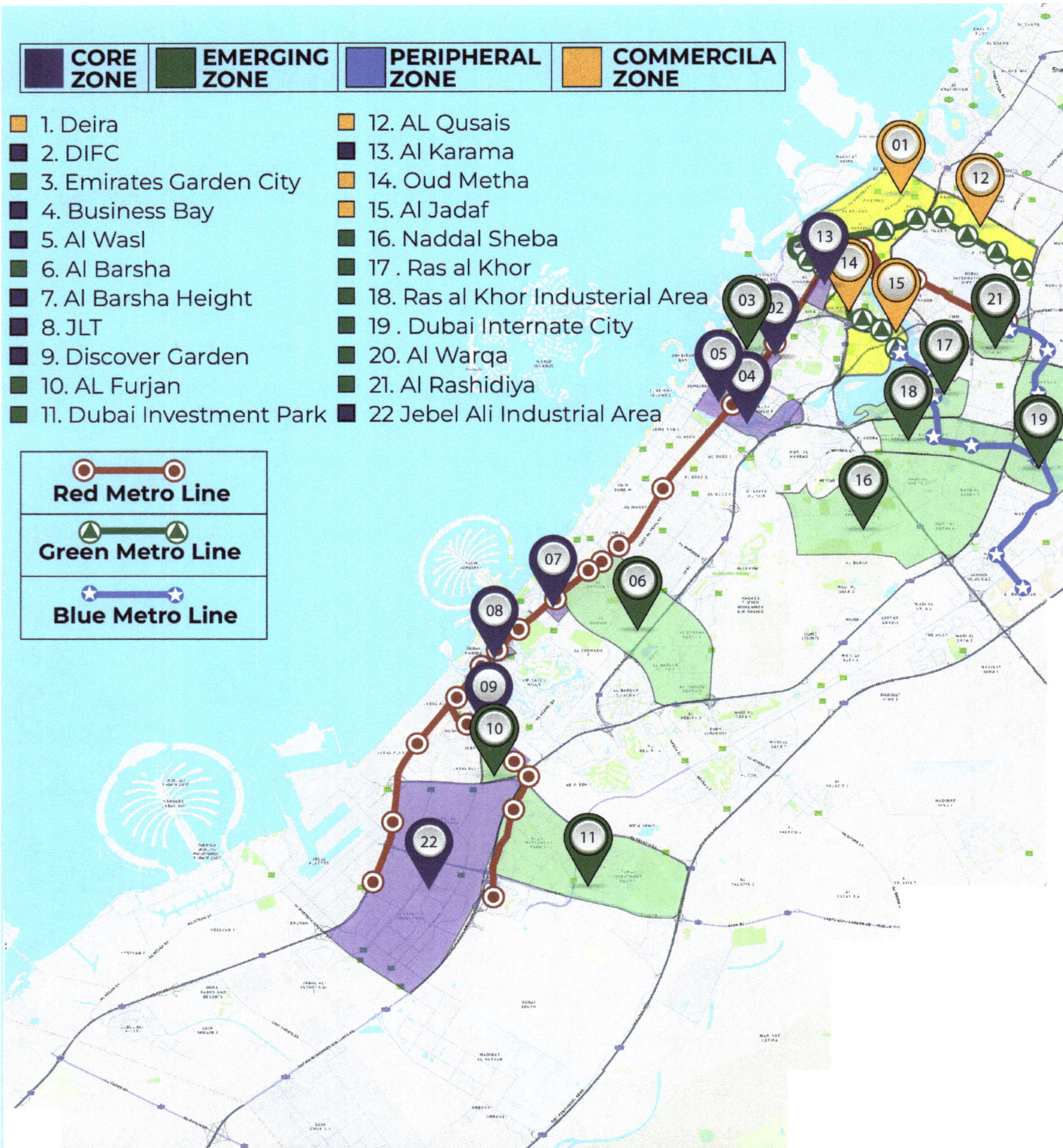

Dubai's Infrastructure Network: Moving Markets

3.10.2. The World's Largest Airport and Metro Expansion

Al Maktoum International Airport (DWC) in Dubai South is on track to become the world's largest airport, with a massive expansion planned to accommodate up to 260 million passengers annually. Backed by an AED 128 billion investment, the project features five parallel runways and over 400 aircraft gates, solidifying Dubai's position as a global aviation and logistics hub.

Surrounding the airport is Dubai South, a vast 145 sq km master-planned city designed to host over 1 million residents and hundreds of thousands of jobs. This expansive ecosystem seamlessly blends aviation, logistics, commercial, and residential zones into a unified urban framework. Sub-districts like the Logistics District, Aviation District, and Residential South are already gaining significant investor momentum.

Why This Matters for Investors:

- Expo City Dubai, now a permanent hub for innovation, continues to anchor institutional activities and events.
- The Blue Line Metro extension will directly link Dubai South to the city, greatly enhancing accessibility and unlocking new value zones.
- Early-mover assets, including land plots, affordable housing, warehouses, and commercial units, are consistently showing strong growth potential near planned transportation hubs and employment clusters.

Table 3.2: Opportunity Zones: Dubai South & Expo Corridor

Zone / Area	Primary Function	Real Estate Investment Potential
Dubai South Residential District	Mid-income and affordable housing	Growing demand from aviation/logistics workers; early-stage capital appreciation
Logistics District	Freight, warehousing, e-commerce	High demand for industrial land and rental yields from warehousing and fulfilment centres
Aviation District	MRO, FBO services, aeronautics cluster	Long-term value in commercial spaces and workforce accommodation
Expo City Dubai	Events, sustainability, innovation hub	Premium mixed-use assets; smart infrastructure attracts global tenants and buyers
Commercial District	Offices, retail, business parks	Strong potential for SME hubs, co-working, and flexible-use commercial properties
Business Park Free Zone	100% foreign ownership	Attractive for office leasing, particularly with startup and tech ecosystem support
Golf District	Leisure, hospitality, and luxury villas	High-end residential potential once the master plan and leisure offerings are launched
Emirates Road (E611) Corridor	Highway linking to other Emirates	Strategic location for logistics, showrooms, and big-box commercial assets

INVESTOR TAKEAWAY

Dubai South is the city's future urban engine, powerfully driven by air traffic, global trade, and long-term government policy. For investors, it offers a rare chance to get in early on the next decade's dominant growth corridor.

3.10.3. The Etihad Rail Network: A New Corridor of Opportunity

While the Dubai Metro has reshaped urban and residential landscapes, the future of national-level connectivity lies with the **Etihad Rail** network. This ambitious railway is a national freight and passenger system designed to connect all seven emirates, linking major ports, industrial zones, and population centers. This railway is a core pillar of the UAE's economic vision, designed to enhance trade, logistics, and inter-city travel. For investors, this creates a powerful new lens through which to view real estate opportunities, particularly along the strategic corridors it serves.

Station Locations & Real Estate Impact

The Etihad Rail network's route through Dubai creates a robust new logistics spine, primarily following the **Emirates Road (E611).** Online research indicates that key freight and passenger stations are planned at strategic locations, transforming these areas into future hubs of activity.

- **Freight Station near Dubai Industrial City (DIC):** An advanced freight terminal with a capacity of 5 million tonnes is located within DIC, a major manufacturing and logistics hub. This station's connectivity to Jebel Ali Port and Al Maktoum International Airport (DWC) is a powerful signal for investors. It is driving demand for **warehouses, industrial plots, and distribution centers** along the E611 corridor, as these are set to become prime locations for freight and e-commerce companies.
- **Passenger Station near Jumeirah Golf Estates:** A passenger station is planned near the existing Jumeirah Golf Estates Metro Station. This location will seamlessly connect to the Dubai Metro Red Line, greatly enhancing accessibility for residents and commuters. This makes properties in and around the **Jumeirah Golf Estates, Discovery Gardens, and Dubai Investment Park (DIP)** highly attractive for commuter-driven residential demand.
- **Passenger Station in Al Jaddaf/Dubai Creek:** A high-speed rail station is planned for the Al Jaddaf area, near Dubai Creek. This will provide direct, high-speed travel between Dubai, Abu Dhabi, and beyond. Properties in **Al Jaddaf, Dubai Creek Harbour, and Business Bay** will benefit significantly from this, as it will create new, highly connected commercial and residential clusters.

Etihad Rail Network - *DUBAI*

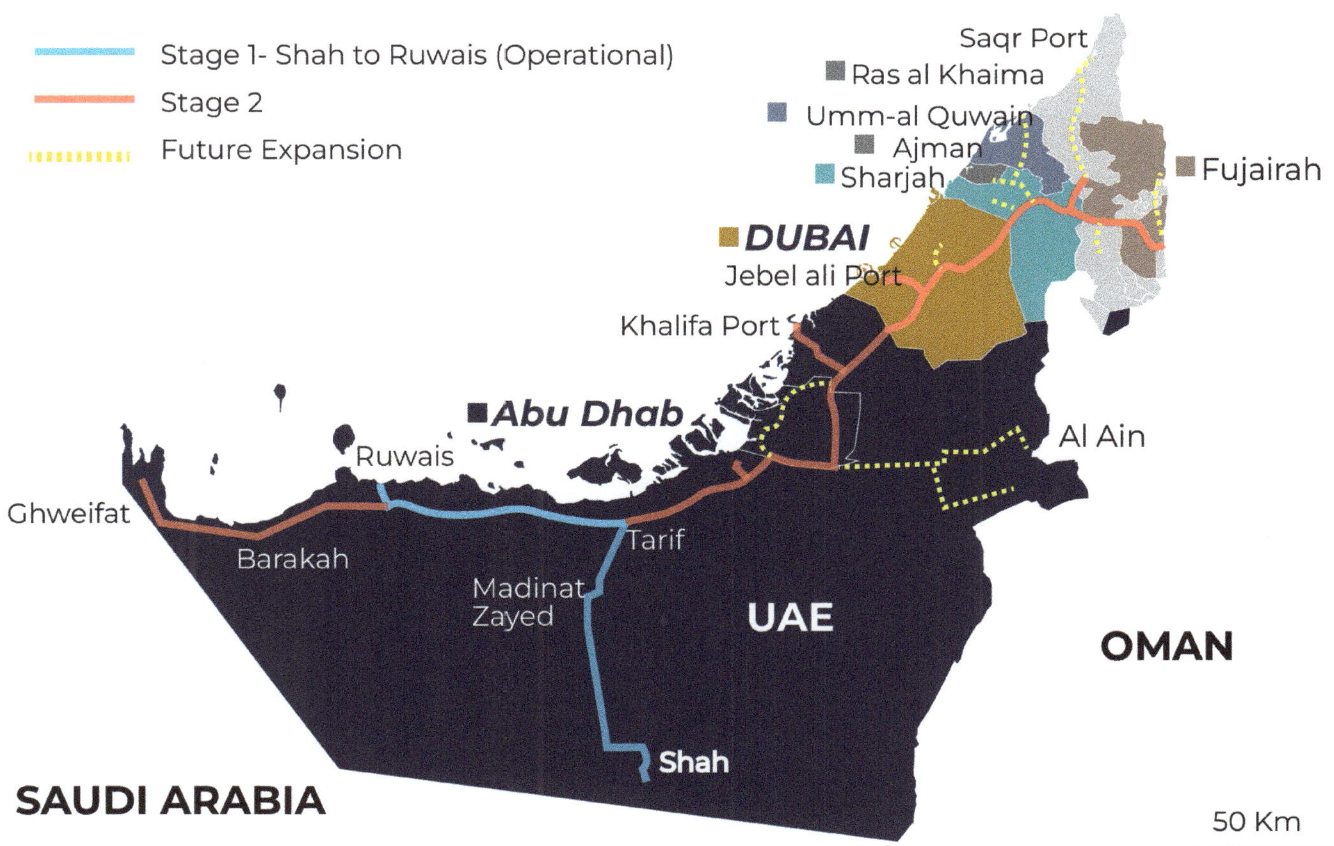

INVESTOR INSIGHT

The Etihad Rail network creates a dual real estate opportunity. First, it drives commercial demand for industrial assets and workforce housing in peripheral logistics zones. Second, the passenger stations create new, highly connected residential hubs, which will likely see significant capital appreciation and increased rental demand from a new class of commuters.

WHY THIS MATTERS FOR INVESTORS

The Etihad Rail network is a long-term catalyst. Investments in logistics and residential assets along its main corridor, particularly E611, are tangible opportunities backed by a national infrastructure project with a clear purpose and a long runway for growth. The project is already fully operational for freight, with passenger services slated to begin in 2026. This offers a clear timeline for investors to position their capital in anticipation of rising demand and property values.

3.11. Waterfront Living & Walkability: Dubai's Lifestyle-Driven Edge

Waterfront real estate consistently commands some of the highest premiums globally, highly prized for its exclusivity, unparalleled lifestyle appeal, and enduring long-term value. Dubai is strategically seizing this opportunity with massive new coastal expansions, firmly anchored by the ambitious Palm Jebel Ali and Dubai Islands projects. These landmark projects are set to deliver:

- 110 kilometres of new coastline
- Over 80 new hotels
- Homes for 35,000 families
- Seamless access to pristine beaches, modern marinas, and luxurious amenities

At the same time, the innovative Dubai Walk initiative is actively redefining urban mobility, adding:

- 6,500 kilometres of pedestrian walkways
- Linking central districts, iconic landmarks, and residential zones citywide

INVESTOR TAKEAWAY

Waterfront and walkable communities are strategic, high-demand assets. Expect strong rental interest, premium pricing, and sustained appreciation as Dubai's shoreline and mobility ecosystem continue to evolve.

Together, these initiatives seamlessly combine lifestyle, wellness, and accessibility, making waterfront zones even more attractive for both short- and long-term residents.

3.12. World-Class Education and Healthcare

Dubai's ambition to become the world's most livable city extends far beyond its impressive skyline and efficient transportation; it's deeply grounded in human capital development. The city is investing heavily in education and healthcare, two fundamental pillars that directly shape quality of life, attract global talent, and robustly support long-term residential demand.

Education Strategy 2033

Dubai plans to open 100 new schools by 2033, adding a substantial 50,000 new student seats. These schools will feature AI-integrated, future-focused curricula designed to meet the evolving needs of a rapidly growing, globally diverse population. This significant push is about uncompromising quality and innovation, actively positioning Dubai as a magnet for skilled families, top-tier professionals, and committed long-term residents.

Dubai Health Authority (DHA) Expansion

The DHA is actively scaling healthcare infrastructure across the emirate:

- 3 new hospitals and 33 clinics are currently in development.
- Significant investment in telemedicine, specialist centres, and public-private partnerships is expanding access.
- A key focus is on emerging residential communities, ensuring healthcare services consistently keep pace with population growth.

These combined efforts are powerfully transforming Dubai into a premier hub for wellness and education, significantly enhancing the appeal of family-friendly, premium residential zones, and reinforcing Dubai's strong long-term investment fundamentals.

Table 3.3: Dubai's Education and Healthcare Expansion

Sector	Initiative / Project	Impact / Outcome
Education	Education Strategy 2033	100 new schools; 50,000+ additional student seats
Education	Premium Schools (2025-2026)	AI-driven curricula, next-gen infrastructure
Healthcare	DHA Strategy	3 hospitals, 33 clinics across key growth areas
Healthcare	Public-Private Partnerships	Expanding care into emerging residential zones

How to Use This as an Investor

- Actively track infrastructure news, follow updates from KHDA (Knowledge and Human Development Authority), DHA, and master developers.
- Map new school or hospital locations to spot overlaps with undervalued residential areas, as these often precede significant price appreciation.
- Enter early capitalise before prices adjust post-completion of new facilities.
- Target family-oriented products, villas, townhouses, and larger units with excellent community access.
- Strategically market to long-term tenants, including healthcare staff, educators, and relocating families who value these amenities.

Dubai's investment landscape is increasingly shaped by quality-of-life infrastructure. Understanding where and why these projects are landing consistently gives you a strategic edge and perfectly positions your capital where the next wave of stable, resilient demand will inevitably emerge.

3.13. Regional Tourism Powerhouses: Disneyland & RAK Casino

Dubai's status as the UAE's tourism capital is poised to receive a significant regional boost, strongly driven by two landmark megaprojects just beyond its borders: Disneyland Abu Dhabi and the Wynn Casino in Ras Al Khaimah. While these highly anticipated attractions are indeed located in neighbouring emirates, their economic ripple effects will directly and powerfully benefit Dubai's already robust real estate, hospitality, and transportation infrastructure.

Dubai naturally serves as the primary gateway city, leveraging its world-class international airport, luxurious hospitality ecosystem, and central connectivity. Just as Anaheim's Disneyland supports Los Angeles, these upcoming regional draws will further amplify Dubai's integral role as the lifestyle and investment anchor of the entire Gulf region.

Disneyland Abu Dhabi (Yas Island)

- **Opening:** Early 2030s
- **Expected:** 13 million visitors per year
- **Impact:** Projected 26 million hotel nights annually, $3-4 billion in annual revenue, and over 25,000 new jobs.
- **Analogy:** Think Anaheim to Los Angeles, expect a surge in short-term stays and residential demand in surrounding hubs.

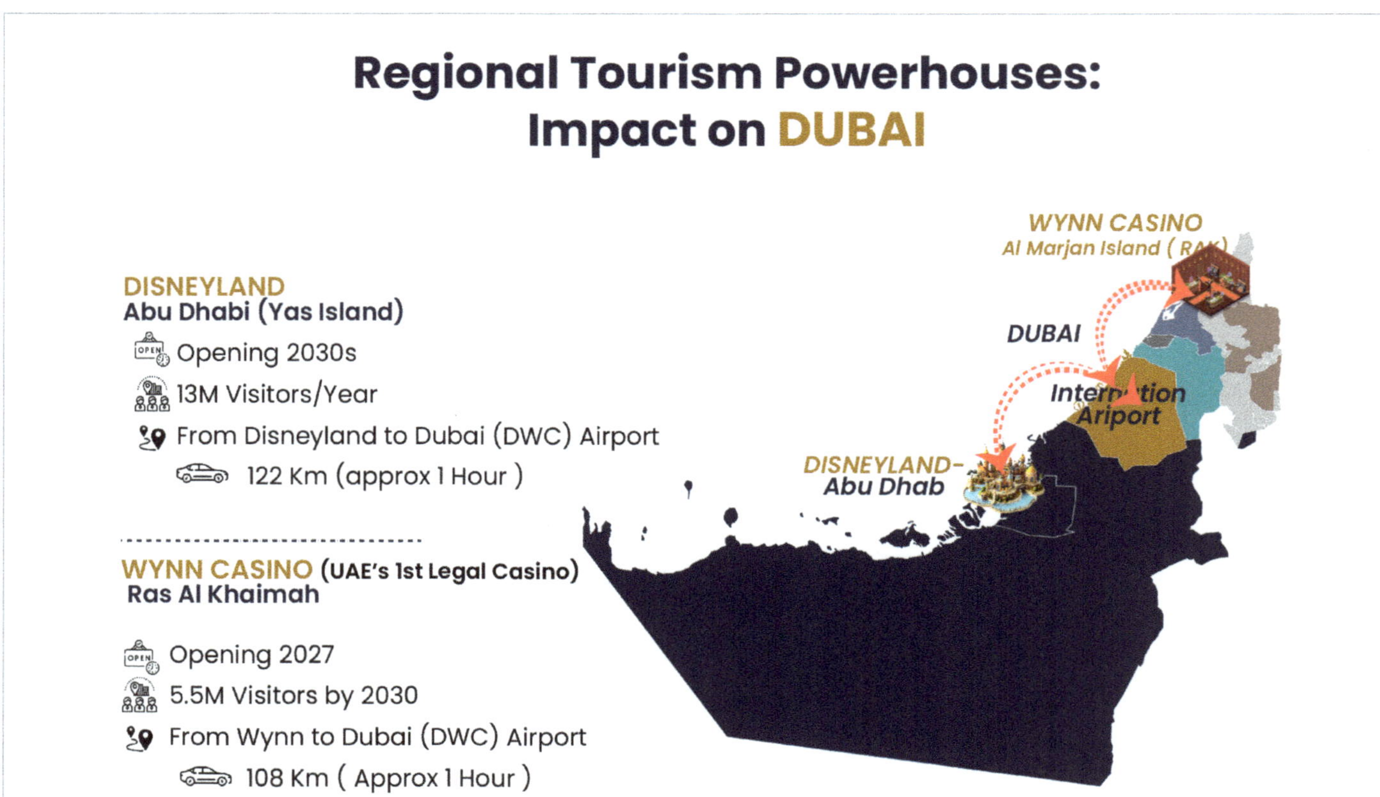

Wynn Casino - Ras Al Khaimah

- **Opening:** 2027
- **Expected:** 5.5 million visitors per year by 2030
- **Significance:** This will be the first legal casino in the UAE, poised to attract high-net-worth global tourists and significant luxury hospitality spending.
- **Analogy:** Think Las Vegas to Los Angeles or Macao to Hong Kong, expect a surge in short-term stays and residential demand in surrounding hubs.

Investor Outlook - Where to Position Capital

- **Jebel Ali & Dubai South:** These are key gateway corridors to both Abu Dhabi and Ras Al Khaimah; expect rising hotel and short-term rental demand.
- **Dubai Marina & Palm Jumeirah:** Highly likely to benefit from overflow luxury tourism and increased high-end residential interest.
- **Hospitality & Mixed-Use Zones:** Watch closely for hotel-branded residences, F&B (Food & Beverage) corridors, and entertainment-linked developments.

INVESTOR STRATEGY

Don't underestimate regional synergy. As tourists increasingly combine visits to Dubai with attractions in Abu Dhabi and Ras Al Khaimah, Dubai's hospitality and real estate sectors will naturally absorb much of the increased footfall and capital flow, particularly in areas near new transit links and lifestyle corridors.

Investor Insight: RAK and Abu Dhabi – Smart Diversification, Not First Base

Many investors often ask me whether they should consider investing directly in Ras Al Khaimah or Abu Dhabi, especially with game-changing developments like the Wynn Casino and Disneyland Abu Dhabi on the horizon. My view is strategic: while these emirates offer exciting long-term potential, they fall firmly within what I call the *Peripheral Opportunity Zone*. They are best suited for portfolio expansion and regional de-risking, rather than as a starting point for new investors.

If you're just entering the UAE market or seeking proven liquidity, faster returns, and established demand cycles, Dubai remains the gold standard. However, for seasoned investors looking to diversify across jurisdictions, tap into government-backed mega-projects, and benefit from capital appreciation before mass uptake, selectively entering RAK or Abu Dhabi can offer powerful long-term upside.

Think of these regions not as competitors to Dubai, but as complementary nodes in a growing regional investment ecosystem where Dubai remains the financial and connectivity anchor.

Chapter Summary

A Blueprint for the City of the Future

Dubai's extraordinary transformation is no accident; it's the direct result of a deliberate, long-range vision that seamlessly fuses ambitious infrastructure, relentless innovation, and broad global appeal. Every project detailed in this chapter fits into a robust, overarching framework: building one of the most future-ready cities on the entire planet.

From the iconic Burj Khalifa to the ambitious Palm Jebel Ali, Dubai's skyline vividly reflects its boundless ambition. However, its deeper strength lies in its master planning. The Dubai 2040 Urban Master Plan envisions a walkable, green, and beautifully balanced city structured around five dynamic urban centres. Simultaneously, the D33 Economic Agenda boldly targets an astounding AED 32 trillion in economic output, propelling Dubai's ascent as a global capital for trade, finance, and innovation.

Mega infrastructure projects, such as the expansive Dubai Metro network, Eithad Railways and the colossal Al Maktoum International Airport (set to become the world's largest), are designed to support large-scale population growth and unparalleled economic activity robustly. Concurrently, sustainability is woven into every layer of development, from vast solar parks and LEED-certified buildings to entire communities designed explicitly for low-carbon living.

Dubai is also pioneering the tokenisation of real estate, actively offering a global model for blockchain-integrated governance. Major attractions like Disneyland Abu Dhabi, the Wynn Casino in Ras Al Khaimah, and revitalised coastal zones powerfully cement Dubai's role as a regional tourism powerhouse. Walkable waterfronts, vibrant cultural districts, and cutting-edge smart infrastructure further enhance the city's compelling lifestyle proposition.

Investor Insight: The genuine real estate opportunity in Dubai is not just about individual assets it lies in strategically aligning with the city's systemic vision. As Dubai continues its evolution into a global benchmark for urban excellence, well-positioned investors will naturally benefit from a rising tide across all asset classes.

Key Highlight: "Dubai's vision is not just for today, it's for the next 20 years and beyond."

Key Takeaways:

- **Vision-Driven Growth:** Dubai's long-term plans (2040 Urban Master Plan, D33 Agenda) are not just slogans; they are strategic blueprints creating investment opportunities.
- **Strategic Zoning:** Understand Core, Emerging, and Peripheral zones to align your property choices with distinct growth profiles.
- **Mega-Projects as Catalysts:** Major infrastructure (Metro, Airports), tourism hubs, and economic zones (DIFC, Expo City) actively drive real estate value.
- **Innovation & Sustainability:** Digital innovation (tokenisation) and green building standards are creating new asset classes and enhancing long-term value.
- **Regional Synergy:** Neighbouring mega-attractions boost Dubai's position as a gateway and tourism anchor.
- **Align with Momentum:** The genuine opportunity lies in positioning your investments in areas and sectors targeted by Dubai's ongoing strategic development.

YOUR JOURNEY
NAVIGATOR

Part 1: Defining the Opportunity

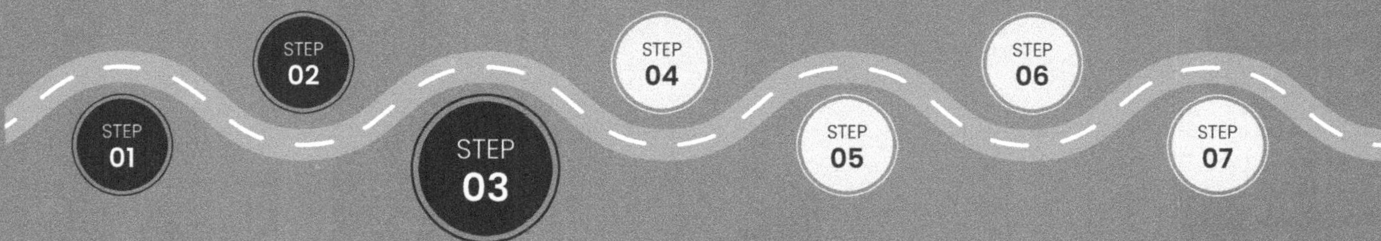

Recap

You have just completed **Chapter 3: Dubai's Vision in Action – Urban Planning and Mega-Projects**, where we explored how Dubai's long-term vision, strategic zoning, and mega-projects shape the city's investment potential. You now understand the difference between core, emerging, and peripheral zones, the infrastructure driving each, and how these areas evolve across the market cycle.

Next Chapter Preview

We now move to the *where* stage at the macro level. **Chapter 4: Market Dynamics – Cycles, Locations, and Investment Timing** examines how real estate cycles work in Dubai, the signals to watch for when entering or exiting, and how location performance changes depending on the phase of the cycle.

You Will Learn

- ☑ How real estate cycles unfold and why they matter for location choice.
- ☑ The key characteristics of high-performing areas at different market stages.
- ☑ Which locations align best with your chosen investment objectives.
- ☑ How to filter areas before narrowing your focus to community or project-level analysis later in the book..

Link to Framework

This chapter strengthens your C.D.R.C. mindset by improving clarity on market movements and timing, and supports the L.E.A.D. approach by showing how to adapt your strategy to different phases while driving value through location selection.

Purpose / Big Picture Link

This is the macro-level *where* stage of your investment journey. Understanding the interplay between location and market cycle ensures that your *when* and *how* decisions later in the book are made with full awareness of geographic and economic context.

CHAPTER 4

Market Dynamics: Cycles, Locations, and Investment Timing

> Markets cycle. Being prepared is more useful than trying to predict.

In Chapter 2, we provided Dubai's foundational blueprint, its policies, people, and economic drivers. That chapter laid the crucial groundwork for understanding *what* makes this market tick. Now, in Chapter 4, we pivot to understanding the dynamic pulse of Dubai's real estate. This is where we delve into *how* the market actually moves through its rhythms and, crucially, **how to time your actions** within these movements. This chapter is your dedicated guide to real estate cycles and the vital inflection indicators that empower you to seize opportunities with precision, rather than guesswork. Understanding *when* to act is just as important as knowing *what* to do. This sets the stage not only for smart entry but also for recognising critical future exit signals.

4.1. Dubai's Real Estate Cycles and Timing Your Entry

Understanding the rhythm of the market is crucial. It's how you move from merely observing to strategically acting.

Understanding Real Estate Cycles - The Pattern Beneath the Price

Real estate doesn't trade daily on a global exchange like stocks, but it is still deeply cyclical. A real estate cycle consistently follows a recurring pattern of expansion and contraction across prices, demand levels, construction activity, and investor behaviour. While the precise timing and intensity of each phase can naturally vary by city or even region, the fundamental drivers remain remarkably consistent: GDP growth, prevailing interest rates, market liquidity, existing supply levels, and significant demographic shifts collectively push the market through four distinct key stages—Recovery, Expansion, Peak, and Correction.

In Dubai, these cycles tend to be more pronounced and dynamic. The market responds quickly due to a highly adaptable construction ecosystem, strong reliance on foreign investment, and active government involvement. Policy shifts like visa reforms, tax changes, new master plans, and crucial freehold announcements often actively spark mini-cycles within the broader trend.

An astute investor doesn't waste time trying to call the exact top or bottom of a cycle. Instead, they focus intently on understanding the ***current*** phase of the cycle, spotting early signs of transition, and strategically adapting their investment approach accordingly. Each phase inherently offers its own unique set of risks and, crucially, opportunities. When you know how the cycle fundamentally works, you can time your acquisitions far more effectively, and just as importantly, decide when to hold, when to exit, and when to pivot between income and growth strategies strategically.

4.1.1. The Four Phases of a Real Estate Cycle

Recovery Phase - Opportunity in the Shadows

The recovery phase begins quietly after a market correction or downturn. Investor sentiment typically remains cautious, but the underlying fundamentals are starting to stabilise. Prices remain attractive, transaction volumes are slowly picking up momentum, and early signals such as increased buyer inquiries and faster absorption of ready inventory subtly suggest growing confidence.

Key Indicators of a Recovery Phase:

- Stabilising fundamentals, though investor sentiment remains cautious.
- Attractive prices with slowly increasing transaction volumes.
- Increased buyer inquiries and faster absorption of ready inventory.

Expansion Phase - The Momentum Builds

The expansion phase is when the market truly transitions from early recovery into broad-based growth. Prices begin to rise steadily, transaction volumes consistently increase, rental yields typically improve, and both investors and end-users become significantly more active. Confidence spreads beyond just early adopters, developers ramp up new activity, banks become more willing to offer financing, and international interest begins to flow in more substantially. This powerful momentum is usually driven by strong economic growth, continuous infrastructure development, clear regulatory clarity, and supportive media narratives.

Key Indicators of an Expansion Phase:

- Steady price increases and rising transaction volumes.
- Improving rental yields and increased activity from both investors and end-users.
- Increased developer activity, readily available financing, and growing international interest.

Dubai's Real Estate Cycle – How to Read The Rhythm and Invest Smart

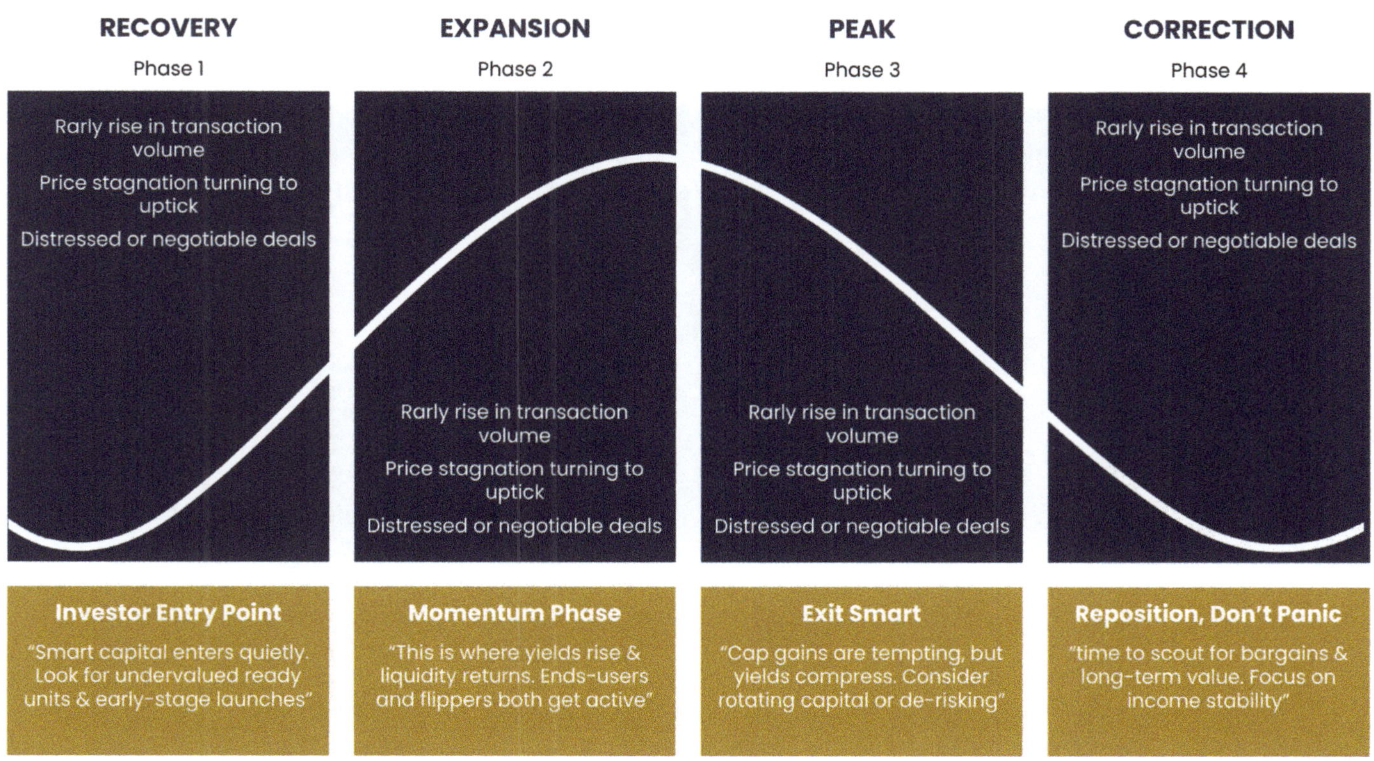

Peak Phase - When Momentum Becomes Mania

The peak phase represents the euphoric high point of the real estate cycle. Prices often hit all-time highs, frequently driven more by rampant speculation, intense media hype, and a strong Fear Of Missing Out (FOMO) rather than by sound fundamental factors. Sales volumes may remain strong, but subtle cracks typically begin to appear, rental yields start to compress, affordability declines for many, and developers often flood the market with new launches, aggressively chasing demand. While liquidity may seem abundant, investment decisions tend to deteriorate as latecomers pile in, pursuing quick returns without thoroughly assessing long-term risks.

Key Indicators of a Peak Phase:

- Prices reach all-time highs, often driven by speculation and hype.
- Substantial sales volumes, but signs of compression in rental yields.
- The market is experiencing declining affordability and developers saturating the market with new launches.

Correction Phase - When the Market Recalibrates

The correction phase is the necessary cooling-off period that inevitably follows the exuberance of a market peak. Prices begin to fall, typically starting in fringe or highly speculative areas, while transaction volumes noticeably slow. Investor sentiment turns cautious, and end-users often take the lead in market activity. This phase is usually triggered by a combination of factors, including oversupply, mounting affordability pressure, broader economic slowdowns, or shifts in global liquidity and policy. While it may feel uncomfortable, this stage plays a crucial role: it resets inflated prices, restores the appeal of rental yields, and effectively clears out the excesses built up during the preceding boom. Corrections are not collapses, they're essential recalibrations. For disciplined investors, this phase actively offers significant opportunities to re-enter the market at more reasonable valuations, renegotiate terms, and strategically position for the next upward cycle.

Key Indicators of a Correction Phase:

- Declining transaction volumes across most segments.
- Inventory build-up and rising days-on-market for sales.
- Developers offering substantial incentives (such as fee waivers, furniture packages, or extended post-handover payment plans).
- Yield compression reverses slightly as prices tend to dip faster than rents.
- Media sentiment noticeably shifts from bullish to cautious.

QUICK FACT

Dubai's real estate market has experienced at least two complete cycles since 2002, each lasting 5–7 years. Understanding where you are in the cycle is key to smart timing.

Sample Market Segment Cycle Status (Mid 2025)

Segment	Phase	Indicator Example
Ultra-Luxury Apartments	Peak	High transaction prices, slowing resales
Mind-Tier Villas in Dubailand	Expansion	Strong rental demand, steady price uptick
Budget Apartments in JVC	Correction	Developer incentives, longer sales cycles
New Launches in Dubai South	Recovery	Increasing launches, early investor participation

4.1.2. Historical Examples in Dubai:

Dubai's market history provides powerful lessons from past cycles

Post-2008 Financial Crisis (2009-2011)

After the speculative boom of 2006-2008, the global financial crisis severely impacted Dubai, exposing overleveraged developers, stalling megaprojects, and triggering sharp price corrections. Property values in Dubai dropped by 40%-60% across many segments, projects were shelved, resale liquidity dried up, and investor capital eroded, particularly in off-plan launches that never reached handover. End-user demand persisted, but financing was scarce, and panic dominated the market. This prolonged correction, while painful, ultimately led to crucial reforms such as escrow laws, RERA standardisation, and stronger investor protections that laid the foundation for a more resilient real estate environment in future cycles.

2015-2019 Cycle

Following a substantial expansion from 2012 to 2014, Dubai entered a soft correction, driven by global macroeconomic headwinds, including falling oil prices, regional tensions, and a strong U.S. dollar that squeezed affordability. Developers had overbuilt mid-income housing in areas such as Al Furjan, Sports City and Dubailand. Sales slowed, off-plan launches were scaled back, and prices declined by 15%-25% over the five years. Unlike 2009, this was a more gradual and controlled adjustment, thanks to improved regulation, better-capitalised developers, and more rational buyers. Secondary market transactions consistently outperformed off-plan, and end-user activity became dominant, quietly setting the stage for the subsequent rebound.

Mature market Late 2023 - Signs of Segmental Correction

Unlike the two complete citywide cycles above, the Dubai market has entered a mature phase where segmental cycles are evident, while the overall market scenario is bullish. By late 2023, although the broader market remained strong, early signs of fatigue began to appear in select areas. The ultra-luxury secondary segment, along with some oversupplied off-plan launches, began to cool. Yields flattened, prices in branded residences plateaued, and capital began to rotate toward ready inventory and undervalued family communities. Analysts began warning against excessive flipping, emphasising the importance of fundamentals. Though not a full correction, this phase underscored the need for cycle awareness even during bullish runs.

Dubai's Cycles: Lessons from history

Post-2008 Financial Crisis (2009-2011)

- » Price crash of 40-60%, projects stalled, investor losses
- » Led to escrow laws, RERA reforms, and tighter regulation

2015-2019 Correction

- » Gradual 15-25% price decline amid global headwinds
- » Rise of end-user market; better regulation avoided crash

Late 2023 - Signs Segmental Correction

- » Ultra-luxury & some oversupplied offplan began cooling
- » Segmental correction in an otherwise bullish market value-driven buying

4.1.3. Timing Isn't Prediction—It's Preparation

Real estate markets don't move in straight lines. They consistently follow cycles that are predictable in their pattern but asymmetric in their precise timing and intensity. In Dubai, they are often amplified by significant global capital flows, rapid local policy shifts, and the city's exceptionally fast development pace.

Truly savvy investors don't waste energy trying to predict exact tops or bottoms. Instead, they build cycle awareness, the crucial ability to accurately read market signals, deeply understand the current phase, and strategically act accordingly.

- **Recovery Phase:** This is the "buy smart" stage. Fear often dominates, but value investors strategically step in quietly, securing distressed or underpriced assets before the broader market rebound.
- **Expansion Phase:** As momentum steadily builds, those holding quality assets are richly rewarded. Yields typically improve, prices rise, and liquidity naturally returns. Strategic off-plan plays in prime areas can often outperform.
- **Peak Phase:** Euphoria typically takes over. Prices spike, but underlying yields often compress. This is when you should strategically de-risk by locking in profits, rotating into safer assets, and actively avoiding FOMO-driven decisions.
- **Correction Phase:** The market inevitably cools, prices soften, and uncertainty rises. However, for well-prepared investors, this presents a golden opportunity to acquire undervalued assets at below-market value. Some of the highest returns in Dubai's history came from investments made during the darkest months of the 2009 and 2020 corrections.

Infrastructure rollouts, international demand, developer behaviour, and robust regulation are the primary forces driving Dubai's market cycles. No two cycles look the same, but the underlying mechanics are consistently predictable. If you can accurately read the cycle, you can stay strategically ahead of the market and consistently make smarter, more confident moves.

4.1.4. Segment Cycles in a Maturing Market: One City, Many Timelines

As real estate markets mature, their cycles tend to become more fragmented. Instead of a citywide boom or bust, different property segments often follow their own distinct timelines, shaped by unique supply-demand dynamics, specific regulations, and varying investor sentiment. This trend is increasingly evident in Dubai, which is evolving from an opportunistic, developer-led market into a more diversified, data-driven investment environment.

For example, since 2021, affordable ready villas in outer zones, such as Town Square and Mudon, have seen steady demand and significant price appreciation, largely driven by end-user migration in the post-COVID era. At the same time, the ultra-luxury apartment segment in prime areas like Palm Jumeirah and Jumeirah Bay experienced a dramatic 30-50% surge from 2021 to early 2024, now showing signs of stabilisation and demand fatigue. Meanwhile, some mid-tier off-plan launches in oversupplied areas, such as JVC and Arjan, are already entering a correction phase, with slower sales and weakening investor appetite, especially for projects with poor locations or weaker developer credentials.

This type of asynchronous cycle behaviour mirrors patterns observed in global hubs such as London, Singapore, and Los Angeles. In London, for instance, while Kensington may be cooling off post-peak, Croydon could be entering an expansion phase due to new transport links and regeneration efforts. Likewise, in Dubai, a resale apartment in Downtown may face softening due to high entry prices and yield compression, while a competitively priced townhouse in Emaar South, backed by solid community development, might be in an early-stage growth phase.

The clear takeaway for investors: segment-level timing matters. Don't assume that "Dubai is booming" means every asset is in an expansion phase, or that a broader correction applies equally to all property types. To succeed, you must map each property's micro-cycle within the city's overall macro trend. Always ask yourself:

- Is this a late-stage off-plan with thin margins, or an early-phase launch in a rising location?
- Are we looking at a stable, low-volatility core area, or a speculative, unproven fringe?
- Has rental demand already peaked, or is there significant upside potential due to impending demographic shifts?

Building a diversified portfolio across segments helps reduce volatility while preserving upside potential. For example, a well-positioned investor might:

- Hold a Downtown Dubai 1-bedroom apartment for stable income with Airbnb flexibility.
- Invest in an early-phase Dubai South launch with Airport & Expo-driven upside.
- Accumulate land or townhouses in Al Furjan or MBR City for medium-term resale potential.

Dubai's maturing market consistently rewards precision, not generalisation. Like managing a stock portfolio across diverse sectors, real estate investing here demands close attention to the asset's micro-cycle, not just the city's headline trend.

INVESTOR INSIGHT

"Dubai is no longer one market, it's many micro-markets moving at different speeds." Segment thinking enables investors to anticipate rather than react. Always ask: Where is this specific property in its cycle?

INVESTOR MISTAKE TO AVOID

Assuming uniform appreciation across all segments. Just because villas in one district are appreciating doesn't mean all villas are. Avoid using "Dubai is booming" as a blanket justification—always dig into the sub-market data.

Table 4.1: Sample Market Segment Cycle Status (Mid 2025)

Segment	Phase	Indicator Example
Ultra-Luxury Apartments	Peak	High transaction prices, slowing resales
Mid-Tier Villas in Dubailand	Expansion	Strong rental demand, steady price uptick
Budget Apartments in JVC	Correction	Developer incentives, longer sales cycles
New Launches in Dubai South	Recovery	Increasing launches, early investor participation

4.2. Timing Entry with Data: Reading Inflection Indicators

While understanding market cycles is one thing, knowing when to act is another. This section introduces the concept of inflection indicators, the precise signals that guide strategic entry and exit.

> **INVESTOR INSIGHT**
>
> "In mature markets, success doesn't come from riding the wave—it comes from spotting the swell."

Real estate investing is often glamorised as a game of bold moves and gut feelings. However, in sophisticated, data-driven markets like Dubai, genuine success stems from identifying early signs long before the headlines even catch up. I call these indicators inflection indicators: subtle yet powerful shifts in market dynamics that clearly hint at a transition is underway, from correction to recovery, or from expansion to peak. Recognising them early empowers you to move with confidence, buying before the crowd, riding the upswing strategically, and stepping back before a correction inevitably bites.

In the following sections, we'll break down the key types of inflection indicators that smart investors can track and, crucially, how to act decisively on them.

4.2.1. Leading vs. Lagging Indicators

It's important to understand that not all indicators operate at the same speed. Some are leading indicators, subtly hinting at future market shifts before they become apparent. These are the earliest clues. Others are coincident indicators, reflecting what's happening in the market right now. And some are lagging indicators, confirming trends that have already passed. Spotting and correctly interpreting the leading signals is where the true edge lies in strategic timing.

Investor Note: Personalised data for your investing edge

I've developed a suite of proprietary tools designed to decode the Dubai market with precision. These tools analyse Dubai data to uncover project-level, community-level, and city-wide trends across both off-plan and secondary markets.

Here's what I track for my clients:

- **Rental Yields** by community, project, and asset type
- **Sales Velocity** (developer-wise and area-wise) a far more insightful indicator than raw sales numbers
- **Capital Appreciation Trends** mapped by developers, communities and projects.
- **Asset Class Breakdown** across both residential and commercial categories — from studios to villas, from offices to warehouses

Whether you're a data-driven investor or just want to stop guessing and start deciding with confidence, I offer **personalised reports** tailored to your investment goals.

Reach out if you'd like real insights, not just headlines.

4.2.2. Transaction Volume Momentum

Transaction volume often leads price movements. A significant uptick can signal renewed interest.

What to Watch:

- 3-6 month rolling averages in transaction counts (both off-plan and secondary).
- Area-specific sales data (e.g., Business Bay vs. Dubai South).
- Volume velocity relative to the previous cycle bottoms or tops.

Why It Matters:

- Volume typically precedes a higher price level. A sudden uptick in ready-unit transactions in a lagging community (e.g., IMPZ, Al Furjan) can signal institutional interest or a return of end-user demand, often marking the early start of a recovery. This makes transaction volume often a leading indicator.

Dubai Example (Q1-Q2 2021):

- Ready villa transactions in communities like Arabian Ranches and Mudon surged by 30% before significant price appreciation caught up in Q3. Early movers actively capitalised on 15-20% value gains within a single year.

4.2.3. Developer Launch Velocity and Payment Plan Trends

Developer behaviour often signals market sentiment and future supply.

What to Watch:

- A significant spike in new off-plan launches across various developers.
- Escalating post-handover payment plans (e.g., 40/60, 20/80, etc.).
- Aggressive incentives such as guaranteed ROI schemes, rent-back offers, or extensive fee waivers.

Why It Matters:

- When developers aggressively launch new projects with increasingly lax payment terms, it often signals growing oversupply pressure or opportunistic behaviour in a late-cycle phase. This is typical in peak or pre-correction phases, where capital inflow remains high but underlying demand may be showing signs of weakening. This can be a leading or coincidental indicator, depending on how early the market detects the shift.

Red Flag Pattern:

- Multiple projects in the same area offering 4-year or longer post-handover payment plans can be a strong liquidity red flag.

4.2.4. Rental Yield Compression

Yields are an accurate measure of a property's income-generating power relative to its price.

What to Watch:

- A consistent decline in gross yields in otherwise high-performing zones.
- Rents are stagnating or showing minimal growth, while capital values (prices) continue to increase significantly.
- Airbnb revenues are plateauing despite substantial and growing tourist traffic in the area.

Why It Matters:

- Yield compression typically occurs when asset prices rise faster than their income potential, often primarily driven by speculative demand. This phenomenon usually signals a late expansion or near-peak scenario, particularly in investment-driven districts. It frequently acts as a coincident or slightly lagging indicator of market overheating.

Example:

- Dubai Marina's average yield notably dropped from 6.2% to 4.8% between 2022 and 2023, even as prices continued to rise, strongly indicating overheating. In contrast, areas like Dubai Silicon Oasis maintained more stable yields, hinting at a more balanced expansion.

4.2.5. Mortgage Uptake Trends

Mortgage activity reflects end-user confidence and sustainable demand.

What to Watch:

- A noticeable spike in mortgage pre-approvals and new loan registrations (data available via the Central Bank of the UAE & DLD).
- An increase in loan-to-value (LTV) utilisation among end-users, suggesting greater willingness to leverage.
- Rising off-plan mortgage-linked approvals indicate banks' confidence in new projects.

Why It Matters:

- Mortgages serve as a proxy for genuine end-user confidence. When more residents commit to long-term financing, it indicates stronger expectations of price stability and more sustainable demand over time. This trend typically marks a recovery or early expansion phase, making it often a leading indicator of market confidence.

Global Parallel:

- In the U.S., Freddie Mac's loan origination volumes are often used to predict housing demand in the years following a recession.

4.2.6. Inventory Accumulation vs. Absorption Rate

Supply-demand balance is critical for price stability.

What to Watch:

- The "Days on Market" are consistently increasing in the secondary market.
- New property listings are outpacing the monthly absorption rate (calculated as the sales-to-inventory ratio).
- Significant developer stock remains unsold after initial launch campaigns, indicating weak initial demand.

Why It Matters:

- When listings increase but transaction velocity slows, it often signals a cooling market, especially after a peak. If the absorption rate drops below 15% in any micro-market, that area may be entering correction territory. This tends to be a coincident or slightly lagging indicator of market slowdown.

Dubai Application:

- Actively track platforms like DXBInteract and Bayut's daily listing flow areas. Popular areas like JVC and Furjan have historically shown inventory surges of over 20% preceding price stagnation.

4.2.7. Policy Catalysts & Regulatory Triggers

Government intervention in Dubai can swiftly reshape market dynamics.

What to Watch:

- Significant visa reforms (e.g., Golden Visa, retirement visas, freelance permits).
- Major infrastructure rollouts (e.g.. new metro line expansions, airport completion).
- Changes in taxation (e.g., VAT expansion, new corporate tax scope, revisions to DTCM fees).

Why It Matters:

- Dubai's real estate is highly policy-sensitive. Regulatory reforms can swiftly spark a new wave of demand or effectively cool speculative heat. For example, the 10-year Golden Visa reform triggered a surge of interest in properties exceeding AED 2 million in 2022-2023, helping pull luxury zones out of stagnation. Policy changes are often strong leading indicators.

Following the government's notification converting the area to freehold status and the announcement of the upcoming Blue Line metro extension, DSO is now back on the radar. The location is also part of Dubai's Urban Master Plan 2040, positioned as a future Innovation Zone, with additional connectivity planned through the Etihad Rail network.

Add to that the growing momentum alcng the E66 Al Ain corridor, and you start to see a cluster effect. Communities like DSO, DLRC, Liwan, Academic City, Warsan, and even International City are moving from overlooked to emerging. These peripheral zones are beginning to come into their own, offering both improved infrastructure and promising upside potential for investors willing to look beyond the core.

INVESTOR INSIGHT

Dubai Silicon Oasis (DSO) was always a well-located community with respectable rental yields, but its capital appreciation remained relatively flat. That's starting to change.

4.2.8. Confluence of Signals: Reading the Whole Story

Relying on a single market indicator is like trying to navigate a ship with only a compass; you know your general direction. Still, you have no information on the wind speed, the ocean currents, or the approaching storm. Expert investors act like seasoned captains; they don't rely on a single instrument. They gather data from every available source to see the complete picture.

This is the power of observing a **confluence of signals.**

Accurate market intelligence comes from identifying multiple indicators that collectively tell a similar story. When transaction volumes, developer incentives, sales velocity, capital appreciation, time on market, rental yields, and mortgage trends start moving in harmony, you have a reliable insight into an impending market shift. This holistic approach minimises the risk of acting on "false positives" and gives you the confidence to make a decisive move, whether that's buying, selling, or holding.

Let's bring this to life with a few practical scenarios showing how you, as an investor, can spot a confluence in the real world.

Putting It Into Practice: Three Market Scenarios

Scenario 1: Spotting a Market Bottom (The "Quiet Turn")

Imagine it's a "buyer's market." Media headlines are cautious, and prices have been flat for over a year. A single indicator, like low prices, isn't enough to act. Here's what a confluence for a bottoming market looks like:

- **Signal #1 (The Obvious):** You see on Property Finder that inventory is high and "Days on Market" for listings are long. Prices are stagnant. (Indicator: Inventory Buildup)
- **Signal #2 (The Early Whisper):** According to available CBUAE data, overall household lending and mortgage credit have remained stable even when sentiment wavers. While pre-approval numbers are not publicly disclosed, a steady uptick in new mortgage lending, even amid a cautious environment, often signals underlying demand momentum.
- **Signal #3 (The First Move):** You use DXBInteract to track specific communities you like (e.g., JVC, Town Square). You notice that while prices haven't moved, the raw number of secondary (ready) property transactions has increased by 15% this quarter. End-users are starting to buy. (Indicator: Surge in Secondary Transactions)

The Confluence: The combination of low prices, rising end-user mortgage demand, and an uptick in transaction volume before prices have started to rise is a powerful signal. The market is quietly turning. This is a classic opportunity to "enter early and target undervalued units."

Scenario 2: Confirming a Healthy Expansion (The "Green Light")

The market is now recovering. You want to know if this is a sustainable trend or just a temporary bounce.

- **Signal #1 (The Momentum):** *Data* confirms that transaction volumes are now substantial across both off-plan and secondary markets.
- **Signal #2 (The Price Action):** Prices are appreciating steadily, not explosively. The *RERA Index* shows that rents are also rising at a similar pace.
- **Signal #3 (The Yield Story):** Because prices and rents are moving together, rental yields are stable or slightly improving. A 1-bedroom in Dubai Marina that was yielding 6% is still yielding 5.8-6%. This is not a speculative bubble. **(Indicator: Stable Yields, not Compression)**
- **Signal #4 (The Developer Mood):** Developers are launching new projects, but their payment plans are still balanced (e.g., 40/60 or 50/50 during construction). They are not yet offering desperate, high-risk incentives.

The Confluence: Strong volume, sensible price growth, stable yields, and rational developer behaviour all point to a healthy, sustainable expansion. This is a green light for investing, especially for long-term yield plays or entering early-to-mid cycle prcjects.

Scenario 3: Identifying a Market Peak (The "Warning Bells")

The market feels euphoric. Everyone is an expert, and stories of quick profits are everywhere. This is when you must be most disciplined.

- **Signal #1 (The Speculative Frenzy):** Prices are accelerating rapidly. You see reports from *Knight Frank* or *JLL* noting 20%+ annual price growth in prime areas.
- **Signal #2 (The Big Red Flag):** You calculate the yields on recent sales and notice they are **compressing significantly**. A property that yielded 7% two years ago now only yields 4.5% at its current sale price. Prices are rising much faster than rents. **(Indicator: Yield Compression)**
- **Signal #3 (The Developer Panic):** You see a flood of new off-plan launches in the same area. To attract buyers, developers are offering extremely aggressive post-handover payment plans (e.g., pay 20% now and the other 80% over 8 years after moving in). This signals they are struggling to find genuinely qualified buyers. **(Indicator: Aggressive Payment Plans)**
- **Signal #4 (The End-User Retreat):** You can detect signs of end-user retreat by watching title deed activity in DXBInteract. In areas like JVC, Dubailand and Dubai Hills Estate, rising off-plan transactions paired with flat or falling ready-property sales often indicate that investors using extended payment plans are dominating the market, whereas genuine buyer demand is cooling.

The Confluence: Euphoric price growth, compressing rental yields, risky developer incentives, and waning end-user demand are a clear and powerful set of warning bells. The market is at or near its peak. The smart move here is to reassess risk, avoid new acquisitions, and perhaps consider taking profits on existing assets.

Table 4.2: Inflection Indicator Matrix - Application Guide

Understanding these critical market indicators helps you align your investment strategy with the current cycle. Here's a quick reference guide to intelligently interpret signals and respond accordingly:

Indicator	Phase It May Signal	Actionable Investor Move
Surge in secondary transactions	Recovery	Enter early; target undervalued, ready units
Spike in off-plan launches	Late expansion / Near peak	Be selective; avoid oversupplied zones
Mortgage uptick (end-user driven)	Bottoming out / Early expansion	Lock in long-term yield plays
Inventory buildup	Correction	Monitor closely; negotiate better terms
Aggressive payment plans	Peak	Reassess risk; verify developer reputation and execution history
Stable rents, rising prices	Yield compression / Peak	Shift focus to income-generating or undervalued rental assets

Table 4.3: Investor Tools to Track Inflection Indicators in Dubai

Use the right tools to stay informed consistently and spot market shifts early. These platforms actively help decode Dubai's real estate cycle in real time:

Tool / Platform	Use Case
DXBInteract	Provides daily transaction data and price heatmaps
Bayut & Property Finder	Offers insights into listing velocity, price drops, and rental trends
CB UAE Mortgage Lending Reports	Details mortgage lending volumes, LTV ratios, and financing sentiment
DLD Smart Apps	Provides information on title deed activity, project launches, and market permits
Colliers / JLL Reports	Analyses absorption rates, occupancy levels, and sectoral performance
My Reports	Across the board, inflection indicator reports are customised to your investment needs.

Table 4.4: Real Estate Market Cycle Tracking Tools - Reference Table

Tool / Data Source	What It Is	Where to Access It	Why It Matters for Investors
Mortgage Data CBUAE	Central Bank data on mortgage lending, Loan-to-Value (LTVs), and interest rates	www.centralbank.ae Statistics Monthly Bulletin	Shows early signals of demand shifts, indicates tightening/loosening credit, and provides insights into interest-rate-driven affordability
DLD Transaction Data	Government records of sales volumes, prices, and types of transactions	Dubai REST App / DLD	Tracks momentum in both off-plan and secondary markets—key for spotting expansion or correction
DXBInteract	Interactive dashboards for project-level transactions and price trends	www.dxbinteract.com	Provides micro-market data, including handovers, launches, and historical cycle trends—ideal for mapping
Property Monitor	Real-time valuation, sales comparables, and area trend analysis	www.propertymonitor.com (paid subscription)	Used by banks and valuers—helps benchmark current versus historic prices and assess when markets overheat
Bayut / dubizzle Trends	Portal data on listing prices, demand trends, and rent changes	www.bayut.com Market Trends	Serves as a sentiment-based indicator—useful for gauging pricing gaps and demand concentration
RERA Index	Rental caps and average area-specific rents	Dubai REST App RERA Index Section	Indicates whether rents are rising faster than prices or vice versa—crucial in yield versus appreciation decisions

Tool / Data Source	What It Is	Where to Access It	Why It Matters for Investors
Knight Frank / JLL Reports	Institutional research on prime markets, supply pipelines, and demand drivers	Knight Frank, JLL MENA	Offers strategic, big-picture insight into market movement—good for macro phase spotting
DIFC Real Estate Reports	Reports on commercial/office performance trends	www.difc.ae	Tracks commercial cycle phase shifts, particularly in Grade A office segments
Emirates NBD Real Estate Insight	Economic sector-specific lending and valuation summaries	www.emiratesnbdresearch.com	Integrates CBUAE data into sector-level analysis—helps detect broader funding appetite and investor optimism
Customised Reports	My proprietary tools, built on Dubai data, include yield tracking, capital appreciation, sales velocity, and liquidity by project or asset class	Available via request (custom reports or dashboards)	Enables deep analysis of off-plan and secondary markets, ranking of top-performing projects, yield compression signals, and heatmaps across all property types
AI-Driven Market Indicators	Predictive tools based on resale cycle patterns, time-on-market, and rental returns	My Internal tools are powered by Dubai data resale history and AI modelling	Identifies inflection points, hot zones, and yield compression or expansion using resale logic—vital for strategic portfolio decisions
Project-Level Secondary Market Reports	Reports on individual buildings and micro-communities, including resale yield, PSF trends, capital gains, and time to exit	My internal analytics suite	Crucial for evaluating exit strategies, flipping potential, and end-user vs investor demand in specific towers or sub-communities

Chapter Summary

Chapter 4, "Market Dynamics: Cycles, Locations, and Investment Timing," is your essential guide to understanding the rhythmic heartbeat of Dubai's real estate market. Moving beyond static observations, this chapter empowers you to interpret and act upon the market's natural ebbs and flows strategically, an essential skill for smart entries and recognising timely exits.

You've developed a deep understanding of real estate cycles, learning to identify the core phases of Recovery, Expansion, Peak, and Correction. Historical examples from Dubai's past illustrated how these cycles unfold in real time, helping you build the foresight to anticipate shifts rather than simply react to them.

A key insight explored was the idea of **segment cycles**, the fact that Dubai's market moves in many micro-markets, each with its own speed and sensitivity. Whether you're looking at studio apartments in JVC or commercial offices in Business Bay, this chapter trained you to view each segment through its cycle lens.

You were also introduced to the vital distinction between **leading and lagging indicators**, and learned how to interpret **inflection signals** like transaction trends, mortgage patterns, rental yields, and policy shifts. These markers help you detect when momentum is building—or fading—long before headlines catch up. More importantly, you learned that no single indicator offers the full picture. Strategic timing relies on recognising the **confluence of multiple signals** acting together.

To help you go further, I've developed a set of **proprietary investment tools**, available on request, that map real-time trends using verified data. These include project-level yield tracking, capital appreciation modules, inventory heat maps, and sales velocity insights for both off-plan and secondary markets. These tools transform market data into visual, actionable intelligence, allowing you to make more confident and timely investment decisions..

Key Takeaways:

- **Cycles Are Predictable in Pattern:** Understand the four phases: Recovery, Expansion, Peak, and Correction—and their typical behaviours.
- **Dubai's Cycles Are Dynamic:** Be aware of how policies, global events, and local factors can accelerate or delay cycle movements.
- **Segment Cycles Matter:** Micro-markets move at different speeds. Analyse property types and communities within their unique timing.
- **Leading vs Lagging Indicators:** Learn to recognise early versus late signals. Use this awareness to anticipate rather than react.
- **Inflection Indicators Are Your Edge:** Monitor confluences in transaction volume, yields, sales velocity, and inventory changes to spot turning points.
- **Confluence Over Single Signals:** The strongest insights come from layered data, not isolated stats.
- **Preparation Trumps Prediction:** Focus on cycle awareness and data fluency. Your readiness is more valuable than trying to time the exact top or bottom.
- **Customised Analytics Available:** My proprietary DLD-powered tools for yield tracking, appreciation heatmaps, and market timing insights are available on request and are designed to support strategic, data-driven decisions.

YOUR JOURNEY
NAVIGATOR

Part 1: Defining the Opportunity

Recap

You have just completed **Chapter 4: Market Dynamics – Cycles, Locations, and Investment Timing**, where we explored how Dubai's real estate cycles work, the signals that indicate when to enter or exit, and how location performance changes at different stages of the cycle. You learned how to identify high-potential areas based on current market conditions and how timing decisions can influence your overall return profile.

Next Chapter Preview

We now move to the *how to analyse* stage, focusing on the financial side of opportunity assessment. **Chapter 5: Essential Real Estate Math – Quantifying Opportunity** gives you the core and advanced formulas needed to evaluate properties, compare investment scenarios, and make data-driven choices with confidence..

You Will Learn

- ☑ The essential real estate metrics every investor must know.
- ☑ How to calculate ROI, yields, and cash-on-cash returns.
- ☑ The difference between gross and net income analysis.
- ☑ How to apply advanced metrics like IRR for strategic decision-making.

Link to Framework

This chapter strengthens your C.D.R.C. mindset by building clarity and confidence in your financial analysis, and supports your L.E.A.D. approach by enabling adaptable, evidence-based decision-making.

Purpose / Big Picture Link

This is the *how to measure* stage of your investment journey. Understanding the numbers now ensures that every *when*, *where*, and *what* decision you make later in the book is grounded in precise, data-backed calculations rather than assumptions.

CHAPTER 5

Essential Real Estate Math: Quantifying Opportunity

> The ability to measure and compare is the foundation of every great investment decision.
>
> **Benjamin Graham**

In real estate, instinct can certainly open doors, but it's math that gives confidence to deals. Consistently successful investors are those who can truly decode the numbers behind every single opportunity. Whether you're considering flipping off-plan units, structuring a complex joint venture, or managing long-term rentals, genuine financial fluency is what unmistakably separates hunches from rock-solid strategy.

Dubai's market is both competitive and highly margin-sensitive. Miscalculating crucial metrics like yield, Return on Investment (ROI), or your breakeven point can swiftly turn a seemingly promising deal into a costly and regrettable error. In reality, most investors don't lack exciting opportunities; what they often lack is the rigorous, accurate analysis required to seize them truly.

This chapter serves as your comprehensive, formula-driven toolkit, designed to guide you from vague guesswork to pinpoint precision. We'll begin with the essential equations every investor absolutely must master, then progressively advance to more sophisticated tools commonly utilised by seasoned professionals and large-scale developers. These aren't abstract finance theories; they are real-world, practical filters that empower you to decide confidently what to buy, when to hold, and how to exit profitably.

What You'll Be Equipped to Do:

- Analyse property deals with clarity and unwavering confidence.
- Compare diverse investment strategies using objective math, not persuasive marketing.
- Actively avoid costly mistakes that frequently trap emotional investors.
- Fluently speak the language of industry professionals - developers, lenders, and analysts.

> **INVESTOR INSIGHT**
>
> In a city often built on dreams, numbers are your unwavering reality check. Always run the math, no matter how polished the pitch or how dazzling the brochure may appear. The spreadsheet should convince you long before the sales agent does.

5.1. Basic Real Estate Math: Essential Tools for Everyday Investors

Before diving into advanced projections, you need to master the fundamental mathematics that powers every savvy real estate move. These aren't just abstract formulas; they are indispensable decision-making tools. Whether you're analysing your very first unit or planning to scale a multi-property portfolio, these core fundamentals will consistently provide you with clarity, control, and unwavering confidence.

Table 5.1: Core Real Estate Math Formulas.

Formula Name	LaTeX Formula	Use Case	Why It Matters
Percentage	$\text{Percentage} = \left(\frac{\text{Part}}{\text{Whole}}\right) \times 100$	Compare part-to-whole metrics	Used in calculating margins, service fees, and ownership splits
Profit %	$\text{Profit \%} = \left(\frac{\text{Profit}}{\text{Purchase Price}}\right) \times 100$	Measure resale or appreciation gains	Clearly shows how much value was created post-purchase
ROI (Return on Investment)	$\text{ROI} = \left(\frac{\text{Net Profit}}{\text{Total Capital Invested}}\right) \times 100$	Evaluate total investment performance	Captures both income and capital gains for a comprehensive view
Gross Yield	$\text{Gross Yield} = \left(\frac{\text{Annual Rent}}{\text{Property Price}}\right) \times 100$	Fast initial rental income screening	Great for quick, initial comparisons of income potential between properties
Net Yield	$\text{Net Yield} = \left(\frac{\text{Annual Rent} - \text{Annual Expenses}}{\text{Property Price}}\right) \times 100$	Measure true post-expense returns	Accurately reflects your real income after all operational costs are accounted for
Cash-on-Cash Return (CoC)	$\text{CoC} = \left(\frac{\text{Annual Pre-Tax Cash Flow}}{\text{Total Cash Invested}}\right) \times 100$	Evaluate cash performance on leveraged deals	A key metric for assessing the efficiency of your cash, especially for mortgage-backed assets
Price per Sq. Ft.	$\text{Price per Sq. Ft.} = \frac{\text{Sales Price}}{\text{Total Sq. Ft.}}$	Standardise pricing across units	Helps compare properties of different sizes and across various locations on a fair, per-unit-area basis

PRO TIP

You don't need to be a mathematician, just a competent decision-maker. Plug these formulas into your property analysis sheets and compare deals purely on objective numbers, not compelling narratives.

5.1.1. Understanding Percentages - The Foundation of All Real Estate Math

Percentages are your very first and most frequently used tool in real estate analysis. They empower you to consistently normalise performance across diverse properties, accurately compare deals of vastly different sizes, and, crucially, spot the accurate returns hidden behind seemingly complex numbers. Master this fundamental concept, and you're already on the way to mastering effective real estate finance.

Formula:

$$\text{Percentage} = \left(\frac{\text{Part}}{\text{Whole}}\right) \times 100$$

Example:

Profit Percentage You invest AED 300,000 and earn AED 60,000 in profit.

Calculation:

$$\text{Profit } \% = \left(\frac{60,000}{300,000}\right) \times 100 = 20\%$$

Why It Matters:

Profit percentages are not just simple math tools; they are the universal language of investment performance. Whether you are analysing a studio apartment in Arjan or a luxury villa on the Palm, percentages remove the distortion of size and reveal the true efficiency of an investment. They help you:

- Evaluate whether a return justifies the capital and risk involved
- Compare deals of very different scales with clarity.
- Benchmark performance against your personal return targets or market norms
- Avoid being misled by large profits that may represent weak returns on capital.

In short, understanding percentages helps you see the real story behind the numbers. A 10 percent return is still 10 per cent, whether it comes from AED 50,000 or AED 5 million. This clarity allows investors to allocate capital effectively and negotiate with confidence.

INVESTOR TIP

Always compare percentage returns, not just absolute AED values. It's consistently the surest way to accurately separate the scale of an investment from its actual performance.

INVESTOR MISTAKE TO AVOID

Confusing total monetary profit with the actual quality of an investment. A gain of AED 200,000 on an AED 5,000,000 deal (which is 4%) significantly underperforms a gain of AED 50,000 on an AED 500,000 deal (which is 10%).

5.1.2. Return on Investment (ROI) – What Your Capital Earned

ROI is your go-to metric for measuring the overall performance of an investment. It comprehensively captures the total return generated on the total capital invested, which includes the initial purchase price, all associated fees, and any subsequent improvements made. This provides you with a complete and accurate view of how efficiently your money has worked.

Formula:

$$\text{ROI} = \left(\frac{\text{Net Profit}}{\text{Total Capital Invested}} \right) \times 100$$

Example: Property Flip ROI

- Purchase Price: AED 1,000,000
- Additional Costs (e.g., DLD fees, broker commission): AED 50,000
- Total Capital Invested: AED 1,050,000
- Resale Price: AED 1,300,000
- Net Profit: AED 250,000 (after accounting for resale costs)

Calculation:

$$\text{ROI} = \left(\frac{250,000}{1,050,000} \right) \times 100 \approx 23.8\%$$

Why It Matters:

ROI seamlessly blends capital gains, various costs, and overall efficiency into a single, comprehensive number. It uniquely allows you to accurately compare different property types and locations on an equal footing, ultimately revealing where your money works the hardest and generates the most effective returns.

Best Use Case: Use ROI for:

- Off-plan flips
- Renovated resales
- Comparing full-cash deals across various communities

INVESTOR TIP

ROI helps you effectively compare performance across different timeframes and investment strategies. A lower ROI in, say, Downtown Dubai might offer greater stability. In comparison, a potentially higher ROI in an emerging area like Arjan might be better suited for short-term, growth-focused investors.

INVESTOR MISTAKE TO AVOID

Don't confuse ROI with yield. ROI encompasses total capital appreciation (and other profits), whereas yield focuses exclusively on rental income. You need to understand both metrics, but they convey fundamentally different aspects of your investment's performance.

5.1.3. Gross Yield vs. Net Yield – The Rental Income Reality

Yields are crucial metrics that measure the amount of income a property consistently generates relative to its price, making them essential for accurately evaluating rental returns. Unlike ROI, which includes the resale profit, yields focus purely on the rental income aspect. There are two primary types:

- **Gross Yield:** Represents the rental return before any expenses are deducted, and is an excellent metric for quick, initial comparisons.
- **Net Yield:** Represents the rental return after all expenses have been accounted for. This gives you your true, actual income.

Gross Yield Formula:

$$\text{Gross Yield} = \left(\frac{\text{Annual Rent}}{\text{Property Price}}\right) \times 100$$

Example:

- Property Price: AED 1,000,000
- Annual Rent: AED 100,000
- Gross Yield: (100,000/1,000,000) x 100 = 10%

Net Yield Formula:

$$\text{Net Yield} = \left(\frac{\text{Annual Rent} - \text{Annual Expenses}}{\text{Property Price}}\right) \times 100$$

Example:

- Annual Rent: AED 100,000
- Expenses (Service Charges, Maintenance, Management Fees): AED 15,000
- Net Yield: ((100,000 - 15,000) / 1,000,000) x 100 = 8.5%

Why It Matters: Yields are indispensable tools that help you:

- Accurately evaluate a buy-to-let property's income potential.
- Precisely compare different locations (e.g., Downtown versus JVC) based on rental profitability.
- Confidently decide between long-term or higher-yield Airbnb-style leasing strategies.

INVESTOR TIP

Always request actual, detailed cost breakdowns before committing to a purchase. A high gross yield can often mask significantly poorer returns once all expenses are factored in.

INVESTOR MISTAKE TO AVOID

Never base crucial purchase decisions solely on gross yield. A property that initially appears to offer an impressive 12% gross yield might realistically drop to just 6% after accounting for all associated costs. Always thoroughly check for:

Service charges (these can be substantial in Dubai).

Property management fees.

Realistic vacancy assumptions.

Gross Yield offers speed in assessment. Net Yield, on the other hand, delivers accuracy and reflects the accurate financial picture.

5.1.4. Cash-on-Cash Return (CoC) – Measuring What Your Money Earns

The cash-on-cash return measures the return specifically on the actual cash you invest, deliberately excluding any borrowed funds. This makes it a critical metric in dynamic markets like Dubai, where mortgages and staged payment plans are prevalent.

Unlike ROI (which includes the total capital, regardless of whether it was borrowed or not), CoC uniquely shows how efficiently *your own money* is actively working, making it an ideal metric for accurately assessing leveraged deals and performing comparative strategy analysis.

Formula:

$$\text{CoC Return} = \left(\frac{\text{Annual Pre-Tax Cash Flow}}{\text{Total Cash Invested}}\right) \times 100$$

Example:

- Purchase Price: AED 1,000,000
- Down Payment (your actual cash invested, e.g., 40%): AED 400,000
- Annual Cash Flow (after all expenses, including mortgage payments): AED 32,000

Calculation:

CoC Return = (32,000 / 400,000) x 100 = 8%

Why It Matters: Use CoC return strategically when:

- You are utilising any form of external financing or mortgages.
- You want to assess how quickly your cash is being recycled within the investment.
- You are actively comparing different rental models, such as Airbnb versus traditional long-term leasing.

CoC powerfully illustrates how hard your money is truly working, rather than the bank's.

Common Pitfall:

Ignoring Leverage Risks. While a high CoC might look incredibly attractive, remember this: it can quickly diminish if interest rates unexpectedly rise or if occupancy rates significantly drop. Never chase yield blindly. Always run downside scenarios, especially when dealing with mortgages.

INVESTOR TIP

Use CoC alongside Net Yield and ROI to gain a comprehensive understanding of both your leverage efficiency and overall profitability.

INVESTOR MISTAKE TO AVOID

Never calculate CoC using the total property value. Always base it strictly on the actual cash you have personally invested. Using borrowed amounts will inaccurately inflate your perceived returns and dangerously mask the exact risk associated with leverage.

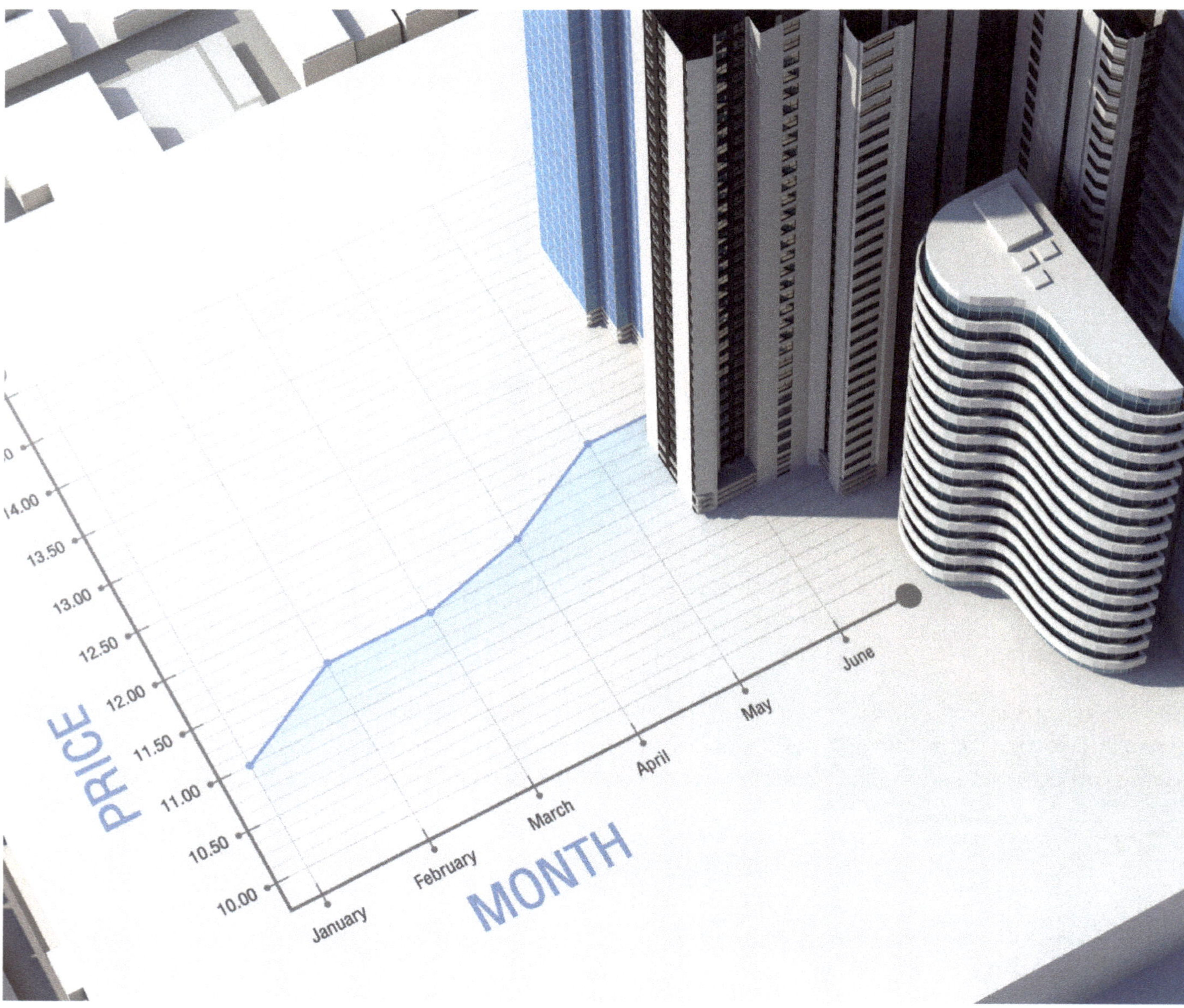

5.1.5. Scenario-Based Strategy Comparison – Align Math with Your Strategy

No two investors are truly identical. Whether you're focused on flipping properties, aiming for consistent rental income, or operating as an Airbnb host, your mathematical analysis must reflect your individual goals. These real-world scenarios powerfully demonstrate how the very same formulas can yield vastly different insights, depending entirely on your chosen investment strategy:

A. Flip Strategy (Short-Term Capital Gain)

- **Investor Profile:** Typically buys an off-plan or discounted ready property with the clear intent to sell it within a short timeframe, usually 1–2 years. The primary focus is on rapid capital gain.
- **Key Metric:** ROI (Return on Investment)
- **Example:**
  - **Purchase Price:** AED 950,000
  - **Sale Price:** AED 1,250,000
  - **Transaction & Agent Fees:** AED 60,000
  - **Net Profit:** AED 1,250,000 – AED 950,000 – AED 60,000 = AED 240,000
- **Calculation:** (Note: Total Capital Invested includes costs)

$$\text{ROI} = \left(\frac{240,000}{950,000 + 60,000}\right) \times 100 \approx 23.8\%$$

- **Insight:** This high short-term ROI is undeniably attractive, but it inherently carries significant timing risk and heavily depends on quick market liquidity at the time of exit.

B. Rental Hold Strategy (Long-Term Income)

- **Investor Profile:** Acquires ready units with the objective of long-term leasing, typically for 5–10 years. Prioritises consistent stability and steady cash flow over rapid appreciation.
- **Key Metrics:** Net Yield and Cash-on-Cash (CoC) Return
- **Example:**
  - **Property Price:** AED 1,000,000
  - **Annual Rent:** AED 100,000
  - **Yearly Expenses (maintenance, service fees):** AED 20,000
  - **Down Payment (your cash, assuming a mortgage):** AED 300,000
  - **Annual Mortgage Payment:** AED 30,000
  - **Net Annual Cash Flow (after expenses and mortgage):** AED 50,000
- **Calculations:**

$$\text{Net Yield} = \left(\frac{100,000 - 20,000}{1,000,000}\right) \times 100 = 8\%$$

$$\text{CoC Return} = \left(\frac{50,000}{300,000}\right) \times 100 \approx 16.7\%$$

- **Insight:** This strategy consistently delivers stable income with a strong CoC return. It is ideally suited for investors who are primarily focused on long-term growth, minimising tenant turnover, and benefiting from asset-backed resilience.

C. Airbnb Play (Short-Term Premium)

- **Investor Profile:** Furnishes and actively operates the unit as a holiday rental, aiming to earn significantly higher income than traditional standard leases. Requires active management.
- **Key Metrics:** Gross Yield, Net Yield, and ROI (including sale after holding period)
- **Example:**
  - **Purchase Price:** AED 1,200,000
  - **Gross Annual Income:** AED 180,000
  - **Annual Expenses (cleaning, management fees, DTCM tourism tax, utilities):** AED 50,000
  - **Net Annual Income:** AED 130,000
  - **Initial Cash Invested (down payment, furnishing):** AED 400,000
  - **Net Profit on Sale (after 2 years, assuming appreciation):** AED 200,000

- **Calculations:**

$$\text{Gross Yield} = \left(\frac{180,000}{1,200,000}\right) \times 100 = 15\%$$

$$\text{Gross Yield} = \left(\frac{180,000}{1,200,000}\right) \times 100 = 15\%$$

$$\text{ROI (on initial cash invested for the entire period)} = \left(\frac{(130,000 \times 2) + 200,000}{400,000}\right) \times 100 = 115\%$$

- **Insight:** Short-term rentals can offer significantly strong yields and excellent resale ROI, but they inherently require active management and strict regulatory compliance. This strategy is ideal for seasoned investors or those willing to use professional property managers.

D. Hybrid Strategy (Yield + Appreciation)

- **Investor Profile:** Holds a property for both consistent rental income and long-term capital appreciation, typically over 5–10 years. Seeks a balanced blend of steady cash flow and eventual resale upside.
- **Key Metrics:** ROI, Net Yield, Cash-on-Cash Return (CoC)
- **Example:**
    - **Purchase Price:** AED 1,200,000
    - **Net Rent over 5 Years (assuming average AED 75,000/year):** AED 375,000
    - **Annual Net Rent:** AED 75,000
    - **Down Payment (your cash invested, e.g., 30%):** AED 360,000
    - **Resale Price:** AED 1,500,000
    - **Net Sale Proceeds (after fees):** AED 1,450,000
    - **Total Inflows:** AED 375,000 (net rent) + AED 1,450,000 (net sale) = AED 1,825,000
    - **Total Investment (initial purchase price + other costs not covered by financing or operations):** AED 1,200,000
- **Calculations:**

$$\text{Return on Investment (ROI)} = \left(\frac{1,825,000 - 1,200,000}{1,200,000}\right) \times 100 \approx 52.08\%$$

$$\text{Net Yield (annual)} = \left(\frac{75,000}{1,200,000}\right) \times 100 = 6.25\%$$

$$\text{Cash-on-Cash Return (annual)} = \left(\frac{75,000}{360,000}\right) \times 100 \approx 20.8\%$$

- **Note:** This simple ROI provides a total return percentage over the five-year period. For a more nuanced, annualised return that accounts for the timing of each cash flow (rent) and the final sale, investors would use the Internal Rate of Return (IRR), which is covered in the Advanced Math section.
- **Insight:** This strategy offers both consistent income and significant long-term upside. ROI captures the total performance across the holding period, Net Yield shows the asset's inherent income efficiency, and CoC illustrates how effectively your actual cash is working annually. Together, these metrics provide a complete and resilient model, particularly well-suited for medium- to long-term investors.

INVESTOR TIP

Always model at least three scenarios, optimistic, realistic, and pessimistic, to test how changes in rent, resale price, or interest rate shifts might affect all your key metrics. This builds a robust understanding of potential outcomes.

PLEASE NOTE

The Cash-on-Cash Return (CoC) calculation above factors in the annual cash flow after mortgage payments. Suppose you wish to factor in yearly payments (like fluctuating EMIs) for a precise time-sensitive analysis across uneven cash flows. In that case, you might consider using the Internal Rate of Return (IRR) as discussed in the Advanced Math section.

5.1.6. Price per Square Foot – Normalise Your Comparisons

In Dubai, unit sizes and layouts can vary wildly. The price per square foot is your indispensable metric for achieving accurate, apples-to-apples evaluations, whether you're considering an off-plan purchase, a ready unit, or a resale property.

Formula:

$$\text{Price per Sq. Ft.} = \frac{\text{Sales Price}}{\text{Total Square Footage}}$$

Where:

- **Sales Price:** The total amount paid or asked for the property.
- **Total Square Footage:** The usable internal area of the property (often referred to as net or Built-Up Area).

Example:

- **Price:** AED 2,000,000
- **Usable Area:** 2,000 sq. ft.
- Result: AED 2,000,000 / 2,000 = AED 1,000 per sq ft.

If the prevailing market average for similar properties in that area is, say, AED 900 per square foot, your AED 1,000 per sq ft. unit might be overpriced unless there's a clearly justified premium for a superior view, a higher floor, or exceptional finishes.

Why It Matters: This metric is crucial because it:

- Consistently normalises diverse unit sizes and configurations, allowing for fair comparisons.
- Instantly flags potentially overpriced or surprisingly underpriced listings.
- Helps you accurately benchmark a property against prevailing local area trends.

INVESTOR TIP

Utilise powerful tools like DXBInteract, Bayut, Property Monitor, and of course, you can request and work with my customised reports, to track trends in AED/sq ft over time. This contextual data is invaluable for verifying whether your specific deal aligns with current market benchmarks.

INVESTOR MISTAKE TO AVOID

Watch out for developers or agents quoting prices based on "gross area" (which might include balconies, external walls, or shared space) instead of the actual "usable area." Your rental returns and living space are based on the net area, so always confirm the exact square footage you're genuinely paying for..

5.1.7. Mind the Measurement – Square Meters vs. Square Feet

Most Dubai property listings and brokers typically quote prices per square foot, but official records, such as title deeds, Oqood certificates, and DLD portals, frequently use square meters instead. Mixing these two units up can lead to serious mispricing and costly errors.

Conversion Formula:

- 1 square meter = 10.7639 square feet
- To convert Square Meters > Multiply by 10.7639
- To convert Square Feet > Divide by 10.7639

Why It Matters for Investors:

- A listing priced at AED 1,100 per square foot is equivalent to approximately AED 11,840 per square meter.
- Misreading or incorrectly converting these units can significantly inflate or understate valuations, particularly when comparing ready-to-move-in inventory versus off-plan projects.
- Additionally, developer brochures, Oqood documents, and final title deeds may list areas as net, gross, or BUA (Built-Up Area), and in either square meters or square feet. Each of these distinctions varies in scope and directly affects your ROI and accurate price benchmarking.

Advance Math Optional Section:

Mastering the basics gives you the power to analyse most standard deals. However, to truly evaluate long-term projects, compare complex leveraged opportunities, or speak the language of professional financiers, you need to upgrade your toolkit. The following advanced metrics are what separate seasoned investors from beginners, allowing you to assess risk and performance with a much deeper level of sophistication.

INVESTOR TIP

Always double-check:

What unit is the price quoted in (sq. ft or sq. m)?

The area includes balconies, walls, or shared common space.

That you're consistently comparing like-for-like areas across all your potential deals.

5.2. Advanced Real Estate Math: Smarter Tools for Bigger Decisions

As your investment journey evolves, simple ROI calculations alone often won't suffice. Larger, longer-term, or intricately leveraged deals demand the application of more advanced analytical tools that factor in time, complex financing structures, and nuanced risk assessments. This section highlights eight key formulas consistently employed by serious investors, astute developers, and professional financiers, each designed to reveal a specific, deeper layer of deal performance.

Use these tools selectively based on your precise investment strategy. You won't necessarily need all of them for every single deal, but knowing when and how to apply the right one accurately can truly be a game-changer for your investment outcomes.

You don't need to use every advanced formula for every deal. Focus on understanding these three powerhouses:

- **Internal Rate of Return (IRR):** Think of it as the 'true' annualised ROI for a project with multiple cash flows over time (like off-plan payments and yearly rent). It's the gold standard for comparing projects with different timelines.
- **Capitalisation Rate (Cap Rate):** This helps you quickly compare the income potential of different properties, assuming you paid all cash. It's the primary metric for valuing commercial and rental-focused assets.
- **Debt Service Coverage Ratio (DSCR):** This is the bank's favourite metric. It simply checks if your property's income is enough to cover its mortgage payments safely. A ratio above 1.25 is typically considered safe."

Table 5.2 – Key Advanced Metrics

Formula Name	LaTeX Formula	What It Does	Why Use It
IRR (Internal Rate of Return)	$\text{NPV}=0=-\text{Initial Investment}+\frac{CF_1}{(1+r)^1}+\ldots+\frac{CF_n}{(1+r)^n}$	Calculates the annualised return across multiple cash flows	Ideal for long-term deals with staggered returns (e.g., off-plan payments) and evaluating capital efficiency over time
Equity Multiple	$\frac{\text{Total Cash Received}}{\text{Total Equity Invested}}$	Measures the total return multiplier on your equity	Great for summarising overall deal performance across multiple years, showing how many times your initial cash investment was returned

Formula Name	LaTeX Formula	What It Does	Why Use It
NOI (Net Operating Income)	NOI = Gross Income - Operating Expenses	Shows pre-debt property profitability	A core number for calculating Cap Rate, DSCR, and for accurate property valuation
Cap Rate	$\text{Cap Rate} = \left(\frac{\text{Net Operating Income (NOI)}}{\text{Property Value}}\right) \times 100$	Evaluates the property's income yield, assuming an all-cash purchase	Use for comparing ready rental assets or commercial properties based purely on income relative to price
GRM (Gross Rent Multiplier)	$\text{GRM} = \frac{\text{Property Price}}{\text{Gross Annual Rent}}$	Provides a quick income check without considering costs	Good for initial screening of rental properties; always follow up with Net Yield or NOI for true profitability
DSCR (Debt Service Coverage Ratio)	$\text{DSCR} = \frac{\text{NOI}}{\text{Annual Debt Service}}$	Tests mortgage viability and risk buffer by showing how well operating income covers debt payments	Critical for securing bank financing and stress-testing the safety of leverage
LTV (Loan-to-Value)	$\text{LTV} = \left(\frac{\text{Loan Amount}}{\text{Property Value}}\right) \times 100$	Measures financing exposure relative to property value	Sets down payment requirements and directly impacts interest terms and lending conditions
YOC (Yield on Cost)	$\text{YOC} = \left(\frac{\text{Net Operating Income (NOI)}}{\text{Total Project Cost}}\right) \times 100$	Calculates return based on actual total investment, including acquisition and development costs	Key for evaluating renovation projects, value-add strategies, or ground-up development projects
Payback Period	$\text{Payback Period} = \frac{\text{Total Investment}}{\text{Annual Cash Flow}}$	Determines the time required to recover the initial investment from cash flows	Useful for liquidity-focused strategies (e.g., Airbnb, value-add projects) where quick capital recovery is a priority

Chapter Summary

Chapter 5, "Essential Real Estate Math: Quantifying Opportunity," is your indispensable toolkit for transforming intuition into precision in Dubai real estate investment. It powerfully asserts that while opportunities may open doors, math is what closes truly profitable deals.

The chapter began by arming you with Basic Real Estate Math, including essential formulas for calculating percentages, ROI, Gross and Net Yields, Cash-on-Cash Return, and Price per Square Foot. Through real-world, scenario-based comparisons, you saw how these core metrics apply to different investment strategies, from short-term flips to long-term rental holds and hybrid approaches, demonstrating how to align your analysis with your specific goals.

You then advanced to Smarter Tools for Bigger Decisions, exploring sophisticated metrics like Internal Rate of Return (IRR), Equity Multiple, Net Operating Income (NOI), Capitalisation Rate (Cap Rate), Debt Service Coverage Ratio (DSCR), Loan-to-Value (LTV), Yield on Cost (YOC), and Payback Period. These advanced formulas equip you to evaluate larger, more complex, or leveraged deals, revealing deeper layers of performance.

This chapter underscores that mastery of these mathematical tools is not just about calculation; it's about confident decision-making, effective risk management, and the ability to distinguish genuine opportunities from mere speculation. By making math your unwavering reality check, you ensure that every investment choice is grounded in objective data, paving the way for truly profitable outcomes.

Key Takeaways:

- **Math is Your Edge:** In a competitive market like Dubai, financial fluency separates profitable strategies from hunches.
- **Master the Basics:** Core formulas like ROI, Yields (Gross and Net), CoC, and Price per Sq. Ft. are indispensable for everyday analysis.
- **Align Math with Strategy:** Different investment goals (flipping, renting, hybrid) require specific metrics for accurate evaluation.
- **Understand Advanced Tools:** For larger or leveraged deals, metrics like IRR, NOI, and DSCR provide deeper performance insights.
- **Quantify Everything:** Always run the numbers objectively to avoid costly mistakes and base decisions on data, not just narrative.
- **Beware of Hidden Costs:** Factor in all expenses (service charges, maintenance, financing) to ensure your calculated returns are realistic.

YOUR JOURNEY
NAVIGATOR

Part 1: Defining the Opportunity

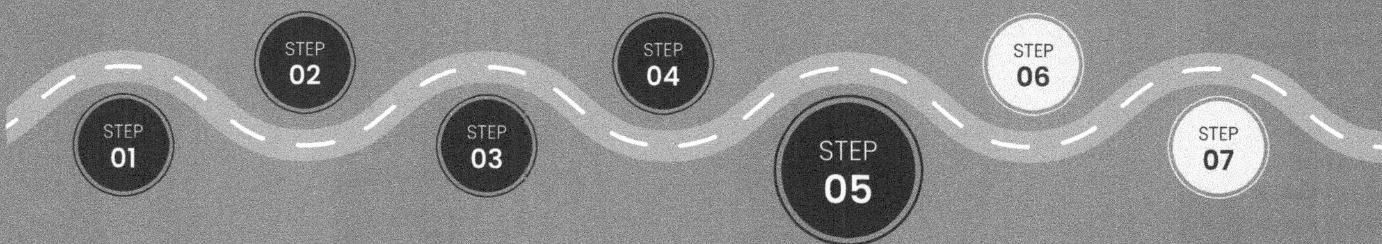

Recap

You have just completed **Chapter 5: Essential Real Estate Math – Quantifying Opportunity**, where you learned the essential and advanced financial metrics that underpin sound investment decisions. You now know how to calculate ROI, yields, cash-on-cash returns, and IRR, and how to apply these tools to compare different strategies and scenarios with accuracy.

Next Chapter Preview

We now move into the *what to invest in* stage. **Chapter 6: Property Types & Investment Opportunities – Residential vs. Commercial** will help you understand the different asset classes available in Dubai, the pros and cons of each, and how to match the right property type to your investment objectives and profile.

You Will Learn

- ☑ The main residential and commercial property types in Dubai and their unique characteristics.
- ☑ How to compare residential versus commercial opportunities.
- ☑ The pros and cons of off-plan versus ready properties.
- ☑ The legal structures of ownership and their implications.
- ☑ How to align property type selection with your investment goals and market outlook.

Link to Framework

This chapter strengthens your C.D.R.C. mindset by clarifying the strategic choices available and supports your L.E.A.D. approach by enabling adaptable selection of property types that drive value in different market conditions.

Purpose / Big Picture Link

This is the *what* stage of your investment journey. Understanding the range of property types and their strategic fit ensures that your decisions in later stages are grounded in a clear match between asset characteristics, market timing, and your investment strategy.

CHAPTER 6

Property Types & Investment Opportunities: Residential vs. Commercial

> The major fortunes in real estate have been made by choosing the right type of property in the right location and holding it.
>
> **Andrew Carnegie**

Not all real estate is created equal. Selecting the right property type isn't just about personal preference; it directly impacts your returns, risks, liquidity, and ultimately, your exit options. Whether you're eyeing a luxury villa for capital appreciation or a compact studio for Airbnb yields, your chosen asset's fundamental structure and its typical market behaviour will broadly define your outcome.

This chapter provides you with a comprehensive framework to evaluate the primary types of real estate investments available in Dubai, including various residential units, commercial properties, and raw land plots. We will also examine the nuances of legal structures, the dynamics of various property transactions, and the suitability of different asset classes for specific investor profiles. By the end of this chapter, you'll be equipped to make more informed decisions about *what* kind of property truly aligns with your investment strategy.

6.1. Residential Property Types in Dubai

Dubai's residential real estate market offers a diverse and compelling range of investment options. From efficient studios, often ideal for high-yield strategies, to sprawling luxury villas that typically anchor long-term wealth, each distinct option serves a unique investment purpose. Let's explore each in detail, referencing actual Dubai examples, typical price ranges, and their strategic positioning within the market.

Residential Property Types at a Glance

Studio	1 Bedroom	2/3 Bedroom	Townhouse	Villas
Airbnb / Student Rental	**Young Professionals / Couples**	**Families / Long-term Tenants**	**Families / Community Living**	**Luxury Living / Long-term Holds**
Pros: High rental yield, low entry price, strong demand in central/student zones.	**Pros:** Balanced demand, flexible for lease or Airbnb, strong liquidity	**Pros:** Higher rental income, stable tenants, better capital growth potential	**Pros:** Strong community demand, mid-ticket pricing, reasonable for end-user	**Pros:** True land ownership, strong capital appreciation, exclusive lifestyle appeal
Cons: Limited capital appreciation, higher tenant turnover, susceptible to oversupply in budget areas	**Cons:** Moderate appreciation possible oversupply in new launches	**Cons:** Higher ticket size, slower resale in downturns	**Cons:** Shared walls, design/expansion limitations, less privacy	**Cons:** High cost, higher maintenance/serv ice charges, lower rental yield

6.1.1. Studio Apartments

Studio apartments are a popular and accessible entry point for investors in Dubai, primarily due to their relatively low prices and their potential for strong rental yields in areas such as Jumeirah Village Circle (JVC) and Dubai Silicon Oasis. These compact units are often ideal for short-term rentals, consistently attracting a diverse demographic including students, young professionals, and tourists. While their appreciation potential may be somewhat limited compared to larger units, studios are excellent at generating solid and consistent cash flow.

Investors should be keenly aware of potential oversupply risks in certain budget areas and note that some zones, like Jumeirah Village Triangle (JVT), no longer permit new studio developments. These specific zoning constraints can increase the value of existing units, particularly in well-connected, high-demand areas. Strategic location choice and an acute awareness of development regulations are key to maximising their potential.

Pros:

- Low ticket size (typically AED 400,000–700,000 in emerging areas).
- High rental yield potential (often 7%–10% gross).
- Strong demand in transient zones, attracting students, solo expatriates, and tourists.

Cons:

- Limited appreciation potential compared to larger units or villas.
- Tend to have higher tenant turnover rates.
- More susceptible to oversupply issues in budget-focused areas.

Where It Makes Sense in Dubai:

- **Discovery Gardens, JVC, International City:** Studio prices range from AED 500,000 to AED 700,000. Yields can be high due to strong demand in these areas.
- **Dubai Silicon Oasis:** Benefits from a stable student and tech tenant base, strategically located close to universities.
- **DLRC (Dubai Land Residential Complex), Liwan, Dubai South:** Characterised by a lower price per sq ft, attracting strong investor interest due to newer off-plan projects.
- **Emirates Garden City Satwa, Dubai Island:** Upcoming areas that show potential for high short-term demand, leading to excellent yield and ROI.

INVESTOR TIP

Many areas in Dubai now impose restrictions on new studio construction. For instance, new developments in JVT are no longer permitted to include studios. Keep an eye out for these zoning restrictions, as they can significantly increase the value of existing projects in those areas due to reduced future supply.

INVESTOR INSIGHT

Studios are your cash-flow machines, ideal for investors looking to test the waters or maximise income with short-term rentals. Always avoid oversaturated buildings and instead focus on properties with proximity to metro lines, academic hubs, or established hospitality zones.

6.1.2. 1-Bedroom Apartments

1-bedroom apartments typically offer an excellent middle ground, balancing affordability with rental stability within Dubai's property market. They are highly liquid assets, appealing to a wide and versatile range of tenants, including singles, young couples, and professionals and are relatively straightforward to lease or resell. With price points typically ranging from AED 850,000 to AED 1.3 million in mid-tier zones, they consistently serve as a go-to option for conservative investors primarily focused on capital preservation alongside moderate yields.

Areas such as Business Bay, JVC, Dubai Hills Estate, and Dubai Marina consistently experience substantial tenant turnover for one-bedroom units due to their central locations and excellent proximity to transit networks, retail hubs, or major employment zones. Historically, 1-bedroom apartments have demonstrated mixed performance during downturns. During the 2015–2016 correction, while luxury and speculative off-plan segments saw significant price drops, well-located 1-bedroom units proved more resilient. This makes them a generally lower-risk choice, but investors must remain diligent regarding unit layout, overall building quality, and potential market saturation when making their selection.

- **Size Range:** Typically 600–900 sq ft.
- **Typical Strategy:** Long-term rental income, personal lifestyle use, or a mixed strategy combining Airbnb and family stays.
- **Investor Profile:** Ideal for first-time buyers, end-users, and hybrid investors seeking balanced returns.

Pros:

- Versatile unit type with broad tenant appeal.
- Relatively more straightforward to sell or lease compared to larger units.
- Offers moderate rental yield (typically 6%–8%), balanced with good liquidity.

Cons:

- The market faces supply competition due to a consistent off-plan development pipeline.
- Offers moderate capital appreciation unless located in prime or high-growth zones.

Analysing some different locations:

- **Dubai Marina:** AED 1.1M–1.4M for sea-facing 1-bedroom units, offering stable yields supported by tourist demand. However, be cautious of ageing buildings or those with inadequate maintenance, which can impact long-term appreciation or leasing.
- **Business Bay:** Close to Downtown and the Metro, boasting a strong rental market. A consistently good option, though achieving a strong yield can be challenging due to higher entry prices.
- **Creek Harbour (Emaar):** Features well-designed new stock with strong future growth potential driven by infrastructure and retail development. Both off-plan and ready options are available here.
- **Town Square & Hessa Stretch:** Demonstrate strong long-term rental and resale demand, particularly from families.

INVESTOR INSIGHT

One-bedroom apartments ideally strike a balance between consistent cash flow and capital security. They effectively attract long-term tenants and are often the easiest unit type to exit in the resale market, making them a solid core component for conservative investors' portfolios..

6.1.3. 2- & 3-Bedroom Apartments

2- and 3-bedroom apartments form the backbone of Dubai's residential market, offering a compelling blend of space, livability, and strong long-term rental appeal. These units are desirable to end-user families, making them a stable option for investors primarily focused on tenant retention and consistent yield. Locations such as Dubai Hills Estate, Al Furjan, JLT and JVC feature well-planned, family-friendly infrastructure, including schools, parks, and retail amenities, which consistently support sustained demand and lower vacancy rates.

While the average gross rental yield for 2-bedroom units typically ranges between 6% and 7.5%, depending on the specific area, they also benefit from lower tenant turnover and reduced management overhead compared to studios or 1-bedroom units. Historically, 2-bedroom apartments have shown greater resilience during market downturns. During the 2015–2016 correction, for instance, while luxury and speculative off-plan properties experienced significant price adjustments, well-maintained 2-bedroom units in established communities generally faced lower price erosion and fewer tenant delinquencies. This makes them suitable for investors seeking downside protection coupled with steady long-term appreciation and income.

- **Size Range:** Typically 1,000–2,000 sq ft.
- **Typical Strategy:** Long-term family rental, focusing on capital appreciation in mixed-use zones.
- **Investor Profile:** Family-focused investors and landlords primarily seeking tenant stability.

Pros:	Cons:
Generally, it commands a higher monthly rent compared to smaller units.	Can be slower to liquidate in down markets compared to smaller units.
Benefits from lower vacancy rates in suburban or master-planned zones.	Involves a higher absolute entry price (typically AED 1.4M–2.5M).
They are highly attractive to the end-user resale market due to their family appeal.	

Analysing some options:

- **Dubai Hills Estate:** 2-3 bedroom units located near schools and parks in areas like Greenside or Executive Residences. Emaar consistently launches new off-plan projects in Dubai Hills, while existing units are well-established and offer good rental yields.
- **Al Furjan:** A rapidly growing family zone known for its large layouts and convenient Metro access.
- **Majan, DLRC, Liwan:** These areas experience strong local family demand and offer good connectivity for working families, with educational institutes nearby and generally lower service charges. They are upcoming areas highly appealing to families.
- **Palm Jumeirah Shoreline or Marina Residences:** Require a higher initial investment but offer premium resale value. These areas generally tend to hold value even in volatile markets where other locations might be oversupplied.

INVESTOR INSIGHT

For investors seeking stable rental income and low tenant turnover, 2–3-bedroom units in family-oriented communities offer powerful fundamentals. These units are highly appealing to end-users upon resale and are typically less sensitive to short-term market noise.

6.1.4. Townhouses

Townhouses are a highly popular property type in Dubai, offering an ideal blend of space, privacy, and community living. Typically featuring two to four bedrooms, private gardens, and dedicated parking, these homes are seamlessly integrated into master-planned communities that provide shared amenities, including parks, swimming pools, and schools. This desirable combination makes them especially appealing to young families and professionals seeking a suburban yet well-connected lifestyle.

For investors, townhouses consistently present strong rental demand and excellent long-term appreciation potential. They primarily attract end-users who desire more space than an apartment can offer, coupled with the comfort and structured environment of an amenity-rich neighbourhood. Communities such as Arabian Ranches, Villanova, and Mudon have consistently seen robust price growth, driven by phased development and continuously improving infrastructure. Dubai's townhouse culture is defined by its strong focus on livability, featuring abundant green spaces, a high sense of safety, and comprehensive family-oriented facilities.

- **Size Range:** Typically 1,800–3,500 sq ft.
- **Typical Strategy:** Buy-to-let within gated communities, targeting end-user resale, and consistent family rentals.
- **Investor Profile:** Investors primarily targeting capital gains with the added buffer of rental income.

Pros:

- High demand among mid-income families.
- Offers desirable community living, often within secure gated developments.
- Features a moderate entry price point (typically AED 1.6M–3.5M).

Cons:

- Generally incur higher service charges compared to apartments.
- Shared walls reduce privacy when compared to standalone villas.

Where It Makes Sense in Dubai:

- **Damac Lagoon/Tilal Al Ghaf:** Along Hessa, many of these townhouses offer a fantastic opportunity in an emerging zone.
- **The Valley (Emaar):** More of a peripheral opportunity, it offers high capital gain potential driven by new infrastructure development.
- **Arabian Ranches 3:** Demonstrates substantial secondary market value due to its established brand and desirable community features. Dubai Land as a whole is a good emerging zone opportunity, with a lot of communities coming alongside that location.
- **Mudon / Mira / Serena:** Popular mid-income family zones, offering good rental stability.

INVESTOR INSIGHT

Townhouses perfectly sit at the sweet spot between apartments and standalone villas. They strongly appeal to long-term tenants and are frequently the first upgrade choice for apartment dwellers, making them highly attractive for 5–7 year hold strategies.

6.1.5. Villas

Villas represent the pinnacle of residential living in Dubai, consistently offering unmatched space, privacy, and prestige. With expansive layouts, private gardens, dedicated maids' rooms, and often private swimming pools, villas cater specifically to high-net-worth individuals, larger families, and discerning long-term residents seeking permanence and an elevated lifestyle. For end-users, especially those with children or multigenerational households, villas provide a serene sanctuary, away from the density of vertical living but still conveniently within reach of key urban zones.

Gated villa communities, such as Arabian Ranches, Jumeirah Park, The Lakes, and more recently, Tilal Al Ghaf and Dubai Hills Estate, offer curated environments that seamlessly blend expansive green spaces, international schools, diverse retail options, and world-class wellness facilities into one cohesive ecosystem. This holistic living experience elevates villas beyond just a property type; it's a comprehensive lifestyle upgrade.

From an investment perspective, villas have consistently shown impressive long-term capital growth, particularly during market cycles when space and privacy become a premium. During the COVID-19 pandemic, for instance, villa prices surged by over 35–40% in some communities as families increasingly prioritised outdoor areas and dedicated home offices. This trend has sustained exceptionally well.

- **Size Range:** Typically 3,000 sq ft and above.
- **Typical Strategy:** Long-term holds for capital appreciation, legacy building, or luxury lifestyle use.
- **Investor Profile:** High-net-worth individuals, large families, and investors seeking significant capital gains.

Pros:

- Offers actual land ownership, a unique and highly valued aspect in Dubai.
- Strong potential for significant long-term capital appreciation.
- Provides an exclusive, private, and prestigious lifestyle appeal.

Cons:

- Involves a much higher entry cost (typically AED 3.5M–30M+).
- Incurs higher maintenance and service charges compared to other residential types.
- Generally offers a lower rental yield compared to apartments.
- Can have longer resale cycles in slower markets.

Maintenance Costs: Beyond the Square Foot

While the *per-square-foot* common area service charges for apartments (especially in high-rises with extensive shared amenities) may seem higher, investors must understand the overall maintenance requirements for different property types. Villas and townhouses, due to their significantly larger sizes, private gardens, and often private swimming pools, will generally incur higher total annual maintenance and upkeep costs. These include expenses for garden upkeep, pool cleaning,

Where It Makes Sense in Dubai:

- **Dubai Hills Estate (Maple, Sidra):** Strong family appeal combined with consistent resale demand. Emaar consistently launches new off-plan villas in Dubai Hills, while existing units are well-established.
- **Palm Jumeirah Frond Villas:** Represents ultra-luxury, waterfront living, commanding premium resale values.
- **Meydan District 11:** This is an upcoming zone due to key location advantage and premium planning, where Villas sell out on launch, and the long-term outlook is positive.
- **Jumeirah Golf Estates, Jumeira Park & Jumeira Islands, Emirates Living:** Known for long-term capital appreciation driven by exclusivity, these are core villa zones where there is a lot of opportunity to redevelop and upgrade the villas to create ongoing value.
- **Emaar, Nakheel & Dubai Properties:** These developers have time and again given priceless gems and great value to early investors. If you can afford a slightly higher entry budget, going with a branded developer is a good idea for a Villa investment.
- **Palm Jebel ALI and Dubai Islands:** Upcoming waterfront living zones which border on peripheral areas as of now, but will soon be vibrant emerging communities

INVESTOR INSIGHT

Villas are inherently long-term plays. They might not generate exceptionally high rental yields. Still, when acquired correctly, especially within branded, master-planned communities, they consistently deliver exceptional capital appreciation and a significant lifestyle ROI over the long run.

6.2. Residential Property Types – Comparison Table (Dubai Context)

Dubai's residential real estate landscape offers a diverse range of investment options tailored to various goals, budgets, and investor profiles.

Studio apartments, with their low entry points and potential for high rental yields, are frequently the go-to choice for first-time investors or those targeting short-term, high-turnover tenants such as students or tourists. However, their often-limited appreciation potential and susceptibility to oversupply risks make them more suitable for income-focused strategies rather than long-term capital growth.

One-bedroom apartments typically strike a compelling middle ground. They offer a desirable mix of liquidity, versatility in usage (whether for consistent leasing or flexible Airbnb operation), and broad tenant appeal, especially among single professionals and young couples. Their appreciation generally tends to be moderate but stable.

Two- and three-bedroom apartments begin to shift the investment focus decisively toward family living. These units consistently command longer leases, exhibit lower tenant turnover, and show more substantial capital appreciation potential, particularly within well-planned mixed-use zones. Investors seeking balanced cash flow with significant potential upside often naturally gravitate towards this segment.

Townhouses present a compelling hybrid, seamlessly blending apartment convenience with villa-style living. With their mid-ticket pricing, strong community appeal, and inherent end-user demand, they consistently perform well in suburban, master-planned areas. Their success, however, hinges heavily on internal positioning within the community and robust build quality, but they offer strong potential when chosen wisely.

Villas, positioned at the top end of the spectrum, are undeniably lifestyle assets. They strongly appeal to long-term end-users and wealth-focused investors seeking legacy properties or prestigious trophy holdings. While they demand higher maintenance costs and typically have longer resale cycles, villas often significantly outperform in capital appreciation over the long term, particularly within blue-chip communities characterised by limited supply and high desirability.

Table 6.1: Residential Property Types – Comparison Table (Dubai Context)

Property Type	Ideal Tenant / Use Case	Pros	Cons
Studio Apartment	Airbnb, student rental	High rental yield, low entry price, strong demand in central/student zones	Limited capital appreciation, higher tenant turnover, susceptible to oversupply in budget areas
1-Bedroom Apartment	Young professionals, couples	Balanced demand, flexible for lease or Airbnb, strong liquidity	Moderate appreciation, possible oversupply in new launches
2/3-Bedroom Apartment	Families, long-term tenants	Higher rental income, stable tenants, better capital growth potential	Higher ticket size, slower resale in downturns
Townhouse	Families, community living	Strong community demand, mid-ticket pricing, reasonable for end-users	Shared walls, design/ expansion limitations, and less privacy
Villa	Luxury living, long-term holds	Actual land ownership, strong capital appreciation, exclusive lifestyle appeal	High cost, higher maintenance / service charges, lower rental yield

INVESTOR INSIGHT

Your chosen property type should always align perfectly with your ultimate investment goal. Studios and 1-bedroom apartments typically suit cash-flow-focused investors; villas, on the other hand, strongly favour capital gain players. Townhouses offer a versatile middle ground for family-focused investors.

6.3. Commercial Property Types – Deep Dive

Dubai's commercial property market is a powerhouse of opportunity, consistently offering investors exposure to business-driven real estate that frequently delivers higher yields than traditional residential options. From high-demand warehouses serving global logistics players to sleek office towers in the heart of Downtown, each commercial asset class presents a distinct investment profile. The following subsections will examine each primary commercial type: plots, warehouses, offices, retail shops, and staff accommodations, providing real-world Dubai examples, key investment characteristics, and actionable insights for building a truly diversified commercial portfolio.

6.3.1. Villa & Townhouse Plots

Villa and townhouse plots offer investors a compelling chance to participate in Dubai's property market from the ground up—literally. These plots are parcels of raw, undeveloped land allocated for low-rise residential use, often situated within master-planned communities or newly emerging corridors. What makes plots particularly attractive is their inherent flexibility and pure exposure to land value appreciation. Without the immediate costs of construction or maintenance associated with a built property, plots allow investors to benefit solely from market growth and strategic infrastructure development over time.

Plots are typically sold directly by master developers or through resale in the secondary market. They can be financed via equity, specific land mortgages, or structured Joint Venture (JV) arrangements. With no rental income generated until development is complete, plot buyers primarily rely on eventual resale value or plan for long-term build-and-hold strategies. Strategic selection and rigorous due diligence are essential to unlocking their full potential.

Where It Makes Sense in Dubai:

- **Al Furjan:** A very popular community for building villas, known for its excellent connectivity.
- **Meydan - Nad Al Sheba:** Look for good deals on plots in these centrally located, premium areas.
- **Jebel Ali Hills by Meraas:** Offers freehold villa plots conveniently located near Dubai Parks and Resorts, featuring no service charges and strong appreciation potential. This represents an early entry opportunity, as the community will be fully developed in a few years.
- **MBR City – District 11:** Select pockets offer villa plot sales with prime proximity to Meydan, Downtown, and elite schools.

Investor Profiles & Use Cases:

- **Developers:** Acquire plots for building custom villa communities or townhouses for sale.
- **End-Users:** Purchase plots with the intent to construct bespoke family homes tailored to their exact specifications.
- **Land Bankers:** Buy undeveloped plots with a long-term strategy to hold them purely for future appreciation.

Key Metrics:

- **Entry Price:** Typically ranges from AED 1M–10M+.
- **Rental Yield:** Not applicable until the plot is developed and rented out.
- **Capital Appreciation:** Potential for high appreciation, particularly in early-stage locations with strong future development prospects.
- **Risks:** Includes zoning delays, unexpected development costs, and potential lags in infrastructure completion.

INVESTOR INSIGHT

Early plot investors in Jebel Ali Hills notably observed prices rise from AED 90 to AED 110 per square foot in 2021 to AED 200 to AED 220 by 2024. With patience for area maturation, these types of investments can yield significant returns.

6.3.2. Warehouses

Warehouse investments in Dubai function very differently from traditional residential real estate. Most are structured on long-term land leases, often for durations of 30 to 50 years rather than offering outright freehold ownership. Investors typically own the built structure (the warehouse itself) on a usufruct basis. Concurrently, the underlying land remains under the control of a master developer such as Dubai Industrial City, Dubai Investment Park (DIP), or Dubai Real Estate Corporation (DREC). This creates a dual-layered asset, where both the built-up property rights and the specific land lease terms must be understood.

In specific projects, strata warehouses offer individually owned units within a larger industrial complex, providing more accessible entry points for small and mid-size investors. These strata units can be leased to logistics firms or utilised for e-commerce storage. However, they also come with associated infrastructure fees, service charges, and zone-specific activity restrictions that must be thoroughly reviewed.

Warehouses in Dubai are primarily industrial storage and logistics facilities, strategically located near major ports, airports, or extensive highway networks to maximise operational efficiency. They are typically used for logistics, distribution, light manufacturing, and e-commerce fulfilment. High-demand areas include Jebel Ali Free Zone (JAFZA), Dubai Investment Park (DIP), National Industries Park (NIP), Dubai Industrial City (DIC), Jebel Ali Industrial Areas 1-4, Al Quoz, Ras Al Khor, Umm Ramool, and Al Qusais. Each of these zones offers specific benefits such as strategic connectivity, labour access, and essential utility infrastructure that must align with your intended tenant profile and investment strategy.

Resale in this asset class frequently requires a No Objection Certificate (NOC) from the master developer, and specific zones may enforce right-of-first-refusal clauses. Since most buyers are yield-driven investors, pricing heavily depends on the net rental income relative to the purchase price.

Investor Alert: Warehouses Are Not Typical Freehold Assets Most warehouse investments in Dubai are structured on a usufruct basis, meaning you own the structure but lease the land from a master developer such as DIP, Dubai South, or Dubai Industrial City.

Key implications:

- **Land Lease Terms:** Typically 30–50 years, renewable at the discretion of the landowner. Be sure to understand the remaining tenure and any associated renewal costs.
- **Power and Utility Limits:** Each industrial zone has specific limits on power load, water usage, and access to infrastructure.
- **Zoning and Activity Approval:** Your tenant's activity must match the licensed use permitted in that zone. For example, cold storage, manufacturing, or chemical storage often requires separate approvals.
- **Transfer Restrictions:** Many master developers require NOCs for resale, and some actively enforce right-of-first-refusal clauses.
- **Compliance Requirements:** Fire safety, staff accommodation standards, and environmental regulations must be consistently maintained, or the property can face penalties or lease termination.

Think Like an Investor: Warehouse assets can deliver high yields (8–12%), but lucrative returns fundamentally depend on deeply understanding the land lease terms, specific regulatory conditions, and the tenant's operational requirements. Rigorous legal and technical due diligence is non-negotiable for this specialised asset class.

Investment Characteristics:

- **Entry Price:** Moderate to high (typically AED 2M–20M+, depending on size and location).
- **Rental Yield:** Generally 8–12% gross, often with long-term leases (3–5 years common).
- **Tenant Profile:** Primarily logistics firms, manufacturers, e-commerce giants, and cold storage operators.
- **Risk Profile:** Moderate demand is closely tied to overall trade volumes, e-commerce growth, and industrial activity.

Who Invests & Why:

- **Institutional Investors:** Pension funds, REITs, and private equity firms seeking stable, high-yield assets.
- **Business Owners:** Entrepreneurs looking to own rather than rent facilities for their logistics, manufacturing, or distribution businesses.
- **Yield-Focused Individuals:** Investors specifically targeting higher, stable returns compared to residential properties.
- **Portfolio Diversifiers:** Investors seeking exposure to the industrial and logistics growth sectors of the economy.

Table 6.2: Warehouse & Industrial Market Overview Report Key Highlights (2023-2024)

Report	Key Highlights	Market Trends & Implications
Knight Frank H1 2024	Demand +185% Year-on-Year (~18 million sq ft) Jebel Ali Grade B rents +38.5% Year-on-Year. Al Quoz Grade A rents doubled to ~AED 65 psf (some units ~AED 100 psf)	**Explosive Demand Growth:** Signified by the sharp increase in H1 2024, driven by logistics, manufacturing, and trade. **Rising Rents Across Zones:** Jebel Ali and Al Quoz indicate strong pricing power in limited supply zones.
CBRE Q1 2024	Dubai industrial rents +14.3% Year-on-Year Registrations +3.2%	**Consistent Growth:** Confirmed by rental increases and registration growth across the industrial sector.
Savills Year-End 2024	Strong rental growth in Grade A across DIP (37.5%), Al Quoz (23%), and Dubai South (22%)	**Grade A Asset Premium:** Highlights that premium, high-spec warehouses in key areas are commanding significantly higher rents. **Scarcity in Grade A Supply:** Shortages of high-quality assets, especially with e-commerce and industrial infrastructure lagging demand, will continue to drive rental growth.

Investment Implications:

- **Strong Rental Upside:** Rapid rent increases and consistent demand growth make warehouse assets highly attractive, especially Grade A properties.
- **Location Matters:** Premium yields are heavily concentrated in established logistics hubs such as Jebel Ali, DIP, and Al Quoz—proximity to major ports and efficient transport links significantly enhances performance.
- **Quality Over Quantity:** High-specification warehouse buildings with superior docking facilities, optimal ceiling heights, and robust sustainability certifications consistently outperform generic stock.
- **Buffer Against Volatility:** Long-term leases with corporate tenants (e.g., logistics providers, manufacturing companies) effectively reduce vacancy risk and enhance investment stability.
- **Development Potential:** With rising industrial land costs, strategically constructing modern Grade A facilities can yield outsized returns.

INVESTOR INSIGHT

Many older areas in Dubai that once housed warehouses are now being converted into residential zones (like parts of Ras Al Khor, where now we have Emaar Creek Harbour) or high-end commercial spaces (e.g., in Al Quoz, where warehouses are transforming into F&B outlets or showrooms for regulated industries only). This ongoing conversion means that demand for dedicated warehouses in industrial areas is inherently bound to grow significantly.

6.3.3. Offices

Office investments in Dubai represent a distinct and continuously evolving segment of the commercial real estate landscape. Unlike warehouses, office units are typically held in freehold formats, particularly within designated commercial areas such as Business Bay, Downtown Dubai, Jumeirah Lake Towers (JLT), and Dubai Silicon Oasis. Investors have the flexibility to purchase individual units or entire floors within commercial towers. Smaller investors can access the market through standalone units, while institutional players more commonly pursue full-floor or entire-building acquisitions.

The performance of office assets is intricately tied to overall business confidence, prevailing occupancy rates, and demand driven explicitly by location. Proximity to Metro stations, ample parking availability, and the uncompromising quality of Grade A buildings significantly impact tenant preferences and command higher rental premiums. In core business districts, the tenant mix (e.g., multinational corporations versus startups) and the lease term structure (e.g., 1-3 years common) must be carefully considered. Investors must also adeptly navigate evolving demand patterns such as the increasing prevalence of hybrid work models and the rise of flexible office spaces, which may influence traditional leasing strategies in the future.

Dubai's office market continues its maturation, characterised by increased transparency and robust demand from both Small and Medium-sized Enterprises (SMEs) and global enterprises, particularly within its various tax-free zones such as the DIFC or DMCC. For those seeking mid- to long-term capital appreciation paired with consistent recurring income, offices remain a core component of a well-diversified commercial portfolio.

Investment Characteristics:

- **Entry Price:** Moderate to high (typically AED 1M–50M+, depending on size and location).
- **Rental Yield:** Generally 7–10% gross, with lease terms often ranging from 1–3 years (potentially longer in free zones).
- **Tenant Profile:** Diverse, including multinationals, SMEs, startups, and individual freelancers.
- **Risk Profile:** Moderate, demand fluctuates directly with overall economic activity and prevailing business sentiment.

Who Invests & Why:

- **Corporate Users:** Companies seeking to own their headquarters rather than rent.
- **Yield Investors:** Individuals or funds specifically targeting stable, mid-yield returns.
- **Tech & Innovation Hubs:** Investors capitalising on the growth in Dubai Silicon Oasis and DIFC.
- **Portfolio Diversifiers:** Investors looking to add commercial exposure to balance overall risk and return.

Key Considerations:

- **Location:** Prime areas consistently command higher rents and exhibit lower vacancy rates.
- **Fit-Out:** Carefully consider whether the unit is Shell & Core (bare interior) or Fitted (ready for occupation); tenant preferences vary significantly.
- **Free Zones:** Some offer 100% foreign ownership and unique tax benefits.
- **Vacancy Risk:** Higher in oversupplied submarkets; monitor absorption rates.

INVESTOR INSIGHT

For savvy investors, business centres, i.e commercial office units subdivided into smaller, independent offices and leased to multiple tenants, are emerging as a high-yield asset class. These setups frequently generate multiple Ejari contracts within a single title, effectively reducing vacancy risk and diversifying rental income streams. Instead of relying on one large corporate tenant, multiple smaller tenants provide greater resilience and more stable monthly cash flow. In popular zones like Business Bay, JLT, and Barsha Heights, well-managed business centres can offer ROIs of 8–12%, mainly when operated with flexible leasing terms and shared amenities. The key lies in precise licensing alignment (e.g., DED versus Freezone), high-quality facility management, and intelligent space planning that maximises rentable area while minimising idle space. For income-focused investors seeking consistent returns with built-in risk mitigation, business centres are a highly compelling option in Dubai's commercial landscape.

Table 6.3: Office Market Overview (2023–2024)

Report	Key Highlights	Trends & Implications
Knight Frank – H1 2024	Lease rates up 22.4% Year-on-Year across 25 zones Prime rents (Downtown/DIFC) reached AED 3,609 psf (+132% since 2020) AED 2.7B in transactions (~1,414 deals)	Strong pricing power in limited supply zones. Downtown & DIFC continue to dominate with record yields. Indicates robust investor confidence.
Knight Frank – H2 2024	Rents rose ~24.3% Year-on-Year in key business districts The Trade Centre District saw top rent growth	Demand shifting to emerging core zones. The Trade Centre is gaining significant investor and occupier attention.
CBRE – Q3 2024	Office rents and occupancy both rose Supply shortage is driving costs up.	Tenants are facing increasing budget pressure. Limited new stock implies long-term rental upside.
CBRE – Q4 2024	Strong commercial investment activity Offices sustained rental and occupancy gains.	Momentum continues across sectors. Offices remain a strong performer.

Key Trends & Implications:

- **Rising Lease Rates:** Consistent 22–24% Year-on-Year growth, primarily driven by tight supply, particularly in Downtown, DIFC, and the Trade Centre. Investors benefit from premium rents and high yields.
- **Prime Locations Lead:** Downtown/DIFC currently command rents of approximately AED 3,600 per sq ft. This signifies a high barrier to entry but offers top-tier ROI potential.
- **High Transaction Volume:** AED 2.7 billion in H1 office deals indicates strong liquidity and robust investor confidence in this asset class.
- **Supply Remains Tight:** Across all reports, there is a persistent lack of quality new office stock. Rental growth is expected to continue, as tenants have fewer options.
- **New Growth Areas:** Trade Centre and co-working zones are gaining significant traction. Early entry into these areas could unlock substantial future appreciation.

6.3.4. Shops (Retail Units)

Retail shop investments in Dubai offer high visibility, steady rental income, and strong tenant loyalty, particularly in busy, high-footfall areas. These retail units can range from small, street-facing community shops to premium spaces within upscale malls, the podium levels of residential towers, or large mixed-use developments. Many of these retail properties are available for individual purchase, giving investors a chance to own and lease out commercial space. They are also compatible with Department of Economic Development (DED) licences, allowing a wide variety of businesses to operate from them.

What makes retail shops particularly attractive to investors is the pass-through nature of many operating costs. Tenants typically cover fit-outs, utility consumption, and frequently even service charges, allowing landlords to retain a high net yield. This is especially true in popular communities like JVC, Arjan, Al Barsha South, International City, and Dubai Silicon Oasis. Well-leased shops can deliver impressive net ROIs of 7%–10%, and specific high-demand sectors such as salons, pharmacies, grocery stores, or F&B (Food & Beverage) outlets often command even higher rental premiums and boast greater tenant stability.

For investors seeking tangible assets with real-use visibility and defensible demand across various business cycles, retail shops present a powerful addition to any real estate portfolio, offering both consistent yield and long-term appreciation, particularly as Dubai's population density continues to rise in suburban communities.

Investment Characteristics:

- **Entry Price:** Moderate to high (typically AED 1M–20M+, depending on size and location).
- **Rental Yield:** Generally 7–12% gross, often with lease terms ranging from 3–5 years.
- **Tenant Profile:** Diverse, including various retailers, F&B operators, and service providers.
- **Risk Profile:** Moderate to high, retail performance is sensitive to foot traffic, tourism levels, and broader economic cycles.

Who Invests & Why:

- **Business Owners:** Entrepreneurs looking to own their shops or franchises.
- **Yield Investors:** Individuals specifically seeking higher returns than residential properties, often with a willingness for active management.
- **Institutional Investors:** Funds targeting prime retail assets within established malls or high-traffic commercial areas.
- **Portfolio Diversifiers:** Investors seeking to add retail exposure to balance overall risk and return within their portfolio.

Key Considerations:

- **Foot Traffic:** Critical importance of location within a mall or community (e.g., anchor store proximity vs. secondary spots).
- **Lease Terms:** Often include provisions for turnover rent (percentage of sales) or minimum guaranteed rent.
- **Licensing:** Ensure the unit is correctly zoned for the intended business type.
- **Tenant Mix:** A complementary tenant mix within a development often drives higher footfall and enhances stability for all businesses.

Table 6.4: Dubai Retail Real Estate – Market Summary (2023–2024)

Source & Report	Summary Trend Highlights	Investor Implications
Savills: Shopping Centre & High Street – Q4 2024	Retail recovery continues as inflation stabilises and consumer spending improves in prime areas More substantial footfall in shopping malls Increased leasing in the F&B and fashion segments Demand stabilising across top-tier high street locations	Prime mall shops (e.g., Dubai Mall, Mall of the Emirates) offer stable income. Focus on well-managed centres for long-term tenant retention.
CBRE: UAE Market Review – Q2 2024	Leasing activity rose significantly, especially in smaller retail units under 2,000 sq. ft. 38% Year-on-Year growth in compact unit leasing 5–21% Year-on-Year rent increases across retail segments High demand in community-centric neighbourhoods	Target smaller shops in high-density communities (e.g., JVC, Arjan). Ideal for yield-focused investors seeking regular rental income.
Savills: Residential Real Estate Market Report – 2024	Residential growth is driving increased local retail demand, particularly in integrated communities Super-regional mall rents rose 14.9% year-over-year in Q3 2024 Population growth in mid-market zones is boosting local shops	Invest in retail spaces within mixed-use zones like Dubai Hills & MBR City. Favours long-term appreciation alongside residential surge.
CBRE: UAE Market Review – Q4 2024	Limited new retail supply and tourism recovery are driving rental gains in premium zones. Rising rents in high-street retail Stable occupancy in malls despite resistance to rent hikes Emerging retail demand near tourist hubs	Focus on areas with upcoming infrastructure/tourism projects (e.g., Dubai Harbour). Lock in long-term leases to hedge against future volatility.

INVESTOR INSIGHT

Retail units consistently thrive on optimal location and the quality of their tenant mix. Prime spots in major malls or bustling communities typically offer stable income, while neighbourhood retail benefits significantly from consistent local demand. Active management and careful tenant selection are key to maximising returns in this sector.

6.3.5. Labour Camps (Staff Accommodation)

Labour camps are a distinct asset class within Dubai's real estate ecosystem, specifically catering to one of the most essential yet often overlooked segments of the economy: the workforce behind construction, logistics, manufacturing, and infrastructure development. These accommodations are typically purpose-built in industrial or peripheral zones and are leased out on a per-room or per-bed basis to contracting companies and labour supply firms. As such, labour camps offer unique income stability closely tied to core economic sectors, and their returns are notably more utility-driven than sentiment-driven. Moreover, they serve a non-discretionary need, making them inherently more resilient during economic downturns and less exposed to consumer sentiment or tourism trends compared to retail or hospitality assets.

Unlike residential assets, labour camps are valued based on their bed capacity, consistent occupancy rate, layout efficiency, and strict compliance with licensing regulations. A well-maintained G+2 or G+3 labour camp facility with 100–500 beds can often offer impressive net ROIs of 8% to 12%, particularly when located in demand-heavy zones such as Jebel Ali Industrial, Al Quoz, Sonapur (Muhaisnah 2), Dubai Industrial City, and DIP. These areas are typically zoned specifically for staff accommodation and come with clear guidelines on room-to-toilet ratios, kitchen facilities, and common area provisions, ensuring regulated quality.

Key Advantages:

- High occupancy rates are often guaranteed via corporate contracts.
- Double-digit yields frequently make them among the top-performing assets.
- They are highly regulated and cater to an essential need, aligning with government infrastructure needs.
- Features lower tenant churn compared to residential or short-let assets.

Overview:

- **Description:** Purpose-built residential complexes specifically designed for company employees, typically located in industrial or logistics zones.
- **Typical Use:** Provides housing for blue-collar workers, drivers, technicians, and various service staff.
- **Areas:** Primarily found in Dubai Investment Park (DIP), Jebel Ali, Al Quoz, and Dubai South.

Investment Characteristics:

- **Entry Price:** Moderate (typically AED 5M–30M+ for multi-unit buildings).
- **Rental Yield:** Generally 8–12% gross, often secured by long-term corporate leases (1–3 years).
- **Tenant Profile:** Primarily companies requiring housing for their workforce.
- **Risk Profile:** Moderate, demand is closely tied to overall industrial and service sector growth.

Who Invests & Why:

- **Institutional Investors:** Funds and corporations actively seeking stable, high-yield assets.
- **Business Owners:** Companies looking to secure reliable housing for their staff.
- **Yield-Focused Individuals:** Investors specifically targeting higher returns with the stability of corporate tenants.
- **Portfolio Diversifiers:** Investors seeking exposure to the essential worker housing segment of the economy.

Key Considerations:

- **Regulatory Compliance:** Must strictly meet RERA and Dubai Municipality standards for worker housing.
- **Location:** Proximity to industrial zones, major transport links, and essential amenities is crucial.
- **Management:** Often requires active management or a partnership with a specialised property management firm.
- **Tenant Stability:** Corporate leases significantly reduce vacancy risk compared to individual rentals.

Table 6.5: Dubai Labour Camp Market Overview Report Key Highlights (2023-2024)

Report	Key Highlights	Trends & Implications
Bayut – Labour Camps	107,112 rentals, AED 2.3B value, rents up 7.6% Year-on-Year	High demand from the construction sector. Attractive rental yields.
Al Taif	Stable demand post-Expo, tied to infrastructure	Long-term occupancy. Socially responsible investment.
Cushman & Wakefield	Rents doubled to AED 500 per month, ROI ~18%	Yields consistently outperform residential. Growing institutional interest.
Bayut & Khaleej Times	Municipality mandates, rent growth beyond core zones	Regulation ensures quality. Limited supply adds value.

Key Takeaways:

- Yields of 8–12% consistently make labour camps top-tier commercial assets.
- Demand is robustly driven by Dubai's ongoing infrastructure development and essential workforce housing needs.
- They are highly regulated and cater to an essential service, making them resilient long-term investments.

INVESTOR INSIGHT

Labour camps are a niche but highly resilient asset class, primarily driven by Dubai's consistently growing industrial and service sectors. Corporate leases provide a stable income, while strict regulatory oversight ensures adherence to minimum standards. They are ideal for investors seeking strong yields with lower volatility.

6.4. Comparing Residential vs. Commercial Investment

Every investor eventually faces a pivotcl choice: residential or commercial? While both types of real estate offer strong opportunities in Dubai, they cater to very different goals, risk appetites, and management needs. This section breaks down the fundamental differences, empowering you to align your strategy accordingly. The core difference isn't just about *what* you're buying (a home versus a shop); it's about *how* that asset typically behaves in the market. Residential properties usually follow population trends, lifestyle shifts, and affordability constraints. Commercial properties, on the other hand, generally respond to specific business cycles, employment trends, and broader economic expansion.

6.4.1. Residential Property: Familiar and Flexible

Residential investments typically include apartments, villas, and townhouses. These assets generally appeal to both individual investors and end-users, thereby creating a broad resale market and consistent rental demand.

Pros:

- Lower entry cost (typically AED 500k–3M).
- Generally easier to finance via banks (especially for end-users).
- Higher liquidity: often quicker to sell due to broader demand.
- Strong rental demand in mid-income zones and established family areas.

Cons:

- Tend to offer lower yields (typically 5–8% on average).
- This can result in higher tenant turnover and more frequent service charge fluctuations.
- Subject to rental caps and specific RERA regulations.
- Can be more susceptible to oversupply in emerging areas.

Use Case Example: A 1-bedroom apartment in JVC, purchased for AED 750,000, could yield 7.5% net annually through long-term rent or even higher through short-term Airbnb rentals.

6.4.2. Commercial Property: Yield-Oriented and Strategic

Commercial investments encompass warehouses, labour camps, office units, shops, and various retail spaces. These assets frequently offer higher rental yields but typically require greater upfront capital and more rigorous due diligence.

Pros:

- Generally offers higher gross yields (typically 7–12%, sometimes more).
- Often feature longer lease terms (especially in warehouses and labour camps).
- Potential for corporate tenants and more predictable cash flows.
- Frequently immune to residential oversupply cycles, driven by distinct demand factors.

Cons:

- Involves a higher entry ticket (typically AED 1M–20M+).
- Financing may require a stronger balance sheet or be primarily cash-based.
- Higher vacancy risk if the location is not prime or the asset is misaligned with demand.
- Lease terms may require specialised legal vetting (e.g., activity-based approvals for shops/warehouses).

Use Case Example: A warehouse in Dubai South, leased to an e-commerce logistics provider at AED 350,000 per year on a 5-year lease, could yield 9% net and typically requires minimal upkeep once leased.

6.4.3. Side-by-Side Comparison Table

Table 6.6: Residential vs. Commercial Property Comparison

Factor	Residential	Commercial
Entry Ticket	AED 500k – 3M	AED 1M – 20M+
Rental Yield	5% – 8%	7% – 12% (or more for labour camps, warehouses)
Vacancy Risk	Lower (especially in family zones)	Higher (especially retail, office)
Liquidity	High (more buyers, end-user demand)	Lower (investor-led sales)
Financing Access	Easier, especially for salaried buyers	More complex, banks assess tenancy strength
Tenant Management	Moderate (renewals, maintenance)	Variable (often managed via long-term leases)
Legal Complexity	Simple (freehold, leasehold)	Complex (license restrictions, zoning)

Think Like an Investor:

Choose residential if you prioritise simplicity, quicker resale, or are just starting out. Opt for commercial if you're ready for the potential of higher returns, longer lease terms, and a more analytical (less emotional) involvement. Many seasoned investors build hybrid portfolios—using residential to maintain liquidity and stability, while commercial assets deliver consistent cash flow and growth. The key is always aligning the asset type perfectly with your personal goals, risk tolerance, and prevailing market outlook.

6.5. A Core Strategic Choice: Off-Plan vs. Ready Property

After deciding between residential and commercial assets, you will face another fundamental choice that will define your entire investment journey: do you buy **off-plan** (a property yet to be built) or a **ready property** (in the secondary market)? This isn't just a matter of preference; it is a strategic decision that impacts your capital outlay, risk exposure, return timeline, and profit potential.

Investing in an off-plan property is an act of **investing in the future**. You are buying a developer's vision and betting on the value of a community that does not yet entirely exist. In contrast, buying a ready property is an act of **investing in the present**. You are purchasing a tangible asset with a proven history, an existing community, and the potential for immediate income.

Neither path is inherently superior, but one will be better aligned with your specific goals, risk tolerance, and financial situation. Understanding the distinct characteristics of each is crucial to making the right choice.

6.5.1. Side-by-Side Comparison: Off-Plan vs. Ready

Table 6.7: This table breaks down the fundamental differences between the two investment paths.

Factor	Off-Plan Property	Ready (Secondary Market) Property
Price & Value	Often priced lower than ready equivalents; potential for "built-in" equity upon completion.	Priced at current market value; what you see is what you pay.
Payment Structure	Highly attractive, staggered payment plans (e.g., 40/60, 50/50). Post-handover plans are common.	Requires a significant down payment (typically 20%+) and immediate mortgage or full cash payment.
Risk Profile	Higher. Risks include construction delays, market downturns before completion, and potential quality discrepancies.	Lower. Tangible assets can be inspected. Community and infrastructure are already established.
Rental Income	Zero during the 2–4 year construction period. Capital remains illiquid and generates no cash flow.	Immediate. Can be rented out from day one, generating instant income.
Capital Appreciation	Higher potential if timed correctly in an emerging area. You benefit from the area's growth and infrastructure.	More stable and predictable, tied to the performance of a known community.
Unit Selection	Excellent. Early buyers get the first choice of the best views, layouts, and positions.	Limited to current listings in the market.
Condition & Costs	Brand new with modern finishes and the developer's warranty. Minimal maintenance initially.	Varies by age. May require renovation or upkeep. Service charge history helps with cost forecasting.
Liquidity	Lower. Flipping before handover may involve developer NOCs and transfer fees.	Higher. It is easier to sell due to broader appeal to end-users and investors.

6.5.2. Who Should Choose Off-Plan?

Off-plan investing is best suited for investors with a specific profile:

- **The Capital Growth Seeker:** If your primary goal is capital appreciation and you have a medium- to long-term horizon, off-plan is ideal. It allows you to enter emerging communities at a lower price point and benefit from the value uplift as the area develops.
- **The Cash-Flow Conscious Buyer:** If you don't have a large lump sum for a down payment, the staggered payment plans offered by developers make the market much more accessible. This allows you to secure an asset with a smaller initial outlay.
- **The Patient, Long-Term Strategist:** Investors who can afford to have their capital tied up for several years without needing immediate returns are perfect candidates. They are betting on the long-term vision of a master community.

6.5.3. Who Should Choose a Ready Property?

Investing in the secondary market is a better fit for those who prioritise certainty and immediate returns:

- **The Income-Focused Investor:** If your goal is to generate rental income from day one, a ready property is the only choice. It starts producing cash flow immediately, which can help cover mortgage payments and other costs.
- **The Risk-Averse Buyer:** If you need certainty about the quality, view, and condition of your property, the secondary market is for you. You can physically inspect the unit and the building, eliminating the risks associated with construction.
- **The End-User:** If you are buying a home to live in, a ready property allows you to move in immediately without waiting for years for construction to finish.

Think Like an Investor:

The decision between off-plan and ready is a classic trade-off between **risk and reward**, and **patience and immediacy**. Off-plan offers the potential for higher returns in exchange for higher risk and a long wait. A ready property offers immediate utility and lower risk in exchange for a higher upfront cost and potentially more modest appreciation.

Your choice should not be based on which is "hotter" in the market right now, but on a clear-eyed assessment of your personal financial goals, your timeline, and your comfort level with uncertainty. Your detailed due diligence process, as we will cover in Chapter 7, will then adapt to the path you choose.

6.6. Legal Structures: Freehold, Leasehold, Usufruct

When you buy property in Dubai, you're not just selecting a location or a design—you're entering into a specific legal framework that fundamentally defines your rights, any limitations, and your future flexibility. The precise ownership model attached to a property significantly affects various aspects, including its resale value, inheritance processes, mortgage eligibility, your control over renovations, and your ultimate exit strategies. Whether you're planning to build a family legacy, maximise capital gains, or secure consistent rental income, understanding the underlying legal structure is essential to aligning with your long-term objectives.

Dubai presents three main ownership structures: Freehold, Leasehold, and Usufruct. Freehold offers perpetual ownership of both land and structure, granting complete control, mortgage eligibility, and full inheritance rights, making it ideal for long-term investors. Leasehold, by contrast, grants usage rights for a fixed period, typically 30 to 99 years, with ownership of the underlying land remaining with the freeholder.

6.6.1. Freehold Ownership

Freehold ownership in Dubai is more than a mere legal label. It represents a seismic shift in the emirate's economic openness and its embrace of global investment. Until the early 2000s, foreign nationals were generally not permitted to own property directly in Dubai. That changed dramatically in 2002, when a landmark decree by the Dubai government introduced freehold zones where non-GCC (Gulf Cooperation Council) nationals could own real estate outright. This pivotal decision was a true game-changer, acting as a catalyst for the city's meteoric rise as a world-class real estate hub.

Under freehold law, investors enjoy full ownership of the unit and a proportional share of the land it stands on, with no expiration date. This mirrors the widely accepted ownership model seen in many mature global markets such as the UK, Canada, Australia, and the United States, where title deeds grant perpetual ownership, full resale rights, clear inheritance rights, and complete transferability. In Dubai, these rights are robustly protected under the Dubai Land Department (DLD) registry, ensuring legal clarity and security for owners.

As Dubai's economy, infrastructure, tourism, and overall economic base continually expand, freehold zones are consistently experiencing increased gentrification and vibrant urban regeneration, which further boosts asset values. However, freehold does come with inherently higher entry costs, especially in prime central areas and carries ongoing service charges as well as community rules enforced by the Owners' Association. Yet, for serious investors, the unparalleled control, robust security, and significant growth potential offered by freehold ownership typically far outweigh these associated costs. In summary, freehold ownership in Dubai aligns exceptionally well with international investor expectations, striking a perfect balance between flexibility and robust legal protection, and remains the cornerstone of long-term wealth creation within the emirate's dynamic real estate landscape.

Pros:

- Provides complete control over the asset, including rights to modify (within building guidelines) and lease.
- Generally eligible for mortgage financing from most banks.
- Comes with full inheritance and resale rights, ensuring long-term value transfer.

Cons:

- Typically involves a higher upfront cost, especially in prime zones.
- Subject to ongoing service charges and adherence to community rules.

INVESTOR INSIGHT

Freehold is often considered the gold standard for foreign investors. If you're planning long-term ownership, aiming for consistent rental income, or intending to pass on as a legacy, freehold provides the most comprehensive legal clarity and security.

6.6.2. Leasehold Ownership

Leasehold ownership in Dubai offers an alternative pathway into the property market, particularly appealing to those seeking affordability, short- to medium-term access, or properties in specific legacy or high-demand locations. Introduced alongside freehold in the early 2000s, leasehold ownership reflects a more conservative structure, often favoured by developers who wish to retain underlying land rights while still monetising building use.

Under a leasehold, the buyer gains the contractual right to use a property for a fixed period, typically ranging from 30 to 99 years, while the underlying land remains under the perpetual control of the original landowner or master developer. This model is common in international markets such as India, Singapore, and parts of the UK, where leasehold structures are well understood and widely accepted. In Dubai, designated leasehold zones include areas such as Deira, Dubai Silicon Oasis, the Green Community, and parts of Jumeirah. Within these zones, buyers receive long-term usage rights but not outright ownership of the land.

The primary advantage of leasehold is its generally lower upfront acquisition cost compared to equivalent freehold properties, making it more accessible. However, the ticking clock of the lease term significantly impacts its long-term investment profile. As the lease shortens, property value can depreciate, resale becomes more challenging (especially for mortgages), and renewal terms can be uncertain. Additionally, leasehold structures often impose restrictions on extensive property modifications. They may require specific approvals for sub-leasing or transfer, providing greater control for developers and authorities, particularly in legacy areas where strategic master planning is paramount.

As Dubai matures as a global real estate market, leasehold remains an essential tool within the legal framework. It enables broader participation in the market but requires careful due diligence, particularly around the remaining term, renewal rights, and resale prospects. For investors aligned with shorter horizons, leasehold may offer decent yields, but long-term capital appreciation and liquidity will always fundamentally favour freehold assets. In summary, leasehold in Dubai offers structured flexibility; you gain access, but not complete control. It appeals to specific investor profiles and budget-conscious buyers, but it's crucial to understand the built-in limits, legal nuances, and the ticking clock behind every leasehold agreement.

Pros:

- Generally involves a lower upfront cost, making properties more accessible.
- Provides access to strategic areas that may not otherwise be open to freehold ownership.

Cons:

- Resale value is limited and depreciates as the remaining lease term shortens.
- The renewal process for the lease can be uncertain or involve additional costs.
- Not ideal for long-term capital appreciation or building intergenerational wealth.

INVESTOR INSIGHT

Do not buy a leasehold property assuming it's equivalent to freehold. Always read the lease terms; some leaseholds may include restrictive clauses or may not be easily renewable.

6.6.3. Usufruct Rights

Usufruct ownership in Dubai is a lesser-known but legally recognised form of property interest that grants the right to use and benefit from a property for a defined period, typically up to 99 years, without owning the underlying land or being able to alter the asset significantly. Rooted in civil law traditions, the term "usufruct" combines two Latin words: ***usus*** (to use) and ***fructus*** (to enjoy the fruits). In real estate terms, this means you can live in, lease out, or generate income from the property during the usufruct term. Still, you cannot demolish, redevelop, or permanently modify it.

In Dubai, usufruct arrangements are most commonly used in corporate developments, government land allocations, or special economic and free zones, areas where authorities retain land ownership but allow individuals or companies to operate or benefit from real estate over the long term. Prominent locations where usufruct is commonly granted include Dubai Healthcare City (DHCC), Dubai Silicon Oasis (DSO), and various specialised industrial parks.

The usufruct right is a temporary, personal right that cannot always be inherited and may carry specific limitations. You cannot sell the underlying land or structure as if it were freehold, and many mortgage providers are unwilling to finance usufruct properties due to the limited ownership rights associated with them. Modifications, redevelopment, and subleasing may also require prior approval from the landholder or regulatory authority. Moreover, once the term expires, the property reverts completely to the original owner, and no compensation is guaranteed for any residual value.

For investors, the key advantage lies in potential yield. Because the upfront investment is generally lower and the operational rights can be extensive, the Return on Investment (ROI) over the usufruct term can be attractive, especially in sectors such as warehousing, healthcare, or hospitality, where consistent cash flows are possible. However, this is best suited for savvy investors or institutions with a clear exit plan and no intention of building a legacy ownership. Globally, usufruct models are used in countries such as France, Egypt, and Thailand, particularly for foreign investors.

Pros:

- Generally involves a lower initial capital outlay.
- It can be a way to access specialised, income-generating assets (e.g., warehouses, corporate staff housing) without complete purchase.

Cons:

- No outright ownership title of the land or permanent structure.
- Typically comes with no resale or mortgage rights for the usufruct itself (only the right to use).
- Often limited to specific business or operational use, as defined by the master developer.
- Cannot be inherited directly; the right extinguishes upon death.

INVESTOR INSIGHT

Usufruct is more akin to a long-term, transferable lease for operational access rather than a traditional property investment. It is helpful for businesses that need facilities without incurring significant upfront capital for full ownership.

6.7. Comparison Table: Legal Structures at a Glance

By now, we've explored the nuances of Dubai's three key property ownership structures: freehold, leasehold, and usufruct, each with its own set of rights, restrictions, and strategic uses. This table serves as a quick-reference snapshot of what you've already learned in detail.

Freehold remains the gold standard for both end-users and long-term investors, offering full ownership rights, inheritance security, and the ability to freely lease, sell, or mortgage the asset, much like mature global markets. It's ideal for those seeking permanence, capital appreciation, and legacy planning.

Leasehold, while limited in duration (typically 30–99 years), provides access to strategic locations that may not be designated as freehold zones. It generally suits investors with medium-term horizons and budget-conscious buyers.

Usufruct, the most time-bound and operational of the three, is better suited for businesses or institutional users needing long-term access to property without the burden of full ownership. It allows use and income generation, but with strict limitations on resale, financing, and inheritance.

In short, your choice of structure should ideally reflect your investment horizon, financial goals, and operational needs. The more control and permanence you seek, the more likely freehold is your best fit, while leasehold and usufruct serve more specialised, strategic purposes within Dubai's evolving real estate landscape.

Dubai Property Legal Structures:

Understanding Your Rights

Structure	Freehold	Leasehold	Usufruct
Can Foreigners Buy?	Yes	Limited	Rare
Right to Sell / Rent?	Yes	Yes (within lease term)	No
Inheritance Rights	Yes	Restricted	No
Typical Zones	Downtown, Dubai Marina, JVC	Dubai Silicon Oasis, Parts of Mirdif, Green Community	Institutional zones (e.g., Dubai Healthcare City)

Think Like an Investor:

If you're planning to pass on property to your heirs, use it for collateral, or sell it easily, freehold is consistently the most secure option. Leasehold may suit short- to mid-term investors in specific zones, but reselling becomes more challenging as the lease term shortens. Usufruct is only strategically viable for businesses seeking low-capital access to space for operational purposes.

6.8. Matching Property Type to Investor Profile

Every investor comes with a unique combination of risk appetite, capital availability, and return expectation. A one-bedroom apartment in JVC isn't the same as a labour camp in DIP—both in inherent structure and in the optimal investment strategy. This section explicitly maps various property types to specific investor goals and personas, helping readers align their investments with their priorities.

Investor Profile Match:

Find Your Asset Fit

Investor Profile	Recommended Property Type	Rationale
First-time Investor	1-Bedroom apartment in JVC, Arjan, or Dubai Hills	Lower entry cost, easier to understand, good resale liquidity
Yield – Focused Investor	Studio Apartment, Labour Camp, Warehouse	Offers high rental yield. Aligns with a cash flow-driven strategy
Capital Appreciation Seeker	Villa plot in Jebel ALI Hills, Townhouse in Dubai South	Focuses on long-term price growth, land value, & strategically located corridors
Short-term Cashflow Hunter	Furnished Airbnb Units in Dubai Marina, Business Bay, JVT	Provides higher monthly rent income & flexibility for quick capital turnover
Portfolio Diversifier	Mix of Commercial (Warehouse or Shop) + Residential	Balances stable income (typically commercial) with liquid assets (typically residential) for overall portfolio stability

INVESTOR INSIGHT

Many investors mistakenly chase the highest advertised yield without truly considering whether the asset aligns with their lifestyle, time commitment, or ultimate exit strategy. An off-plan studio might be easy to enter but harder to exit profitably. A villa may hold value exceptionally well but take longer to resell. Always align your chosen investment type perfectly with your long-term plan, not just with fleeting short-term returns.

6.9. Market Data & Future Outlook

Understanding broader market data and future outlooks is crucial for any strategic investor. It allows you to anticipate trends and align your investments with where the market is genuinely heading.

Why It Matters

Before diving into the numbers, it's essential to understand the crucial role this data plays in your investment decision-making. The figures presented, transaction volumes, yield ranges, and price growth bands, are not forecasts or explicit investment tips. Instead, they serve as a powerful lens to help you think like a truly strategic investor: someone who identifies patterns, asks the right questions, and aligns capital with underlying market momentum.

Markets shift. Yields compress. Appreciation cycles peak and then inevitably reset. That's why this section is not about chasing today's "hot area" or this year's "best performer." It's fundamentally about teaching you ***how to analyse market data effectively***. What asset types consistently dominate transaction volume? Where is rental demand deepest and most consistent? What price bands are showing genuine organic growth, and which zones exhibit supply constraints that might effectively fuel future appreciation? Savvy investors don't just react to headlines or social media hype; they evaluate macro indicators to inform their decisions.

Residential Market Overview (2023–2024)

	Market Share	Typical Appreciation	Typical Yield
Apartment	~60%	5-8%	6-9%
Townhouse	~20%	8-12%	5-7%
Villa	~10%	10-15%	4-6%

Top Performing Areas – Price Appreciation:

- **Villas:** Dubai Hills, Arabian Ranches III, Tilal Al Ghaf, The Valley.
- **Townhouses:** Mudon, Town Square, Damac Lagoons.
- **Apartments:** JVC, Business Bay, Downtown.

Trend Highlights:

- Apartments consistently dominate in transaction volume but tend to exhibit more modest capital appreciation, unless they are strategically located in prime or rapidly emerging areas.
- Townhouses are increasingly favoured by mid-income families actively seeking community living and long-term ownership.
- Villas consistently remain the strongest appreciation class, particularly within established gated and beachfront communities that offer inherent land component value and limited supply.

INVESTOR TAKEAWAY

Investors primarily seeking appreciation should focus on master-planned communities with upcoming infrastructure developments. Apartment buyers should prioritise consistent rental income and strong liquidity, while villa investors should anticipate longer holding periods and significant value uplift driven by scarcity and prime location.

Commercial Market Overview (2023–2024)

	Market Share	Typical Yield	Growth Drivers
Plots	**~30%**	**N/A** (Capital Gain)	Dubai South, Jebel Ali Hills, Land Banking opportunities
Warehouse	**~25%**	**8-12%**	E-commerce, logistics & manufacturing demand
Offices	**~20%**	**7-10%**	DIFC, Downtown, tech & financial services growth
Retail Shops	**~15%**	**7-12%**	Tourism recovery, community football & F&B expansion
Labour Camps	**~10%**	**8-12%**	Infrastructure boom, Expo legacy, industrial labour housing

Top Performing Commercial Corridors:

- **Warehouses:** Jebel Ali Free Zone, Dubai Industrial City, Al Quoz, Dubai Investment Park.
- **Offices:** Downtown Dubai, DIFC, Trade Centre District, Dubai Silicon Oasis.
- **Retail:** Marina Walk, JBR, Business Bay retail clusters, Town Square Centre.
- **Labour Camps:** Dubai Investment Park, Al Quoz Industrial, Jebel Ali South.

Future Outlook

Residential Forecasts:

- Upcoming infrastructure (Metro Blue Line, Al Maktoum Airport expansion, and Expo City upgrades) is expected to significantly enhance demand in Dubai South, The Valley, and nearby zones.
- Townhouse communities like Mudon and The Valley are consistently maturing into high-demand family neighbourhoods.
- Affordable apartment zones (JVC, Arjan, Sports City) are expected to maintain strong rental yield momentum due to robust population growth and favourable price-to-income alignment.

Commercial Forecasts:

- Warehouse demand is expected to remain consistently robust, fuelled by GCC-wide e-commerce and logistics expansion.
- Prime office spaces in the DIFC and Downtown will continue to attract premium tenants due to their scarcity of supply and unparalleled global positioning.
- Retail performance is expected to diverge; neighbourhood retail will benefit significantly from increasing population density, while tourism-linked F&B will remain more cyclical.
- Labour camps are projected to offer consistent rental cash flow with strong long-term stability within regulated industrial zones.

INVESTOR INSIGHT

Smart investing isn't just about current price; it's about aligning your investment thesis with prevailing infrastructure trends, consistent tenant demand, and the overall economic direction. Those who strategically positioned themselves early in post-Expo growth corridors or adapted to shifting commercial demand centres are already realising above-market returns.

Chapter Summary

Chapter 6, "Property Types & Investment Opportunities: Residential vs. Commercial," is your essential guide to understanding that choosing the right asset class is a core strategic decision, directly impacting your investment's returns, risks, liquidity, and future exit options.

You've gained a comprehensive understanding of Dubai's diverse Residential Property Types, from efficient studios and versatile 1-bedroom apartments to family-friendly 2- and 3-bedroom units, spacious townhouses, and prestigious villas. We explored their typical characteristics, pros, cons, and ideal investor profiles.

The chapter then delved into the powerful world of Commercial Property Types, including villa and townhouse plots, high-yield warehouses, dynamic office spaces, strategic retail units, and resilient labour camps. You learned about their unique investment characteristics, target tenant profiles, and specific considerations for each.

A direct comparison of Residential vs. Commercial Investment highlighted their fundamental differences in entry cost, yield potential, vacancy risk, and legal complexities, empowering you to choose the sector that best aligns with your goals.

Crucially, you gained insights into the nuances of Legal Structures, understanding the distinctions between Freehold, Leasehold, and Usufruct ownership, and their significant implications for control, inheritance, and resale.

Finally, the chapter provided a strategic framework for Matching Property Type to Investor Profile, ensuring your investment choices perfectly align with your individual risk appetite, capital availability, and return expectations. We also reviewed current Market Data & Future Outlook for both residential and commercial sectors, equipping you with insights into prevailing trends and future growth drivers.

By understanding the unique profiles of different property types and their legal structures, you are now equipped to make highly informed decisions about *what* to invest in, confidently selecting assets that best serve your specific investment strategy in Dubai.

Key Takeaways:

- **Diverse Asset Classes:** Dubai offers a wide range of property types, each with distinct income streams, regulatory requirements, and capital appreciation timelines.
- **Strategic Alignment:** Choosing the right property type requires alignment with your personal investment goals—whether that's long-term yield (e.g., warehouses), capital growth (e.g., plots), or a lifestyle-driven strategy (e.g., villas or branded residences).
- **Legal Structure is Paramount:** Understanding Freehold, Leasehold, and Usufruct is critical as it impacts your rights, control, and long-term investment flexibility.
- **Residential vs. Commercial:** Weigh the pros and cons of each sector based on your risk tolerance, capital, and management preference.
- **Match Profile to Property:** Align your investment with your investor profile for optimal fit and performance.

YOUR JOURNEY
NAVIGATOR

Part 1: Defining the Opportunity

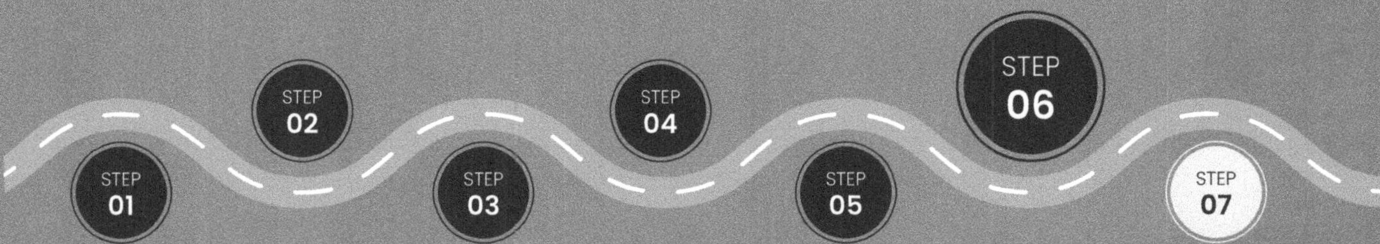

Recap

You have just completed **Chapter 6: Property Types & Investment Opportunities: Residential vs. Commercial**, where you examined Dubai's key residential and commercial property categories, compared their investment profiles, and learned how to select between off-plan and ready units. You also explored ownership structures and matched property types to specific investor profiles, building a solid understanding of what to invest in.

Next Chapter Preview

We now move into the final step of Part 1: **Chapter 7: Research & Due Diligence: From Guesswork to Game Plan**. This chapter equips you with the investigative frameworks, tools, and verification steps needed to move from potential opportunity to well-vetted, investment-ready property decisions.

You Will Learn

- ☑ How to apply financial metrics like ROI and IRR to real deals.
- ☑ Macro and micro-level location research techniques.
- ☑ How to research and compare off-plan and secondary market properties.
- ☑ Step-by-step due diligence processes for different property types.
- ☑ Tools, trackers, and common pitfalls to avoid when assessing opportunities.

Link to Framework

This chapter strengthens your C.D.R.C. mindset by embedding discipline and thoroughness into your selection process, and supports your L.E.A.D. approach by providing adaptable, evidence-based methods for narrowing opportunities to only those that deliver long-term value.

Purpose / Big Picture Link

This is the how to verify stage of your investment journey. By mastering research and due diligence, you ensure that every property you consider is backed by solid data, regulatory compliance, and clear risk assessment, closing Part 1 with the confidence to transition into the execution phase in Part 2.

CHAPTER 7

Research & Due Diligence: From Guesswork to Game Plan

> You can't improve what you don't measure, and in real estate, what you measure defines what you buy.

In Chapters 1 through 6, you've built a robust foundation: cultivating a strategic investor mindset, understanding Dubai's economic and policy blueprint, aligning with its visionary future, mastering market entry & cycles, and quantifying opportunities with essential real estate math. You've also gained clarity on various property types and investment opportunities. Now, it's time to bring all these pieces together and dive into the critical phase of **Research & Due Diligence**.

This chapter is where the theoretical knowledge transforms into actionable insights, moving you from potential "guesswork" to a concrete "game plan" for assessing real deals. It's about ensuring that every investment decision is backed by solid data and rigorous verification, rather than intuition alone. This chapter serves as your practical guide to understanding specific locations, evaluating properties, validating claims, and building your research system. It's how you confidently transition from identifying an opportunity to thoroughly investigating it, truly earning your "license to deal."

7.1. Applying Investment Math to Real Deals

Knowing formulas like Return on Investment (ROI), Internal Rate of Return (IRR), or Net Yield isn't enough. What truly separates experienced investors from amateurs isn't just the ability to calculate, but the skill to accurately *apply* these numbers in the complex context of real deals. Whether it's a ready apartment or an off-plan townhouse, each investment involves choices about timing, cash flow, strategy, and structure. And each of these choices fundamentally shifts the potential returns. This section focuses on applying those critical formulas to real Dubai-based investment scenarios, showing how math becomes your most powerful decision-making tool.

7.1.1. Why ROI Isn't Everything: The Power of IRR

ROI (Return on Investment) is one of the most widely used metrics in real estate. It's easy to understand: how much profit did you make relative to how much capital you invested? But here's the crucial catch: ROI is blind to time. It doesn't care whether your returns came in 1 year or 5. And in a business where cash flow timing significantly defines your opportunity cost and risk, that's a considerable limitation. To gain a more comprehensive understanding, investors often rely on the Internal Rate of Return (IRR). IRR is a time-sensitive metric that evaluates how efficiently your capital is being deployed over the entire investment horizon. Let's explore this through two real-world-inspired examples:

Case Study: Investor A vs. Investor B

Detail	Investor A (Ready Property)	Investor B (Off-Plan Property)
Purchase Price	AED 1,000,000 (paid upfront)	AED 1,000,000 (staggered payments)
Rental Income	AED 50,000/year for 5 years	AED 70,000/year for 2 years (Years 3 & 4)
Sale Price	AED 1,200,000	AED 1,310,000
Capital Gain	AED 200,000	AED 310,000
Total Profit	AED 450,000	AED 450,000
ROI	45.0%	45.0%
IRR (approx.)	9.1%	10.3%

Cash Flow Breakdown for IRR

Investor A – Ready Property Cash Flows:

- **Year 0:** -1,000,000
- **Years 1–4:** +50,000 per year
- **Year 5:** +50,000 (rent) + 1,200,000 (sale) = +1,250,000

IRR Calculation (using LaTeX):

$$0 = -1{,}000{,}000 + \frac{50{,}000}{(1+r)^1} + \frac{50{,}000}{(1+r)^2} + \frac{50{,}000}{(1+r)^3} + \frac{50{,}000}{(1+r)^4} + \frac{1{,}250{,}000}{(1+r)^5} \quad UsingExcel's = IRR()function, IRR \approx 9.1$$

Investor B – Off-Plan with Staggered Payments Cash Flows:

- **Year 0:** -200,000
- **Year 1:** 0
- **Year 2:** -500,000
- **Year 3:** -100,000 (payment) + 70,000 (rent) = -30,000
- **Year 4:** -100,000 (payment) + 70,000 (rent) = -30,000
- **Year 5:** -100,000 (payment) + 1,310,000 (sale) = +1,210,000

IRR Calculation (LaTeX):

$$0 = -200{,}000 + \frac{0}{(1+r)^1} + \frac{-500{,}000}{(1+r)^2} + \frac{-30{,}000}{(1+r)^3} + \frac{-30{,}000}{(1+r)^4} + \frac{1{,}210{,}000}{(1+r)^5} \quad UsingExcel's = IRR()function, IRR \approx 10.3$$

INVESTOR INSIGHT

Although both investors earned the same total profit and ROI, Investor A tied up all the capital upfront. Investor B, however, spread capital payments across 5 years, crucially keeping more cash liquid for longer. IRR accurately captures this time advantage, showing Investor B had a more efficient investment.

Table 7.1: ROI vs. IRR Summary Table

Metric	What It Shows	Strength	Strength
ROI	Return as % of invested capital	Simple to calculate and compare	Ignores time and payment structure
IRR	Annualised return over time	Accounts for the time value of money and cash flow timing	More complex; requires a spreadsheet or calculator

7.1.2. Scenario-Based Comparison – Flip vs. Rent + Sell

Investors often face a critical choice: should they sell the unit at handover or hold it and rent it out before selling later? This section compares both strategies using real numbers, helping you understand how ROI and IRR are applied in actual Dubai investment scenarios. Let's use a 1-bedroom apartment in Jumeirah Village Circle (JVC) as a case study.

Assumptions:

- **Purchase Price:** AED 850,000
- **Total Investment (including fees):** AED 900,000
- **Handover in:** 2 years
- **Flip Price:** AED 1,050,000
- **Annual Rent:** AED 65,000
- **Holding Duration for Rent:** 3 years
- **Service Charges (total):** AED 30,000
- **Final Sale Price (after rent):** AED 1,050,000

Scenario A: Flip at Handover

Capital Gain: 1,050,000 - 900,000 = 150,000

Return on Investment (ROI):

$$\text{ROI} = \left(\frac{150,000}{900,000}\right) \times 100 = 16.7\%$$

Cash Flows for IRR:

- **Year 0:** -900,000
- **Year 1:** 0
- **Year 2:** +1,050,000

Excel IRR Formula: = IRR ({-900000, 0, 1C50000}) ⇨ IRR ≈ 8.0%

Scenario B: Rent + Sell

Total Rent Collected: 3 x 65,000 = 195,000

Net Rent After Service Charges: 195,000 - 30,000 = 165,000

Total Gain: 165,000 (net rent) + 150,000 (capital gain) = 315,000

Return on Investment (ROI):

$$\text{ROI} = \left(\frac{315,000}{900,000}\right) \times 100 = 35.0\%$$

Cash Flows for IRR:

- **Year 0:** -900,000
- **Year 1:** +65,000
- **Year 2:** +65,000
- **Year 3:** +65,000 + 1,050,000 = +1,115,000

Excel IRR Formula: = IRR ({-900000, 65000, 65000, 1115000}) ⇨ IRR ≈ 8.5%

Table 7.2: Strategy Comparison: Flip vs. Rent + Sell

Strategy	Total ROI	Annualised IRR	Liquidity	Risk Exposure (Example)	Complexity
Flip at Handover	16.7%	8.0%	High	High (market timing)	Low
Rent + Sell	35.0%	8.5%	Medium	Medium (tenant risk)	Medium

INVESTOR INSIGHT

Although both strategies yield the same sale price, the rental income makes a significant difference in total returns. The Rent + Sell option nearly doubles the ROI and slightly improves the IRR. This example clearly illustrates why investors shouldn't rely solely on ROI. IRR incorporates time, providing a more accurate measure of investment performance when cash flows are spread across multiple years..

7.1.3. How to Adjust ROI for Payment Plans

Not all AED 1 million properties are created equal, especially when it comes to how and when you pay for them. Many off-plan deals in Dubai offer payment plans that span from the initial booking to handover, and sometimes even extend into post-handover years. That staggered payment schedule directly affects your ROI, IRR, and overall risk exposure. Two properties might have the same total price, but the one that lets you defer payments offers more flexibility and liquidity along the way. Let's explore this with a side-by-side example.

Scenario: Two Units in the Same Project

	Total Price	Payment Structure
Unit A	AED 850,000	60/40 with post-handover plan
Unit B	AED 800,000	100% during construction

Which is the better deal? At first glance, Unit B is the more affordable option. However, in real investing, timing is crucial. Let's break it down.

Unit A: Post-Handover Plan (60/40)

- **Booking:** AED 100,000 (Year 0)
- **Under Construction:** AED 410,000 (Years 1–2)
- **Post-Handover:** AED 340,000 (Years 3–5)
- **Rent:** AED 70,000/year (Years 3–5)
- **Sale:** AED 950,000 (Year 5)
- **Total Rent Collected:** 3 x 70,000 = 210,000
- **Total Investment:** 850,000 (across 5 years)
- **Net Profit (Rent + Capital Gain):** (210,000 + 100,000) = 310,000
- **Return on Investment (ROI):**

$$\text{ROI} = \left(\frac{310,000}{850,000}\right) \times 100 = 36.5\%$$

- **Cash Flows for IRR:**
    - **Year 0:** -100,000
    - **Year 1:** -200,000
    - **Year 2:** -210,000
    - **Year 3:** -115,000 (payment) + 70,000 (rent) = -45,000
    - **Year 4:** -115,000 (payment) + 70,000 (rent) = -45,000
    - **Year 5:** -110,000 (payment) + 70,000 (rent) + 950,000 (sale) = +910,000
- **Excel IRR Formula:** = IRR ({-100000, -200000, -210000, -45000, -45000, 910000}) ⇨ IRR ≈ 9.7%

Unit B: Fully Paid Upfront

- **Full Payment:** AED 800,000 (Year 0)
- **Rent:** AED 70,000/year (Years 3–5)
- **Sale:** AED 950,000 (Year 5)
- **Total Rent Collected:** 210,000
- **Total Gain:** 210,000 + 150,000 = 360,000
- **Return on Investment (ROI):**

$$\text{ROI} = \left(\frac{360,000}{800,000}\right) \times 100 = 45.0\%$$

- **Cash Flows for IRR:**
    - **Year 0:** -800,000
    - **Year 1:** 0
    - **Year 2:** 0
    - **Year 3:** +70,000
    - **Year 4:** +70,000
    - **Year 5:** +70,000 + 950,000 = +1,020,000
- **Excel IRR Formula:** = IRR ({-800000, 0, 0, 70000, 70000, 1020000}) ⇨ IRR ≈ 8.8%

Table 7.3: Payment Plan Strategy Comparison

Metric	Unit A (Post-Handover)	Unit B (Upfront)
ROI	36.5%	45.0%
IRR	9.7%	8.8%
Upfront Capital	Low	High
Cash Flow Timing	Staggered	Delayed income
Flexibility	High	Low

7.1.4. Real-World ROI – Villa vs. Apartments

When investors have AED 2 million to allocate, a common dilemma is whether to buy a villa or multiple apartments. Both options present strong arguments. Villas typically demonstrate greater long-term appreciation, while apartments often offer superior yield and liquidity in the shorter term. In this section, we'll compare these two investment approaches over 5 and 10 years using realistic Dubai market data, one scenario for a villa and the other for an apartment portfolio of similar value.

Asset Type	Initial Investment	Handover Year	Initial Rent Yield	Expected Rent Growth	Sale Year Options
Villa	AED 2,000,000	After Fourth Year	6%	5% annually	Year 5 or 10
Apartment	AED 2,000,000	Year 2.5	7.5%	5% annually	Year 10 only

Villa Investment: 5-Year and 10-Year Projection

- **Rent Accumulation (Years 5 to 10):**
  - Year 5 Rent = AED 2,000,000 x 0.06 = 120,000
  - Year 6 Rent = AED 120,000 x 1.05 = 126,000
  - Year 7 Rent = 132,300 (and so on for 6 years)
  - **Using a geometric series with annual 5% growth:**

$$\text{Total Rent (Years 5–10)} = 120{,}000 \times \frac{1.05^6 - 1}{0.05} \approx \text{AED } 816{,}230$$

- **Appreciation:**
  - Year 5 Sale Value = AED 2,500,000
  - Year 10 Sale Value = AED 3,934,641 (5% CAGR)

- **IRR Calculation (Year 10 Sale):**
  - **Year 0–3:** -2,000,000 (no rent)
  - **Year 4:** 0
  - **Year 5–9:** +120,000, +126,000, +132,300. +138,915, +145,861
  - **Year 10:** +153,153 + 3,934,641 = +4,087,794
  - = IRR ({-2000000, 0, 0, 0, 0, 120000, 126000, 132300, 138915, 145861, 4087794}) ⇨ IRR ≈ 19.5%

- **IRR (5-Year Exit):**
  - **Year 5:** Sale + Rent = AED 2,500,000 + 120,000 = AED 2,620,000
  - = IRR ({-2000000, 0, 0, 0, 0, 2620000}) ⇨ IRR ≈ 5.5%

Apartment Investment: 10-Year Projection

- **Rent Accumulation (Years 3 to 10):**
  - Year 3 Rent = AED 2,000,000 x 0.075 = 150,000
  - Apply 5% growth annually for 8 years

$$\text{Total Rent (Years 3–10)} = 150{,}000 \times \frac{1.05^8 - 1}{0.05} \approx \text{AED } 1{,}432{,}366$$

- **Sale Price (Year 10):**
  - Assuming modest appreciation: AED 2,500,000

- **IRR Calculation:**
  - **Year 0–2:** -2,000,000
  - **Year 3–9:** Rent increases
  - **Year 10:** 211,065 + 2,500,000 = AED 2,711,065
  - = IRR ({-2000000, 0, 0, 150000, 157500, 165375, 173644, 182326. 191442, 201014, 2711065}) ⇨ IRR ≈ 8.1%

- **IRR (5-Year Exit Not Applicable):**
  - Since most of the apartment's value is in rental return, an early exit would significantly lower the ROI.

Table 7.4: Villa vs. Apartment Investment Comparison

Metric	Villa (10-Year)	Villa (5-Year)	Apartment (10-Year)
Total Rent	AED 816,230	AED 120,000	AED 1,432,366
Sale Price	AED 3,934,641	AED 2,500,000	AED 2,500,000
Total Value	AED 4,750,871	AED 2,620,000	AED 3,932,366
IRR	9.5%	5.5%	8.1%
Rent Start Year	5	5	3
Strategy	Long-term growth	Flip	Early returns

INVESTOR INSIGHT

Villas truly shine over the long term, offering strong capital appreciation and consistent rent growth, especially once handed over and the community has stabilised. However, you must be prepared to wait longer to realise those returns. Apartments, on the other hand, begin generating income earlier, making them an excellent choice for investors primarily seeking consistent cash flow, greater liquidity, or earlier exit potential. Your decision should always perfectly match your investment horizon and specific capital goals.

7.1.5. When ROI Is More Practical Than IRR

While IRR is a potent tool for evaluating time-based performance, it's not always the most practical or straightforward metric, particularly in short-term or highly uncertain scenarios. There are indeed cases where a simpler, more static measure like ROI can provide faster clarity and minimise unnecessary confusion. This section helps you understand when not to overcomplicate your analysis.

1. Short-Term Flips (Under 12 Months)

For rapid flip projects, especially those with no rental income and a holding period of less than a year, IRR can become overly sensitive to even small changes in timing. Because IRR annualises returns, it can sometimes create artificially inflated and misleading numbers.

Example: You buy a property for AED 1,000,000 and sell it for AED 1,150,000 within 6 months. The ROI is:

$$\text{ROI} = \frac{1,150,000 - 1,000,000}{1,000,000} = 15\%$$

IRR would attempt to annualise this 6-month return: = IRR ({-1, 000, 000, +1, 150, 000}) ≈ 32.0%

The 32% figure sounds incredibly impressive, but it can be highly misleading unless you are genuinely confident you can repeat such a swift, high-percentage flip consistently multiple times within a year.

2. Projects With No Cash Flow

If a property generates no rental income, like undeveloped land, certain distressed assets, or delayed off-plan projects, there is often only one significant cash flow event: the eventual sale.

Example: A plot is bought for AED 2,000,000 and sold 4 years later for AED 2,600,000:

$$\text{ROI} = \frac{2,600,000 - 2,000,000}{2,000,000} = 30\%$$

While trying to calculate IRR on a single outflow and a delayed inflow makes mathematical sense, the additional insight it provides is often no greater than what ROI already tells you in such a scenario = IRR ({-2,000,000, 0, 0, 0, 2,600,000}) ≈ 6.7%.

In cases with no intermediate cash flows, ROI often provides sufficient clarity.

3. Uncertain Cash Flow Projections

IRR inherently assumes that you can forecast future rents and sale prices with reasonable accuracy; however, in scenarios where cash flows are highly speculative (e.g., highly volatile Airbnb income) or heavily dependent on future, uncertain regulations, ROI can often offer a more conservative and easily understandable framework.

For example, if rents are highly volatile (e.g., Airbnb income) or significantly dependent on future regulations, using varying projections like: Expected Rent = AED 100,000/year (best case) versus Conservative Rent = AED 60,000/year will result in different ROIs. But trying to use IRR with such uncertain data introduces a false sense of precision that may inadvertently mislead less experienced investors.

4. Investor Psychology and Simplicity

ROI is inherently intuitive and straightforward. Many first-time investors find themselves feeling more confident and comfortable comparing deals using simple percentage returns. While IRR is mathematically superior in certain complex instances, the sheer clarity and immediate grasp of ROI often drives faster, more decisive actions, particularly for new investors.

INVESTOR INSIGHT

Use IRR when:

- You anticipate multiple, uneven cash flows across several years.
- Your capital will be deployed and returned in stages (e.g., off-plan payment plans).
- Payment plans, rental incomes, and eventual exits are all highly time-sensitive elements of your strategy.

Use ROI when:

- The investment involves a single, straightforward capital cycle.
- There is no significant cash flow generated during the holding period.
- Simplicity and immediate clarity matter more than the precision of compounding over time.

7.1.6. How to Model IRR in Excel

Internal Rate of Return (IRR) is undoubtedly one of the most powerful tools in a real estate investor's toolkit. Yet, it's often frustratingly underused simply because investors find its calculation intimidating. Fortunately, readily available tools like Microsoft Excel and Google Sheets make it incredibly easy to compute IRR, as long as you grasp the basic structure of the cash flows involved.

Now with ChatGPT, Gemini and other tools, it's even easier. You can throw in the numbers and experiment with the AI prompts. While there is a slight learning curve to get the prompts right, it would really make IRR and ROI comparisons easier for investors who don't want to open Excel spreadsheets. The only thing to look out for is that with the wrong prompt or incomplete data, AI can get calculations wrong, even with the right prompt. If there seems to be something off about the output, you have to recheck.

In this section, we'll walk you through the step-by-step process of building an IRR model using a real off-plan property scenario, explaining the logic behind each entry.

Step 1: Understand What IRR Needs

IRR calculates the precise discount rate at which the Net Present Value (NPV) of your investment's cash flows equals zero, accounting for all inflows and outflows across the entire life of the deal. You don't need to know the discount rate upfront; Excel will compute it for you. What you do need is a complete, chronological list of year-by-year cash flows, which must include:

- Negative cash flows (representing investments or payments made).
- Positive cash flows (representing rental income received or resale proceeds).
- Zeros in any year with no transactions or cash movements.

Step 2: Prepare Your Cash Flow Data

Organise your cash flows in a single column or row in your spreadsheet. Remember that the initial investment (Year 0) must be entered as a negative number. Subsequent payments should also be negative, while incomes and sale proceeds are positive.

Example: Off-Plan Property Cash Flows (from Section 7.1.1 Investor B)

- **Year 0:** -200,000
- **Year 1:** 0
- **Year 2:** -500,000
- **Year 3:** -100,000 (payment) + 70,000 (rent) = -30,000
- **Year 4:** -100,000 (payment) + 70,000 (rent) = -30,000
- **Year 5:** -100,000 (final payment) + 1,310,000 (resale income) = +1,210,000

The precise cash flow series to input into Excel or Sheets would be: (-200,000, 0, -500,000, -30,000, -30,000, 1,210,000)

Step 3: Use Excel's IRR Formula

In Excel, simply use the formula: =IRR (range) Where range is the continuous cell range containing your year-by-year cash flows (e.g., A1:A6). Ensure each year's cash flow is in a separate cell and in the correct chronological order.

Step 4: Read the Output Carefully

Excel will return a percentage; this is your annualised IRR. It tells you how efficiently your capital is working over time, factoring in any delays, staggered payments, consistent rental income, and the final resale amount. If your calculated IRR is above your target return (say, 8–10%), it's certainly worth investigating further. If it's below, critically ask why, and whether the proposed timeline or your rental assumptions might be dragging it down.

INVESTOR INSIGHT

IRR Powerfully Reveals Value Hidden in Timing. You might encounter two seemingly identical deals with the same headline ROI, but vastly different IRRs. Why? One might tie up your money significantly from the very start, while another strategically allows you to pay gradually, thereby freeing up your capital for other lucrative uses. IRR makes that crucial distinction visibly clear, empowering you to optimise for capital efficiency, not just headline returns.

Troubleshooting IRR Calculations:

- **Too Few Cash Flows?** IRR fundamentally requires at least one negative cash flow (an investment) and at least one positive cash flow (a return).
- **Non-Converging Result?** If your cash flows are too erratic or complex, Excel's standard IRR() function might struggle to find a solution. In such cases, consider using the XIRR() function, which allows you to input exact dates for each cash flow, providing greater precision for irregular timing.

INVESTOR MISTAKE TO AVOID

Over-Reliance on ROI One of the most common pitfalls in real estate investing is relying solely on ROI as the single metric to evaluate a deal. While ROI is undeniably simple, fast, and easy to communicate, it can also be dangerously misleading, particularly when comparing properties with different timelines, payment structures, or rental profiles.

The Problem: ROI Ignores Time and Timing

Let's say you invest AED 1 million and get AED 1.4 million back in 5 years. That's a 40% ROI. Now imagine another deal where you invest the same AED 1 million and get AED 1.4 million back in just 2 years. Same ROI, but which is the better investment? The second one. Your money came back significantly faster, allowing you to reinvest it sooner. That crucial aspect is what ROI doesn't tell you: how long your cash was tied up and how efficiently it worked over time. This is where IRR becomes an indispensable tool.

INVESTOR INSIGHT

The worst ROI trap is one that feels incredibly good initially but performs poorly over time. Savvy investors consistently dig deeper; they look beyond the surface numbers and model the precise flow of money across years, not just the static totals.

INVESTOR WARNING

ROI may make a deal look attractive on the surface, but it dangerously hides the most crucial variable in wealth building: time.

7.2. Research Begins with Location

In Chapter 3, we explored Dubai's long-term vision and strategic zoning, introducing Core, Emerging, and Peripheral areas. Now, we dive deeper into location from a research perspective, moving from the strategic 'what' to the investigative 'how.' Since the property's location is the single most critical aspect of any real estate investment, it fundamentally overshadows the unit type and any amenities that come with it. In this section, we'll guide you through how to evaluate both macro-level (city-wide) and micro-level (community-specific) location factors, empowering you to make confident, high-conviction decisions.

Location Research
Macro to Micro

Zoom-in Checklist from City Zones to Plot-Level Analysis

City Level

Macro Trends

- Economic growth rate (Dubai vs. other Emirates)
- Population growth & migration trends
- Strategic mega projects (e.g. Expo, Dubai 2040 Plan)
- Governance & real estate regulations
- Transport connectivity (airports, metro plans)

District Level

Investment Pockets

- District reputation (Business hub, family-friendly?)
- Infrastructure maturity (roads, hospitals, schools)
- Demand-supply metrics (vacancy rate, rental yield)

Zone / Community Level

Master Planning Quality

- Developer profile (Emaar, Nakheel, Damac etc.)
- Community type (Freehold, Leasehold, Mixed-use)
- Ementies & lifestyle (parks, schools, mall, beach access)
- Service charges & maintenance quality
- Planned vs delivered infrastructure

Particular Property Level

Micro Feasibility

- Plot orientation (sunlight, wind, direction)
- Plot size & FAR/GFA rules
- Title deed & ownership structure
- Proximity to noise, power lines, drainage
- Zoning permission & future construction nearby

7.2.1. Macro-Level Location Research

This focuses on the broader context and future trajectory of an area.

Factor	What to Look For
City-Wide Trends	Is the area strategically located within a designated growth corridor? Is the government actively investing in significant infrastructure development in this vicinity?
Infrastructure Plans	Investigate upcoming Metro extensions, new major highways, future malls, planned economic zones, and any significant public transport expansions.
Zoning Announcements	Pay close attention to any upcoming changes from RERA or DLD that might affect specific land use, density regulations, or building rules in the area.
Area Positioning	Determine whether the area is already saturated with development, actively emerging with new growth, or currently undergoing a transition phase.
Inflection mapping	Check the location's market cycle and outlook, as discussed in Chapter 4, with data.

TIP

Areas with significant, confirmed infrastructure investment typically see 10–25% higher appreciation within 3 years of completion.

7.2.2. Micro-Level Location Research

Once you've intelligently shortlisted a broader area, it's time to zoom in. Micro-level research focuses on what it's ***actually like*** to live in, or rent out, a specific unit within a particular community or even on a specific street. These are the everyday realities that influence tenant demand, end-user appeal, and a property's long-term value.

Factor	What to Evaluate
Proximity to Essentials	Are there readily accessible supermarkets, quality schools, clinics, pharmacies, or medical centres conveniently located within a comfortable 5–10 minute radius?
Transport Access	Is there a nearby Metro station, a convenient highway exit, or an efficient public transport link easily accessible from the property?
Construction Status	Are internal roads within the community fully complete? Is the area still noisy or dusty due to ongoing construction? Are nearby plots still actively under development?
Noise, Traffic, Livability	Visit the property at different times of the day (morning, afternoon, evening), during both weekdays and weekends, to accurately assess the noise levels, traffic, and overall living comfort.
Community Profile	Identify who typically lives in the area. What is the approximate mix of owners versus tenants? Are units predominantly sold to end-users or to short-term flippers?

INVESTOR INSIGHT

Gentrifying zones like Al Jaddaf, DSO, Liwan or Dubai South may offer significantly more upside potential than already saturated prime areas. Always look for early infrastructure signals; these often precede a substantial increase in property appreciation. A slightly less polished area with a Metro line actively under construction can frequently outperform a highly polished area with stagnant pricing.

INVESTOR MISTAKE TO AVOID

Focusing solely on the unit or project without thoroughly assessing the location's fundamental strengths. You might find an impressive floor plan or a flashy launch offer, but if the surrounding community lacks adequate infrastructure or future growth catalysts, your investment may struggle.

Tool Tip for Smarter Research:

Combine various tools to gain a real-time and historical understanding of the area:

- **Google Maps Timeline:** Use this to check typical commute times and assess walkability.
- **Bayut Area Maps:** Visually observe listings distribution and price heatmaps.
- **DXBInteract:** Compare historical transaction data and market movement within the same building or on the same street.

Further Distinction of Location Types (Reiteration from Chapter 6, here for research context):

Mature locations, such as Downtown Dubai, Business Bay, and Dubai Marina, offer stability, established infrastructure, strong rental demand, and higher liquidity. Emerging areas such as Jumeirah Village Circle (JVC), Arjan, or Meydan typically have ongoing development and rising investor interest, offering greater appreciation potential with moderate risk. Future-facing zones like Dubai South, Dubai Islands, and parts of Dubailand represent early-stage opportunities where returns may take time but could be significant over the long term. Each type presents a different risk-return profile, so matching your strategy to the lifecycle of a location is key. Capital flippers, yield seekers, and long-term investors will all choose differently, depending on their timing, goals, and risk tolerance.

7.2.3. Types of Master Communities in Dubai

A master community refers to a large-scale, pre-planned development that includes residential buildings, roads, retail spaces, parks, and comprehensive community facilities, all delivered in coordinated phases by a single developer or consortium. These communities boast their own internal infrastructure, amenities, and sometimes even dedicated schools and clinics. However, different master communities are built to fulfil specific criteria, allowing us to distinguish them based on these inherent characteristics.

By Landmark or Feature

Lifestyle features shape these communities. Whether it's a championship golf course, a prime waterfront property, or a sprawling public park, these landmarks exert a significant influence on property values, rental demand, and buyer preferences. This table categorises four major community types based on natural or man-made features, providing insight into their investment appeal, illustrative examples, and strategic positioning.

Community Type	Feature	Appeal
Golf	Golf courses	Luxury lifestyle, green space, exclusivity
Park & Lake	Parks, lakes	Family-friendly, affordable, walkable public areas
Equestrian	Horse riding	Quiet setting, privacy, suits mid to upper segments
Waterfront	Beaches, marinas	Waterfront views, skyline appeal, strong ROI and tourism draw

TIP

Waterfront and golf communities tend to have higher purchase prices and lower yields initially. In contrast, park and lake communities often strike a better balance between rentability and price entry

By Community Structure

Neighbourhoods also vary significantly in their underlying structure and management. Exclusive gated enclaves, open-access zones, and mixed-use developer layouts each impact property values, yields, and overall resident experiences. This table breaks down key community structures, highlights relevant examples, and explains their investment implications.

Structure Type	Examples	Key Features
Gated	Dubai Hills, Arabian Ranches, Damac Hills	Controlled access, enhanced security, internal amenities, strong end-user appeal
Park & Lake	Motorcity, Furjan, Town Square	Easier access, lower perceived restrictions, often more diverse and vibrant
Mixed-Developer	JVC, Arjan, Liwan, DLRC, Jadaf, Majan	Architectural diversity and developer competition often keep prices realistic and foster innovation
Single-Developer	Dubai Hills, Downtown (Emaar)	Consistency in quality, cohesive master-planned execution, centralised upkeep and community management

INVESTOR MISTAKE TO AVOID

Assuming a gated investment automatically means a better investment. Open communities, such as JVC, can frequently outperform gated ones in terms of ROI and resale liquidity, particularly when price points are more accessible.

By Housing Mix

You can also distinguish communities based on their prevalent housing mix. Some communities lean heavily toward villas, naturally drawing families and offering long-term stability. Others are predominantly apartment-driven, appealing more to transient renters and investors prioritising liquidity. Hybrid zones seamlessly blend both types, providing greater flexibility in exit and leasing strategies. Whether you're targeting end-users, long-term tenants, or short-stay guests, the mix of property types will directly impact your pricing strategies, achievable yields, and desired holding horizon.

Housing Mix	Examples	Key Appeal
Apartment Dominant	JLT, Dubai Marina, Business Bay	Offers greater liquidity, lower entry cost, and strong potential for short-term rentals
Mixed (Apartments + Townhouses)	JVC, Dubai Hills, Al Furjan	Possesses broad appeal; suits both end-users and investors, providing flexibility for resale or lease strategies

By Function – Commercial, Mixed-Use & Transit-Oriented Communities

Business hub-oriented communities are those strategically located around major employment hubs, key commercial zones, and significant transit corridors. These areas typically attract working professionals and business tenants, consistently offering substantial rental turnover and reliable income stability. This makes them an excellent fit for investors primarily focused on yield and shorter holding periods.

Community Type	Examples	Key Appeal
Business/Commercial Districts	Business Bay, DIFC, Barsha Heights, Downtown Dubai	Proximity to offices and financial hubs, consistent rental demand, and opportunities for executive rentals
Mall-Linked Urban Zones	Dubai Mall, Dubai Hills Mall, Festival City Mall	Strong footfall, high family appeal, seamless retail integration, and attractiveness for long-term tenants
Airport-Connected Zones	Dubai South (Al Maktoum Airport), DXB (Current airport), Al Jadaf, Mirdif	Logistical advantages, appeal to aviation-linked workers, Expo City legacy, and future-proof infrastructure
Transit-Oriented Developments (TOD)	Areas directly linked to Metro: JLT, Discovery Gardens, Furjan, Tecom	Offers a car-free lifestyle, high ROI on rentals due to accessibility, and excellent walkability
Mixed-Use Urban Hubs	JLT, Dubai Hills, Wasl 1, Downtown, Business Bay, Barsha Heights	Provides a balanced lifestyle: ideal for Live-Work-Play zones, appealing to both investors and end-users

7.2.4. Location Analysis Checklist

As we've seen, various community characteristics can significantly help us chart out the potential appeal of a property. Here is a handy reference to map out property options based on both macro-level and micro-level checklists, as discussed earlier.

Look for locations along clearly defined growth corridors, zones specifically prioritised for future development, like Dubai South. Actively scan for government announcements that signal future upside, such as the confirmed construction of new Metro lines, major roads, shopping malls, or hospitals. Understand where the area sits in the broader market cycle: is it emerging (with a low entry point), saturated (stagnant), or actively transitioning?

Macro-Level Checks

Factor	What to Look For
Growth Corridor	Is the location part of a significant infrastructure plan or within a designated development axis?
Government Announcements	Are there any upcoming road projects, Metro lines, malls, hospitals, or zoning revisions confirmed for the area?
Position in the Market Cycle	Is the area emerging (offering a low entry point), saturated (experiencing stagnation), or actively transitioning?
Proximity to Economic Drivers	Is the property conveniently located near a major business district, airport, large shopping mall, hospital, or significant school hub?

After the macro picture is clear, micro-level checks help assess daily convenience, community quality, and the precise fit for your investment. This table outlines essential criteria, like access, noise levels, service charges, and tenant profile, to ensure your chosen property aligns with both your lifestyle and investment strategy.

Micro-Level Checks

Factor	What to Assess
Daily Life Needs	Is there convenient access to supermarkets, schools, clinics, and parks within a comfortable 5–10 minute radius?
Connectivity	How close is the property to Metro stations, arterial roads, and major airports?
Community Feel	Is the community primarily end-user driven (families), transient (attracting short-term rentals), or a balanced mix?
Noise & Disruption	Are there ongoing construction activities, nearby highways, active flight paths, or consistently busy roads that could negatively affect quality of life?
Developer Mix	Is it a single developer (implying consistency) versus a mixed developer environment (implying variation and potentially a wider resale range)?
Service Charges	Are the annual service charges (AED/sq.ft rate) transparent and fair? What is included? What are existing residents saying about maintenance quality?
Unit Types & Tenant Base	Are typical tenants professionals, families, or students? What type of units (e.g., studios, villas) are in the majority?
Legal and Ownership Type	Is the property freehold, leasehold, or designated for GCC nationals only?

TIP

Always visit the site in person; if you're unable to, thoroughly check it out on Google Street View. Observe traffic patterns during peak hours, assess walkability, evaluate landscaping quality, and note real-time activity. This approach will consistently provide you with better insight than relying solely on marketing materials, especially when faced with multiple options and trying to make a final choice.

7.2.5. Key Investment Corridors in Dubai

When thinking about location for real estate investment in Dubai, it's incredibly valuable to consider the city in terms of its major **investment corridors**—the key arteries along which development and value often flow. These corridors are more than just roads; they represent strategic growth paths, shaping pricing tiers, influencing accessibility, and defining the character of the communities they serve. Thinking in terms of these corridors, rather than just isolated postcodes, will provide you with a richer, more strategic understanding of investment potential.

You'll see that the city's development follows a pronounced north-south spine, expanding inland from the coast. Prime areas began near Jumeirah and Sheikh Zayed Road, then systematically moved east toward Al Khail Road (E44), E311, and finally E611. Concurrently, major west-east corridors, such as Hessa Street and Al Ain Road, significantly shape secondary growth patterns. Crucially, Metro lines further define valuable clusters, especially the Red Line and the upcoming Blue Line. Generally, property prices tend to decline as you move inland from the coast and south from Downtown, making this layout a powerful predictor of pricing tiers and growth potential. Understanding this strategic grid helps investors position themselves intelligently across the city's expanding landscape.

INVESTOR INSIGHT

Thinking of Dubai in terms of investment corridors is incredibly useful. You will slowly gain insight into how the pricing of property per square foot transitions from high to low as you move further inland from the shore, along the key corridors.

Table 7.5: Key Investment Corridors in Dubai

Corridor / Zone	Key Communities Served	Investment Impact / Insights
Dubai Metro – Red Line	JLT, Dubai Marina, Business Bay, Downtown, Deira, Rashidiya, Jebel Ali	Offers premium rents, high resale demand, and an excellent tenant pool; strong for mixed-use developments and consistent rental yields.
Dubai Metro – Green Line	Al Qusais, Mirdif, Al Nahda, Deira, Bur Dubai, Dubai Creek Harbour, Al Jaddaf	Drives affordable housing growth and urban regeneration; offers long-term uplift with improved transport access.
Dubai Metro – Blue Line (Planned)	Discovery Gardens, Mirdif, Dubai Hills, Dubai Silicon Oasis, Emaar Creek Harbour	Presents early-mover upside and significant value uplift expected post-Metro launch.
Sheikh Zayed Road (E11)	Downtown, DIFC, Business Bay, JLT, Marina, Al Barsha, Jebel Ali, Dubai South	The prime corridor, signifying prestige and stability, offers strong rents and consistent resale activity.
Al Khail Road (E44)	Business Bay, Dubai Hills, Meydan, JVC, JVT, Al Quoz	Known for fast connectivity, serves maturing mid-tier communities.
Sheikh Mohammed Bin Zayed Road (E311)	Dubailand, Silicon Oasis, Al Furjan, Jebel Ali Village, Dubai South	An emerging corridor, offering affordable housing and direct access to logistics hubs.
Emirates Road (E611)	DAMAC Lagoons Island, DAMAC Sun City, Reem Communities, DAMAC Hills 2, DIC, Dubai South	Represents outer-belt villa/logistics/tourism zones; offers undervalued entry points with strong growth potential.
Al Ain Road (E66)	Dubailand (north), Al Barari, The Valley, Silicon Oasis	A family-oriented villa/townhouse belt, characterised by strong end-user and investor interest.
Hessa Street Corridor	JVC, Arjan, Al Barsha, Motor City, Studio City, Tilal Al Ghaf, Town Square, DAMAC Hills	Connects various mid-market communities; benefits from improving infrastructure and accessibility.
Sheikh Zayed Bin Hamdan Street	Arabian Ranches, Al Barari, Villa Lantana, The Sustainable City, Dubailand	A quieter suburban villa zone, known for strong appreciation and high quality of life appeal.
Al Qudra Road	The Valley, DAMAC Hills 2, Tilal Al Ghaf, Dubai South, Sports City, Al Furjan	A lifestyle-centric corridor, demonstrating strong villa/townhouse investor demand.
Dubai Creek & Canal Corridor	Dubai Creek Harbour, Ras Al Khor, Creek Island, Al Safa, Business Bay extension, Al Jaddaf	Represents waterfront living with Metro access; offers iconic views and strong long-term ROI potential.

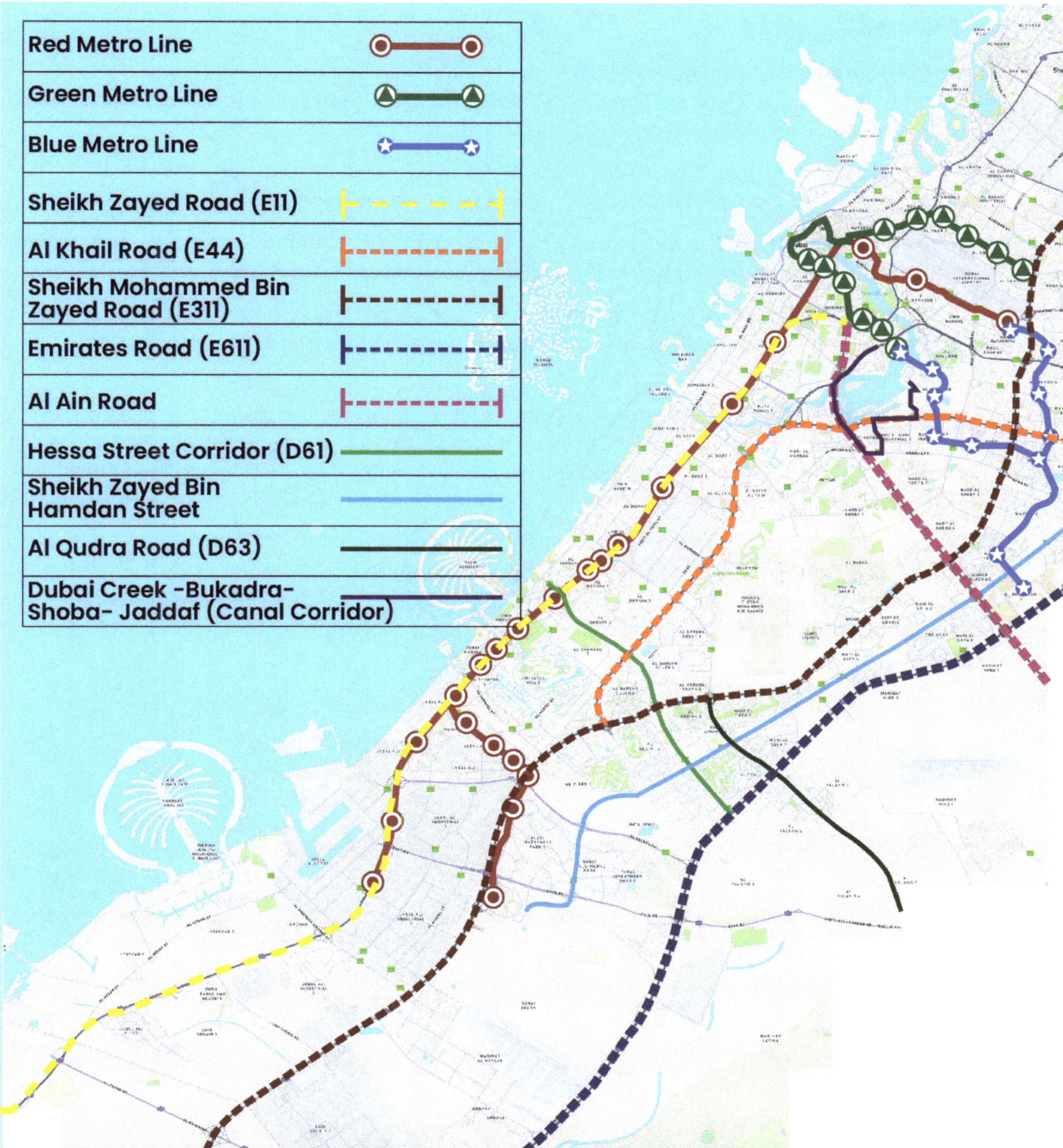

Key Investment Corridors in Dubai

Corridor Highlights:

- **Metro Corridors:** Properties located within 500m of Metro stations consistently enjoy higher rental rates, lower vacancies, and superior resale demand. The Red Line is especially valuable for commercial and residential mixed-use zones.
- **Sheikh Zayed Road (E11):** As the primary spine of Dubai, proximity here directly translates to prestige and excellent accessibility for both businesses and residents.
- **Al Khail Road (E44):** This is the most rapidly developing east-west corridor, efficiently connecting central business hubs to emerging residential neighbourhoods.
- **Hessa Street & Sheikh Zayed Bin Hamdan Street:** These secondary arteries have become vital lifelines for mid-market and suburban communities, making them perfect for families and value investors.
- **Emirates Road:** E611, this is the strongest peripheral zone, especially the stretch starting from Al Ain Road up to Dubai South. On the east side of this road, expect to see continuous development with new communities being announced. For investors looking for future villa and townhouse developments with long-term play, this is a good place to start checking for really good-priced options.
- **Dubai Creek & Canal:** This represents the next significant mixed-use waterfront frontier. With the development of Dubai Creek Harbour, the ongoing regeneration of Al Jaddaf, and the extension of the canal towards Safa Park, this corridor offers iconic views and substantial long-term upside potential.

7.3. Off-Plan vs. Secondary: Research Paths Differ

When it comes to real estate research, one size does not fit all. A significant mistake investors frequently make is applying the very same due diligence process to both off-plan and secondary market properties. These are fundamentally different investment types, each with unique timelines, inherent risks, and distinct data sources, so your evaluation approach must adapt accordingly.

Off-plan properties inherently require forward-looking research. Since the asset doesn't yet physically exist, your primary focus should be on the developer's proven credibility, their historical delivery record, the specific payment terms offered, and the ongoing construction progress. Pricing for off-plan units is often set by the developer, with limited real-time transaction data available. Instead, you'll need to rely on indirect signals, such as Oqood registrations and broader launch trends. My sales velocity index is a strong indicator of developer and location performance for off-plan and can be an incredibly useful metric for this research.

Secondary market properties, on the other hand, offer complete visibility into historical transaction records, actual rental yields, and current market activity. Here, your research revolves around comparable sales (comps), detailed resale history, verified service charges, and precise tenant profiles. I have developed a capital appreciation comparison indicator which can tell you how the resale activity in communities is rewarding the investors. Also, my yield comparison indicator is a good way to research secondary markets.

In this section, I break down how your research approach must fundamentally differ for each type of property.

INVESTOR MISTAKE TO AVOID

Don't apply the same research lens to off-plan and secondary properties. With off-plan, focus on delivery timelines, developer reputation, and payment plan flexibility. With secondary, scrutinise actual transaction data, service charge history, and tenancy status.

Table 7.6: Off-Plan vs. Secondary Research Paths

Aspect	Off-Plan Property (Under Construction)	Secondary Market Property (Ready/ Resale)
Asset Status	Physical property does not yet exist; it relies on future development.	Physical property exists; it is often occupied or ready for immediate use.
Developer Track Record	Critical research delivery timelines, project history, and overall reputation.	Less relevant unless the developer still actively manages the community or has ongoing liabilities.
Payment Plans	Directly impacts ROI, cash flow, and liquidity; usually involves structured instalment plans over time.	Typically requires full payment (cash or mortgage); offers fewer financial levers for staggered payments.
Pricing Transparency	Controlled pricing, sometimes with early-bird discounts or specific launch offers from the developer.	Market-driven pricing is heavily influenced by current supply, prevailing demand, and recent transaction history.
Availability of Data	Limited to marketing brochures, Oqood registration records, and indirect demand signals.	Comprehensive historical transaction data, actual rental records, and extensive listing comparables are readily available.
Resale / Exit Liquidity	Uncertain until handover or project completion; resale governed by No Objection Certificate (NOC) and developer approval process.	Benefits from market-tested demand; liquidity can be assessed by checking average "Days on Market" and historical resale performance.

7.3.1. A Deep Dive into Off-Plan Investing: Research, Risks, and Rewards

In Dubai's dynamic real estate landscape, the term "off-plan" represents one of the most exciting and widely discussed investment avenues. Off-plan investing is the act of purchasing a property directly from a developer before its construction is complete. Essentially, you are buying a promise based on architectural blueprints, 3D renderings, and a detailed sales and purchase agreement (SPA). You invest in a property that does not yet physically exist, often securing it at a competitive price with a structured payment plan.

This forward-looking approach is a cornerstone of Dubai's growth story, allowing developers to fund ambitious new projects while offering investors an early entry point into the city's future communities. However, because you are investing in a promise, your research must extend far beyond mere marketing materials. This guide equips you with the tools to protect yourself and make an informed decision.

7.3.1.1. The Safety Net: How Dubai's Regulations Protect Off-Plan Investors

The idea of paying for something that isn't built yet can seem risky. However, Dubai has established one of the world's most robust regulatory frameworks to protect off-plan buyers, spearheaded by the Real Estate Regulatory Agency (RERA) and the Dubai Land Department (DLD).

Here are the key policies that make off-plan investing in Dubai significantly safer:

- **Mandatory Escrow Accounts (Law No. 8 of 2007):** This is the most critical piece of legislation protecting your investment. Developers are legally required to open a separate, DLD-monitored escrow account for each project. Your payments go directly into this account, and the developer can only withdraw funds to cover construction costs after reaching specific, verified project milestones.
- **Oqood Registration:** When you purchase an off-plan property, the transaction is registered on a provisional property register called "Oqood" (Arabic for "contracts"). This provides you with a government-issued certificate that legally secures your claim to the property long before the final Title Deed is issued.
- **Strict Developer & Project Requirements:** A developer cannot launch a project without proving they own 100% of the land and have either deposited 20% of the construction cost as a bank guarantee or completed 20% of the construction, ensuring only financially sound developers can enter the market.
- **RERA Approval for All Marketing:** Every aspect of an off-plan project, from brochures to payment plans, must be officially approved by RERA before being advertised, preventing misleading claims.

7.3.1.2. The Off-Plan Advantage: The Pros

When executed correctly, off-plan investing can be incredibly lucrative.

- **Significant Capital Appreciation Potential:** The primary allure is buying at today's price with the expectation that the property's value will be significantly higher upon completion, once the community matures and infrastructure is in place.
- **Attractive Payment Plans:** Dubai developers are famous for offering flexible payment plans (e.g., 40% during construction, 60% on handover) and even Post-Handover Payment Plans (PHPP), which allow you to use rental income to help pay off your investment.
- **Lower Initial Capital Outlay:** You commit a smaller initial deposit and pay in instalments, making it easier to enter the market.
- **Choice of Best Units:** As an early investor, you get to pick the best available units, those with premium views, optimal layouts, or better locations.
- **Brand New Asset:** You receive a new property with modern amenities, minimal initial maintenance, and often a developer warranty.

7.3.1.3. The Calculated Risk: The Cons

Off-plan investing is not without its risks, which demand careful consideration.

- **Market Timing Risk:** The market cycle could turn. If the market is in a downturn when your property is handed over, its value could be lower than what you paid.
- **Construction Delays:** Delays can still happen, meaning your capital is tied up for longer than anticipated without generating rental income.
- **Quality and Finishing Risk:** The final product may not match the glossy brochure or the luxurious showroom perfectly.
- **Zero Initial Rental Income:** During the 2-4 year construction period, your invested capital is not generating any cash flow.
- **Liquidity Risk:** Selling an off-plan property before completion ("flipping") can be challenging in a slower market and usually requires developer approval (NOC) and fees.

7.3.1.4. The Due Diligence Blueprint: How to Research Off-Plan Properties

It's simply not enough to rely solely on a developer's reputation or a broker's enthusiasm. You must verify licenses, confirm escrow protections, read the fine print, and understand where your money is going.

- **Validate Developer Credibility.** Never get swayed purely by strong branding or flashy sales booths; these do not inherently guarantee reliable delivery. Your absolute first step should always be to check the developer's historical track record. Go beyond the basic information: look into their history of completed projects, how they've handled any past delays or disputes, and how closely their finished projects genuinely matched the promises initially made.
  Whenever feasible, make it a point to visit at least one of the developer's previously finished projects. Speak directly with existing residents or local agents to accurately gauge the quality of the build and the standards of ongoing maintenance. These invaluable firsthand observations will frequently reveal crucial details that marketing materials conveniently omit.

When you meet the sales team, pay acute attention to how they handle your questions. Are they genuinely transparent, or do they rigidly stick to a pre-defined script? Always request draft agreements, detailed escrow information, and other crucial project documents. A reputable developer will consistently provide these without hesitation. For instance, when I spoke with a relationship manager at Binghatti, he proudly pointed out their impressive record of zero delays and zero complaints registered with the DLD. This exemplary track record truly sets a developer apart.

- **Check Demand Velocity:** A key indicator of a project's actual viability is its demand velocity. Don't just take "selling fast" at face value.
  - **Observe Sales Centre Activity:** Is there a consistent queue for bookings, or is it empty? Is there genuine buzz, or are agents simply standing around?
  - **Verify Oqood Registration:** Check actual DLD Oqood registration numbers for the project (via the Dubai REST App). This tells you how many units are genuinely being registered, not just reserved.
  - **Cross-Check Listing Portals:** Use Bayut or Property Finder to cross-check demand by filtering to the specific project and sorting by "Popularity" or "Most Viewed."
- **Check Marketing Momentum:** Avoid confusing marketing momentum with real, sustainable demand. Flashy "Sold Out" signs may not accurately reflect actual DLD-registered sales. Always verify the underlying data.
- **Compare Price and Payment Plan:** Price per square foot is merely one piece of the puzzle. The real leverage frequently lies in the payment timeline.
  - **Compare Launch Price:** Rigorously compare the launch price with nearby ready properties to accurately assess if the premium for off-plan is truly justified.
  - **Review Payment Schedule:** Determine if it's front-loaded (more upfront), back-loaded (more at handover), or involves extended post-handover plans.
  - **Check for Waivers:** Diligently check if registration fees, DLD charges, or service fees are waived; these can significantly impact your actual entry cost.
- **Track Construction Progress and Escrow:** It is always better to verify physical construction progress.
  - **Check DLD Project Tracker:** Regularly monitor the project's progress on the DLD Project Tracker.
  - **Verify Escrow Account:** Confirm that the developer has a DLD-registered escrow account for your specific project. Your payments should only go into this account.
  - **Request Updates:** Don't hesitate to ask the developer or your broker for the latest site progress reports or drone footage.

PRO TIP

Projects with delayed escrow disbursement reports or stagnant construction updates often signal underlying funding or permitting issues.

INVESTOR INSIGHT

If a developer has a documented history of delayed projects or consistently delivers specifications that fall notably short of promises, even significant price discounts won't compensate. The long-term exit value will inevitably be negatively impacted.

7.3.1.5. Strategic Framework for Off-Plan Success

- **Market Timing & Confluence:** The ideal time to buy off-plan is during the Recovery or early Expansion phases of the real estate cycle. Buying at the Peak is extremely risky. Use the confluence of indicators from Chapter 4 to assess the cycle phase before committing.
- Strategic Zoning: Off-plan opportunities are most abundant and have the highest growth potential in Emerging and Peripheral zones where new master-planned communities are being built (e.g., Dubai South, The Valley, Dubai Land).
- **Developer Due Diligence:** This is non-negotiable. Top-tier developers (e.g., Emaar, Nakheel) command a premium price but offer lower risk. For mid-tier developers, you must check their history, previous projects, and financial stability.

7.3.1.6. Integrating Off-Plan Investing with Your Mindset

This high-stakes, high-reward strategy requires a disciplined mindset.

- **SMART Goal:** An off-plan investment must be highly specific.
  - **Example:** "To acquire a one-bedroom, 750 sq. ft. off-plan apartment in Emaar's Creek Harbour for under AED 1.8M (Specific, Measurable, Achievable), with a 40/60 payment plan, to achieve at least 30% capital appreciation by its handover in Q4 2028 (Relevant, Time-bound)."
- **CDRC Mindset:**
  - **Clarity:** This is your foundation. It means knowing your "why" and defining clear objectives for the investment, whether it's capital growth, passive income, or a future home. Your purpose guides every decision.
  - **Discipline:** This is paramount. It involves diligently researching the developer, visiting the location, understanding every clause in the SPA, and verifying escrow details. Discipline means trusting your research and holding steady, ignoring market noise during the long construction phase.
  - **Resilience:** Have the financial buffer to withstand potential delays or a market dip at handover. This financial strength prevents you from being forced to sell at a loss and gives you holding power.
  - **Curiosity:** The market constantly evolves. Stay updated on new regulations, upcoming infrastructure projects, and economic trends that could impact your investment. Continuous learning is your competitive edge..
- **LEAD Mindset:**
  - **Long Game:** View off-plan as an entry point into a long-term hold in a future prime location.
  - **Embrace Calculated Risk:** Use diligence to quantify and mitigate the inherent risks to chase outsized returns.
  - **Anticipate:** This is the core of a successful strategy. Anticipate where the city's growth is heading, where the next metro station or mall will be, and invest there before it becomes obvious.

INVESTOR INSIGHT

Treat off-plan investing as a strategic *timeline play*. Your returns are tied not just to the property itself, but to the stage at which you enter and exit the project. Monitor construction progress, payment milestones, and secondary market demand for each delivery phase. Enter early in credible developments to lock in lower pricing, but balance this with a realistic understanding of construction timelines and your own liquidity needs.

7.3.2. The Existing Asset: A Deep Dive into Researching Secondary Market Properties

Secondary market properties, those already built and available for resale, offer the distinct and powerful advantage of tangibility. Unlike the promise of an off-plan unit, here you can see, touch, and verify the asset. The research path shifts from forecasting a developer's promise to investigating a property's past performance and present condition.

The data available for ready properties is richer and more immediate. However, this transparency comes with its own set of challenges. Your goal is to uncover the complete story of the asset, its transaction history, its actual running costs, and its physical health, to ensure you are buying a proven winner, not someone else's problem.

The Due Diligence Blueprint: A Step-by-Step Guide

7.3.2.1. Step 1: The Digital Deep Dive – Mastering Data Analysis

Your research begins online, not with asking prices, but with the hard data of actual, closed deals.

A. Beyond Asking Prices: Focusing on Actual Transactions. Your most reliable tool is historical transaction data. Use platforms like DXBInteract and the DLD's official Dubai REST app to see exactly what comparable units in the same building or community have sold for. Asking prices on portals can be inflated; sold prices are the market's unvarnished truth.

B. Focus on Recent Data: Concentrate on transactions from the last 6 to 12 months to get an accurate pulse of the current market. Data older than a year may not reflect today's values.

C. The Art of the "Comp": Finding True Comparables. Not all "two-bedroom apartments" are created equal. To make an accurate comparison, you must drill down into the details:

- **View:** Marina view vs. road view can create a 15-20% price difference in the same building.
- **Floor Level:** Higher floors typically command a premium.
- **Layout & Size:** Compare the exact square footage and floor plan. A "two-bedroom" can range from 900 sq. ft. to 1,800 sq. ft.
- **Condition:** Is the unit in its original condition, or has it been recently upgraded or renovated? A modern kitchen or upgraded flooring adds real value.

INVESTOR INSIGHT

When resale units are trading significantly below the developer's launch prices for new, similar units, it may signal either a unique value opportunity for you or a broader loss of confidence in the project. If you paid keen attention to Market Cycles (Chapter 4), you would possess a better understanding of the underlying dynamics.

7.3.2.2. Step 2: Gauging the Market Pulse – Analysing Liquidity and Demand

How easily can you sell this property if you need to? The data on listing portals provides crucial clues.

A. Decoding Days on Market (DOM) This powerful indicator reveals seller urgency and market health. Observe how long similar listings remain active on portals like Bayut and Property Finder before being sold or removed.

B. Interpret DOM Rapid sales (under 45 days) signal strong market liquidity and demand. A consistently long DOM (90+ days) indicates an overpriced listing, low demand, or potential issues with the building itself.

C. The "Ask vs. Sold" Spread Diligently compare initial asking prices with the final sold prices from DXBInteract. A large gap suggests a buyer's market where you have strong negotiating power. A small gap indicates a seller's market where you may need to act more decisively.

TIP

Bayut and Property Finder prominently display the "added-on" field, which indicates how long a listing has been live. Cross-reference this with transaction data for the same project for a comprehensive view.

7.3.2.3. Step 3: The Physical Inspection – Beyond the Photos

This is a non-negotiable step. A property can look perfect in professional photos but reveal its flaws in person. If you cannot visit yourself, hire a trusted representative or a professional snagging company.

Your On-the-Ground Checklist:

- **Unit Condition:** Check for signs of water damage (on ceilings and under sinks), test the AC in every room, check water pressure, and inspect the quality of the finishing, fixtures, and appliances.
- **Building Common Areas:** The condition of the lobby, elevators, hallways, gym, and pool is a leading indicator of the quality of the building management and the Owners' Association. Worn-out common areas suggest neglect and potentially poor management of funds.
- **Noise & Environment:** Visit at different times. Is there noise from a nearby highway, construction site, or busy retail area below? Are the neighbours noisy?
- **Parking:** Check the location and accessibility of the designated parking spot. A spot far from the elevator is less desirable.

7.3.2.4. Step 4: Due Diligence on Documentation & Costs

Every ready property comes with a history. Your job is to uncover it.

A. Verifying the Paper Trail Before making an offer, request key documents from the seller or their agent:

- A copy of the Title Deed to verify ownership.
- We need to confirm whether a No Objection Certificate (NOC) is required from the developer for resale, and the associated fees.

B. Uncovering the True Cost of Ownership: Service Charges. This is one of the most critical research points in Dubai. A low purchase price can be a trap if the service charges are exorbitant.

- **Demand Invoices:** Do not rely on the advertised rate. Request the actual service charge invoices from the seller for the past two years. This will show you the real costs and any special assessments.
- **Benchmark:** Use the RERA Service Charge and Maintenance Index to see if the charges are in line with similar properties in the area.

7.3.2.5. Step 5: Assessing the Tenancy Situation

Understanding the property's tenancy status is crucial as it directly impacts your cash flow and usage rights.

Is the Property Vacant or Tenanted?

- **If Tenanted:** The existing tenancy contract transfers to you, the new owner. Its terms legally bind you. You must understand:
  - **The Rent Amount:** Is the tenant paying at, above, or below the current market rate?
  - **The Contract Expiry Date:** When can you legally increase the rent or issue a notice?
  - **Eviction Notice:** In Dubai, you can only issue a 12-month eviction notice upon expiry of the tenancy contract for specific reasons (such as moving in yourself or selling), and it must be delivered via Notary Public or Registered Mail. This process must be followed.
- **If Vacant:** This offers maximum flexibility. You can move in immediately, rent it out at the current market rate, or furnish it for short-term lets.

PRO TIP

Look for properties where an eviction notice has been given for a tenant paying significantly below market price. Here, you can get a yield advantage as you will be able to rent out the unit at the current price after the tenant vacates. Such properties can offer significant value in the long term

INVESTOR INSIGHT

In the secondary market, you are buying performance data as much as you are buying the property. Analyse past rental yields, occupancy trends, and transaction history for comparable units in the same building or community. This data-driven approach reduces uncertainty and allows you to price in realistic returns before committing capital.

7.4. Advanced Insights – Reading Between the Lines

Once you've competently covered the basics of property research, the next level involves uncovering unspoken signals, those subtle yet powerful indicators of underlying demand, potential distress, or pricing inefficiencies that typically don't show up in official brochures or standard transaction logs. These advanced techniques are what truly separate sharp, seasoned investors from casual browsers, and can help you spot lucrative opportunities that others might easily miss.

7.4.1. Use Listing Platform Tools Smartly

Most investors use popular platforms like Bayut or Property Finder simply to browse listings, but these powerful tools can reveal hidden demand signals if you know how to leverage them.

- **Sort by "Most Popular":** This feature displays which properties are being viewed most frequently; high interest here often indicates high future liquidity.
- **Track New Listings:** Observe how quickly new units are added to, and then subsequently disappear from, the platform. Rapid removals usually indicate fast sales or strong rental interest.
- **Map-Based Search:** Examine location clusters to identify specific areas where supply is becoming oversaturated or, conversely, where inventory is rapidly drying up.

INVESTOR INSIGHT

Data from listing platforms can reveal real-time shifts in buyer sentiment and demand, long before official transaction reports are published. Pay attention to properties that are consistently "Most Contacted" or "Most Viewed."

7.4.2. Validate Listings and Spot Fakes

In competitive or oversupplied markets, fake listings are unfortunately a common tactic used as bait.

- **Be Wary of "Too Good to Be True":** Watch out for listings that appear unrealistically attractive (e.g., a Dubai Marina 2-bedroom for AED 1.1M fully furnished with a sea view).
- **Request Proof:** Always request a copy of the Sale and Purchase Agreement (SPA) or Ejari contract as initial proof of ownership or rent history before engaging in any deeper discussion or commitment.
- **Look for Red Flags:** Listings without clear unit photos, detailed floor plans, or overly vague descriptions are often strong red flags that warrant extreme caution.

INVESTOR MISTAKE TO AVOID

Believing the first number or claim you hear. Cross-check everything, from square footage to handover dates, through official portals and your tracking. Validate, validate, validate.

7.4.3. Use Proxy Metrics When Data is Missing

Not every listing or transaction will have every detail readily available. Learn to use proxy data intelligently when official information is missing:

- **No price per sq. ft.?** Calculate it manually by dividing the total price by the advertised area.
- **No rent data?** Estimate from nearby units with the same layout.
- **No recent comps?** Look at neighbouring towers or communities with similar developer profiles and amenities.

PRO TIP

Build a dedicated reference sheet for frequently researched buildings or communities. After documenting 3–5 entries, clear patterns will often emerge, significantly speeding up your analysis.

7.5. Tools and Trackers – Building Your Research System

In property investing, robust structure consistently beats fleeting instinct. Professional investors do not rely on casual conversations or glossy brochures; they build and use sophisticated systems. A personal research tracker, focused on key metrics, is essential for consolidating scattered information, objectively comparing various options, and maintaining unwavering objectivity. This tracker effectively becomes your decision dashboard. It seamlessly integrates data on pricing, rental yields, developer history, area trends, and resale performance. Used consistently, it empowers you to accurately benchmark deals, monitor market shifts, and identify any gaps between asking prices and actual, underlying value.

You don't necessarily need complex, expensive tools; a well-organised Excel spreadsheet, a structured Notion database, or even a basic CRM (Customer Relationship Management) system can work perfectly fine. What truly matters is consistently tracking the correct and relevant data. Over time, this systematic approach will inevitably sharpen your judgment and significantly accelerate your decision-making process. The table that follows lists the key fields you should aim to capture, including construction status, precise service fees, detailed payment plans, historical performance data, and other highly relevant details.

Table 7.7: Essential Fields in Your Research Tracker

Attribute	What to Include
Project & Developer	Name of project, developer background (e.g., reputation, financial stability), and past delivery performance.
Unit Size & Layout	Number of bedrooms, total square footage (usable area), specific floor plan details (e.g., corner unit, sea view, layout efficiency).
Sale Price Range	Current list price and recent actual sold prices (obtained from DXBInteract or DLD records).
Rental Estimate	Market rental range for similar units and expected gross/net yield.
Sale Transactions History	Table or summary of past 6–12 months' sales in the same building or area, including price per sq ft.
True Estimate Range	Your own independently estimated resale value based on robust market benchmarks and comps. Bayut has the TrueEstimate feature you can use.
DOM (Days on Market)	Average time similar listings take to sell or rent.
Payment Plan (if off-plan)	Detailed breakdown of payment structure (e.g., 20/60/20 post-handover), and any incentives offered (e.g., fee waivers). Sometimes you will get secondary units, i.e. ready units, also with developer payment plans. If you are buying in cash, rather than with a mortgage, these can add to your IRR boost and provide you with a cash flow advantage.
Construction Status	Percentage completed, recent site photos, DLD escrow verification status.
Service Charges	Annual AED/sq ft rate and whether it aligns with similar communities. Gather resident feedback on maintenance and request actual invoices.
Resale Liquidity	Are resales frequent in this project? How long do units typically stay on the market? What is the predominant buyer type, investors or end-users?

INVESTOR INSIGHT

Savvy investors combine off-plan and ready properties in a single portfolio to balance risk and reward. Off-plan offers potential for early-stage appreciation, while ready properties provide immediate rental income and liquidity. The right mix can deliver both growth and cash flow, making your portfolio more resilient to market shifts.

Example Snapshot: Secondary Research Tracker

Attribute	Example Entry (June 2025)
Project & Developer	Wellington Park, Ellington – Sobha Hartland
Unit Size & Layout	2BR, 1,300 sq ft, corner layout
Sale Price Range	AED 2,200,000 – AED 2,500,000
Rental Estimate	AED 100,000 – AED 120,000/year
Sale History	DXBInteract: 4 transactions last 3 months @ AED 1,780/sq ft
TrueEstimate	AED 2,300,000 (based on surrounding comps)
DOM	30–40 days (Bayut + Property Finder)
Service Charges	Estimated AED 16/sq ft/year
Resale Liquidity	High; 4 sales in the last 3 months. Primarily investor-to-investor.

7.6. Common Pitfalls and How to Avoid Them

Even seasoned investors can make costly mistakes when emotion, undue pressure, or unverified claims take precedence. Common pitfalls include rushing into off-plan launches due to pervasive hype, thoughtlessly copying others' investment strategies without proper contextual understanding, or confusing the distinct assessment criteria for secondary and off-plan properties. Overlooked costs, such as unexpectedly high service charges or relying solely on incomplete listings and unqualified agent claims, can also severely erode returns.

The most effective solution is consistently structured, data-backed research. Always utilise official tools like DXBInteract, Bayut's comprehensive market data, and the DLD's verified transaction records to validate every detail before you commit any capital. Simple, yet powerful habits, such as applying a 24-hour pause rule before making impulsive decisions, checking actual service charge invoices, or reviewing how long similar units have genuinely been on the market, can protect you from making poor decisions. Research isn't a one-time task; it's a continuous, disciplined process. Treat each potential deal as if your capital is already irrevocably committed, and you'll naturally begin investing with unwavering clarity instead of impulsive compulsion.

Table 7.8: Common Pitfalls and How to Avoid Them

Pitfall	What Happens	How to Avoid It
Emotional Urgency	A broker creates a false sense of urgency, pressuring you to "buy now or miss out" without adequate research.	Apply a strict 24-hour pause rule before making any offer or payment. Conduct your independent research and verification.
Hidden Costs	You overlook or underestimate significant expenses like service charges, DLD fees, mortgage registration fees, or maintenance.	Always request a detailed breakdown of all costs (upfront and ongoing). Ask for actual service charge invoices for the past year.
Mixing Research Criteria	You evaluate an off-plan unit using resale metrics, or vice versa. You compare projects without accounting for payment plans, handover timelines, or liquidity differences.	Rigorously adjust your metrics depending on the specific property type (off-plan vs. secondary). Use separate, tailored trackers for each. Understand that "price per sq. ft." for off-plan may matter less than future liquidity.
Ignoring Service Charges	A unit appears to be a high-yield bargain until you realise the service charge consumes 25% of your annual rent.	Always ask for the AED/sq ft service charge rate and compare it with the average for that community. If possible, request the actual service charge invoice from the Owners' Association.
Relying Only on Listings/ Agents	You base your entire research on what agents say or what's listed online, without checking actual transaction data.	Always use real, verified transaction data from DLD (via Dubai REST App or DXBInteract) to confirm actual sold prices and market trends, not just asking prices.
Assuming Uniform Appreciation	You assume that because one segment (e.g., luxury villas) is booming, all property types (e.g., budget apartments) will appreciate equally.	Delve into micro-market data. Understand that Dubai comprises many micro-markets, each with unique supply-demand dynamics and cyclical behaviours.
Ignoring Developer Track Record	You invest in an off-plan project solely based on flashy marketing, without verifying the developer's history of delivery, quality, or past delays.	Thoroughly research the developer's past projects. Check DLD project completion rates and read independent reviews. Visit previous developments to assess quality firsthand.
Trusting Verbal Promises	You rely on verbal agreements or informal WhatsApp confirmations for crucial terms related to payment, handover, or repairs.	Always ensure all critical terms, conditions, and agreements are in writing and part of the official Sale and Purchase Agreement (SPA) or a legally binding addendum. Verbal promises are rarely enforceable.

Chapter Summary

Chapter 7, "Research & Due Diligence: From Guesswork to Game Plan," is the pivotal culmination of Part 1, transforming your foundational knowledge into a concrete game plan. This chapter armed you with the investigative toolkit to move from insight to actionable investment, ensuring every decision is rooted in validated facts, not assumptions

You have now mastered the essential pillars of rigorous due diligence:

- **Applied Financial Analysis:** You learned to move beyond simple ROI and use metrics like IRR to accurately assess deals with staggered cash flows and different timelines, turning math into an accurate decision-making tool.
- **In-Depth Location Research:** You delved into location analysis, evaluating areas from both a macro (city-wide trends, government plans) and micro (community specifics) perspective. Crucially, you learned to see the city through the strategic lens of its Key Investment Corridors.
- **The Two Paths of Property Research:** The chapter provided comprehensive deep dives into the distinct research required for Dubai's two main investment types:
    - **Off-Plan Investing:** You were equipped with a complete blueprint, from understanding the **regulatory safety net** (Escrow, Oqood) and weighing the pros and cons, to investigating developer credibility.
    - **Secondary Market Investing:** You learned the step-by-step process for researching ready properties, focusing on historical transaction data, physical inspections, and verifying the actual costs of ownership.
- **Advanced Diligence & System Building:** You gained insights into reading between the lines of market data, spotting red flags, and were guided in building your research tracker to turn scattered information into a decision dashboard. Finally, you were briefed on the most common pitfalls and how to avoid them.

This chapter underscores that true mastery in real estate comes from systematic, data-backed investigation. By embracing this rigorous approach, you empower yourself to make confident, informed choices, thereby earning your proper "license to deal" in Dubai's dynamic property market.

Key Takeaways:

- **Math Validation:** Apply real estate math, such as IRR, to actual scenarios to accurately account for cash flow timing.
- **Location is King, with Nuance:** Understand location through the lens of macro vision, micro specifics, and Key Investment Corridors.
- **Master the Two Paths:** Off-plan research hinges on the developer's promise and future potential; secondary research is about verifying an asset's past performance and present condition.
- **Data Over Hype:** Leverage tools like DXBInteract and DLD apps to access real transaction data, not just marketing claims.
- **Build Your System:** Use research trackers and checklists to organise information and compare deals objectively.
- **Due Diligence is Your Insurance:** Rigorous verification protects your capital, minimises risks, and ensures clarity before committing.
- **Avoid Common Pitfalls:** Be wary of emotional urgency, hidden costs, and unverified claims; always prioritise disciplined research.

PART 2

From Plan to Purchase

02

Executing Your Strategy –
The Execution Phase

With your preparation complete, it is time to move from theory to action. In Part 1, you built the foundation by understanding how to think like an investor, why Dubai presents compelling opportunities, where to focus your search, when to act, and how to analyse the numbers.

Part 2 is the execution phase of your investment journey. This is where you take your well-researched plan and put it into motion, following a structured process that ensures every move is safe, compliant, and aligned with your goals.

From selecting the right property to securing the deal, navigating legal requirements, and taking possession, this part of the book provides a step-by-step framework for successful transactions. Each chapter builds on the last, guiding you through the critical stages of execution so you can invest with confidence and control.

In this part, you will:

The Buying Process: Step by Step
Learn how to progress from property selection to signed agreement, ensuring nothing is missed along the way (**Chapter 8**).

Due Diligence and Deal Safety
Master the checks and safeguards that protect your capital and reduce transactional risk (**Chapter 9**).

Legal Structures, Taxation and Ownership Options
Understand the legal framework, ownership models, and tax implications that directly affect your investment (**Chapter 10**).

Taking Handover
Navigate the final steps to ownership, from inspections and snagging to receiving the keys (**Chapter 11**).

By the end of Part 2, you will have the complete toolkit for executing a purchase in Dubai's real estate market, knowing exactly what to do, in what order, and how to protect yourself at every stage. This is where your preparation turns into tangible results.

CHAPTER 8

The Buying Process – Step by Step

> The property is the prize, but the process is the path.

In **Part 1**, you prepared your investor mindset and gained a deep understanding of Dubai's real estate landscape, from its economic drivers to market dynamics and research methodologies. Now, in **Part 2**, your journey transitions from planning to precise execution. This chapter is your indispensable guide to the formal path of property acquisition in Dubai.

Whether you're buying an off-plan unit, a ready property from the secondary market, or taking over an off-plan resale (a "flip"), the process is governed by a well-defined legal and regulatory structure under RERA (Real Estate Regulatory Agency) and the Dubai Land Department (DLD). While Chapter 9 will delve into the critical aspects of due diligence and transactional safety, this chapter ensures you know exactly how to execute your deal accurately, efficiently, and legally.

Why It Matters:

An excellent investment opportunity can quickly fall apart with poor execution. Delays in payments, incorrect paperwork, or critical misunderstandings during the transfer stages can lead to significant financial loss, challenging legal disputes, or even complete forfeiture of your investment. Knowing the process cold protects your capital and your future.

8.1. Step Onto the Property Ladder with DLD's First-Time Buyer Program

In early July 2025, the Dubai Land Department (DLD), in partnership with the Dubai Department of Economy & Tourism (DET), introduced a landmark programme aimed at making homeownership more accessible than ever before to both UAE nationals and expatriates.

Purpose and Strategic Alignment

This initiative serves as a key pillar of both the Dubai Economic Agenda (D33) and the Dubai Real Estate Strategy 2033, robustly reflecting the government's ambition to grow the city's population significantly, deepen community roots, and consistently maintain a vibrant real estate market. Its core goal is to empower first-time buyers and actively support Dubai's long-term growth plans.

Who's Eligible?

Applicants must be UAE residents, aged 18 or older, and hold a valid Emirates ID. They must not currently own any freehold residential property in Dubai; however, ownership of other properties in the UAE is permitted. The specific property being purchased must be valued at AED 5 million or below.

What Are the Benefits?

The programme offers priority access to a curated portfolio of pre-approved properties from leading developers, often including exclusive offers like DLD fee waivers (which can save 4% of the property value) and extended payment plans. It also provides tailored mortgage packages featuring improved interest rates, faster approvals, and reduced fees, all delivered through partner banks.

Participating Developers & Banks

The initiative unites over a dozen of Dubai's major developers, such as Emaar, DAMAC, Nakheel, Azizi, Binghatti, Ellington, Meraas, Danube, Palma Holding, Wasl, Beyond Developments, and others, alongside five prominent banks: Emirates NBD, Emirates Islamic, Dubai Islamic Bank, Commercial Bank of Dubai, and Mashreq Bank.

How It Works

Interested applicants register online via the DLD website or the Dubai REST app. Brokers can also register their clients as first-time buyers. Eligible buyers receive a QR code, which unlocks access to exclusive benefits with participating developers and banks. Purchases include off-plan units through developers and ready properties through banks, with the scheme tailored to meet individual preferences.

Pros:

- DLD Waiver is a key benefit for the program, offering significant upfront savings.
- Some developers may release special launches exclusively for programme participants.

Cons:

- This programme does not cover all developers; buyers should still compare options in the broader market, as better deals may exist even with the DLD waiver.
- A limited number of banks under this program are available for mortgage plans; buyers may find better options from other lending institutions not participating in the programme.

One-Time Privilege

Once a purchase is made under this programme and the property is registered, the buyer's "first-time" status is no longer valid. Even if the property is later sold, participants are not eligible for the programme again.

In Summary, Dubai's First-Time Home Buyer Initiative represents a powerful combination of government support, private-sector collaboration, and technology, all designed to remove common barriers, from upfront costs to financing, for those ready to own their first home. With exclusive access, financial flexibility, and significant potential savings, the programme offers a clear pathway for residents to step onto the property ladder.

8.2. Mortgage Financing and Pre-Approval: Your Buying Power

For many investors, securing a mortgage is a crucial step in acquiring property in Dubai. Understanding your borrowing capacity and obtaining pre-approval before you start property hunting is paramount. This defines your actual budget and allows you to act swiftly when the right opportunity arises. Without pre-approval, you might find your dream property, only to lose it to a cash buyer or face delays that jeopardise the deal.

WHY IT MATTERS

Mortgage pre-approval is your financial green light. It confirms your eligibility, sets your maximum budget, and gives you a significant advantage in negotiation.

8.2.1. Understanding Pre-Approval

A mortgage pre-approval is a conditional commitment from a bank to lend you a specific amount of money for a property purchase. It's based on an assessment of your financial standing, income, credit history, and existing liabilities.

Process of Obtaining Pre-Approval:

- **Application Submission:** You submit a mortgage application to a bank, providing personal and financial documents (passport, Emirates ID, visa, salary certificate, bank statements, and credit report).
- **Income & Credit Assessment:** The bank assesses your debt-to-income ratio, credit score (via Al Etihad Credit Bureau), and overall financial health.
- **Conditional Approval:** If approved, the bank issues a pre-approval letter stating the maximum loan amount, interest rate, and validity period (typically 60-90 days).

PRO TIP

Pre-Approval Validity: Mortgage pre-approval letters typically have a validity of 60 to 90 days. Ensure your property search aligns with this timeframe, or be prepared to renew your pre-approval if needed.

8.2.2. Mortgage Availability: Residents vs. Non-Residents

Mortgage availability and terms in Dubai can vary significantly based on your residency status.

Table 8.1: Mortgage Availability & Typical LTVs in Dubai

Category	Residency Status	Typical Loan-to-Value (LTV)	Key Requirements
UAE National	Resident	Up to 85%	Stable income, good credit score
Expatriate Resident	Resident	Up to 80% (first property)	Stable employment, clear credit history
Non-Resident	Non-Resident (Overseas)	Up to 50%	International credit check, proof of income from home country, usually higher interest rates

INVESTOR INSIGHT

Off-Plan vs. Secondary Market Mortgages:

- **Secondary Market Properties:** Generally readily financeable. Once a property is complete and has a title deed, banks are typically willing to lend against it, provided the property and buyer meet their criteria.
- **Off-Plan Properties:** Mortgages for off-plan units are usually only possible near completion or handover (e.g., when the project reaches 80-90% completion and has a Building Completion Certificate - BCC). Banks typically do not finance early construction phases due to higher risk. This means you will need to pay developer instalments out of pocket until the property is eligible for a mortgage. However, for some developers, the bank will finance after 50% of the construction is complete, and 50% of the amount has been paid. Please keep in mind that this is a highly variable situation, and you need to check with the bank, a mortgage agent, or the developer itself if they offer this support.

Mortgage Availability & Typical LTVs in Dubai

UAE National (Resident)

Up to 85% stable income good credit score

Expatriate Resident (Resident)

Up to 80% (first property) stable employment, clear credit history

Non-Resident (Overseas)

Up to 50% international credit check, proof of income from home country, usually higher interest rates

8.2.4. Types of Mortgages in Dubai: Conventional vs. Islamic Finance

- **Conventional Mortgages:** These are interest-based loans where the bank lends you capital, and you repay the principal plus interest over a set tenure.
- **Islamic Mortgages (Sharia-compliant):** These avoid interest (riba) and adhere to Islamic finance principles. Common structures include:
  - **Murabaha:** The bank buys the property and then sells it to you at a pre-agreed higher price, which you pay in instalments. The bank makes a profit from the resale, not interest.
  - **Ijarah:** The bank buys the property and leases it to you, with ownership gradually transferring to you over the lease period.
  - **Musharaka:** A partnership between you and the bank, where both contribute capital and share profits/losses.

Key Differences for Investors:

- **Interest vs. Profit Rate:** Conventional mortgages have an interest rate; Islamic finance has a profit rate or fixed repayment amount.
- **Asset Ownership:** In Islamic finance, the bank typically owns the asset (or a share of it) during the repayment period, before transferring full ownership.
- **Fees:** Both types will have setup fees, valuation fees, and DLD registration fees.

8.2.5. General Prevalent Rates, Tenures, and What to Look Out For

Mortgage rates in Dubai are typically influenced by the Emirates Interbank Offered Rate (EIBOR), similar to how global rates are tied to LIBOR or SOFR.

Typical Rates & Tenures:

- **Interest Rates:** Currently range from 4.0% to 7.5% annually, depending on the bank, your profile, LTV, and current market conditions. Rates can be fixed for an initial period (e.g., 1-5 years) or variable (tied to EIBOR).
- **Tenure:** Up to 25 years for residents, and often shorter (e.g., 15 years) for non-residents. Max loan term is generally until the borrower turns 65 years old (for residents) or 70 (for UAE nationals).

What to Look Out For:

- **Fixed vs. Variable Rates:** A fixed rate provides predictability but might be higher initially. Variable rates can be lower but expose you to EIBOR fluctuations.
- **Early Settlement Fees:** Understand the penalties for paying off your mortgage early (typically 1-2% of the outstanding balance, or a maximum of AED 10,000 in the UAE).
- **Pre-Approval Validity:** As mentioned, pre-approvals have a limited validity period.
- **Pre-Approval vs. Offer Letter:** Pre-approval is conditional; the final offer letter comes after the property valuation.
- **Foreclosure Clauses:** Understand the bank's rights in case of default.

INVESTOR TIP

Compare multiple banks and engage with a reputable mortgage broker. They can help you navigate the complexities and find the most competitive terms that align with your investment strategy and risk tolerance.

8.3. Off-Plan Buying Process – Step by Step

Acquiring an off-plan property in Dubai follows a structured sequence. Understanding each step ensures a smooth transaction and protects your investment.

8.3.1. Step 1: Expression of Interest (EOI)

Before a formal project launch, many Dubai developers initiate a soft pre-launch phase by collecting Expressions of Interest (EOI) from potential buyers. This non-binding step enables serious investors to signal their intent and secure early access to select units. The EOI typically involves a flat fee ranging from AED 10,000 to AED 50,000 or, in some cases, up to 10% of the anticipated unit price. While this amount is generally refundable before unit confirmation, specific policies can vary by developer. Importantly, the EOI does not guarantee a particular allocation of units, especially with large developers such as Emaar, Nakheel, and Wasl, which often only confirm allocations at the official launch. Smaller or emerging developers may offer pre-launch lock-ins as a marketing incentive, particularly for VIP or bulk investors. Submission is typically done through the developer's portal or an authorised sales agent. Investors should always clarify refund and allocation rules upfront.

PRO TIP

Some developers (like Emaar, Nakheel, Wasl) do not confirm unit allocation at the EOI stage, only at the official launch. With smaller developers, you may be able to secure a pre-launch unit lock-in, especially for bulk deals or VIP previews.

At this point, usually you will have a receipt to show the EOI payment which will clearly mention that it is refundable.

8.3.2. Step 2: Unit Booking & DLD Fee Payment

Once the developer officially launches the project and unit selection opens, the booking phase begins. At this stage, buyers are required to make two key payments: the first instalment of the purchase price, typically 20% of the unit value, and the mandatory Dubai Land Department (DLD) registration fee, which is 4% of the unit price, plus an administrative charge (which can vary from AED 580 to AED 2,500). While the initial purchase down payment has to be made into the project's escrow account, DLD and Admin charges may be requested to be paid directly to DLD using Noqoodi, via a manager's cheque to DLD, or, if the developer is handling the registration on your behalf, to the developer's corporate account. This process varies from developer to developer. It is crucial to understand that payments should never be made directly to a broker's account. Rushing into payment without thoroughly reviewing the exact floor plan, view orientation, and draft Sale and Purchase Agreement (SPA) can lock you into an unfavourable unit. Always reconfirm all details with your agent. The booking form is generated after confirming the property at launch or payment of the initial down payment and DLD fees. This is your first document, which confirms your transaction.

8.3.3. Step 3: SPA (Sales and Purchase Agreement) Signing

The Sales and Purchase Agreement (SPA) is the cornerstone legal contract that formally binds the buyer and the developer in an off-plan transaction. It outlines the full spectrum of terms and obligations governing the purchase, including the payment schedule, construction timeline, handover date, penalties for project delays, developer responsibilities, and precise unit specifications. Signing the SPA marks a shift from mere intent to a firm legal commitment; it represents the buyer's enforceable claim to the property and the developer's obligation to deliver as agreed. Developers may require in-person signing at their office or may permit digital execution via email using digital signing, depending on their internal policies and regulatory permissions. Critically, the SPA also includes explicit provisions regarding assignment rights, your ability to resell the unit before its completion and handover. You generally need to get the developer's signed copy and maintain it with you.

8.3.4. Step 4: Oqood Registration & Progress Payments

After signing the Sales and Purchase Agreement (SPA), the developer is legally obligated to register the property under the buyer's name with the Dubai Land Department (DLD). This registration generates an **Oqood Certificate**, which serves as the official record of ownership for off-plan properties in Dubai. The word "Oqood" means "contracts" in Arabic, and in real estate, it represents your recognised legal interest in a unit that is still under construction. Although the title deed is only issued upon project completion, the Oqood offers essential protection during the construction phase, confirming that your purchase has been acknowledged and recorded by the DLD. Registration must typically be completed within 60 days of unit booking, and the Oqood is linked to your Emirates ID or passport. Investors can verify the status of their Oqood through the Dubai REST app, available on both iOS and Android. Logging in with your passport number, Emirates ID, or email allows you to view property registration details, escrow account records, and your portfolio. Failure by the developer to register the Oqood within the stipulated period is a red flag and may indicate internal issues or regulatory non-compliance. For buyers, confirming that the Oqood has been issued and is digitally accessible is a critical due diligence step. This certificate is your only recognised proof of ownership during the construction phase.

How to Authenticate Your Oqood Certificate

Step	Dubai Residents	International Investor	Tools / Notes
1. Download the App	Download the Dubai REST App from the iOS/Android Store	Same for international investors	Dubai REST – iOS / Android
2. Log In	Use Emirates ID or passport number	Use your passport number	Must match the info used in SPA
3. Navigate to Property Portfolio	Tap "My Properties" > View off-plan unit details	Tap "My Properties" > Access overseas-owned property data	Use search by project name/unit number if needed
4. Check Oqood Status	Confirm the Oqood Certificate is listed under the unit	Confirm the Oqood status is displayed	If not shown, contact the developer or DLD
5. Verify Developer Registration	Ensure the developer name matches the SPA	Same as residents	Registration date should be within 60 days of booking
6. Review Escrow Details	Check the linked escrow account and project details	Same process	Cross-reference with DLD escrow info portal
7. Save or Screenshot Record	Save certificate details for the record	Take a screenshot/ email confirmation	Useful for bank loans or resale verification
8. Contact DLD if Missing	Call 800-DLD (353) or visit the DLD office	Use the DLD website's live chat	

Once the Sales and Purchase Agreement (SPA) is signed and the initial booking and DLD fees are settled, the remaining payments in an off-plan purchase follow a milestone-based payment plan as specified in the SPA. These payment schedules are typically construction-linked, meaning payments become due when specific stages of the development, such as foundation, superstructure, cladding, or handover, are completed. Developers are legally required to notify buyers when a milestone is reached, often accompanied by progress reports or DLD-approved construction certificates. However, it is the buyer's responsibility to monitor these milestones and ensure timely payments, even if notifications are delayed or missed. All payments must be made exclusively to the project's escrow account, a legal safeguard overseen by the Dubai Land Department (DLD). This ensures that funds are released to the developer only upon verified progress through registered contractors and DLD inspections, thus protecting your investment. Consistently keeping up with the payment schedule is not just an administrative task; it's a critical part of safeguarding your investment and maintaining your rights under the SPA.

What To Do	Why
Pay only to the escrow account	Ensures the developer can't misuse funds
Collect all payment receipts	Required for resale or mortgage
Use bank disbursement if mortgaged	Most banks release stage-wise payments

> **PRO TIP**
>
> Set up payment reminders for milestone triggers. Missing a payment deadline, even by a few days, can result in penalties or cancellation of the SPA under specific contracts.

Off-Plan Buying Process: Step-by-Step

8.4. Step-by-Step Secondary Market Process (Ready Properties)

Buying a ready (completed) property in Dubai, commonly referred to as a secondary market transaction, is a legally intensive and procedurally distinct process from off-plan purchases. Regulated by the Real Estate Regulatory Agency (RERA) and the Dubai Land Department (DLD), the secondary market operates under a strictly regulated ownership transfer system, which involves immediate registration, formal legal documentation, and enhanced scrutiny at every stage. Unlike off-plan transactions, where the developer handles much of the legal framework, secondary market deals typically require coordination between multiple independent entities: the seller, buyer, appointed brokers, DLD trustee offices, mortgage banks (if applicable), and sometimes conveyancing companies.

The transaction begins with the appointment of licensed real estate agents, as mandated by RERA, through the submission of mandatory forms (Form A for the seller and Form B for the buyer). These forms must be digitally executed via the Dubai REST app, with identity confirmation via OTP-based verification, ensuring legal traceability and transparency. Each action taken throughout the secondary transaction, whether a mortgage pre-approval, a No Objection Certificate (NOC) request, or a Title Deed transfer, must align with regulatory compliance under DLD protocols. All ownership records are updated in real-time through the central government system.

Due to the permanent and high-value nature of ready property purchases, any mistake in documentation, broker representation, or payment sequencing can lead to legal complications, registration rejection, or financial loss. As such, secondary market investors must take a more hands-on, documentation-heavy approach, with a clear understanding of their legal protections and agent responsibilities from the outset. This chapter outlines the whole, step-by-step journey of a secondary property acquisition, from broker appointment to Title Deed issuance, ensuring buyers are fully informed, protected, and prepared for a secure transaction.

8.4.1. Understanding Form A and Form B – The Brokerage Contracts That Frame Your Deal

In Dubai's regulated real estate market, Forms A and B are standardised contracts issued by RERA (Real Estate Regulatory Agency), designed to establish formal relationships between clients and brokers. These forms are not optional paperwork; they're the foundation of a legal, enforceable brokerage engagement and are crucial to both compliance and client protection.

Form A: Seller's Listing Agreement

- **Who Signs:** Only the property owner signs Form A.
- **Purpose:** Appoints a licensed real estate broker to list and market the property for sale. Form A legally empowers the broker to advertise and sell the property on behalf of the owner.
- **Types:** It can be signed as either:
  - **Exclusive listing:** Only that specific broker can market the property.
  - **Open listing:** Multiple brokers may market the same property.
- **Mandatory Attachments:**
  - Title Deed or Oqood
  - Emirates ID or Passport of the Seller
  - Floor Plan and Location Map (for marketing)
  - Service Charge Statement (if applicable)
- Once signed and uploaded, Form A generates a unique Trakheesi ID, mandatory for all property advertisements in Dubai.

NOTE

If a seller attempts to market a property without Form A, it is considered a violation, and platforms such as Property Finder or Bayut will not allow the listing without the Trakheesi ID.

Form B: Buyer's Agent Agreement

- **Who Signs:** The buyer signs Form B with a broker.
- **Purpose:** Appoints a broker to represent the buyer's interests in locating and negotiating a suitable property. Form B formalises the broker's fiduciary duty to the buyer, meaning they are legally required to act in the buyer's best interest.
- **Includes:**
  - Buyer's specific criteria (budget, preferred location, desired unit type).
  - Commission expectations (typically 2% + VAT).
  - Defined representation scope (e.g., off-plan only, secondary market, commercial).
- Like Form A, it is digitally executed via the Dubai REST App with OTP verification, creating a secure digital audit trail.
- **Without Form B, there is no binding agreement between buyer and agent, meaning:**
  - The broker has no legal obligation to represent the buyer's best interest.
  - The buyer has no recourse if something goes wrong.
- Brokers are prohibited from charging the buyer a commission if a valid Form B is not in place.

IMPORTANT NOTE

The Disclosure Form (Dual Agency). If a single agent represents both the buyer and the seller in the same transaction (known as dual agency), a Disclosure Form must be completed and signed by both parties. This form explicitly acknowledges the potential conflicts of interest and ensures careful neutrality in negotiations.

8.4.2. Step 1: Appointing a Broker – Forms A & B

- The seller signs Form A with a RERA-licensed listing broker, giving exclusive or open authorisation to sell (this is not required if the Seller is selling directly without a broker).
- The buyer signs Form B with a broker to represent their interest (this is not required if the buyer doesn't have a broker representing them).
- Both forms are completed digitally on the Dubai REST App and require OTP verification by the respective sellers and buyers for security.
- If the same agent represents both parties, ensure transparency via the mandatory disclosure acknowledgement.

Why It Matters:

These forms legally bind brokers to specific duties and disclosure requirements. They also protect you from unauthorised listings or fake agents, establishing a transparent chain of accountability.

APPLY NOW

Use the DLD Trakheesi system or the Dubai REST App to verify your broker's license.

INVESTOR MISTAKE TO AVOID

Never proceed with a property buying deal without a signed Form B. Without it, you lack critical legal protection, and your agent has no fiduciary responsibility to you.

8.4.3. Step 2: Form F (MOU) & Offer Finalisation

Once the buyer and seller agree on the basic terms of the deal, the next critical legal step is the signing of Form F, the Memorandum of Understanding (MOU) mandated by the Dubai Land Department (DLD). This document formalises the offer and outlines all key contractual terms, including the agreed sale price, deposit amount (usually 10% of the purchase price), transfer timeline, and the allocation of various fees. Form F is a legally binding document; once signed, it commits both parties to the transaction under clearly defined conditions and timelines. It also initiates an electronic "unit lock" in the DLD registry, ensuring that the property cannot be resold or modified without mutual cancellation of the agreement.

Notably, the MOU includes a guarantee cheque, typically held by the seller's broker as security against default. This cheque is not encashed during this stage. If there is no broker involved in the transaction, it is highly recommended to use a third-party conveyancer or a DLD-approved escrow service to hold the cheque securely. Critically, avoid providing any post-dated cheques directly to the seller, as this can expose you to unnecessary risk. Because Form F governs the financial and legal obligations of both parties, it is essential that buyers read the document carefully and clarify all fee responsibilities upfront. Ambiguities regarding commission, DLD fees, trustee charges, or mortgage costs can easily lead to disputes at the time of transfer. Buyers are strongly advised to consult a conveyancer or legal expert, particularly when inserting conditional clauses such as "subject to mortgage approval" or requesting custom handover terms. While Form F may appear standardised, its implications are significant; it is the very foundation of your secondary market transaction.

What Form F (MOU) Includes and Why It Matters

- **Binding Contract:** Once signed, Form F is fully enforceable in court. It locks both parties into the agreed terms.
- **Unit Lock in DLD System:** The property cannot be resold, assigned, or altered unless mutually cancelled via DLD.
- **Details Captured:** It outlines the final sale price and payment timeline. It details the deposit amount (usually 10%). It specifies all fee allocations, including:
    - DLD registration fee.
    - Broker commissions.
    - Trustee office charges.
    - Mortgage setup fees (if applicable).
- **Guarantee Cheque:** Typically 10%, held securely by the seller's broker (not encashed). If there's no broker, use a third-party conveyancer or escrow service. Avoid giving post-dated cheques directly to the seller.
- **Digital Execution:** Can be completed via the Dubai REST App for digital signing. OTP-based verification ensures security and creates a digital audit trail, expediting the deal.
- **Custom Clauses Allowed:** Can include conditions like: "Subject to Mortgage Approval" or "Subject to NOC Clearance." These clauses and others if applicable, should be mentioned; legal review is highly advised.
- **Legal Risks if Ignored:** Misunderstood fee responsibilities can cause last-minute conflicts. An invalid or unsigned Form F can completely invalidate the transaction.

PRO TIP

Form F is legally binding. Read it thoroughly and clarify who pays which fees to avoid any unpleasant surprises at transfer

8.4.4. Step 3: Mortgage Clearance and Developer NOC – Unlocking the Path to Transfer

Once the Memorandum of Understanding (Form F) is signed and the property is registered in the Dubai Land Department (DLD) system, the transaction proceeds to the compliance and clearance phase. At this point, two major components critically affect the transaction timeline and determine the earliest possible transfer date:

- Mortgage clearance (either on the buyer's or seller's side).
- Issuance of the No Objection Certificate (NOC) from the developer.

Both must be resolved before the deal can proceed to the final transfer at the trustee's office.

A. Seller Has an Existing Mortgage on the Property

When the seller has an outstanding mortgage with a bank, the property cannot be legally transferred until the loan is fully cleared and the bank formally releases the title.

- **Process:**
  - **Liability Letter Request:** The seller must request and provide this letter addressed to the buyer or the buyer's bank. This document states the exact outstanding loan amount, along with clear instructions on how to clear it. Liability letters are typically valid for only 7 to 15 days, depending on the issuing bank. A delay beyond this period will require reissuance.
  - **Loan Settlement:** The buyer (or buyer's bank) prepares a manager's cheque in the name of the seller's bank for the outstanding mortgage amount. Once received, the bank issues a clearance letter and releases the original title deed or ownership document to the seller or their authorised broker. (This process happens via Real Estate Trustee, not directly.)

LEGAL NOTE

The buyer should not release any purchase payment to the seller until the title is fully cleared. Always use a trustee office or escrow service to facilitate these financial exchanges securely.

B. Buyer Requires Mortgage Financing

If you, as the buyer, require a mortgage to finance the purchase, the following steps are crucial:

- **Process:**
  - **Pre-Approval Submission:** The buyer must submit a valid mortgage pre-approval from their bank, ideally before signing Form F. Pre-approval involves an income assessment, a thorough credit check, and an eligibility review.
    (This process is detailed in Section 8.2. Mortgage Financing and Pre-Approval: Your Buying Power)
  - **Property Valuation:** After signing Form F, the buyer's bank will appoint a third-party valuation company (approved by the bank) to assess the fair market value of the property. Banks typically lend 70-80% of the lower of the sale price or the bank's valuation. If the valuation is lower than expected, the buyer must make up the shortfall in cash.
  - **Final Approval & Cheque Issuance:** Once the valuation is cleared and the loan is approved, the bank prepares manager's cheques: one to the seller for the balance purchase amount; one to the seller's bank (if there is an existing mortgage); one for the buyer's broker (if required); and one for DLD and trustee fees. These cheques are submitted at the DLD trustee transfer appointment, where the title legally changes hands.

PRO TIPS FOR SMOOTH EXECUTION

Request the seller's mortgage details upfront (bank name, loan account number) to expedite the liability letter process. Also, ensure all service charges are settled well in advance of the NOC application.

INVESTOR MISTAKE TO AVOID

"My bank is taking care of everything, I don't need to follow up." That assumption can cause costly delays. Banks operate on their internal timelines, and unless you proactively push at every step (valuation, cheque preparation, NOC coordination), the deal can miss critical deadlines, leading to penalty deductions from your deposit or even cancellation of the transaction.

8.4.5. Step 4: Final Transfer at the DLD Trustee Office – Completion & Ownership Registration

The final and definitive step in a Dubai property transaction is the transfer of ownership at one of the authorised Dubai Land Department (DLD) Trustee Offices. This is the official moment when the buyer becomes the legal owner and receives the title deed in their name. To proceed, all documents, necessary clearances, and manager's cheques must be in order; there are no partial transfers or pending dues allowed at this critical stage.

The Role of the Trustee Office

DLD operates through licensed Trustee Centres; private offices specifically authorised to facilitate property transactions under strict DLD oversight. These centres serve as neutral venues for rigorous document verification, secure fund exchange, and the legal transfer of property title.

Key Trustee Offices: Conveniently located in key areas such as Al Barsha, Downtown, Business Bay, Al Twar, and Dubai Marina.

Required Documents & Cheques – Buyer's Responsibilities

The buyer, or their authorised Power of Attorney (POA), must bring the following to the appointment:

- **Manager's Cheque in Seller's Name:** Covers the agreed sale price as per Form F. The buyer's bank issues this cheque and it is non-reversible once submitted.
- **DLD Fees Payment: Typically:** 4% of the sale price (mandatory). Paid via manager's cheque in favour of "Dubai Land Department."
- **Agent's Commission Cheque:** Usually 2% + VAT (AED 2,000 minimum). Paid directly to the broker's company (as named in Form B).
- **Original NOC from the Developer:** Must be within its validity window (usually 10–15 days). Verifies that there are no service charge arrears or disputes.
- **Valid Emirates ID & Passport Copies:** For both buyer and seller. A POA copy (if applicable) must be pre-attested by DLD.

The Transfer Process – What Happens at the Appointment

- **Document Verification:** The Trustee officer verifies the identities of all parties, Form F, the NOC, and all cheques. Any missing or expired documentation will immediately halt the process.
- **Cheque Exchange:** Manager's cheques are handed over and recorded. The seller physically receives the cheque during this meeting unless pre-arranged escrow arrangements are used.
- **Title Deed Issuance:** A new electronic title deed (Mulkiya) is generated immediately by DLD under the buyer's name. The deed is sent via email and/or can be downloaded instantly from the Dubai REST App.
- **Confirmation of Transfer:** DLD issues an official receipt and a confirmation email. This marks the legal completion of the transaction.

Post-Transfer – Handover of Unit and Documents

After the transfer is completed:

- **The seller hands over:** Physical access (keys, access cards, remote controls) and original documents, including: a copy of the old title deed, original NOC, last DEWA (Dubai Electricity and Water Authority) bill or clearance, and the most recent service charge receipt.
- **The buyer should:** Immediately apply for the DEWA connection and service charge account transfer. Also, register with the developer's community portal for building access.

Record-Keeping & Legal Safety

Always request and store:

- A soft and hard copy of the previous title deed.
- The original NOC.
- A copy of all managers' cheques issued.
- Service charge payment history from the seller.
- A copy of Form F and the final transfer receipt from DLD.

These documents are essential for:

- Future resale of the property.
- Any necessary legal verification.
- Protection against service charge disputes.
- Future mortgage applications or portfolio audits.

PRO TIP

Always request copies of the old title deed and previous service charge receipts for your records. This can be invaluable down the line.

8.4.6. Step 5: Optional – Hire a Conveyancer

In case of mortgage-related purchases, hiring a professional conveyancing service can significantly simplify and de-stress the transaction process. A good conveyancer can:

- Streamline all the complex paperwork involved.
- Effectively coordinate between banks, DLD, and developers.

APPLY NOW

Ask your agent or brokerage for referrals to a reputable conveyancer. Look for RERA-compliant legal service providers who specialise in Dubai property transactions.

INVESTOR MISTAKE TO AVOID

Don't underestimate the complexity of a property transaction, especially if you are overseas, require a bank loan, or are managing multiple stakeholders. A conveyancer can save you time, stress, and potentially costly errors.

Table 8.2: Typical Charges in a Secondary Sale

Charge	Amount / Range	Paid By
DLD Transfer Fee	4% of the sale price	Buyer
DLD Admin Fee	AED 580	Buyer
NOC Fee	AED 500–5,000 (varies by developer)	Seller
Broker Commission	2% of the sale price (or as agreed)	Buyer (typically)
Mortgage Registration Fee	0.25% of loan + AED 290	Buyer
Conveyancing Fees (Optional)	AED 5,000–10,000	Buyer (optional)

8.5. Off-Plan Flip (Resale Before Handover)

An off-plan flip, also commonly known as a pre-handover resale or an assignment transaction, involves buying a unit from an investor who originally booked it directly from the developer. The property is still under construction, and the final title deed has not yet been issued. As a result, this transaction is legally and operationally distinct from both a regular off-plan booking and a ready property resale. This type of deal seamlessly combines elements of the developer's assignment process with secondary sale mechanics, introducing specific risks and documentation requirements that investors must thoroughly understand.

8.5.1. How It Works

In a typical off-plan flip:

- The seller is the first buyer, who originally booked the property at the launch or EOI (Expression of Interest) stage.
- You, the new buyer, agree to purchase that unit before its official handover.
- **You pay:**
  - The premium (i.e., the profit margin the original seller wants over their original price).
  - The remaining payments are then to be made directly to the developer as per the original payment schedule outlined in the initial Sale and Purchase Agreement (SPA).

Example Calculation:

- Original Price: AED 1,000,000
- Seller Paid to Developer: AED 400,000 (e.g., first few instalments)
- Seller's Asking Price for Assignment: AED 1,150,000 (meaning a premium of AED 150,000 over the original price)
- You, the new buyer, would pay AED 400,000 (reimbursement for seller's paid portion) + AED 150,000 (seller's premium) = **AED 550,000** directly to the seller.
- You then assume the responsibility for the **Remaining AED 600,000** (from the original AED 1,000,000 price) to be paid to the developer in future instalments as per the original SPA.

8.5.2. Steps in an Off-Plan Flip Transaction

Step 1: Review Original SPA and Payment Status

- Request a copy of the original Sale and Purchase Agreement (SPA) directly from the seller.
- Request a copy of the Oqood and passport copies, and details of the seller. Confirm the names on the Oqood with the owner details you are entering into form F.
- **Verify:**
    - All unit details (size, view, floor, orientation) as per the original booking.
    - The original payment plan schedule.
    - Crucially, whether the SPA explicitly allows for assignment (resale) at the current stage.
- Obtain a Statement of Account from the developer to see what has been paid by the seller to date and what remains outstanding.

Why It Matters: You are stepping directly into someone's shoes. You must know what they've paid, what you'll owe, and whether the project allows for resale before handover.

Step 2: Verify Assignment Eligibility and NOC

- **Not all developers permit resale before handover.** Even if they do, they often impose specific conditions.
- **Some require:** A minimum payment threshold (typically 30% to 50%) to have been made by the seller before assignment is allowed, specific approval from the developer's legal and sales team.
- **The developer will charge:** An assignment administration fee (typically AED 1,000–5,000).
- The developer ultimately issues a **No Objection Certificate (NOC)** to officially proceed with the assignment.

APPLY NOW

Contact the developer's customer service or relationship manager to confirm their resale policies for the specific project explicitly. Get it in writing to avoid any ambiguity.

INVESTOR MISTAKE TO AVOID

Don't agree to an off-plan resale deal without a developer-issued NOC. Without this, the assignment can be rejected, even if both buyer and seller agree to the terms.

Step 3: Obtain NOC and Prepare for Assignment Registration

Once you have verified that the developer permits off-plan resale for the specific unit and that all payments are entirely up to date, the next critical step is to obtain the No Objection Certificate (NOC) from the developer.

- **What the NOC Means:** It formally confirms that the developer has no objection to the transfer of the unit from the original seller to you, the new buyer. It verifies that the seller has met the minimum payment threshold (e.g., 30%–50% of the total amount paid) required for assignment. It also discloses any assignment or administration fees, which must be settled before the NOC is issued.
- **Developer May:** Charge an assignment fee (typically a flat administration fee). Require clearance of all dues and instalments up to date. These payments will be made by the Seller.

INVESTOR MISTAKE TO AVOID

Don't agree to a resale deal without a developer-issued NOC. Without this, the assignment can be rejected, even if both buyer and seller agree.

Step 4: Finalising the Assignment at the DLD Trustee Office

This is the official step where the contractual rights to the off-plan property are transferred to you, and the DLD records your ownership.

- **Booking the Appointment:** You or your appointed broker must book an appointment at an approved DLD Trustee Office. Some developers may require the physical presence of their representative during the registration, so coordinate accordingly.
- **Parties Present:** The buyer (you), the seller (the original investor), the developer's representative (optional, depending on the project and developer policy), and the broker or conveyancer (optional but highly recommended).
- **Documents to Bring:** Original and a copy of the buyer and seller's passports & Emirates IDs. Original SPA and Assignment Agreement. NOC from Developer. Statement of Account from the developer. Payment receipts for the 4% DLD fee and the developer's administration fees. Manager's cheque for the amount to be paid to the seller.
- **Payment & Fees:** The 4% DLD transfer fee must be paid in manager's cheque or on the spot (some Trustee offices accept card payments). You will also need to pay trustee service fees, which are typically AED 4,200 (including VAT) for transactions under AED 500,000 and AED 5,250 for transactions exceeding AED 500,000.
- **Signing & Registration:** The Assignment Agreement is signed in the presence of the Trustee (some projects require biometric verification). The new Oqood registration is issued in your name by the Trustee after verification and stamping.
- **Document Handover:** You receive a stamped receipt and a copy of the Oqood certificate in your name. All paperwork is uploaded into the DLD system, formally updating interim ownership.

WHY THIS STEP MATTERS

This is the legal registration of your off-plan ownership; without it, DLD does not recognise you as the unit owner. It ensures title clarity, payment traceability, and protects against future ownership disputes.

INVESTOR MISTAKE TO AVOID

Do not transfer funds to the seller or assume ownership is complete until this step is done. Without DLD registration, you are not the legal owner, even if you've paid.

Table 8.2: Key Documents Checklist for Off-Plan Assignment Deals

Document / Item	Purpose
Original SPA (from seller)	Review legal terms, payment schedule
Statement of Account (from developer)	Confirm paid vs. due amounts
NOC from Developer	Approves transfer and confirms no outstanding dues
Assignment Agreement (Tripartite)	Legal document to execute the flip
Buyer Passport + Emirates ID	Required for new Oqood registration
4% DLD Fee Receipt + Admin Charges	Must be paid for the ownership transfer
Proof of Premium Paid to Seller (e.g., cheque)	Reflects the resale price and transfer value

Off-Plan Flip:
Assignment Transaction Flow

Step 1

REQUEST OKKOD, SPA, SOA, OWNERS DOCS (PASSPORT ETC) FORM F, FORM A, FLOORPLANS & BROUCHERS

Check & verify all Documents

Step 2

VERIFY ASSIGNMENT ELIGIBILITY & NOC

Confirm that the developer permits resale before handover

Step 3

OBTAIN NOC & PREPARE FOR ASSIGNMENT REGISTRATION

Get the NOC from the developer & settle any applicable fees before the assignment registration

Step 4

FINALISNG THE ASSIGNMENT AT THE DLD TRUSTEE OFFICE

Book an appointment, prepare the required documents, and pay the transfer fee at the trustee office

Chapter Summary

Chapter 8, "The Buying Process – Step by Step," is your indispensable guide to navigating the precise mechanics of property acquisition in Dubai. It serves as the vital bridge from your strategic planning in Part 1 to the decisive execution of a deal. The chapter begins by highlighting the

DLD's First-Time Buyer Program offers valuable incentives for eligible residents to step onto the property ladder.

Crucially, you gained a comprehensive understanding of **Mortgage Financing and Pre-Approval**, learning how to assess your buying power, the process of obtaining pre-approval, key factors banks consider, and the associated costs and availability for both residents and non-residents across off-plan and secondary markets. This section is vital for defining your budget and acting swiftly in a competitive market.

You then gained a step-by-step understanding of the three primary acquisition paths:

- The **Off-Plan Buying Process**, from Expression of Interest (EOI) to Oqood registration and progress payments, emphasising the importance of developer credibility and escrow protection.
- The **Secondary Market Process**, detailing the roles of RERA Forms (A, B, F), mortgage clearance (for both buyer and seller), developer NOCs, and the critical final transfer at the DLD Trustee Office.
- The **Off-Plan Flip (Resale Before Handover)**, which requires careful verification of original SPAs, payment status, and mandatory assignment eligibility through the developer.

This chapter underscores that accurate execution is paramount. It provides clear checklists and highlights common pitfalls to avoid, such as relying on verbal promises or skipping crucial verification steps. By mastering these formal procedures, you protect your investment from day one, ensuring a smooth and legally sound transaction. This knowledge is your ultimate practical tool, translating your readiness into confident, real-world property acquisition.

Key Takeaways:

- **Process is Paramount:** An excellent investment can fail due to poor execution; understanding each step is critical.
- **Mortgage Pre-Approval is Key:** Define your buying power early, understanding availability, rates, and terms for residents and non-residents across different property types.
- **First-Time Buyer Program:** A valuable initiative offering incentives for eligible residents.
- **Off-Plan Clarity:** Follow EOI, booking, SPA signing, Oqood registration, and progress payments.
- **Secondary Market Rigour:** Master Forms A, B, and F, secure mortgage clearance and NOCs, and navigate the DLD Trustee Office transfer.
- **Off-Plan Flip Nuances:** Verify original SPAs, payment status, and assignment eligibility through the developer.
- **Document Everything:** Maintain a complete paper and digital trail of all agreements, receipts, and clearances.
- **Conveyancers are Allies:** Consider professional help for complex transactions.
- **Avoid Shortcuts:** Stick to mandated legal and procedural steps to safeguard your investment.

YOUR JOURNEY

NAVIGATOR

Part 2: From Plan to Purchase

Recap

You have just completed **Chapter 8: The Buying Process – Step by Step**, where you learned how to progress from initial property selection through to securing an agreement. You now understand how to navigate both off-plan and secondary market transactions, work effectively with brokers and developers, handle contracts such as Forms A, B, and F, and manage the legal and financial steps required to reach a signed deal.

Next Chapter Preview

We now move into the deal protection stage. **Chapter 9: Due Diligence and Deal Safety** gives you the critical tools and verification processes that safeguard your capital and reduce risk before you commit fully to the purchase. You will learn how to identify red flags, confirm compliance, and ensure that every aspect of the property, seller, and documentation stands up to scrutiny.

You Will Learn

- ☑ How to verify developer credibility and project legitimacy.
- ☑ The due diligence steps for off-plan, secondary, and leasehold commercial properties.
- ☑ How to assess tenancy situations, market positioning, and exit potential.
- ☑ The checklists and frameworks that act as your deal insurance.

Link to Framework

This chapter strengthens the discipline element of your C.D.R.C. mindset by ensuring no step is skipped in your verification process. It also supports your L.E.A.D. approach by enabling you to embrace calculated risks with clarity, adapt your process to different transaction types, and drive long-term value through well-protected purchases.

Purpose / Big Picture Link

This is the protection stage of your investment journey. The work you do here ensures that all the research, strategy, and negotiation from earlier chapters result in a transaction that is both safe and strategically sound.

CHAPTER 9

Due Diligence and Deal Safety

> Your best deal can become your worst liability if you skip even one verification step..

In **Part 1**, you prepared your investor mindset, gained a deep understanding of Dubai's real estate landscape, and mastered the math and research frameworks for identifying opportunities. Chapter 8 then walked you through the step-by-step transactional processes. Now, as you prepare to commit capital, this chapter serves as your **ultimate safety net**.

Due diligence isn't just a box to tick; it's your best defence against costly mistakes. No matter if you're considering an off-plan apartment, a finished villa, or a leased warehouse, every opportunity comes with its own set of risks. You can't erase them all, but you can learn to spot and manage them proactively.

Beyond mere checklists, this chapter aims to help you cultivate the critical eye of an auditor, a lawyer, a property manager, and a data analyst, all rolled into one. You'll gain crucial insights on how to vet developers, scrutinise complex documents, accurately assess real project demand beyond marketing hype, and, crucially, how to ask the tough questions, especially the uncomfortable ones, before you commit any funds. The more thorough your due diligence process, the more assured and protected your decisions will ultimately be. Sometimes, the wisest move in property investing is simply to step back. Knowing when to say "no" is just as important as recognising a good opportunity. Protecting your capital frequently means resisting pressure and trusting your research.

Why It Matters:

Your best deal can become your worst liability if you skip even one verification step.

HOW TO APPLY THIS

Use this chapter's step-by-step structure to identify risks before you pay, even if the agent insists "everyone's already bought."

INVESTOR MISTAKE TO AVOID

Believing developer brochures or agent reassurances without verifying information through official channels.

9.1. Off-Plan Property Due Diligence

> Buying off-plan isn't just a transaction, it's a trust exercise. Make sure that trust is earned, not assumed.

Dubai's off-plan market holds obvious appeal: lower entry prices, flexible payment plans, and the potential for capital appreciation before handover. But with those rewards comes a distinct set of risks that don't exist in ready properties. When you buy off-plan, you're not purchasing what you can physically see; you're buying a promise. And promises, in real estate, absolutely require validation. This section equips you with the indispensable tools to protect yourself at every stage of an off-plan deal. It's simply not enough to rely solely on a developer's reputation or a broker's enthusiasm. You must verify licenses, confirm robust escrow protections, read the fine print in contracts, and thoroughly understand where your money is going, and, crucially, *why*. We will look into due diligence in five essential categories.

Essential Off-Plan Due Diligence

01. Developer Vitals

- Check RERA & DLD registration.
- Visit their past projects.

02. Project & Escrow

- Verify on DLD REST App.
- Confirm the Escrow account is active.

03. Payment Plan

- Demand construction-linked terms.
- Scrutinize for hidden fees.

04. Contract (SPA)

- Factor in DLD transfer fees and developer assignment fees.

05. Market Check

- Evaluate future demand and location.
- Don't buy based on brand hype.

9.1.1. Validate Developer Credibility

Your absolute first step should always be to validate the developer's formal credentials and legal standing. Never get swayed purely by strong branding or flashy sales booths; these do not inherently guarantee reliable delivery. Check their active RERA licence and DLD registration to confirm their legitimacy. Understanding their historical track record is also vital: look into how closely their finished projects genuinely matched the promises initially made and their approach to quality.

Why It Matters:

A flashy showroom means nothing if the developer lacks proper licensing or has a history of poor-quality handovers.

HOW TO APPLY THIS

Use the DLD Project Tracker and RERA portal to verify their licence and registration. If possible, visit at least one past project by the same developer to assess build quality firsthand.

INVESTOR MISTAKE TO AVOID

Trusting that a "big name" developer automatically means guaranteed quality. Even top-tier developers may face project delays or changes to specifications; always verify.

9.1.2. Project Legitimacy and Escrow Safeguards

No matter how attractive the brochure or how compelling the payment plan, an off-plan property in Dubai is only as safe as the legal framework behind it. That's where project legitimacy and robust escrow protection come into play. These aren't just formalities; they are foundational safeguards built into Dubai's regulatory system specifically to protect buyers like you.

By law, every off-plan project must be officially registered with the Dubai Land Department (DLD), and a dedicated escrow account must be established for that specific development. Critically, the developer does not directly control this account; it is monitored by the DLD and strictly regulated to ensure that funds are released only when specific construction milestones are independently verified. In short, the developer cannot spend your money unless the project is actively progressing. These legal structures, escrow, project registration, and Oqood, are what truly separate serious developments from purely speculative ventures. Verifying them gives you more than just peace of mind; it provides you with solid legal ground to stand on if things do not go as planned.

Key Verifications:

- **Escrow Account Status:** Always ask for the Escrow Account Number and verify its status through the DLD REST App.
- **Oqood Registration:** Ensure your unit is properly registered under Oqood, which is the interim ownership system used until the property is handed over.
- **Master Community NOC:** Confirm the project has obtained the necessary approval (No Objection Certificate) from the master developer (e.g., Emaar, Nakheel, etc.).

Why It Matters:

Your funds are inherently at risk until construction milestones are genuinely achieved. Escrow protection is a vital legal safeguard, but you must verify its presence and proper functioning.

HOW TO APPLY THIS

Always ask for the escrow account number, the bank name, and the project registration number. Then, validate all this information on the DLD REST App.

INVESTOR MISTAKE TO AVOID

Assuming escrow is active just because it's mentioned. Without DLD verification, your funds may not be protected as intended.

Table 9.1: Dubai Off-Plan Due Diligence Checklist (Summary)

Verification Point	Action to Take
The project is registered with DLD	Check on DLD REST App
Dedicated Escrow Account is active	Verify escrow status on the REST App
The developer is RERA licensed	Check the licence on Trakheesi
Developer Track Record is solid	Review past project completions, delays, and disputes (DLD Tracker, site visits)
Visit the Past Projects of the Developer	Assess delivery quality first-hand, speak to owners or agents
Sales Centre Visit (Evaluation)	Evaluate how organised and informative the developer's front-line staff are
Project Model Inspection	Review the master plan, apartment sizes, and unit types at the sales gallery
Site Visit (Physical Confirmation)	Confirm fencing, signage, groundwork, or any construction activity (in person or via drone)
Relationship Manager Feedback	Ask relationship managers about past launches, how quickly they sold out, resale demand, and cancellation rates
Request Documentation	Obtain brochures, floor plans, draft SPA, and escrow bank details (cross-check with DLD)

9.1.3. Payment Plan and Financial Transparency

As you saw in Chapter 5 (the Math Section), the time value of money is a key factor in any investment decision. When selecting off-plan properties, one of the most important factors to scrutinise is the payment plan itself. In Dubai, developers offer a wide range of payment plans, from top-heavy structures where most of the payment is due during construction, to highly flexible plans that extend years beyond handover. These plans are usually presented by the Relationship Manager (RM) or broker in a ratio format, such as 60/40 or 80/20. The first number typically refers to the percentage paid during construction, and the second is the amount due at handover.

Example: Emaar Dubai Creek Harbour – 80/20 Payment Plan

- **Down Payment:** Most developers typically require a 20% down payment, usually due at the time of booking or within a few days. You can often negotiate this timeline; developers generally allow up to 30 days. Additionally, a 4% DLD (Dubai Land Department) transaction fee is due at this stage.
- **Oqood Registration:** This is typically completed after approximately 24% of the total payment has been made. If a developer offers a lower initial payment, it's crucial to confirm when the Oqood registration will take place. This is a vital legal safeguard for your investment.
- **Under Construction Payments:** For an 80/20 plan like Emaar's, instalment percentages and specific due dates are clearly listed. A total of 80% (which includes your initial down payment) must be paid before the handover.
- **Handover Payment:** The remaining 20% is paid upon the successful completion of construction and the official initiation of the handover process.

Key Due Diligence Point: Calendar vs. Construction-Linked Plans - Your initial layer of analysis should always be to determine whether the payment milestones are explicitly tied to physical construction progress or merely to fixed calendar dates:

- **Construction-linked plans are generally safer;** they directly align your payments with actual, verifiable progress on site.
- **Date-based plans can be inherently risky.** You might be contractually required to make payments even if the project experiences significant delays, creating financial strain without tangible progress. In some cases, such as the Emaar launch mentioned, developers may offer hybrid structures that combine elements of both.

Multiple Payment Options in the Same Project - It's pretty common for developers to offer multiple payment plans within a single project. Always proactively ask if alternative plans are available; some might come with attractive incentives like discounts for faster or larger upfront payments.

Example: Reportage Taormina Village:

Reportage is known for aggressive discounting strategies. In this specific project, they offered up to a 40% discount if the buyer committed to a 100% upfront payment within three months. Concurrently, they also provided several other plans with varying discount levels, depending on the initial upfront amount committed.

Example: Meteora Vivanti, JVC Post-Handover Plan:

This offer included:

- Precise Escrow account details.
- Transparent registration and administration fees.
- A payment split of 50% up to handover, 10% at handover, and the remaining 40% spread over 40 months post-handover.

In a Nutshell: Off-plan payment plans in Dubai can be a powerful tool for entering the market with lower upfront capital. But never be fooled by surface-level ratios like "60/40 post-handover." Always model the actual cash flow requirements and assess how potential penalties or construction delays could impact your investment. A detailed understanding of the precise structure, including specific registration timelines, handover triggers, and all late fee clauses, is essential.

Key Checks:

- **Payment Milestones: Are** they genuinely construction-linked or merely time-based?
- **Hidden Costs:** Are DLD registration fees, potential service charges, and any community fees fully and transparently disclosed?
- **Escalation Clauses:** Are there any specific conditions under which the developer reserves the right to raise the agreed price?

Why It Matters:

The precise payment plan and Sale and Purchase Agreement (SPA) clauses are essential checks. A fixed-date payment plan can create significant financial exposure if construction delays occur. On the other hand, ignoring agreed payment dates can render you liable to penalties or even trigger a cancellation procedure due to a missed deadline.

APPLY

HOW TO APPLY THIS

Rigorously cross-check all terms in the Sale and Purchase Agreement (SPA) with the developer's verbal claims and any payment plan brochures. scrutinise the small print for any hidden clauses.

9.1.4. Contract Review (Sale and Purchase Agreement - SPA)

The Sale and Purchase Agreement (SPA) is the single most important legal document in your off-plan investment journey. It defines the entire relationship between you and the developer, and every right, responsibility, and risk rests within its clauses. Yet, regrettably, many investors merely skim it, relying instead on the verbal promises of sales agents or the allure of flashy brochures. This is where easily avoidable and costly mistakes are frequently made.

Your SPA should include:

- **Payment milestones tied to actual progress or fixed dates?** Ensure payments align with tangible structural milestones (e.g., floor completion), not arbitrarily scheduled calendar dates.
- **Grace periods & late-payment penalties?** Precisely identify if there's a buyer grace period for payments and what exact fines or interest rates will apply if you are late.
- **Developer delay penalties & buyer termination rights?** Does the contract specify compensation for developer delays (e.g., daily/monthly penalties)? Define your right to terminate the SPA in cases of continuous, unreasonable developer delays.
- **Escrow, Oqood & title registration?** The SPA must explicitly note the use of the escrow account, the precise Oqood registration conditions, and who is responsible for DLD registration fees (typically 4% plus any associated administrative fees).
- **Fittings & specification guarantees?** Insist that the exact kitchen, bathroom, flooring, doors, and appliances match the brochure or an annexed specification sheet, and that these are legally binding.
- **Defect liability & snagging period?** Clearly define the inspection window post-handover (the "snagging" period) and the developer's explicit commitment to rectify any identified defects.
- **Force majeure scope?** Clarify which unforeseen events (e.g., pandemics, natural disasters) genuinely pause deadlines, and limit any vague contractual escape clauses that could unfairly disadvantage you.
- **Jurisdiction, dispute resolution & governing law?** Confirm that the UAE/Dubai legal framework applies, clarify RERA/DLD mediation paths, specify arbitration versus court resolution, and state the applicable jurisdiction for disputes.
- **Termination/default conditions?** Precisely identify both buyers' and developers' rights to terminate the SPA (e.g., for non-payment versus continuous, unjustified delays beyond grace periods), with specified notice periods and a clear 30-day cure period.
- **Liquidated damages for delays?** Ensure the developer is explicitly liable for daily/monthly penalties if they fail to meet agreed-upon handover dates.

These are the critical financial, legal, technical, and space-related clauses your SPA should include. Review them with extreme care, ideally with the indispensable assistance of legal counsel, to robustly protect your investment. In essence, your SPA is your legal seatbelt. It's designed to keep you protected in both smooth and turbulent conditions, but only if you fully understand and actively enforce its precise terms. Always consider having the SPA reviewed by a property lawyer, especially for high-value purchases, and never accept verbal guarantees that are not explicitly echoed and made binding in writing. In real estate, what's signed fundamentally matters more than what's said.

Why It Matters:

This is your only binding agreement. Any marketing claims mean nothing unless they are explicitly written and agreed upon in the SPA.

HOW TO APPLY THIS

If the investment value is substantial (over AED 2 million), strongly consider obtaining a professional legal review of the SPA.

INVESTOR MISTAKE TO AVOID

Assuming the contract protects you just because it's lengthy. Many SPAs are primarily written to favour developers; read every clause.

9.1.5. Demand and Market Position

A project can have flawless architecture, impeccable finishes, and even a strong developer name, yet still underperform if underlying demand isn't genuinely there. In real estate, desirability isn't built with concrete; it's built with optimal location, precise market fit, and astute buyer psychology. As an investor, your very first question should always be: "Who truly wants this property after me?" That candid answer fundamentally determines both your resale potential and your achievable rental yield.

Even premium developments can struggle if strategically located in areas with poor connectivity, limited essential amenities, or a significant oversupply of similar units. You should proactively track sales velocity, total transaction volumes, average prices per square foot, and listing saturation within the specific project and its surrounding area. If a project's recent launches show sluggish resale movement or consistently discounted listings shortly after handover, that's a clear red flag, not a bargain. Location should always be evaluated not just by what's currently built, but by its future potential in terms of infrastructure and connectivity. Suppose your confident answer isn't a clear and resounding "yes" to the question of future demand. In that case, it may be wiser to redirect your capital to a project with demonstrably stronger fundamentals.

Research Essentials:

- **Demand Tracking:** Proactively monitor sales velocity, average price per sq ft, and resale listings for similar projects.
- **Project Location:** Confirm it is conveniently near highways, Metro stations, schools, retail centres, or upcoming government infrastructure.
- **Developer Premium Check:** Rigorously assess if the pricing is fair, or if you are paying an unjustified extra solely for a brand name.

Why It Matters:

A beautifully designed project in a weak or unsustainable location can leave you holding an unsellable or unrentable asset, eroding your investment.

HOW TO APPLY THIS

Compare your potential purchase with nearby launches. Always ask yourself: Would a tenant or buyer genuinely choose this property over others? If so, why?

INVESTOR MISTAKE TO AVOID

Buying purely based on a developer's name or initial launch hype, without checking how similar projects performed post-handover.

9.2. Off-Plan Resale (Assignment) Due Diligence

An off-plan resale, also referred to as an assignment transaction, involves acquiring a unit from another investor who originally booked it directly from the developer, with the property still under construction. In essence, you, the new buyer, are stepping into the original seller's shoes and taking over their existing obligations under the original Sale and Purchase Agreement (SPA). This transaction involves the legal transfer of contractual rights rather than a direct title deed transfer, making document verification critical.

Start by requesting a copy of the original SPA between the seller and the developer. This document will outline key details, including the unit number, the total original purchase price, the payment schedule, and all specific terms related to assignment or resale. Then, insist on a developer-stamped payment statement that confirms how much the seller has paid to date and what remains outstanding. This is crucial because the developer will not permit an assignment to proceed if the seller has defaulted on payments or hasn't met the required minimum payment threshold (which often ranges from 30–80% of the property's value). Finally, request receipts for any DLD (Dubai Land Department) or Oqood registration fees already paid by the seller.

Off-Plan Resale Due Diligence (Assignment)

01. Verify All Paperwork

- Get the Original SPA.
- Demand a developer-stamped payment statement.
- Get all DLD/Oqood receipts.

02. Get Developer Approval

- Confirm assignment rights in the SPA.
- Secure a formal Developer NOC.
- Clarify all assignment fees (e.g., 2%-5%) ..

03. Benchmark the Price

- Compare the asking price to new developer launches.
- Check recent transaction data for similar units.

04. Calculate Total Costs

- Factor in DLD transfer fees and developer assignment fees.
- Ensure the Oqood registration will be updated in your name.

9.2.1. Essential Paperwork for Assignment Deals

Always insist on obtaining the following key documents from the seller for a thorough review:

- A copy of the original Sale and Purchase Agreement (SPA) between the seller and the developer.
- A developer-stamped payment statement (confirming how much the seller has paid).
- Any receipts for DLD or Oqood registration fees already paid by the seller.

Table 9.2: Essential Paperwork for Assignment Deals

Document	Why It Matters
Original SPA	Confirms all unit terms and obligations
Developer Statement	Verifies total payments made and outstanding
DLD / Oqood Receipts	Confirms registration with authorities
Assignment Application	Initiates official resale process with the developer

How To Apply This:

Visit the sales centre of the developer and ask for an updated payment certificate to verify the seller's claim. Request a copy to include in your deal folder.

KEY INSIGHT

Whether the unit is pre-handover or has already been handed over under a payment plan, the absence of a final title deed means your only legal position fundamentally stems from the SPA and subsequent developer-issued documents.

INVESTOR MISTAKE TO AVOID

Never rely solely on the seller's word regarding payments made. You *must* verify payment history directly with the developer and obtain official documentation

9.2.2. Assignment Rights and Developer NOC

Not all developers permit resale before handover, and even if they do, they frequently charge fees or impose specific conditions.

- **Check the original SPA** for any clauses about assignment or resale rights.
- **Confirm that assignment is allowed** at the current stage of construction with the developer.
- **Request a formal developer NOC (No Objection Certificate)** to proceed with the assignment.
- **Inquire about the assignment fee**, which can range between 2% to 5% of the original unit price or be a fixed amount.

Why It Matters:

Assignment rights are not automatically guaranteed. Some developers actively block resale until a significant percentage (e.g., 50–80%) of the unit price has been paid.

HOW TO APPLY THIS

Use the DLD REST App to verify the project status. Crucially, visit the developer's office with the seller to confirm eligibility for assignment and clarify all conditions.

INVESTOR MISTAKE TO AVOID

Agreeing to a price and signing a deal before confirming assignment rights and fees can lead to significant legal and financial complications.

9.2.3. Updated Market Positioning and Pricing

You are buying a unit that is part of a live, evolving market. The value of an off-plan assignment can be influenced by new competing launches, changes in market sentiment, or shifts in the developer's pricing strategy.

Why It Matters:

The seller's asking premium should reflect current market demand, not just their initial speculation. Always compare your potential purchase price with current developer rates for new launches and prevailing market rates for similar assignments.

HOW TO APPLY THIS

Benchmark your deal against live listings and recent transaction data for similar units within the same project. Utilise tools like DXBInteract for transaction insights and Bayut/ Property Finder for active listings

INVESTOR MISTAKE TO AVOID

Overpaying for a resale unit simply because the seller "got in early." Continually evaluate based on the current market value and future potential, not past booking prices.

9.2.4. Financial and Exit Considerations

Assignment deals may incur DLD transfer fees, developer assignment fees, and brokerage commissions. Factor these into your total investment cost. Also, clarify:

- Will the Oqood be updated directly in your name as the new owner?
- What specific resale restrictions (if any) apply post-assignment (some developers may re-impose lock-in periods)?
- The estimated time frame for assignment completion (this process can take several weeks).

Table 9.3: Assignment Deal Due Diligence Checklist

Item Verified	Status
Original SPA Reviewed	
Developer Payment Statement Obtained	
Assignment Rights Confirmed	
Developer NOC Issued	
Assignment Fee Disclosed	
Oqood Status Checked	
Market Pricing Benchmarked	
All Costs Calculated	

9.3. Secondary Market Due Diligence

Buying a ready (completed) property in Dubai's secondary market may initially seem like a safer and simpler investment. After all, you're purchasing a tangible, existing unit, often with existing tenants or immediate occupancy potential. But never mistake visibility for certainty. The secondary market brings its own distinct set of hidden risks that require just as much, if not more, due diligence than off-plan transactions.

In these deals, no single developer is guiding the entire transaction or holding your hand. Instead, you're primarily relying on brokers, the seller, and your attention to detail. Every ready property carries a financial and legal history, sometimes perfectly spotless, and sometimes problematic. From verifying the seller's accurate ownership title and checking for any outstanding service charges to thoroughly understanding the existing tenant's legal rights and ensuring clean regulatory documentation, your role as the investor is to confirm every aspect of the property package: legal title, financial dues, tenancy obligations, and ongoing community costs. This section will walk you through what to look for, from title deeds and RERA forms to Ejari checks and occupancy clauses so that you can approach the secondary market with unwavering confidence and clarity, rather than dangerous assumptions or impulse.

9.3.1. Seller and Documentation

Before entering into any secondary market transaction, the first and most crucial step is verifying the seller's legitimacy. You're not just buying bricks and mortar; you're inheriting its complete legal and financial history. That means confirming the seller truly owns the unit, ensuring there are absolutely no unpaid service charges, outstanding mortgages, or hidden title encumbrances, and collecting all necessary documents upfront. Skipping this step can lead to severe delays in transfers, accumulate unexpected hidden costs, or even jeopardise the entire deal. Treat this as your impenetrable legal firewall, because once the sale moves forward, the liabilities transfer with it.

Checklist: Document Verification Method

Document	Verification Method
Title Deed	Obtain a copy from the seller and verify its authenticity and the owner's name on the Dubai REST App.
Service Charge Clearance	Request a "No Objection Certificate" (NOC) from the Owners' Association (OA) or developer confirming all dues are paid. Also, ask for recent service charge invoices.
Mortgage Clearance	Obtain a "Liability Letter" from the seller's bank detailing the outstanding loan amount and instructions for its settlement.

Why It Matters:

You're not just buying bricks and mortar; you're buying legal title, financial obligations, and tenancy rights.

HOW TO APPLY THIS

Use the Dubai REST App to validate title details. Cross-check the property service charge status directly with the Owners' Association (OA).

INVESTOR MISTAKE TO AVOID

Failing to verify any unpaid service charges or outstanding mortgages can significantly delay the transfer process or, worse, saddle you with unexpected debt.

9.3.2. Property Condition

A thorough physical walkthrough of the property is not optional; it's mandatory.

- **Inspect the Unit:** Look for any signs of water damage, potential electrical issues, mould, or poor-quality past renovations.
- **Review Floor Plan:** Ensure the physical property accurately matches the advertised layout and dimensions.
- **Snagging Report (Optional):** For high-value purchases, consider hiring a third-party inspector to conduct a professional snagging report. This ensures optimal protection against hidden defects.

Why It Matters:

While minor issues can be easily fixed, undetected structural problems or poor-quality fit-outs could lead to substantial and unexpected long-term costs.

HOW TO APPLY THIS

Take timestamped photos during your initial property tour or when you sign Form F (the MOU). Use these photos as a visual reference for comparison at the time of final handover.

Secondary Market Due Diligence

What Every Smart Buyer Must Check

Seller & Documentation – your legal firewall	Property Condition – Spot Legal Firewall	Tenancy & Occupancy Know Who's inside	Legal & regulatory No Paperwork, No Deal	Market Pricing & Yield Think Ahead
Verify Title Deed on Dubai REST App	Do a full unit inspection (damage, fit-out, mold)	Review Ejari contract for validity & terms	Ensure all RERA forms A, b & F are used	Compare actual sales prices in area (DXBinteract)
Get Service charge clearance from OA/Developer	Cross-check floor plan vs actual layout	Understand tenant rights & eviction rules	Get NOC from Developer (no dues)	Calculate Net Rental Yield, not just gross
Request mortgage liability letter from seller's bank	Optional: Hire snagging inspector for major purchases	Ensure "Vacant on Transfer" clause is in Form F	Confirm service charge clearance certificate is valid	Check vacancy rates & tenant turnover risk

9.3.3. Tenancy Status and Occupancy

If the unit you are considering is currently rented, it is essential to understand the legal implications involved fully.

- **Ejari Contract:** Request a copy of the current rental agreement and check its validity and registration status on the Ejari System.
- **Tenant's Rights:** If the existing tenant is within the first two years of their tenancy, specific eviction rules and notice periods apply. It's crucial to understand your legal obligations as the new landlord.
- **Vacant on Transfer Clause:** If the seller has promised the property will be vacant upon transfer, ensure this crucial condition is explicitly included and legally binding within the Form F agreement.

Why It Matters:

Buying a tenanted unit could significantly delay your intended occupancy or alter your investment timeline, depending on existing lease terms.

HOW TO APPLY THIS

Have your broker obtain a formal tenant confirmation letter or clear proof of the tenant's stated intent to vacate

INVESTOR MISTAKE TO AVOID

Relying solely on verbal promises regarding vacancy timelines. Only written terms explicitly included in Form F are legally enforceable in a dispute.

9.3.4. Legal and Regulatory Compliance

Secondary market deals require a standard set of RERA forms and clearances to ensure legal compliance:

- **Required Forms:**
  - **Form A:** The seller's exclusive listing agreement with their broker.
  - **Form B:** The buyer's agreement with their broker.
  - **Form F:** The Memorandum of Understanding (MOU) outlining the agreed sale terms.
- **NOC from Developer:** Mandatory clearance from the master developer confirming no outstanding dues.
- **Service Charge Clearance Certificate:** Proof that all service charges are paid up to date.

Why It Matters:

Missing crucial paperwork can halt the transfer process, incur penalties, or even render your entire transaction legally invalid.

HOW TO APPLY THIS

Always use RERA-registered brokers who are highly familiar with completing these forms. Ensure that all documents are correctly signed in the presence of the DLD-authorised trustee.

INVESTOR MISTAKE TO AVOID

Skipping Form B or using informal methods like WhatsApp to confirm crucial terms. Only DLD-approved forms are officially recognised in dispute resolution proceedings.

9.3.5. Market Pricing and Yield

You're buying at today's price, but a truly savvy investor evaluates tomorrow's potential return.

- **Comparative Sales:** Utilise platforms like DXBInteract or Property Monitor to review recent actual sales in the specific building or community.
- **Rental Yield:** Accurately estimate the annual net rental income versus the property price. While a gross yield over 6% might be typical, always calculate the *Net yield* after all service fees and other ongoing costs are deducted.
- **Vacancy Trends:** Carefully consider the typical vacancy duration and the tenant turnover risk for similar properties in the area.

APPLY

HOW TO APPLY THIS

Rigorously run all numbers using the formulas learned in Chapter 5. Create a comprehensive financial model that includes all potential costs and income streams.

Why It Matters:

Your ultimate ROI (Return on Investment) is directly dependent on both the achievable rental yield and the property's capital appreciation potential over your holding period.

Key Documents for Secondary Market Due Diligence:

- Original Title Deed or Oqood Certificate (if off-plan with owner-held Oqood).
- Service Charge Clearance Certificate.
- Mortgage Liability Letter (if the seller has an existing mortgage).
- Ejari Rental Contract (if the property is currently tenanted).
- RERA Forms A, B, and F.
- No Objection Certificate (NOC) from the developer.

9.4. Leasehold Commercial Property Due Diligence

Commercial leasehold investments, such as offices, warehouses, and retail spaces, are governed by typically longer lease terms, specific zoning restrictions, and unique tenant turnover dynamics. Unlike freehold residential properties, leasehold commercial assets usually require more hands-on management and a more specialised approach to due diligence. Because commercial units may not be registered under the standard Title Deed/Oqood framework, verification heavily depends on specific lease contracts, trade licences, and strict compliance with usage regulations. Whether you're purchasing an already leased asset or acquiring vacant commercial space for your own business use or income generation, this section outlines key considerations before committing.

9.4.1. Lease Terms and Tenancy Status

Understanding the precise lease terms is foundational to accurately assessing the value and inherent risk of any commercial property.

What to Verify:

- **Lease Duration:** Precisely confirm the remaining years on the current lease and any available renewal options.
- **Rental Agreements:** Review all existing lease agreements for details on rent escalation clauses, payment frequency, and any specific tenant obligations.
- **Payment History:** Request historical payment proofs (e.g., bank statements, receipts) to verify consistent rental income.
- **Tenant Quality:** Assess the creditworthiness and operational stability of the existing tenant.

INVESTOR MISTAKE TO AVOID

Assuming a "rented" property is profitable without analysing the sustainability or legality of the lease.

9.4.2. Zoning and Permitted Usage

You cannot simply operate any business from any unit; Dubai's zoning laws are strict and specific.

What to Check:

- **Zoning Classification:** Use Dubai Municipality or the relevant Free Zone authority to verify the officially permitted usage for the property (e.g., retail, F&B, warehouse).
- **Trade Licence Compatibility:** Ensure that the tenant's current trade licence, or your intended trade licence, aligns with the property's designated zoning.
- **Special Approvals:** Be aware that certain business types (e.g., clinics, restaurants, educational institutions) require additional specific permits or precise layout approvals from relevant authorities.

Why It Matters:

Acquiring a commercial space that cannot legally host your intended business or a potential tenant's activity can result in severe fines or even forced closure.

HOW TO APPLY THIS

Request a copy of the DED (Department of Economic Development) or Free Zone compliance certificate. Additionally, visit the planning department (or use the DubaiNow app) to confirm the zoning classification.

INVESTOR MISTAKE TO AVOID

Overlooking zoning regulations. A seemingly perfect commercial unit is worthless if it cannot legally operate the desired business

9.4.3. Service Charges and Maintenance Liabilities

In commercial properties, understanding who bears maintenance costs is critical for net yield.

What to Check:

- **Service Charge History:** Request a complete history of service charges for the unit or building from the management or Owners' Association (OA).
- **Outstanding Dues:** Confirm there are no unpaid service charges or utility bills from the previous owner.
- **Fit-Out Responsibility:** Clarify who bears the cost of ongoing maintenance, repairs, and fit-outs—i.e., the tenant or the landlord.
- **Common Area Maintenance (CAM):** Check CAM charges, particularly within retail or office complexes, as these can be substantial.

Why It Matters:

Unforeseen service charge liabilities or unexpected maintenance burdens can significantly erode rental yield and turn an otherwise attractive ROI into a substantial cash drain.

HOW TO APPLY THIS

Obtain a service charge clearance letter from the building management or the Owners' Association. Always factor these anticipated costs into your ROI model.

INVESTOR MISTAKE TO AVOID

Ignoring potential service charge escalations or consistently poorly maintained common areas, as these will inevitably hurt long-term capital appreciation and tenant satisfaction

9.4.4. Legal and Financial Ownership Structure

Unlike freehold residential property, commercial leasehold may be owned under longer-term lease agreements or held within specific corporate structures.

Key Verifications:

- **Title Documentation:** Request the precise lease contract or long-term usufruct agreement. This is often registered with the Free Zone authority, DLD, or the specific regulating authority, such as DXB Healthcare City Authority.
- **Company Status (if applicable):** If a corporate entity owns the property, verify the company's registration status, licence validity, and the authority of the selling signatories.
- **Encumbrances:** Confirm there are no financial liens or legal encumbrances registered against the commercial leasehold interest.

INVESTOR MISTAKE TO AVOID

Skipping legal due diligence simply because the unit "looks ready" for lease or appears to be a good deal. Documentation is inherently more complex in commercial property deals.

Callout Summary: Key Checks for Leasehold Commercial Property

Item	What to Do
Lease Agreements	Review lease terms, rent history, and duration
Rental Consistency	Cross-check income with payment proofs
Zoning Compliance	Confirm legal use via DED/Free Zone authority
Trade Licence Alignment	Check that the business activity matches the zone
Service Charges	Obtain full history and clearance
Legal Ownership	Review leasehold agreements and company documents
Pending Dues	Clear all utility, OA, and authority fees
Maintenance	Inspect premises and shared areas

9.5. Quick Reference Checklists

Every investor should treat these checklists as their personal safety net. Whether you're buying off-plan, flipping before handover, entering the secondary market, or analysing a commercial property, these lists transform vague promises into verifiable facts. Keep them saved, printed, or bookmarked for future reference. This is your essential "Don't Sign Until You've Done This" guide.

INVESTOR INSIGHT

"Due diligence is not paranoia; it's precision."

9.5.1. Off-Plan Property Checklist

Verification Point	Action to Take
The project is registered with DLD	Check on DLD REST App
Dedicated Escrow Account is active	Verify escrow status on the REST App
Developer Reputation is solid	Use DLD Project Tracker and visit past projects to assess quality
The developer is RERA licensed	Check the licence on Trakheesi
Visit Sales Centre	Evaluate transparency, Relationship Managers' knowledge, and availability of documentation
Project Model and Site Visit	Confirm marketing materials reflect real plans and verify the physical presence of construction
Construction Fence & Signage	Drive by the site to verify physical presence and any ongoing construction activity.

9.5.2. Off-Plan Resale (Assignment) Checklist

Verification Point	Action to Take
Original SPA Reviewed	Obtain the seller's signed contract with the developer and review all terms.
Payment History	Ask for official payment receipts from the seller and cross-verify with the developer's statement of account.
Oqood Transferability Confirmed	Confirm with the developer if resale is permitted at this stage, and if your Oqood will be updated in your name.
Developer NOC for Assignment Issued	This is required before resale approval; ensure it's obtained
Assignment Fee Disclosed	Clarify the exact percentage or AED value of the assignment fee with the developer.
Profit Margin Comparison	Compare the seller's asking price to current project listings and recent assignment transaction data for similar units.
Escrow Status Reverified	If applicable, re-verify that funds are held in escrow and no discrepancies exist.
Timeline for New Oqood	Ask the developer how long reassignment and issuance of the new Oqood certificate typically takes
Market Resale Liquidity	Use DXBInteract or other portals to gauge current resale demand for similar assignments.

9.5.3. Secondary Market Property Checklist

Verification Point	Action to Take
Title Deed / Oqood Match	Must exactly match the seller's name as verified on the DLD REST App
Service Charge Clearance	Obtain the latest invoices and a clearance letter from the Owners' Association or developer confirming no outstanding dues
Mortgage on Property Checked	Check with the seller's bank; confirm the exact settlement method for any outstanding loan
Physical Inspection Conducted	Visit the property to inspect the condition, layout, and identify any issues or discrepancies with advertised features.

9.5.4. Leasehold Commercial Property Checklist

Verification Point	Action to Take
Lease Duration & Escalation Terms	Review the full lease contract to understand the remaining term, renewal options, and rent escalation clauses
Rental Income Consistency	Cross-check historical income with payment proofs (e.g., bank statements, receipts) from the previous tenant/owner
Tenant Quality Evaluation	Assess the tenant's size, financial stability/creditworthiness, and operational history
Zoning & Permitted Use Confirmed	Verify legal use via Dubai Municipality or the relevant Free Zone authority for the specific property
Trade Licence Alignment	Check that the business activity (seller's or potential tenant's) is compatible with the zone's licensing requirements
CAM History & Arrears Checked	Obtain previous Common Area Maintenance (CAM) invoices and a clearance letter from the building management
Legal Ownership Structure Reviewed	Ask for the leasehold title documentation and master agreement to understand the precise ownership structure
Utility and Service Dues Cleared	Obtain all clearance certificates for utility (DEWA, chiller) and other service dues
Exit Terms & Resale Options	Clarify if subleasing or resale of the leasehold interest is allowed under the existing contract and any associated conditions.

9.6. Final Reminder: Due Diligence is Your Deal Insurance

It's easy to be swept away by the pace and passion of Dubai's dynamic real estate market. Developers launch fast, buyers queue early, and listings get snapped up in days. But savvy investors know this truth: "In real estate, the deal you don't do is sometimes your best deal."

Your final filter before committing to any investment is your due diligence. It's a rigorous process that empowers you to move with confidence, clarity, and control, safeguarding your capital against hidden risks.

Chapter Summary

Chapter 9, **"Due Diligence and Deal Safety,"** served as your ultimate safety net, providing the indispensable verification processes required to protect your capital in Dubai's real estate market. It established that thorough due diligence is not just a formality but your most critical risk-control tool, transforming potential deals into protected, fact-based investments.

You learned the distinct due diligence paths for the four primary transaction types. For **Off-Plan Properties**, the chapter detailed how to verify developer credibility, confirm project registration and escrow account status via the DLD, scrutinize payment plans, and meticulously review every clause in the Sale and Purchase Agreement (SPA). For **Off-Plan Resales (Assignments)**, you learned to verify the original SPA, confirm the seller's payment history, and secure the mandatory developer NOC before proceeding.

The chapter then provided a complete framework for **Secondary Market** deals, emphasizing the verification of the seller's title deed, obtaining service charge clearance certificates, assessing the property's physical condition, and navigating the legalities of existing tenancy contracts. Finally, it offered specialized guidance for **Leasehold Commercial Properties**, highlighting the critical importance of checking zoning laws, permitted usage, lease terms, and complex legal ownership structures..

Ultimately, Chapter 9 equipped you with actionable **Quick Reference Checklists** for each scenario, creating a practical "deal insurance" policy. By moving beyond marketing claims and mastering these verification steps, you learn to identify red flags, avoid costly assumptions, and ensure every decision is rooted in validated facts. This rigorous process is what empowers you to invest with confidence and control, truly safeguarding your journey in Dubai's dynamic market.

Key Takeaways:

- **Due Diligence is Your Deal Insurance:** Rigorous verification of every detail is not optional; it is your most critical protection against hidden risks and costly mistakes.
- **Off-Plan Vigilance:** Before committing, scrutinize the developer's credibility, confirm the project's escrow account status, analyze the payment plan, and meticulously review every clause in the Sale and Purchase Agreement (SPA).
- **Assignment Scrutiny:** For off-plan resales, verify the original SPA, the seller's payment history directly with the developer, and secure a formal No Objection Certificate (NOC) confirming your right to the assignment.
- **Secondary Market Reality Check:** Confirm the seller's title deed on the DLD app, obtain clearance for all service charges and mortgages, and thoroughly assess the property's physical condition and current tenancy status.
- **Commercial Property Compliance:** For any commercial unit, verify the specific zoning and permitted usage and carefully analyze all existing lease terms, as these are more complex than residential deals.
- **Official Documents Over Verbal Promises:** Never proceed based on verbal assurances; your entire deal must be supported by official, verifiable documents like NOCs, title deeds, and legally binding contracts.
- **Use the Checklists:** Treat the checklists for each transaction type as your non-negotiable final filter to ensure no critical verification step is ever missed before you commit capital..

YOUR JOURNEY
NAVIGATOR

Part 2: From Plan to Purchase

Recap

You have just completed **Chapter 9: Due Diligence and Deal Safety**, where you mastered the verification steps that protect your capital before committing to a purchase. You learned how to validate developers and projects, check compliance with escrow and RERA requirements, assess tenancy situations, analyse market positioning, and use structured checklists for off-plan, secondary, and leasehold commercial properties.

Next Chapter Preview

We now move into the legal framework stage. **Chapter 10: Legal Structures, Taxation, and Ownership Options in Dubai Real Estate** explains the types of ownership available, the tax environment, and how to structure your investment for protection and optimisation. You will also learn about powers of attorney, wills, probate, and strategies to reduce tax exposure while safeguarding your legacy.

You Will Learn

- ☑ The different ownership structures in Dubai, including individual, joint, company, trust, and foundation setups.
- ☑ How powers of attorney work and when they are necessary.
- ☑ Will and probate processes for protecting your real estate assets.
- ☑ Key taxes, fees, and tax optimisat on strategies relevant to property investors.

Link to Framework

This chapter builds the confidence and clarity elements of your C.D.R.C. mindset by removing uncertainty about legal and tax obligations. It also supports your L.E.A.D. approach by enabling you to adapt your ownership model to different investment goals, embrace calculated risks through legal safeguards, and ensure your investment retains value over time.

Purpose / Big Picture Link

This is the structuring stage of your investment journey. Getting the legal and tax setup right is critical to protecting your returns, minimising liabilities, and ensuring your investment supports your long-term objectives.

CHAPTER 10

Legal Structures, Taxation, and Ownership Options in Dubai Real Estate

> “ Ownership is not just about having a title deed; it’s about understanding the legal framework that secures your legacy.

You’ve embarked on a remarkable journey: cultivating a strategic mindset, mastering market dynamics, quantifying opportunities, and navigating the step-by-step acquisition process in Dubai. Now, as you hold that title deed (or Oqood certificate) for your new property, a crucial new phase begins: **understanding the legal and financial structures that secure your ownership and shape your long-term returns.**

Real estate investment extends far beyond the moment of purchase; it involves planning for the entire lifecycle of your asset, from how you hold it today to how it’s taxed during your ownership, and, critically, how it will be transferred or managed as part of your legacy. Ignoring these vital legal and tax considerations can quickly erode your profits, create unforeseen liabilities, or complicate inheritance for your loved ones. This chapter is designed as your indispensable guide to navigating Dubai’s legal landscape with clarity and confidence.

We’ll explore the various ownership structures available, from individual and joint ownership to corporate Special Purpose Vehicles (SPVs) and sophisticated trusts. You’ll gain a clear understanding of Dubai’s tax environment, including its unique zero-tax benefits on property income and capital gains, and learn about the crucial role of Wills and Powers of Attorney in protecting your legacy. This knowledge is not just about compliance; it’s about optimising your investment for maximum security and efficiency, ensuring your asset truly works for you and your future.

10.1. Types of Ownership Structures in Dubai

When you acquire real estate in Dubai, you're faced with a choice about how to hold that property. This decision, whether to register it in your name, jointly with others, or through a corporate entity, carries significant implications for your tax obligations, legal liabilities, mortgage eligibility, and estate planning. Each ownership structure offers distinct advantages and disadvantages, and aligning the right one with your investment goals is crucial for long-term success and peace of mind.

A. Individual Ownership (Personal Name)

This is the most straightforward and standard method of holding property in Dubai. You simply register the property directly in your name, as an individual.

Pros:

- Simplicity in setup and management. Lower initial transaction costs (no corporate registration fees). It is easier for first-time buyers and those seeking direct control.

Cons:

- Personal assets may be exposed to liabilities. Inheritance follows Sharia law for non-Muslims without a specific Will.

Best For: Individuals, end-users, first-time investors.

B. Joint Ownership

Joint ownership involves two or more individuals (e.g., spouses, family members, business partners) holding title to the exact property.

Pros:

- Shared investment burden and costs. Can simplify family ownership

Cons:

- Potential for disputes if not documented. Requires mutual consent for major decisions (e.g., sale, mortgage)

Best For: Married couples, family investments, business partners.

Types: Usually "Joint Tenancy" (with right of survivorship, meaning the surviving owner automatically inherits) or "Tenancy in Common" (where each owner has a distinct share that can be bequeathed). This specific distinction needs to be explicitly chosen and registered.

C. Company Ownership (SPV or Corporate Entity)

Holding property through a corporate entity, typically a Special Purpose Vehicle (SPV), involves establishing a local or free zone company (e.g., in DIFC, JAFZA, RAKICC) solely to own real estate.

Pros:

- Can offer corporate tax efficiencies (especially for multiple properties or professional investors). Provides asset protection and liability segregation. Allows for more effortless transfer of ownership (by selling shares rather than the property directly), potentially avoiding DLD fees on transfer of underlying property. Simplifies complex inheritance for professional investors

Cons:

- Higher setup and annual maintenance costs (licence fees, audit fees). More complex administration. Corporate ownership may affect mortgage eligibility depending on the bank and structure.

Best For: Professional investors, high-net-worth individuals with multiple properties, those seeking asset protection, or where tax optimisation is critical.

Table 10.1: Comparing Common Real Estate SPVs in the UAE

SPV Type	Jurisdiction	Key Features	Cost (Approx.)	Control	Audit Requirement
RAKICC SPV	Ras Al Khaimah International Corporate Centre	Most cost-effective, ideal for holding non-UAE assets	AED 15,000	100%	Low
JAFZA Offshore SPV	Jebel Ali Free Zone Authority	Dual licensing can hold onshore and offshore assets	AED 25,000	100%	Medium
DIFC SPV	Dubai International Financial Centre	Fully regulated, strong legal framework, ideal for institutional and high-value assets	AED 35,000+	100%	High

D. Trusts and Foundations

Trusts and Foundations are sophisticated estate planning tools that involve transferring property ownership to a legal entity (the trust/foundation), which then holds and manages the assets for the benefit of designated beneficiaries.

Pros:

- Provides strong asset protection and privacy. Facilitates seamless, private wealth transfer across generations without probate (if structured correctly). Offers flexibility in managing assets according to the founder's wishes.

Cons:

- Complex to set up and administer. High initial costs. Requires professional legal and fiduciary advice.

Best For: High-net-worth individuals, family wealth management, complex estate planning.

Offshore Ownership via JAFZA, DIFC, RAKICC: These jurisdictions facilitate the establishment of offshore companies, trusts, and foundations that can own onshore Dubai property. This strategy is often used for privacy, asset protection, and streamlined inheritance planning, as the ownership of the property shifts from an individual to a corporate or trust structure governed by a specific jurisdiction's laws.

INVESTOR INSIGHT

" For sophisticated investors, a robustly structured SPV (Special Purpose Vehicle) or a trust can be significantly more efficient for property management and succession planning compared to direct individual ownership. While it involves higher setup costs, the long-term benefits in terms of asset protection, privacy, and streamlined inheritance can be substantial

10.2. Types of Power of Attorney in Dubai

A Power of Attorney (POA) is a critical legal document that grants one individual (the "agent" or "attorney-in-fact") the authority to act on behalf of another (the "principal") in legal or financial matters. In Dubai real estate, POAs are frequently used to facilitate property transactions (buying, selling, leasing), manage assets, or represent owners in legal proceedings, especially for overseas investors. Understanding the different types and their implications is crucial for both granting and accepting a POA.

General Power of Attorney (GPA)

A GPA grants broad authority to the agent to act on behalf of the principal in a wide range of financial, legal, and property matters. It's comprehensive but requires careful consideration due to its extensive scope.

Special Power of Attorney (SPA)

An SPA grants specific, limited authority for a particular task or transaction (e.g., selling a specific property, signing a specific tenancy contract, or managing a single bank account). It is highly recommended for real estate transactions due to its precise and narrow scope, which limits potential misuse.

Key Considerations for POAs:

- **Authenticity:** POAs issued outside the UAE must be attested by the Ministry of Foreign Affairs (MOFA) in both the issuing country and the UAE.
- **Clarity:** The POA must specify the exact powers granted and the properties involved (e.g., "to sell Plot No. XXX, located in Downtown Dubai").
- **Validity:** A POA can be issued for a specific period or until revoked. It typically becomes invalid upon the death of the principal.
- **Revocation:** The principal can revoke a POA at any time by issuing a formal revocation document.
- **Notarisation:** All POAs for property transactions in Dubai must be officially notarised by a Public Notary in Dubai.

INVESTOR INSIGHT

For property matters, always use a **Special Power of Attorney (SPA)**. It provides precise control and clearly defines the exact scope of authority granted to your agent, thereby significantly minimising the risk of misuse or misinterpretation. Never grant a General Power of Attorney for property transactions unless essential and with trusted legal counsel.

Power of Attorney in Dubai
Key Types & Considerations

What is a POA?

Legal authority to act for another
Common in Dubai property deals

Types of POA

General Power of Attorney (GPA)

- Grants broad powers (financial, legal, property)
- Useful for full asset control.
- Risk of misuse due to wide authority.
- Avoid for property sales unless essential and legally advised.

Special Power of Attorney (SPA)

- Grants limited, specific powers (e.g, sell one property)
- Ideal for real estate transactions
- Safer- defines exact task, property, or purpose.
- Minimizes misuse or legal disputes.

Key POA Considerations

- **Authenticity:** POAs issued outside the UAE must be attested by MOFA in both the issuing country & UAE.
- **Clarity:** Must clearly specify the powers granted and exact property (e.g., "Sell Plot 123, Downtown Dubai").
- **Validity:** Can be valid for a specific time or until revoked. Ends on death of principal.
- **Revocation:** Can be revoked anytime via a formal revocation document.
- **Notarisation:** All real estate POAs in Dubai must be notarised by a Dubai Public Notary.

10.3. Wills and Probate: Protecting Your Real Estate Legacy

For non-Muslim expatriates owning property in Dubai, understanding the legal framework surrounding Wills and probate is paramount. Without a properly executed Will in the UAE, your assets, including real estate, may be distributed according to Sharia law, which can differ significantly from common law jurisdictions and may not align with your wishes or family arrangements. Proactively planning your estate ensures your property is passed on according to your intentions, safeguarding your loved ones from complex and lengthy legal processes.

10.3.1. Legal Will Options for Non-Muslim Property Owners in the UAE

Non-Muslim expatriates in the UAE have several options for creating a legally valid Will to govern the distribution of their Dubai-based assets. Each option offers different benefits and suitability depending on your circumstances:

Wills in UAE:

Protecting Your Legacy Options

Compare Will Registration Options for Non-Muslim Property Owners in the UAE

DIFC Wills Service Centre	ADGM Wills Centre	Local UAE Courts
Common law (Expat-friendly, predictable)	Common law (similar to DIFC)	UAE Civil Law (can apply Sharia principles)
English	English	Arabic
Approx. 1-2 months (fast, structured process)	Approx. 1-2 months	Can take 6 months or longer, may be unpredictable
Guardian appointment, onshore/offshore coverage	Cross-emirate coverage, legal certainty	Local access, but may face interpretation challenges
Highly recommended for non-Muslims in Dubai	Good option for assets in Abu Dhabi or UAE-wide	Not recommended for primary real estate wills

Dubai International Financial Centre (DIFC) Wills Service Centre

- **Overview:** Established in 2015, the DIFC Wills Service Centre (WSC) provides a common law-based framework for non-Muslims to register their Wills. It is widely regarded as the most straightforward and reliable option for protecting Dubai-based assets.
- **Benefits:** Offers predictability and certainty, as it operates under common law principles familiar to many expatriates. Allows for the appointment of guardians for minor children. Can cover both onshore (mainland UAE) and offshore assets if structured correctly.
- **Suitability:** Highly recommended for all non-Muslim property owners in Dubai seeking to avoid Sharia law application.

ADGM Wills Centre

- **Overview:** Similar to the DIFC WSC, the Abu Dhabi Global Market (ADGM) also offers a Wills Centre that allows non-Muslims to register Wills for both onshore and offshore assets. It operates under common law principles.
- **Benefits:** Provides another robust option, particularly for those with assets across different emirates or who prefer the ADGM's specific legal framework.
- **Suitability:** A viable alternative or complementary option to the DIFC WSC.

Local UAE Courts

- **Overview:** While it's technically possible to register a Will with local UAE Notary Publics, such Wills are typically governed by UAE Civil Law (which can reference Sharia principles) and may face challenges if they contradict public order.
- **Risks:** Often subject to judicial interpretation, which can be less predictable than common law frameworks. May still be subject to Sharia law for aspects not explicitly covered or if challenged.
- **Suitability:** Generally not recommended as the primary method for property assets in Dubai due to potential complexities compared to DIFC/ADGM Wills.

INVESTOR INSIGHT

Proactively securing a DIFC Will is your strongest defence against the unintended application of Sharia law. It's a small investment today that provides monumental peace of mind for your legacy and ensures your family's financial security tomorrow.

10.3.2. Probate in the UAE: What You Need to Know

Probate is the legal process of proving the validity of a deceased person's Will (if one exists) and formally distributing their assets to the rightful beneficiaries. In the UAE, the probate process for non-Muslims without a registered Will can be particularly complex and lengthy.

- **Without a Will:** In the absence of a UAE-registered Will, Sharia law principles will generally apply to the distribution of assets. This means assets are divided according to fixed Quranic shares, which may not align with the deceased's wishes or the expectations of their family (e.g., specific shares for male vs. female heirs, no automatic inheritance for non-blood relatives). The process can involve freezing assets until heirs are legally confirmed, causing significant delays and financial hardship for dependents.
- **With a DIFC/ADGM Will:** A properly registered DIFC or ADGM Will significantly streamlines the probate process. It allows for assets to be distributed according to the deceased's stated wishes, avoiding the default application of Sharia law. While a court order is still required to give effect to the Will, the process is generally faster and more predictable.
- **Asset Freezing:** Until a Grant of Probate is issued (either based on a Will or Sharia law), the deceased's assets, including bank accounts and properties, may be frozen. This can leave dependents in a precarious financial situation, especially if they relied on the deceased's income.
- **Executor Appointment:** A Will allows you to appoint an executor to manage the distribution of your assets, whereas without one, the court appoints an administrator, which may cause delays.

THINK LIKE AN INVESTOR

Don't delay. If you own property in Dubai, consult with a qualified Wills and estate planning expert in the UAE to ensure your assets are protected and your family's future is secure. This simple step protects your legacy more than any investment decision.

10.3.3. Beyond the Will: Estate Planning Through Structures

While a Will is crucial, advanced estate planning often involves leveraging corporate structures, such as SPVs or Foundations (as discussed in Section 10.1), to hold real estate assets.

- **Foundations:** These can hold assets in perpetuity for specific beneficiaries, avoiding the need for probate upon the founder's death. This offers continuity and privacy.
- **SPVs:** If a property is owned by an SPV, the shares of the company can be easily transferred to beneficiaries (subject to the company's Articles of Association and a specific Will for the shares), rather than the property itself needing to go through the probate process. This is often a faster and more private method of transfer.

10.4. Taxation for Property Owners in Dubai

Dubai is renowned globally for its highly investor-friendly tax environment, offering significant advantages that directly enhance the profitability of real estate investments. Unlike many other major global cities, Dubai maintains a very favourable tax regime, which substantially contributes to its appeal as a magnet for international capital. This section breaks down the key tax implications for property owners, ensuring you understand exactly what you're liable for—and, crucially, what you're not.

No Property Tax

Unlike many international markets where annual property taxes (council tax, municipal tax, property rates) can be substantial and significantly erode rental yields, Dubai has **no annual property tax** on freehold residential or commercial properties. This absence is a significant financial advantage for investors.

No Capital Gains Tax

Dubai currently imposes **no capital gains tax** on the profit generated from the sale of real estate. This means that if you buy a property and sell it for a higher price, the entire profit is yours, tax-free. This policy actively encourages long-term investment and reinvestment within the market.

No Income Tax

The UAE generally has **no personal income tax.** This applies to rental income generated from properties in Dubai. All rental earnings are yours, without being subject to income tax deductions at the individual level.

VAT (Value Added Tax)

VAT in the UAE is currently 5% and primarily applies to commercial property transactions and the sale of new residential properties within three years of completion. Resale of residential properties after three years, and residential rents, are generally exempt from VAT.

Transfer Fees

The primary government fee on a property transaction is the **Dubai Land Department (DLD) transfer fee,** which is 4% of the property's sale value. The buyer typically pays this fee, though sometimes it can be split between the buyer and the seller.

Service Charges

These are not taxes but annual fees paid to the Owners' Association (OA) for the maintenance and upkeep of common areas (e.g., pools, gyms, security, landscaping, building structure). They are typically calculated per square foot and are mandatory.

Tourism Dirham Fee (for short-term rentals)

If you operate your property as a short-term rental (e.g., Airbnb, holiday home), you will be liable for a "Tourism Dirham Fee" (also known as "Tourism Dhs" or "Tourism Levy"), which is a per-night fee paid to the Dubai Department of Economy and Tourism (DET). This is passed on to the guest.

Corporate Tax

Introduced in June 2023, Corporate Tax (CT) at a rate of 9% applies to businesses (including SPVs) with taxable income exceeding AED 375,000 per year. Property held by individuals in their name for passive rental income is generally exempt. However, if an individual is deemed to be "carrying on a business" (e.g., actively managing multiple properties, providing services beyond basic rental), they might be subject to CT. SPVs are generally subject to CT if their taxable income exceeds the threshold.

10.5. Tax Optimisation Strategies

While Dubai's tax environment is already incredibly favourable, strategic planning can further optimise your investment returns. Understanding the nuances of holding structures and income types can significantly impact your net profitability.

SPV Ownership for Corporate Tax

If you are a professional investor or plan to build a substantial portfolio, holding properties through an SPV (Special Purpose Vehicle) is a key consideration.

- **Benefits:** An SPV can provide asset protection and liability segregation. It also offers potential Corporate Tax benefits. If the SPV's taxable income from rental activities exceeds AED 375,000, it would be subject to Corporate Tax. However, if structured correctly, certain expenses might be deductible, potentially reducing taxable income.
- **Consideration:** This requires professional advice to ensure the structure aligns with your investment strategy and complies with tax regulations.

Long-Term vs. Short-Term Rental Income

The *type* of rental income you generate can have different tax and regulatory implications.

- **Long-Term Rental Income (Ejari registered):** Generally simpler, as the income is personal and typically not subject to Corporate Tax for individual owners.
- **Short-Term Rental Income (Holiday Home):** While potentially higher yielding, it involves additional regulations (DTCM licensing), Tourism Dirham fees, and generally falls under "business activity," which might trigger Corporate Tax applicability if the owner's activities are deemed to be "carrying on a business."

Timing of Sale

While there is no capital gains tax, understanding market cycles (as discussed in Chapter 4) and macroeconomic trends can help you time your sale to maximise your profit before any potential market corrections or oversupply.

Leveraging DLD Fee Waivers

During particular new project launches or government initiatives (like the First-Time Buyer Program mentioned in Chapter 8), developers or the DLD may offer waivers on the 4% DLD transfer fee. These waivers significantly reduce your upfront costs and can substantially boost your net ROI on the deal. Always inquire about these opportunities when purchasing off-plan.

INVESTOR INSIGHT

Tax laws, while stable in Dubai, can evolve. Always consult with a qualified tax advisor in the UAE before structuring complex ownerships or making high-value investment decisions to ensure full compliance and optimal tax efficiency.

10.6. Common Mistakes to Avoid

Navigating Dubai's legal and tax landscape for property ownership requires attention to detail. Overlooking key aspects can lead to costly errors, legal complications, or unintended tax liabilities. Here are some common mistakes and how to avoid them:

Table 10.2: Common Mistakes in Legal & Tax Aspects of Property Ownership

Mistake	Consequence	How to Avoid It
Not Having a UAE Will	Assets distributed according to Sharia law, potentially contrary to wishes; lengthy, complex probate process for non-Muslims.	Draft and register a specific UAE Will (DIFC or ADGM recommended) covering Dubai assets.
Ignoring Corporate Tax for SPVs/ Businesses	Unforeseen tax liabilities and penalties for non-compliance; potential audit risks.	Consult a UAE tax advisor to determine if your SPV or rental activity is subject to Corporate Tax and ensure compliance.
Misunderstanding Leasehold/Usufruct	Depreciation of asset value over time, limited resale options, complex inheritance, and inability to mortgage.	Thoroughly understand the specific rights and limitations of leasehold/ usufruct before purchasing; seek legal advice on renewals/resale.
Using a General POA for Property Deals	Risk of misuse of power by the agent; lack of clear boundaries for specific property transactions.	Always use a Special Power of Attorney (SPA) specifically for the property transaction. Ensure it is notarised in Dubai and clearly defines the scope.
Unregistered Rental Contracts	Lack of legal enforceability in tenant disputes; inability to register claims with RERA.	Ensure all rental contracts are formally registered with Ejari.
Not Knowing Service Charge Trends	Unexpected increases in annual running costs can erode net yield.	Request historical service charge invoices from the Owners' Association (OA) and inquire about planned increases.
Ignoring Inheritance Planning for Joint Ownership	Automatic transfer to surviving joint owner (in Joint Tenancy) might not align with the overall estate plan; potential delays in transferring specific shares (in Tenancy in Common).	Explicitly define inheritance wishes for jointly held property in a Will; consider a trust structure for complex situations.

Table 10.3: Summary Chart – Tax Treatment by Property Type (Based on Common Scenarios)

Property Type	Income Tax	Property Tax (Annual)	Capital Gains Tax	VAT (5%) on Sale	Corporate Tax (9%)	Tourism Dirham
Residential (Long-Term Rental - Personal Name)	No	No	No	Exempt	No	No
Residential (Long-Term Rental - SPV/Company)	No	No	No	Exempt	Yes (if > AED 375k)	No
Residential (New Sale by Developer - < 3 yrs)	No	No	No	Zero-rated	No	No
Commercial (Sale / Rent)	No	No	No	Yes	Yes (if > AED 375k)	No
Short-Term Rental (Holiday Home - Personal Name)	No	No	No	Yes	Yes (if deemed business)	Yes
Short-Term Rental (Holiday Home - Company)	No	No	No	Yes	Yes (if > AED 375k)	Yes

Table 10.4: Summary Table of Ownership and Taxation Structures

Structure	Key Features	Taxation Aspects	Estate Planning / Inheritance
Individual Ownership	Simplest, direct control	No income tax, no property tax, no capital gains tax on personal property income/sale. Potentially subject to Corporate Tax if "carrying on a business."	Default Sharia law applies for non-Muslims without a UAE Will.
Joint Ownership	Shared control, shared costs.	Same as individual ownership.	Varies by type (Joint Tenancy vs. Tenancy in Common). It can be complex without a Will.
Company Ownership (SPV)	Asset protection, liability segregation, and easy share transfer.	No income tax, no property tax, no capital gains tax on property sale. SPV's income may be subject to 9% Corporate Tax if taxable income > AED 375k. VAT applies to commercial activity.	Inheritance of shares via a specific Will (DIFC/ADGM) for the shares, or via the company Articles. Can avoid property probate.
Trust / Foundation	Ultimate asset protection, privacy, and flexible distribution to beneficiaries.	No income tax, no property tax, no capital gains tax on property sale. Trust/Foundation itself may be subject to Corporate Tax depending on structure and activities.	Seamless, private transfer of assets to beneficiaries as per the Trust/Foundation deed; avoids probate process for property.

Chapter Summary

Chapter 10, **"Legal Structures, Taxation, and Ownership Options in Dubai Real Estate,"** is your essential guide to securing your property investment beyond the moment of acquisition. It highlights that actual ownership involves understanding the intricate legal and financial frameworks that secure your asset and shape your long-term returns.

The chapter began by detailing the various **Types of Ownership Structures** available, from straightforward individual and joint ownership to strategic company ownership (SPVs) and sophisticated trusts/foundations. You learned the distinct advantages and disadvantages of each, and how to align your choice with your investment goals for optimal tax, liability, and legacy planning.

You then gained critical insights into **Types of Power of Attorney (POA)**, distinguishing between General and Special POAs and understanding their crucial role in facilitating transactions and managing assets, particularly for overseas investors.

A significant focus of the chapter was on **Wills and Probate: Protecting Your Real Estate Legacy**. You explored the essential Will options for non-Muslims in the UAE (DIFC, ADGM, Local Courts), understanding how a properly executed Will can prevent the default application of Sharia law and streamline the probate process, safeguarding your family's financial future.

Finally, the chapter provided a comprehensive overview of **Taxation for Property Owners in Dubai**, underscoring its highly investor-friendly environment with typically no property tax, no capital gains tax, or personal income tax on rental earnings. It also covered Corporate Tax implications for businesses and SPVs, along with other relevant fees like VAT and Tourism Dirham Fee. You were also equipped with **Tax Optimisation Strategies** and insights into **Common Mistakes to Avoid**, ensuring you can navigate the legal and tax landscape with confidence and clarity.

By mastering the legal structures, understanding tax implications, and proactively planning your estate, you ensure your Dubai property investment is not only profitable but also securely held and efficiently managed for generations to come.

Key Takeaways:

- **Choose the Right Structure:** Align your ownership (individual, joint, SPV, trust) with your tax goals, liability concerns, and estate planning needs.
- **Utilise SPVs Strategically:** Consider company ownership for asset protection, tax efficiency (if applicable), and streamlined transfers, especially for professional portfolios.
- **Wills Are Essential:** For non-Muslims, a UAE-registered Will (DIFC or ADGM recommended) is crucial to ensure assets are distributed according to your wishes, avoiding Sharia law application and simplifying probate.
- **Leverage Tax Advantages:** Dubai offers significant benefits like no property tax, no capital gains tax, and no personal income tax on rentals. Understand Corporate Tax implications for businesses.
- **Power of Attorney:** Use Special POAs for specific property transactions to grant limited, controlled authority.
- **Avoid Pitfalls:** Proactively plan for inheritance, understand all ownership limitations (especially leasehold/usufruct), and seek professional tax/legal advice for complex situations.

YOUR JOURNEY
NAVIGATOR

Part 2: From Plan to Purchase

Recap

You have just completed **Chapter 10: Legal Structures, Taxation, and Ownership Options in Dubai Real Estate,** where you explored the ownership models available to investors, from individual and joint ownership to company and trust structures. You learned about powers of attorney, wills, and probate, and how they safeguard your investment. You also examined the tax landscape in Dubai, including VAT, service charges, transfer fees, and strategies for optimising your tax position.

Next Chapter Preview

We now progress to the final stage of purchase execution. **Chapter 11: Taking Handover – Final Steps to Ownership** walks you through the process of receiving your property, ensuring it meets agreed standards, and completing all legal, financial, and operational steps for full possession. Whether your property is off-plan or secondary market, this chapter provides a clear roadmap to closing your transaction and activating your asset.

You Will Learn

- ☑ The step-by-step handover process for off-plan properties, including snagging inspections and title deed issuance.
- ☑ How to manage handover for secondary market properties, from final inspections to utility transfers.
- ☑ Key documents, payments, and deadlines that ensure a smooth completion.
- ☑ How to address defects and post-handover issues effectively.

Link to Framework

This chapter strengthens your C.D.R.C. mindset by building discipline in finalising transactions and resilience in resolving any issues before they become costly. It also enhances your L.E.A.D. approach by enabling you to drive value through a smooth activction process, adapt to varying handover procedures, and safeguard your long-term investment from the outset.

Purpose / Big Picture Link

This is the closing stage of your execution phase. A flawless handover ensures your investment journey moves into the ownership and income stage without delays, disputes, or avoidable expenses.

CHAPTER 11

Taking Handover – Final Steps to Ownership

> “ The keys in your hand are just the beginning; true ownership lies in the activation of your asset.

In **Part 1**, you prepared your investor mindset, understood Dubai's market blueprint and visionary future, and quantified opportunities. In **Part 2**, you then mastered market dynamics, essential real estate math, property types, and the precise legal and transactional steps for acquisition. Chapter 10 armed you with the critical knowledge of legal structures, taxation, and ownership options for your asset.

Now, you stand at the final, pivotal step of the acquisition process: **taking handover of your property**. This isn't merely receiving keys; it's the coordination of physical inspection, financial settlements, utility transfers, and legal registrations that truly activate your asset for its intended purpose, whether for personal use or immediate rental.

Why It Matters:

A seamless handover ensures your investment begins generating value without unnecessary delays or hidden costs. Overlooking key checks during this phase can lead to disputes over defects, unexpected utility bills, or delays in getting your property ready for market. This chapter ensures you complete the acquisition journey with confidence, protecting your asset from day one.

11.1. Off-Plan Property Handover – From BCC to Key Collection

The handover of an off-plan property marks the exciting culmination of months, or even years, of anticipation. It's the moment your promised vision transforms into a tangible asset. However, it's a critical phase that requires attention to detail. This section guides you through the process, from the issuance of the Building Completion Certificate (BCC) to the final key collection, to ensure a smooth activation of your property.

The BCC (Building Completion Certificate)

The Building Completion Certificate (BCC) is a crucial document issued by the Dubai Municipality. It formally confirms that a building or project has been constructed in strict accordance with approved designs, building codes, and safety regulations. The issuance of the BCC officially signals that the building is structurally complete, safe for occupancy, and ready for connections to essential services such as DEWA (Dubai Electricity and Water Authority), gas, and telecommunications. For off-plan buyers, the BCC is the green light for the final handover process to commence.

Key Due Diligence:

Always verify the BCC issuance via the Dubai REST App or directly with the Dubai Municipality. This ensures the building has met all regulatory requirements and is fit for habitation.

Pre-Handover Snagging Inspection

Before accepting the handover of your new off-plan property, conducting a comprehensive **snagging inspection** is mandatory. This is your opportunity to identify any defects, unfinished work, or deviations from the Sale and Purchase Agreement (SPA) specifications. Developers are legally obligated to rectify documented defects either before handover or within the Defect Liability Period (DLP), which typically spans 12 months from the handover date. A detailed, documented snagging report is your best tool for ensuring accountability during this crucial developer warranty period.

What to Look For:

- **Cosmetic Defects:** Scratches on windows, chipped tiles, paint imperfections, and damaged cabinetry.
- **Functional Issues:** Non-working light switches or sockets, leaking taps, drainage problems, issues with air conditioning, and faulty appliances (if included).
- **Structural Concerns:** Cracks in walls (beyond hairline), uneven flooring, issues with doors or windows.
- **Deviation from SPA:** Check if all promised specifications (e.g., specific brands of appliances, type of flooring) match what has been installed.
- **Area Verification:** Though less common, ensure the usable area aligns with the SPA.

Off-Plan Handover Process Step-by-Step

From BCC to Title Deed

01 BCC Issued

Document:

Building Completion Certificate (Dubai Municipality)

Purpose:

Confirms structural completion & safety

Action:

Verify via Dubai REST App

02 Snagging Inspection

Document:

- Snagging
- Report

Check For:

- Cosmetic & Functional defects
- Structural issues
- SPA specification match

Tip:

Hire a professional snagging company

Warning:

Skipping this can cost you later

03 Final Payment & Utilities Setup

Documents:

- Final SPA invoice
- DLD fee receipt
- Service charge invoice

Also Required:

- Security deposit
- Mollak registration
- DEWA / gas / chiller activation

Tip:

Set up UAE bank account in advance

04 Key Collection

Documents:

Final clearance + ID + snagging approval

Receive:

Keys, access cards, remote controls

Action:

Register with OA / Community Portal

Pro Tip:

Get property insurance immediately

05 Title Deed Issuance

Document:

Mulkiya (via Dubai REST App)

Timeframe:

~2-3 months post-handover

Purpose:

Legal proof of ownership

Action:

Store securely (digital + physical)

Process:

- **Developer Notification:** The developer will typically notify you when your unit is ready for snagging inspection.
- **Conduct Inspection:** You can conduct the inspection yourself, or, for larger investments, I highly recommend hiring a professional snagging company. They provide a detailed report with photos.
- **Submit Report:** Present the snagging report to the developer. They are legally obliged to rectify defects within a reasonable timeframe (typically 30-90 days, as per SPA).
- **Re-inspection:** Re-inspect the property after the developer has addressed the issues to ensure satisfactory completion.

INVESTOR MISTAKE TO AVOID

Skipping the snagging inspection. This is your only chance to document defects before taking possession. Once you accept handover, rectification for non-structural issues typically becomes your financial responsibility outside the Defect Liability Period.

Final Payment and Post-Handover Cheques

As the project approaches BCC and handover, the final payment on your off-plan property becomes due. This usually constitutes the last major instalment outlined in your Sale and Purchase Agreement (SPA). For investors who opted for post-handover payment plans, this marks the commencement of those scheduled payments, often extending over several months or years post-handover.

Key Considerations:

- **DLD Registration Fee:** Ensure the 4% DLD registration fee (already paid at booking or due now) is accurately reconciled.
- **Service Charges:** The developer will issue an invoice for the first year's service charges, due upon handover. Confirm the AED/sq ft rate aligns with the RERA Index and is reasonable for the community.
- **Utilities Activation:** You will need to apply for DEWA (Dubai Electricity and Water Authority), gas (if applicable), and cooling (chiller) connections in your name.
- **Security Deposit:** Developers typically require a security deposit for utilities and potential minor damages.
- **Mollak Registration:** Ensure your property is registered on the Mollak system for transparent service charge management.

Why It Matters:

Timely final payments are crucial to avoid penalties or delays in key collection. Understanding all upfront and ongoing costs ensures no hidden surprises.

HOW TO APPLY THIS

Request a clear breakdown of all charges from the developer well in advance of handover. Budget for utility deposits and initial service charges.

PRO TIP

For overseas (non-resident) investors, ensure you have a local UAE bank account set up well in advance of handover. This will streamline the payment of service charges, utility bills, and the receipt of any rental income.

Key Collection and Oqood or Title Deed Issuance

Upon final payment clearance and the resolution of any snagging issues, you will be invited for the ultimate step: key collection. This is when you physically receive the keys, access cards, and remote controls to your new property. For off-plan purchases, the DLD will formally issue the:

Title Deed (Mulkiya) in your name upon completion and handover, replacing the interim Oqood Certificate as your permanent proof of ownership. The Title Deed is typically issued **within 2-3 months** of handover completion [Adjusted based on fact-check].

Process:

- **Final Clearance:** Ensure all payments are cleared, and any snagging rectifications are complete and approved.
- **Appointment:** Schedule key collection with the developer's handover team.
- **Receive Keys:** Take physical possession of your property.
- **Title Deed:** The DLD issues the final Title Deed (Mulkiya), which you can access and download via the Dubai REST App.

INVESTOR INSIGHT

The Title Deed is your ultimate proof of ownership. Ensure it's issued in your name and securely stored, both physically and digitally, on the Dubai REST app. Also, remember to register with your community management / Owners' Association (OA) portal promptly to gain full access to community services and understand rules regarding fit-out..

PRO TIP

Property Insurance is Paramount: As soon as you take physical possession of your property, it is critical to obtain comprehensive property insurance (building insurance and landlord insurance if renting it out). This protects your asset from fire, water damage, theft, and liability, complementing any master building insurance your Owners' Association might hold.

Table 11.1: Handover Checklist for Off-Plan Property

Action	Status	Notes
Building Completion Certificate (BCC) verified		Confirm the building is officially approved for occupancy.
Property Snagging Inspection completed.		Check for defects and unfinished work; submit a detailed report to the developer.
All snagging issues rectified.		Re-inspect the property to ensure all identified defects have been fixed to your satisfaction.
Final payment to the developer cleared.		Ensure the last instalment and any post-handover cheques are settled as per SPA.
Service charges paid		Pay the first year's service charges to the Owners' Association (OA); verify the AED/sq ft rate.
Utility accounts activated (DEWA, chiller, gas)		Apply for DEWA (electricity and water), gas connection (if applicable), and district cooling (chiller) in your name.
Key collection completed		Obtain all keys, access cards, and remote controls for the property and community amenities.
Title Deed (Mulkiya) issued and verified.		Confirm the final title deed is registered in your name on the Dubai REST App.

11.2. Secondary Market Handover

The handover of a secondary (ready) property is a distinct process from off-plan, primarily because the unit already exists and is likely to have existing utility connections and potentially even tenants. While the legal transfer of ownership occurs at the DLD Trustee Office (as detailed in Chapter 8), the physical handover involves a separate set of crucial steps to ensure a smooth transition of possession and responsibilities.

11.2.1. Final Property Inspection – Before Key Collection

Before physically collecting the keys and taking possession, conduct a final inspection of the property with the seller or their representative. This inspection, akin to a detailed snagging process for a new build, is your last opportunity to ensure the unit is in the agreed-upon condition and that any terms outlined in your Memorandum of Understanding (MOU) or Sale and Purchase Agreement (SPA) regarding repairs or included fixtures are met.

What to Check:

- **Agreed Repairs:** Confirm any repairs or rectifications promised by the seller have been completed satisfactorily.
- **Included Items:** Verify all fixtures, fittings, and appliances (if specified in the MOU) are present and in working order.
- **Property Condition:** Look for any new damage or significant issues that may have occurred between your last inspection and the handover date.
- **Utilities Functioning:** Briefly check that electricity, water, and air conditioning are functioning.

HOW TO APPLY THIS

Take timestamped photos during your initial property tour or when you sign Form F (the MOU). Use these photos as a visual reference for comparison at the time of final handover. Budget for initial deep cleaning or minor aesthetic improvements (e.g., painting) if the property was previously tenanted or is older, to make it move-in/rent-ready.

WHY IT MATTERS

Once you accept the keys, you typically assume responsibility for the property's condition. Any issues discovered later become your burden.

Secondary Market Handover Process

Smooth Transition

01 Final Property Inspection

- Confirm repairs & included items (from SPA/MOU)
- Check condition, utilities (AC, water, power)
- Take timestamped photos
- Tip: Budget for deep cleaning / painting if needed

02 Utility & Service Charge Transfers

- Transfer DEWA, chiller, gas (if any)
- Update service charge account with OA
- Use DubaiNow or in-person with Title Deed
- Seller must clear all dues & show clearance

03 Key Collection & Physical Access

- Collect all keys, access cards, remotes
- Confirm appliance manuals / warranties (if transferred)
- Tip: Get property & landlord insurance immediately
- Tip: Register with OA / Community Management

04 Tenanted Property Handover Nuances

- Existing Ejari contract remains valid
- You inherit all lease, terms & rent structure
- 12-month legal notice required for eviction (via notary / mail)
- Review lease terms before purchase

05 Role of Conveyancer or Agent

- Coordinates utilities, keys, documents
- Resolves last-minute, issues
- Saves time & stress-ideal for overseas buyers

11.2.2. Utility & Service Charge Transfers

After the DLD transfer is complete, prompt transfer of utility accounts and service charges into your name is critical to avoid service interruptions or accumulating outstanding bills under the previous owner's name.

What to Transfer:

- **DEWA (Dubai Electricity and Water Authority):** This is essential for electricity and water. You will need your new Title Deed and Emirates ID/passport. The previous owner must clear their final DEWA bill.
- **District Cooling (Chiller):** If your property has district cooling (e.g., Empower, Emicool, or a developer-specific chiller provider), you must transfer this account.
- **Gas (if applicable):** For properties with gas connections, ensure the gas connection is transferred.
- **Service Charges:** The Owners' Association (OA) account needs to be transferred to your name, and you'll typically pay for the upcoming period. Ensure the seller has cleared all previous dues.

HOW TO APPLY THIS

The seller should obtain final clearance certificates for DEWA and other utilities. As the buyer, promptly visit the respective service providers (or use online apps like DubaiNow) with your new Title Deed to initiate the transfer

WHY IT MATTERS

Delayed transfers can lead to service disconnections, penalties, or you being held liable for the previous owner's bills.

11.2.3. Key Collection & Physical Access

Once all legal transfers are complete and utilities are in your name, the physical key collection takes place.

What to Receive:

- All sets of keys (main door, utility boxes, storage units).
- Access cards for building entry, parking, and community facilities (gym, pool).
- Remote controls for gates or garage doors.
- Any relevant manuals or warranties for appliances (if transferred).

HOW TO APPLY THIS

Ensure you receive all necessary keys and access tools during the final walkthrough. Test them immediately if possible.

WHY IT MATTERS

Full physical control allows you to secure the property and begin renovations, furnishing, or tenanting.

Pro Tip: Activate Your Insurance Policy: The seller's insurance does not transfer to you. To avoid any gap in coverage, ensure your own comprehensive home or landlord insurance policy is active the moment you take possession (building insurance and landlord insurance if renting it out). This protects your asset from fire, water damage, theft, and liability, complementing any master building insurance your Owners' Association might hold.

Pro Tip: Community Management / Owners' Association Registration: Immediately after handover, register with your community management company or Owners' Association (OA). This is crucial for obtaining building access, understanding community rules, paying service charges, and ensuring compliance for any future fit-out work or tenant applications.

11.2.4. Tenanted Units – Rights, Timelines, and Handover Nuances

If a tenant currently occupies the secondary property you've purchased, the handover process has specific legal nuances in Dubai. You, as the new owner, inherit the existing Ejari-registered tenancy contract. You cannot simply evict the tenant; their rights are protected under Dubai's RERA tenancy laws.

Key Considerations:

- **Ejari Contract:** The existing Ejari contract remains valid until its expiry date. You step into the shoes of the previous landlord.
- **Notice Period:** If you intend to use the property for personal use or sell it vacant, you must provide the tenant with a 12-month written notice to vacate, sent via public notary or registered mail. This notice can be served at any time, but the tenant has the right to remain in the property for the full 12 months after the notice is received.
- **Inherited Terms:** You inherit all terms and conditions of the existing lease, including rent amount, payment schedule, and any clauses regarding maintenance responsibilities.

HOW TO APPLY THIS

Thoroughly review the existing Ejari contract before purchase. Factor in any required notice periods into your investment timeline.

WHY IT MATTERS

Misunderstanding tenant rights can lead to legal disputes and significant delays in gaining vacant possession or re-leasing at market rates.

11.2.5. Role of the Conveyancer or Agent at Handover

While you can manage the handover yourself, a professional conveyancer or an experienced real estate agent can significantly streamline the process. They can:

- Coordinate utility transfers.
- Facilitate key collection.
- Ensure all documents are properly exchanged.
- Handle any last-minute issues that arise.

HOW TO APPLY THIS

Discuss their exact scope of services and fees upfront.

WHY IT MATTERS

Their expertise can save you time, reduce stress, and prevent costly administrative errors, especially for overseas investors.

11.2.6. Summary - Getting the Handover Right

A seamless handover is the final critical step that transforms your investment from a legal document into a functioning asset. Whether it's an off-plan handover with its specific snagging and payment milestones, or a secondary market handover with its utility and tenancy transfer nuances, attention to detail is paramount. By understanding each step, coordinating effectively with all parties, and leveraging professional support where needed, you ensure your property is ready to generate income or serve its purpose without unexpected hitches. Your due diligence doesn't end with the purchase agreement; it culminates in a successful handover.

Chapter Summary

Chapter 11, **"Taking Handover - Final Steps to Ownership,"** is your essential guide to navigating the precise physical and administrative steps involved in taking possession of your acquired property in Dubai. It highlights that handover is the critical culmination of your acquisition process, ensuring your asset is fully activated and ready to generate value.

The chapter began by detailing the **Off-Plan Property Handover process**, from the issuance of the Building Completion Certificate (BCC) and the crucial pre-handover snagging inspection, to managing final payments, post-handover cheques, and the issuance of your official Title Deed (noting the typical 2-3 month timeframe for issuance).

You then explored the distinct steps for **Secondary Market Handover**, which involves a final property inspection (functioning as a snagging process), the prompt transfer of utility and service charge accounts, physical key collection, and a thorough understanding of nuances related to **tenanted units** and their protected rights. The chapter also touched upon the valuable **role of a conveyancer or agent** in streamlining this process.

Crucially, this chapter emphasised vital post-handover protections: the importance of **obtaining comprehensive property insurance** immediately upon possession, and **registering with your community management/Owners' Association** for ongoing operational readiness and to understand community rules.

By mastering the intricacies of both off-plan and secondary market handovers, you ensure your investment's transition into a functioning asset is smooth, legally sound, and free from unexpected complications. This knowledge is your practical tool for completing the acquisition journey with confidence and protecting your asset from day one.

Key Takeaways:

- **BCC is Your Green Light:** For off-plan, verify the Building Completion Certificate before handover.
- **Snagging is Mandatory:** Always inspect for defects before accepting property, applying this diligence to both new and secondary units.
- **Final Payments & Utilities:** Ensure all final dues are cleared and utility accounts are promptly transferred into your name.
- **Title Deed is Final Proof:** For off-plan, the Title Deed replaces Oqood upon handover (typically within 2-3 months); for secondary, it confirms ownership transfer.
- **Tenanted Units Require Nuance:** Understand and respect existing tenant rights and notice periods in secondary market purchases.
- **Conveyancers Simplify:** Consider professional assistance for a smoother, error-free handover process.
- **Handover Completes Acquisition:** This final step is crucial for activating your property and ensuring it begins generating value.
- **Insure Your Asset Immediately:** Secure comprehensive property insurance (building/landlord) right after taking possession to protect against unforeseen risks.
- **Engage with Community Management:** Register with your OA/community management to understand rules, service charges, and ensure operational readiness.

PART 3

Maximising Ownership Value

Making Your Property Work for You – The Growth Phase

With the purchase completed and the keys in your hand, your journey as a property owner truly begins. This is the growth phase. It is the stage where your focus shifts from acquiring the asset to maximising its potential, ensuring it delivers the returns and benefits you planned for during the preparation and execution phases.

Part 3 is about what happens after ownership. You will learn how to manage, protect, and enhance your property's value while ensuring compliance with Dubai's regulations. Whether your aim is steady long-term rental income, higher-yield short-term leasing, or preparing for an eventual sale, this section equips you with practical strategies to achieve it.

In this part, you will:

Your Property is Yours - Now What?
Organise post-handover essentials including utilities, property management setup, and ongoing maintenance (**Chapter 12**).

Renting it Right - Long-Term Leasing
Build a solid rental strategy, from pricing and tenant selection to contracts and legal compliance (**Chapter 13**).

Renting it Right - Short-Term and Holiday Letting
Unlock the potential of Dubai's short-term rental market, understanding licensing operations, and maximising occupancy (**Chapter 14**).

By the end of Part 3, you will know how to operate as a confident and capable property owner, with systems in place to generate consistent returns, protect your investment, and adapt to changing market conditions.

CHAPTER 12

Your Property Is Yours: Now What?

> What you do after you hold the keys determines the kind of return you'll get.
>
> **Investor Axiom**

The transaction is done. The keys are in your hand. But the real journey of ownership begins now. Whether you've taken possession of a brand-new off-plan unit or purchased a ready property from the secondary market, this chapter is your operations manual. It walks you through every essential post-handover task, utility setup, AC/chiller activation, Owners Association (OA) registration, service charges, insurance, telecom, gas, documentation management, and even smart home basics.

These are the foundational steps that make your property livable, rentable, and financially efficient. Done right, they enhance returns, reduce tenant complaints, and prevent costly surprises. Think of this chapter as your onboarding into the role of a successful real estate owner in Dubai.

12.1. Post-Handover Essentials: Overview

Once the handover is complete, whether from a developer (off-plan) or a private seller (secondary market), your immediate priority is to transition from legal ownership to operational readiness. This involves activating essential services, confirming your ownership with community management, and ensuring your property is fully functional and ready for occupancy or rental.

From setting up DEWA for electricity and water, to coordinating AC/chiller service, registering with the Owners Association (OA), and initiating telecom, gas, and service charge billing, each task plays a critical role in making your asset livable and income-generating. Delaying these steps can lead to access issues, tenant frustration, or even regulatory fines. While some processes can be completed online, others require direct coordination with building management or service providers.

Table 12.1: Essential Post-Handover Tasks (Applies to All Owners)

Utility/Task	How	Action	Docs Needed
DEWA Activation	Water & electricity setup	Apply on DEWA website	Title deed/Oqood, ID, Passport copy
AC/Chiller	Check billing	Contact Empower/ Emicool/OA	Title deed, DEWA number
OA Registration	Register ownership	Email or contact OA	Title deed, ID,, contact info
Telecom Setup	Internet & phone	Contact DU/Etisalat	Emirates ID, DEWA NO., Tenancy (if any)
Gas Connection	Cooking/ water heating	Contact Emirates Gas/private	DEWA No., Emirates ID
Service Charges	Confirm billing	Via Mollak or with OA	Title deed, contact info
Access Cards	Get building/ parking cards	From developer or OA	Handover form, proof of ownership

12.2. Chiller Systems in Dubai

Air conditioning is one of the most significant operating expenses for any property in Dubai, particularly during the long, hot summer months. In many mid- to high-rise buildings, cooling is not managed through individual split units, but through centralised systems known as chillers. These systems distribute chilled water throughout the building to cool individual units, offering greater efficiency at scale, but also introducing a layer of complexity in billing and budgeting.

There are two standard billing models:

- **Chiller-Free:** In this model, the cost of cooling is included in the building's annual service charges. Owners and tenants pay a predictable amount regardless of actual usage. This is generally more attractive to tenants as it simplifies budgeting, and it gives landlords a pricing advantage in the rental market. However, this may result in higher overall service charges for the building.
- **Chiller-Paid:** In this model, cooling is billed separately by a third-party provider (e.g., Empower, Emicool) based on actual consumption. Tenants are usually responsible for these charges, similar to DEWA bills. This model offers greater transparency in consumption but introduces a variable cost for the tenant.

Table 12.2: Chiller-Free vs. Chiller-Paid: What Dubai Property Investors Should Know

Chiller Type	Features	Impact
Chiller-Free	Included in the service charge	Predictable cost, easy to market to tenants
Chiller-Paid	Billed monthly/quarterly by the provider	Variable cost requires tenant education

Major Providers:

- Empower
- Emicool
- Tabreed
- DEWA Cooling

12.3. Insurance: Don't Skip the Safety Net

Insurance is not legally required for cash buyers in Dubai; however, it is compulsory for financed (mortgaged) properties. If you're purchasing a property using a mortgage, the lending bank will mandate two types of insurance:

- **Property (Building) Insurance** – to protect the asset against damage
- **Mortgage Life Insurance** – to ensure the loan is repaid in case of the borrower's death or disability

These policies are a condition of loan disbursal, and banks typically require proof of coverage before completing the title deed transfer.

Even for cash buyers, insurance is one of the most affordable and effective ways to safeguard your investment. Whether your property is off-plan, ready, or a villa, risks such as fire, water damage, theft, and tenant-related liability are real and growing. The 2024 flood events in Dubai, which resulted in tens of millions of dirhams in insurance payouts, serve as a potent reminder that damage can occur suddenly and with significant financial consequences.

- **Building insurance:** Typically covers the full replacement cost of the structure.
- **Mortgage life insurance:** A term policy that repays the outstanding loan in case of your death or total permanent disability.

Banks may offer their own bundled insurance at a premium or allow you to use an approved third-party policy. Either way, the policy must meet their minimum coverage standards before they disburse the loan.

12.3.1. How to Select the Right Property Insurer in the UAE

With several reputable insurance providers operating in the UAE, choosing the right policy comes down to balancing coverage, credibility, cost, and claims service. Whether you're a cash buyer voluntarily insuring your asset or a mortgage borrower meeting mandatory requirements, selecting an insurer is key.

Key Coverage and Policy Terms:

- **Perils Covered:** Look for named perils such as fire, flood, water leakage, theft, and accidental damage.
- **Contents Insurance (Optional):** For furnished units, ensure contents insurance is included and based on replacement value, not depreciated cost.
- **Add-Ons & Exclusions:** Some policies exclude flood, mould, and electrical surges unless explicitly added. Always read the fine print.
- **Landlord Liability:** If you lease to tenants, inquire about landlord liability and loss of rental income coverage.

Claims Reputation & Service:

- Look for insurers with a strong claims payout record.
- Online reviews and forums can reveal common delays or disputes.

Bank Compatibility (for Mortgage Buyers):

- If you have a mortgage, confirm whether your bank accepts third-party insurance or if you're required to use their partner insurer.
- If allowed, a third-party policy may be more affordable and offer greater flexibility.

PRO TIP

You don't have to go directly to each insurer; aggregation platforms and licensed brokers in the UAE can provide comparative quotes across multiple providers, helping you find the best value and coverage. Some property developers also have tie-ups with preferred insurers for off-plan handovers; these can be convenient, but not always the most cost-effective option.

Table 12.3: Typical Costs of Property Insurance in Dubai

Property Type	Annual Building Insurance	Contents Insurance (Optional)
1-Bed Apartment	AED 250 – AED 500	AED 150 – AED 300
2-Bed Apartment	AED 400 – AED 700	AED 250 – AED 500
3-Bed Apartment/Villa	AED 600 – AED 1,200	AED 400 – AED 800

- Premiums vary based on property value, location, chiller systems, furnished status, and whether the unit is occupied or rented.
- Mortgage-linked policies may have additional life insurance premiums bundled into your EMI (typically 0.03%–0.07% of the loan amount annually).

PRO TIP

Bundling property and mortgage life insurance through a broker can save time and reduce cost, but always ask for breakdowns and the option to choose separate providers if needed.

12.3.2. Mortgage Life Insurance – Mandatory Protection for Financed Properties

While property insurance is optional for cash buyers in Dubai, mortgage life insurance is mandatory for properties financed through a mortgage. Suppose you're purchasing a property with a bank loan. In that case, your lender will require you to take out a life insurance policy that covers the outstanding loan amount in the event of death, and in some cases, total and permanent disability. This ensures that the bank is repaid and your family is not burdened with the remaining mortgage.

Mortgage life insurance can be structured in two ways:

- **Single premium:** A one-time, upfront fee, often built into your mortgage loan amount.
- **Annual or monthly premium:** A recurring cost based on your outstanding loan balance, age, and health.

Table 12.4: Typical Mortgage Life Insurance Pricing Overview

Category	Estimated Range
Single Premium	AED 2,500–5,000 per AED 1M loan (one-time)
Annual Premium	AED 1,200–2,000/year per AED 1M loan
Monthly Premium	AED 100–170/month for AED 1M loan

- **Influencing Factors:** Age, smoker status, loan term, insurer, and medical history.

INVESTOR TIP

Compare mortgage insurance quotes independently before accepting your bank's offer. Opting for an external provider can reduce long-term costs and offer better terms, just ensure the policy is assignable to the bank. This segment is especially relevant if you're investing with leverage. Just as we urge you to do technical due diligence on the unit, you should also do financial due diligence on your insurance policy. This isn't just a regulatory formality; it's a risk shield for your family and your portfolio.

12.4. Owner's Document Folder: What to Keep

Ownership doesn't just come with keys; it comes with paperwork. As a real estate investor in Dubai, one of the most important habits you can build is organising your critical property documents from day one. These records are essential not just for legal and operational continuity, but also for smooth resale, tenant onboarding, or even insurance claims.

Think of this as your property's medical file, a combination of original documents, receipts, confirmations, and agreements that together form the complete ownership record. You should maintain both a physical folder (in a secure location) and a cloud-based digital folder (such as Google Drive, Dropbox, or iCloud) for backup and ease of access.

Table 12.5: Essential Documents for Your Property Folder

Document / Item	Why You Need It
Title Deed / Oqood	Proof of ownership
Sale & Purchase Agreement	Legal transaction reference
DEWA / Chiller Receipts	Service setup confirmation
OA Registration Confirmation	Proof of community rights
Insurance Policy	Claim reference and coverage terms
Telecom/Gas Confirmations	For utility continuity
Access Card Receipts	Evidence in the case of replacement is needed

INVESTOR INSIGHT

Organised documentation saves you time during resale, protects you in disputes, and enhances your professional reputation. Think of this folder as your property's second title deed; only this one speaks when something goes wrong.

PRO TIP

Label your digital folder with the property name and unit number for quick reference (e.g., Downtown Blvd 2506). Keep a running checklist inside to update any missing documents after move-in.

12.4.1. Documents Accessible via Dubai REST App

Once your transaction is completed and your unit is registered, these documents will typically be visible in your Dubai REST App dashboard:

Table 12.6: Documents Automatically Available (Post-Transaction or Registration)

Document	Description
Title Deed (for completed units)	Final ownership certificate for secondary or 100% paid-off-plan properties
Oqood Certificate (off-plan)	Interim ownership record until the title deed is issued
Unit Registration Details	Specifics of your property and its DLD registration status
Trakheesi Permit (if reselling/ advertising)	Required for listing property for resale or rent
Broker & Agency Information	Linked to Form A or B agreements and approved RERA brokers

Many official documents related to your property purchase and ownership in Dubai are now managed through the Dubai Land Department's (DLD) integrated digital ecosystem. This includes platforms like:

- **Dubai REST App** – Your main portal to access ownership records, title deeds, and utility setup support.
- **Oqood System** – For off-plan property registrations and payment progress.
- **Mollak Platform** – For service charges and Owners Association-related financials.

You'll only be able to view or download these documents once they are uploaded by the relevant parties, typically your developer, bank, broker, or conveyancer. These entities are authorised to sync documents with DLD's backend systems, which ensures that the record is up-to-date and legally binding.

Table 12.7: Documents Accessible via DLD Integration

Document	Source	Platform / App
Payment Ledger	Developer / OA	Mollak
Title Deed / Oqood	DLD (post-transfer)	Dubai REST
Mortgage Liability Letter	Bank	Dubai REST (via bank sync)
Service Charge Clearance	OA / Developer	Mollak / Dubai REST

12.5. Owners Association (OA): Get Involved

Every freehold community in Dubai, whether a high-rise apartment tower or a gated villa enclave, has an Owners Association (OA) formed to manage the shared spaces, maintenance, budgeting, and governance of the building or community. These OAs are regulated under the Jointly Owned Property (JOP) Law and must be registered and overseen by the Real Estate Regulatory Agency (RERA). The OA is legally empowered to act in the collective interest of property owners, managing service providers, collecting service charges, and ensuring the property's upkeep aligns with Dubai's building management standards.

Owners Association (OA): Your Community Governance

Owners Association (OA)

Responsibilities

- Attend AGMs & Vote – Approve budgets, contracts, and community decisions
- Monitor OA Budgets – Check reserve fund use, vendor payments.
- Submit Suggestions & Complaints Improve community life and resolve issues.

How to Engage

- Mollak System - Verify OA registration, budgets, payments, vendor contracts.
- Document Request – Get audited statements, AGM minutes, vendor contract list.
- Physical Inspection – Check common area upkeep, amenities, and maintenance quality.

Red Flags of a Poorly Managed OA

- Unregistered on Mollak or missing budgets.
- Frequent unexplained service charge hikes.
- Poor maintenance of common areas.
- Unresponsive to complaints.
- Delayed or missing financial reports.

As an owner, your involvement in the OA isn't optional; it's part of your investment responsibility. Your active participation impacts everything from the quality of standard amenities to the level of security, and, crucially, the efficiency of your annual service charges.

Key Responsibilities & Benefits of OA Involvement:

- **Attend AGMs and Vote:** Influence budgets, approve maintenance contracts, and shape decisions about the property.
- **Update Contact Details:** Receive notices, AGM invitations, urgent community updates, and legal correspondence.
- **Monitor OA Budgets:** Understand where your money is going, check reserve fund usage and vendor payments.
- **Submit Suggestions or Complaints:** Help shape the quality of community life and bring concerns to the board's attention for action.

INVESTOR INSIGHT

YA proactive, well-run OA protects your long-term asset value. A poorly run one leads to deferred maintenance, disgruntled tenants, and falling rents. Conducting this check can help you avoid high-risk buildings, even if the unit itself looks perfect.

In newly completed buildings, the developer typically appoints the OA management firm for the first year. However, once 10% or more of the building is sold and registered, owners can initiate the process to vote and replace or reappoint the management company.

Table 12.8: Top OA Management Companies in the UAE

OA Management Firm	Speciality or Notes
Kaizen	One of the largest and most experienced
Provis	Abu Dhabi-based, known for high standards in integrated OA and FM services

Some OAs also have resident owner boards working with these companies, giving you a direct voice in operations.

12.5.1. How to Check OA Registration and Budget

Understanding how your Owners Association is registered and how your service charges are being utilised is a key responsibility of every real estate investor in Dubai. Fortunately, the Dubai Land Department has introduced a transparent, centralised digital system called Mollak - meaning "Owner" in Arabic - that allows property owners to verify OA compliance, budgets, and financial performance. Mollak is the official RERA-regulated Jointly Owned Property (JOP) system, where all OA management companies are required to register their buildings, budgets, and vendor contracts. It ensures that every dirham collected in service charges is accounted for and that OAs are operating within approved limits.

What You Can Do on Mollak:

- **Verify OA Registration Status:** Confirm if your OA management company is officially registered with RERA.
- **Access Budgets:** View approved service charge budgets and audited financial statements.
- **Monitor Payments:** Track your service charge payments and common area expenses.
- **Check Vendor Contracts:** Review the OA's contracts with service providers (e.g., cleaning, security).

How to Use Mollak:

- Visit the Mollak portal online (www.mollak.gov.ae) or access via the Dubai REST App.
- Sign in using your Emirates ID, property ownership details, or with help from your broker or OA manager.
- Navigate to the "Owner Services" section.
- Input your unit number or title deed reference to access building-specific data.

INVESTOR INSIGHT

If your OA budget is not visible or the management company is not listed on Mollak, this could be a red flag. Always ensure your community is being managed under RERA oversight. Lack of registration may affect the legal enforceability of service charges.

12.5.2. Red Flags of a Poorly Managed OA

When assessing a property for investment, most buyers focus on location, layout, and price, but often overlook the quality of the Owners Association (OA). Yet a mismanaged OA can erode rental income, inflate service charges, and make resale difficult. As part of your pre-purchase due diligence, it's essential to evaluate the OA's transparency, maintenance standards, and financial health.

Here's how to conduct a practical OA assessment before signing:

- **Mollak Check:** Log in to the Mollak system (or ask your broker) to check the building's registered service charge rates, historical increases or reserve fund contributions, and whether the OA is registered with RERA and the current management company.
- **Document Request:** Request key OA documents through the seller or broker: Audited financial statements for the last two years, Minutes of the latest Annual General Meeting (AGM), and a summary of active vendor contracts (e.g., cleaning, security).
- **Physical Inspection:** Physically inspect common areas during your viewing: Look for signs of deferred maintenance in elevators, lighting, or air conditioning; evaluate amenities like pools, gyms, and landscaping for functionality and upkeep; note odours, water stains, or signs of pest infestation in shared areas.
- **Resident/Staff Talk:** Talk to existing residents or building staff to understand whether service complaints are handled quickly, if there are issues with cleaning, chiller supply, or parking disputes, and how involved and responsive the OA is.
- **Governance Inquiry:** Ask about governance practices: Are AGMs held regularly with documented decisions? How are vendors selected, through open bidding or fixed contracts? Are any significant repairs or special assessments planned shortly?

INVESTOR TIP

Think of the OA as your building's CEO. A strong OA builds value; a weak one bleeds it. Conducting this check can help you avoid high-risk buildings, even if the unit itself looks perfect.

What Is a Reserve Fund?

A reserve fund is a legally mandated savings account maintained by the Owners Association (OA) to cover major future repairs, like roof replacement, façade refurbishment, or elevator upgrades. It's separate from the day-to-day service charge budget.

12.6. Maintenance Planning - AMC or DIY

Owning a property in Dubai is not just about collecting rent or watching values rise; it also means taking responsibility for your unit's ongoing health. A neglected apartment or villa can quickly accumulate hidden damage, including clogged drains, inefficient cooling, pest infestations, or worse, water leakage that spreads to neighbouring units, triggering insurance claims or even legal disputes. As an investor, you have two broad approaches: handle the maintenance yourself (DIY) or outsource it via an Annual Maintenance Contract (AMC) or a dedicated property management company.

12.6.1. Self-Managed Maintenance: What It Takes

If you prefer to stay hands-on or have a single unit, you can manage upkeep manually. Here's what this typically involves:

- **Creating a Service Calendar:** Schedule quarterly AC service, bi-annual plumbing and electrical checks, and periodic pest control.
- **Using a Maintenance Log:** Track repairs, costs, technician details, and warranty records in a shared document or cloud folder.
- **Hiring Individual Vendors:** You'll need to source and supervise reliable electricians, plumbers, and cleaning teams yourself.
- **Responding to Emergencies:** Be prepared for urgent calls from tenants, especially during the summer when AC breakdowns are common.

INVESTOR TIP

Even if you manage maintenance yourself, always keep dated receipts and before/after photos of repairs. These are invaluable during resale or tenancy disputes.

12.6.2. Annual Maintenance Contracts: When to Outsource

If you travel often, live overseas, or simply want peace of mind, outsourcing to an FM company via an Annual Maintenance Contract (AMC) can be a wise investment. These contracts provide comprehensive coverage and professional management of your property's upkeep.

- **Services Included in AMCs:**
  - AC servicing and repairs (preventive and breakdown)
  - Plumbing and electrical repairs
  - Pest Control (scheduled treatments, especially for villas or vacant units)
  - Emergency Support (24/7 hotline for urgent repair dispatch)
  - Digital Reporting (maintenance logs and technician notes via online portal, if available)
- **Typical Cost Range (for AMCs):**
  - **Apartments:** AED 1,200–2,000 per year (studio to 2-bed)
  - **Villas:** AED 2,500–6,000 per year (depending on size and inclusions)

12.7. Owner vs. Tenant Responsibilities – Avoiding Maintenance Disputes

In Dubai, maintenance responsibilities are a common source of confusion and conflict between landlords and tenants. Many issues arise not from bad intent but from unclear expectations or vague tenancy agreements. As an investor, proactively clarifying who is responsible for what not only prevents disputes but also protects your ROI by avoiding surprise costs, vacancy periods, or tribunal complaints. Let's break down who typically pays for which type of repair and how to set expectations clearly from the start.

Table 12.10: General Rule of Thumb for Maintenance Responsibilities

Type of Repair	Responsible Party
Minor maintenance (e.g., light bulb replacement, clogged drains)	Tenant
AC servicing or breakdown (normal wear)	Owner
Water heater failure	Owner
Plumbing blockages (unless caused by tenant misuse)	Owner
Structural repairs (roof, foundation)	Owner

INVESTOR TIP

The AED 500 threshold is a commonly accepted standard in Dubai and is often written into tenancy agreements. However, it is not a legal rule; you must explicitly include it in your lease to enforce it

12.7.1. How to Prevent Maintenance Disputes

- **Include Clear Maintenance Clauses in the Lease:** The standard tenancy agreement (registered with Ejari) allows for customised addenda. Include a clause that outlines:
  - The AED threshold for minor repairs.
  - Who pays for appliance servicing?
  - AC servicing frequency (e.g., quarterly).
  - Is pest control shared or landlord-only?
  - Contact point for emergencies and the approval process for repairs.
- **Conduct Move-In & Move-Out Condition Reports:** Use a checklist and take photos of walls, ceilings, flooring, all appliances, bathroom and kitchen fittings, and AC vents and units. Both the landlord and the tenant should sign the condition report. This reduces disputes significantly during the move-out process.
- **Schedule Mid-Term Inspections:** For long-term leases, consider adding a mid-term inspection clause (typically at 6 months). This enables the early detection of issues such as moisture buildup, leaks, or misuse before they become costly.
- **Maintain a Digital Maintenance Log:** Use shared folders (Google Drive, Dropbox) to store repair bills, photos of issues (before/after), technician details, and warranty cards. This transparency benefits both parties and builds trust.

12.7.2. RERA Perspective on Maintenance

Dubai's Rental Dispute Centre follows a general precedent:

- Landlords are responsible for structural and major systems (AC, plumbing, electrical).
- Tenants must return the property in the same condition, less reasonable wear and tear.
- If disputes arise and no clause is present, responsibility defaults to the owner.

LEGAL NOTE

Tenants cannot withhold rent due to maintenance disputes. Even a minor AC breakdown in July can escalate into a tenancy-ending dispute if communication is unclear. Utilise professional leasing agents or property managers to establish standards from the outset. In long-distance arrangements, an AMC with tenant hotline access can serve as a neutral bridge, keeping everyone accountable.

12.8. Safety, Security & Smart Home Setup

Today's homes are smarter, but that also means they're more vulnerable if not properly secured after handover. Many new units in Dubai come equipped with smart locks, digital thermostats, surveillance cameras, and integrated automation systems. However, these conveniences can pose a risk if passwords are not reset or the seller, developer, or contractor still controls app access. As the new legal owner, you must immediately take control of all access points, digital and physical. This isn't just about privacy; it's about liability and tenant safety.

Table 12.11: Security Checklist for Your Smart Home

Item	Action
Smart locks & devices	Reset passwords and factory settings
Security Cameras	Ensure app access is transferred from the seller/developer
Parking Access	Collect all passes/cards from OA or the seller
Alarm/Monitoring	Set up with the service provider (if applicable)

INVESTOR TIP

Take control of all connected devices and reset the devices to your credentials, even if you don't plan to use the innovative features immediately. Missed handovers of digital access have led to security breaches and even tenant disputes. Smart homes offer comfort, but they require clever transitions. Secure your asset fully, digitally and physically, from day one.

Chapter Summary

Chapter 12, **"Your Property Is Yours: Now What?,"** serves as your essential operations manual for successfully managing your property after handover in Dubai. It fundamentally asserts that actual ownership transcends the acquisition, beginning with operational diligence to ensure long-term returns.

The chapter began by detailing **Post-Handover Essentials**, guiding you through activating crucial utilities like DEWA and chiller systems, and understanding the implications of "chiller-free" versus "chiller-paid" models. A key emphasis was placed on the critical importance of **Property Insurance** (building and mortgage life insurance) as a non-negotiable safeguard for your asset, with practical advice on selection and cost.

You then learned about effective **Owner's Document Folder management**, highlighting which vital records to keep and how to leverage digital platforms like the Dubai REST App for easy access and verification. A significant section was dedicated to **Owners Association (OA) involvement**, explaining their role in community management, how to check their registration and budget via Mollak, and critical red flags of poorly managed OAs that can impact your investment's value.

The chapter provided comprehensive guidance on **Maintenance Planning**, comparing self-managed (DIY) approaches with Annual Maintenance Contracts (AMCs), and offered clear rules on **Owner vs. Tenant Responsibilities** to prevent disputes. Finally, it covered **Safety, Security & Smart Home Setup**, advising new owners on securing physical and digital access points post-handover.

By following the operational and management principles outlined in this chapter, you ensure your Dubai property is not just a valuable asset but a fully functional, secure, and efficiently managed part of your investment portfolio, ready to perform and generate optimal returns.

Key Takeaways:

- **Operational Readiness is Key:** Activating utilities, registering with community management, and understanding chiller systems are immediate post-handover priorities.
- **Insurance is Non-Negotiable:** Secure comprehensive property (building/landlord) and, if mortgaged, mortgage life insurance immediately upon possession.
- **Organise Documents:** Maintain a physical and digital folder of all property-related documents.
- **Engage with the OA:** Understand your Owners Association's role, monitor their budget (via Mollak), and actively participate to protect your asset's long-term value.
- **Plan Maintenance:** Decide between self-management and an AMC, and clearly define owner vs. tenant maintenance responsibilities in the lease.
- **Secure Smart Homes:** Immediately reset passwords and transfer access for all smart devices and security systems.

YOUR JOURNEY
NAVIGATOR

Part 3: Maximising Ownership Value

Recap

You have just completed **Chapter 12: Your Property Is Yours: Now What?**, where you established the operational foundation for your newly acquired property. You learned how to connect utilities, arrange insurance, organise ownership documentation, engage with the owners' association, and set up a maintenance plan. Your asset is now stable, compliant, and ready to start generating income

Next Chapter Preview

We now move into the income activation stage. **Chapter 13: Renting It Right: Long-Term** takes you through the full process of securing and managing reliable tenants for sustained rental income. You will learn how to prepare your property for leasing, market it effectively, screen tenants, negotiate terms, and comply with all legal requirements.

You Will Learn

- ☑ How to prepare a property for leasing, including furnished vs. unfurnished strategies.
- ☑ Effective listing, marketing, and tenant screening methods.
- ☑ How to set the right rent using RERA's Rental Index and market data.
- ☑ Key clauses and documentation for tenancy agreements.
- ☑ Ejari registration and compliance with Dubai rental laws.
- ☑ Lease renewal, rent adjustment, and tenant dispute resolution.

Link to Framework

This chapter strengthens the Clarity and Discipline pillars of your C.D.R.C. mindset by focusing on systematic leasing practices, and supports your L.E.A.D. approach by enabling you to Drive Value through consistent occupancy, Adapt to tenant needs and market shifts, and secure your Long Game with stable cash flow.

Purpose / Big Picture Link

This is the revenue generation stage of your investment journey. A well-executed long-term rental strategy provides predictable income, strengthens tenant relationships, and preserves your property's condition for the years ahead.

CHAPTER 13

Renting It Right: Long-Term

> The right tenant is an asset; the wrong one is a liability. Screening, pricing, and process make all the difference.

Owning property is only the first half of the investment journey. The real challenge, and opportunity, begins when you transition that property into a steady, well-managed source of income. In Dubai's fast-evolving rental landscape, this means going far beyond simply listing a unit online. Whether you aim to lease long-term to families or professionals, this chapter offers the insights, real-world examples, compliance tips, and investor-focused advice to help you convert keys into consistent cash flow while preserving the long-term value of your real estate asset.

13.1. Pre-Leasing Prep: Getting the Property Ready

Before a single rent dirham is earned, your property must be prepared to meet the expectations of your target tenant. This preparation is not merely cosmetic; it reflects the operational readiness of your asset. Whether you're leasing a one-bedroom apartment in Business Bay or a villa in Arabian Ranches, your first task is to understand who your likely tenant is, what they value, and how your property can be optimised to attract and retain them. Tenant profiles vary widely: a long-term family renter may prioritise proximity to schools and low maintenance costs, while a corporate client or digital nomad may expect high-speed internet, sleek furnishings, and flexible terms. Your leasing strategy, furnishing decisions, and even the tone of your listing should reflect these tenant needs.

A poorly prepared property, dirty, incomplete, or mismatched to the market, can lead to prolonged vacancy, tenant dissatisfaction, or premature wear and tear. Professional landlords treat pre-leasing preparation as a strategic phase. This includes layout planning, cosmetic upgrades, safety inspections, furnishing (if applicable), and functional testing of all systems. A small investment at this stage can often improve rental yield and reduce post-move-in complaints.

13.1.1. Furnished vs. Unfurnished: Strategic Trade-Offs

In Dubai's rental market, the decision to furnish your unit, or leave it bare, is not just about convenience. It directly influences your target tenant profile, your achievable rent, and the speed at which your property leases. The key is to furnish strategically, not extravagantly, and understand what level of furnishing commands a premium.

Table 13.1: Furnished vs. Unfurnished Unit Comparison

Factor	Furnished Unit	Unfurnished Unit
Target Tenant	Short-term guests, expats, and corporates	Families, long-term residents
Setup Cost	High (AED 15K–35K)	Low (paint, minor repairs)
Rental Yield	Higher (7%–12%)	Moderate (5%–8%)
Maintenance	Frequent turnover, higher wear	Lower turnover, minimal damage
Marketing Time	Shorter, visual appeal drives fast leasing	Longer, it requires tenants who are willing to furnish themselves

INVESTOR TIP

Unsure which route to choose? Start with light, neutral furnishings that can appeal to both ends of the market. A clean, partially furnished unit offers flexibility and a faster leasing process.

13.1.2. Pre-Lease Readiness Checklist

Before handing over keys, ensure the property is move-in ready, clean, and functional. Here's your preparation checklist:

- **Deep Cleaning:** Hire a professional cleaning company to clean floors, bathrooms, kitchens, windows, and air vents.
- **AC Servicing:** Have the air conditioning cleaned and filters changed. Share the service receipt with the tenant.
- **Pest Control (if applicable):** Optional, but advisable before long-term tenancies.
- **Painting & Touch-Ups:** Repaint walls if there are visible marks, scuffs, or old patchwork. Neutral tones work best.
- **Functional Check:** Test all appliances, lights, water heaters, faucets, flushing systems, and door locks.
- **Furnishing Setup (for furnished units):** Ensure all items match the agreed inventory, no mismatched or broken pieces.
- **Maintenance Receipts:** Collect and keep records of all work done before handover for your file and tenant trust.

Best Practice: Formal Move-In Condition Report:

After preparing the property, conduct a thorough "Move-In Condition Report" with the tenant present before they take possession of the keys. Document the property's state with timestamped photos or a video walkthrough, and have the tenant sign off on it. This formalises the condition at the start of the lease, which is crucial for managing security deposit deductions at move-out and avoiding disputes.

Optional - Hire a Snagging Company:

For new handovers, especially off-plan units or villas, consider hiring a professional snagging company. This helps identify latent defects developers may have overlooked. **Chapter 11** provides a thorough handover checklist.

INVESTOR MISTAKE TO AVOID

Many landlords rush to list a unit the day they receive keys, without final paint touch-ups, utility connections, or staging. These premature listings result in poor tenant impressions, longer vacancies, and avoidable rent losses. Your property should be 100% ready before you show or list it

13.2. Listing, Marketing & Tenant Selection

Once your property is fully prepped, it's time to take it to market, but don't be fooled into thinking that visibility alone guarantees results. In Dubai's rental market, effective leasing requires more than just a listing; it demands a strategic approach to marketing and tenant screening.

13.2.1. Listing Routes: Broker vs DIY

Option	Advantages	Considerations
Broker	Access to agent networks, MLS platforms, pricing expertise, and tenant screening	Commission is usually paid by the tenant (5% of annual rent, minimum AED 5,000); the landlord may need to coordinate Form A and allow property access.
DIY	Complete control over listing, tenant selection, and no commission involvement	Requires time investment, legal understanding, and direct DLD compliance knowledge.

Form A Requirement (Broker Route): If you choose a broker, signing Form A is mandatory. This authorises the broker to advertise the property and is registered with RERA. Always verify broker licences on the Trakheesi portal via dubailand.gov.ae.

13.2.2. Creating High-Impact Listings

Great listings don't just describe, they attract. In a competitive market, clear listings that feature strong visuals and include specific callouts consistently outperform the rest.

Checklist for a Professional Property Listing:

- Use wide-angle, high-resolution photos and/or a 3D tour.
- Include a clear floor plan.
- Write a compelling description highlighting unique selling points (e.g., "Burj Khalifa view," "Metro walk distance").
- State inclusions (e.g., "Chiller Free," "Appliances Included").
- Provide all essential property details (size, bedrooms, bathrooms, parking, community amenities).

Marketing Insight:

Listings with professional photos and a floor plan receive 40–60% more inquiries on platforms like Bayut, Property Finder, and Dubizzle.

13.2.3. Screening Tenants Like a Professional Landlord

Finding a tenant is easy. Finding the *right* tenant is what separates professionals from amateurs. Poor screening can result in late payments, damages, and legal headaches, risks that a structured evaluation process can easily mitigate.

Tenant Screening:
Professional Landlord's Playbook

Documents You Must Request:

- Passport and Emirates ID
- UAE residency visa
- Salary certificate or bank statements (last 3-6 months)
- Employer details and length of employment
- Previous landlord reference (if applicable)

Soft Interview Questions to Ask:

- How long do you plan to stay?
- Do you have pets?
- Do you or anyone in your household smoke?
- Will other people be staying at the property regularly?

Sample Tenant Evaluation Matrix

(Scoring Method)

Item	Score (Max 3 points)
Employment Stability (>2 years in current job)	+3
Income Level (≥3x monthly rent)	+3
Family or Solo Tenant (Solo/couple = +2, Large family = 0-1)	+0-1
Pets (None = +2, Small pets = +1)	+1-2
Rental History (Verified, no issues)	+3
Communication Style (Responsive, clear)	+2

Documents You Must Request:

- Passport and Emirates ID
- UAE residency visa
- Salary certificate or bank statements (last 3–6 months)
- Employer details and length of employment
- Previous landlord reference (if applicable)

Soft Interview Questions to Ask:

- How long do you plan to stay?
- Do you have pets?
- Do you or anyone in your household smoke?
- Will other people be staying at the property regularly?

INVESTOR INSIGHT

A high income doesn't equal a high-quality tenant. Look for consistency, transparency, communication, and the ability to follow clear agreements.

Table 13.3: Sample Tenant Evaluation Matrix (Scoring Method)

Item	Score (Max 3 Points)
Employment Stability (>2 years in current job)	+3
Income Level (≥3x monthly rent)	+3
Family or Solo Tenant (Solo/couple = +2, Large family = 0–1)	+0-1
Pets (None = +2, Small pets = +1)	+1-2
Rental History (Verified, no issues)	+3
Communication Style (Responsive, clear)	+2
Total (Max 15)	

INVESTOR MISTAKE TO AVOID

Never lease in a hurry to avoid a few weeks of vacancy. A poorly matched tenant can cost far more than a delayed rent payment.

13.2.4. Best Platforms for DIY Advertising

If you opt for the DIY route, here are some of the most effective platforms for advertising your long-term rental property in Dubai:

Table 13.4: Best Platforms for DIY Advertising

Platform	Use Case
Bayut.com	High-traffic portal with premium exposure
PropertyFinder.ae	Professional listings and investor tenants
Dubizzle	Budget-conscious tenants, direct visibility
Facebook Groups	Community listings and relocation leads (e.g., "Dubai Expats")

Digital Advantage:

Consider investing in a Matterport 3D tour or 60-second video walkthrough. These tools improve engagement, especially for overseas tenants or relocation clients.

13.3. Professional Property Management Companies (Long-Term Rentals)

For landlords seeking a truly hands-off investment for their long-term rental properties, partnering with a professional property management company is often the most effective strategy. These companies take on the day-to-day operational burden, allowing you to focus on portfolio growth rather than tenant calls or maintenance issues.

Services Typically Offered:

- **Tenant Sourcing & Screening:** Advertising, conducting viewings, and thorough vetting of applicants (credit checks, employment verification, references).
- **Lease Agreement & Ejari Registration:** Drafting comprehensive tenancy contracts and managing their official registration with Ejari.
- **Rent Collection:** Collecting post-dated cheques, depositing them, and managing rent finance platforms.
- **Maintenance Coordination:** Handling all tenant maintenance requests, scheduling repairs, and often providing 24/7 emergency support (sometimes with an Annual Maintenance Contract built in).
- **Inspections:** Conducting move-in, mid-term, and move-out inspections to document property condition.
- **Dispute Resolution:** Acting as a liaison in minor tenant disputes or preparing documentation for the Rental Dispute Centre if needed.
- **Legal & Compliance:** Ensuring adherence to RERA laws, managing Ejari renewals, and handling notices (e.g., rent increase, eviction).
- **Reporting:** Providing regular financial statements and property performance reports.

Typical Fees

Property management fees for long-term rentals in Dubai usually range from **5% to 8% of the annual rent**, plus VAT. Some companies may also charge a separate "finding fee" (e.g., 50% of one month's rent) for securing a new tenant.

INVESTOR INSIGHT

While professional management incurs a fee, the peace of mind, time saved, and potential for higher tenant retention and fewer disputes can significantly enhance your net returns, especially for overseas or busy investors. Always ensure the management company is RERA-licensed.

13.4. Rental Pricing, Payment Terms & Negotiation

> "The price you set today defines your income tomorrow; make it data-driven, not emotional.

Once your property is ready and potential tenants begin to inquire, your next step is to set the rent and negotiate the terms. But pricing isn't a guessing game. It's a strategic decision that shapes your yield, vacancy period, and long-term cash flow. This section will guide you through the art and science of rental pricing in Dubai, including how to structure payment terms and the negotiation levers you can use to stay competitive without compromising control. Whether you're dealing with a family seeking a two-year lease or a corporate tenant with specific needs, your approach should combine market data, tenant psychology, and contractual safeguards.

13.4.1. Using the Smart Rental Index to Price and Adjust Rents

One of the most practical tools available to landlords in Dubai is the RERA Smart Rental Index. It's an official reference for average rental prices across different property types and areas. It's not just a regulatory reference; it's a strategic guide for setting and adjusting your leasing prices.

The Smart Rental Index, updated regularly by the Dubai Land Department (DLD), provides a rental price range for each unit type in every community. It's accessible via the DLD's Ejari platform or through apps like Dubai REST. As a landlord, here's how you should use it:

- **Set a Competitive Rent:** When listing a new unit, check the current index to avoid overpricing or undervaluing. Pricing within the recommended band increases tenant interest while keeping you compliant.
- **Justify Rent Increases:** If you're planning a rent increase, the index gives you a legal and market-accepted benchmark. Dubai's rental laws only allow increases if your current rent is below the index average by a certain percentage threshold.
- **Preempt Tenant Disputes:** By referencing the index during lease negotiations or renewal notices, you provide transparent, data-backed justification for your pricing.

1. Use the 3-Pillar Pricing Strategy

Don't rely on broker estimates alone. Smart landlords triangulate rent using three verified sources:

3-Pillar Pricing Strategy:
Optimising Your Rent

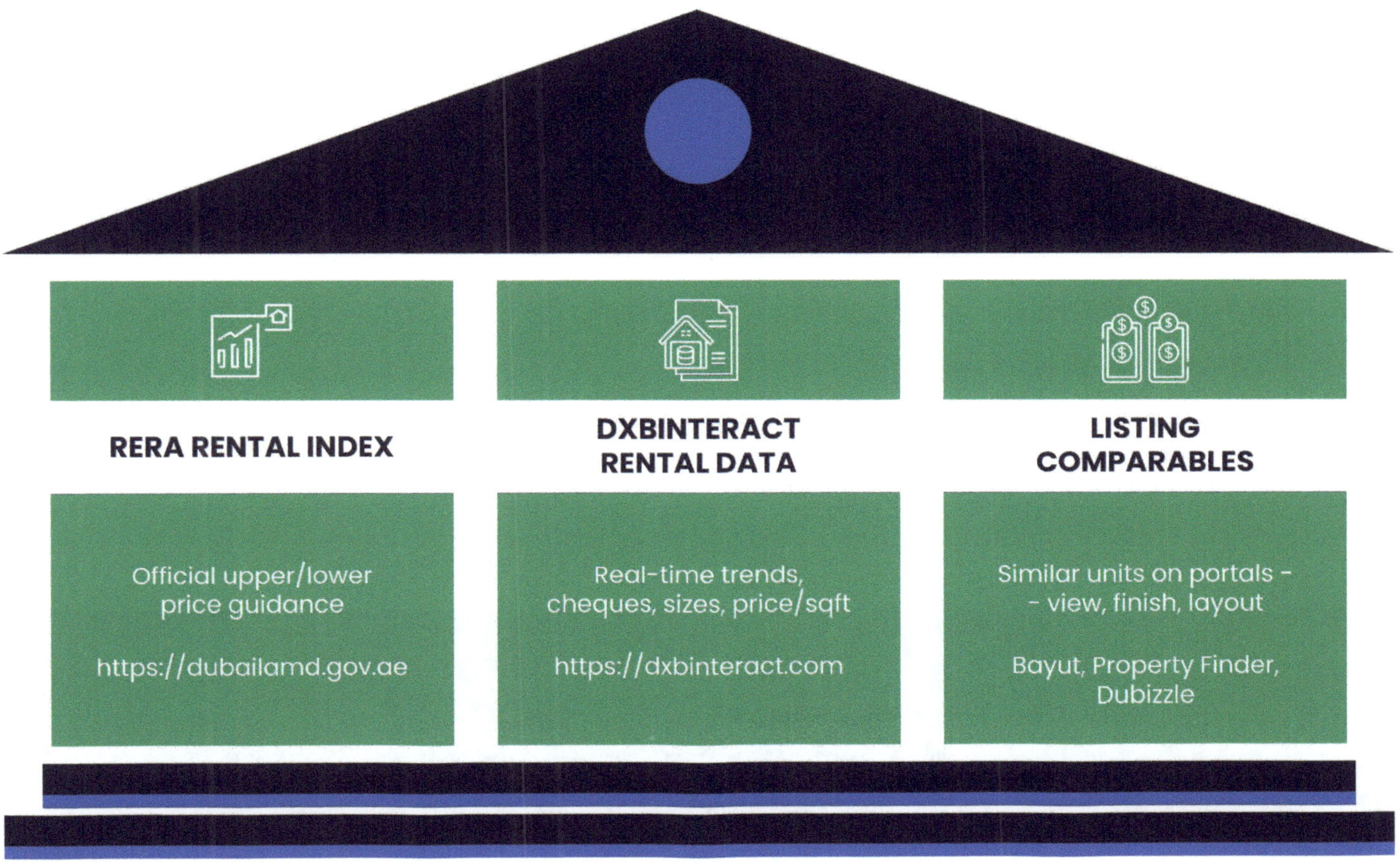

INVESTOR TIP

Compare your unit to same-tower listings first, then expand to the same community. Ensure you match on floor height, size, furnishings, and included amenities.

2. Key Variables That Influence Rent

Rent isn't just a number per square foot. Tenants pay attention to these differentiators:

- View and floor height (marina, lake, park, road).
- Furnishing status.
- Balcony orientation and usable space.
- Inclusions (e.g., chiller-free, DEWA cap, maintenance).

You can price your unit 5–10% higher if it includes chiller-free AC, all utilities covered, or comes with high-speed Wi-Fi.

3. Real Example: Pricing a 2BR in JVC

Let's say you own a 2-bedroom, 1,150 sqft unit in JVC, located on a mid-floor, unfurnished.

- **RERA Index:** AED 90,000 - AED 100,000
- **DXBInteract avg:** AED 95,000 with three cheques
- **Current listings in your tower:** AED 105,000 asking with four cheques

Final Listing Strategy: AED 100,000 with two cheques, or AED 105,000 with four cheques. You offer flexibility with incentives, not blindly preserving both value and tenant appeal.

13.4.2. Furnished vs. Unfurnished: Price Premiums

> Furnishing is not just an expense:
> it's a pricing strategy.

Furnishing your property is a key lever for maximising rental income. Each level, from partially furnished to fully serviced, attracts a different tenant and justifies a specific price premium over the baseline unfurnished rate.

Table 13.6: Rental Premiums by Furnishing Type

Platform	Use Case	Use Case
Unfurnished	Base Rate	Families, long-term residents
Partially Furnished	+5% – 10%	Expats, professionals
Fully Furnished	+10% – 20%	Short-term guests, corporates, digital nomads
Fully Serviced	+20% – 40%	Corporate stays, luxury travellers

LANDLORD INSIGHT

Dubai's diverse tenant base means that furnished units move faster in areas with younger or international populations, such as Dubai Marina, Downtown, and Business Bay. In contrast, unfurnished units are more prevalent in family areas such as JVC, Mirdif, or Silicon Oasis.

1. What "Furnished" Should Mean

Simply placing a sofa and a mattress does not count as a furnished listing in the eyes of a discerning tenant. If you're offering a furnished unit, ensure:

- Neutral, durable furniture (not overly personal or flashy).
- Essential appliances: fridge, washing machine, cooker, AC.
- Basic kitchenware: plates, pans, utensils (optional but adds value).
- Working lighting and curtains/blinds. For serviced or high-premium rentals, you'll also need:
- Weekly cleaning service.
- Fresh linens and towels.
- TV, Wi-Fi, and hotel-grade finishes.

INVESTOR TIP

Stick to a furnishing budget of AED 15,000–35,000, depending on unit size and location. Overspending rarely results in proportionate rent gains. Focus on function, neutrality, and ease of maintenance.

2. Hybrid Strategy: Partially Furnished

If you're unsure whether to furnish or not, consider offering a partially furnished unit, fitted wardrobes, curtains, and appliances, but skip the sofas and beds. This appeals to both ends of the market: those who bring their furniture, and those who want to avoid setup hassles.

3. Real Example: Yield Comparison

Let's say you own a 1BR in Dubai Hills Estate. Based on an assumed property value of AED 1,000,000, the gross yield for each furnishing level is calculated as follows:

Table 13.7: Yield Comparison by Furnishing Type (Based on AED 1M Property Value)

Setup	Annual Rent	Setup Cost	Gross Yield
Unfurnished	AED 70,000	AED 5,000	6.40%
Furnished	AED 82,000	AED 25,000	8.00%
Fully Serviced	AED 100,000	AED 40,000	9.62%

While the gross yield increases significantly, you also take on more vacancy risk, turnover, and management effort as the level of furnishing increases.

13.4.3. Payment Terms: Cheques, Discounts, and Strategy

> Your rental income flow is shaped not just by how much you charge, but when and how you collect it.

In Dubai, rent is primarily paid through post-dated cheques, a system that reflects both the tenant's liquidity and the landlord's risk tolerance. While this may seem unusual to investors from other markets, cheque-based rent is a legally accepted norm and one of the most flexible tools in your negotiation toolkit. This section helps you understand how to use cheque terms strategically, structure your payment agreements, and leverage timing to your advantage.

1. Understanding Cheque Structures

Table 13.8: Cheque Options and Their Impact

Cheque Options	Landlord Advantage	Tenant Perception	Rent Impact
1 Cheque	Full year cash in hand	High initial outlay	-5% to -10% discount
2 Cheques	Good compromise	Common and accepted	Neutral
4 Cheques	More flexibility for the tenant	Preferred for budgeting	+3% to +5% on rent
12 Cheques	Monthly payments (rare)	Corporate or managed tenants only	+5% to +10% on rent

INVESTOR INSIGHT

Offering flexible cheque terms increases your pool of potential tenants, but each extra cheque introduces more risk. Use rent pricing to offset that risk.

2. Strategy: Use Cheques to Adjust Rent

Instead of offering blind discounts or waiving fees, use cheque frequency as a leverage point in your negotiation:

- **Tenant Request (Wants lower rent):** Offer a 1-cheque option in exchange for a discount.
- **Tenant Request (Asks for more cheques, e.g., 6):** Increase rent slightly to compensate for the delay.
- **Tenant Offer (Offers 1 cheque):** Provide a faster move-in or a minor appliance gift.
- **Tenant Profile (Corporate lease, monthly):** Demand higher rent and stricter documentation.

3. Cheque Logistics: Do's and Don'ts

- Cheques should be addressed to the landlord's name or company name as on the title deed.
- Ensure dates are staggered according to the agreed rent schedule (monthly, quarterly, etc.).
- Always issue receipts after each cheque is cleared, even if the process is done automatically.
- Never accept handwritten or incorrectly dated cheques; this can cause legal issues.

Legal Caution: Bouncing a rent cheque is a criminal offence in the UAE, but landlords must still follow legal notice protocols before filing any complaint. Do not act without proper process.

4. Optional: Direct Debit and Bank Transfers

Some landlords and tenants prefer to avoid cheques entirely by setting up recurring bank transfers or direct debits through specific banks, or using property management company collection services. These alternatives offer more automation and fewer risks of bounced payments, but must be agreed upon in writing in the tenancy contract.

Best Practice: Include a clause in your lease stating: "Rent shall be paid via post-dated cheques unless otherwise agreed in writing. Late cheque clearance will incur a penalty of AED ___ per day."

5. When Your Tenant Pays in EMIs, but You Still Get Full Rent Upfront

As a landlord, don't be alarmed if your prospective tenant mentions paying rent via EMIs (Equated Monthly Instalments). This simply means they are using a third-party service that will pay you the full annual rent upfront, while the tenant repays that amount in monthly instalments to the provider. These "rent finance" platforms have emerged as a valuable tool in Dubai's rental market, particularly for young professionals, salaried residents, or newcomers who prefer to manage their cash flow on a monthly basis.

Why it works for you:

- You receive your rent as a single lump sum, as per your tenancy agreement.
- You deal with no added risk or follow-up; your contract is still directly with the tenant.
- It widens your tenant pool, attracting financially responsible clients who would otherwise be unable to afford a bulk cheque.

Table 13.9: Rent Finance Companies and Key Features

Company	Key Features	Website
Keyper	Pay rent in 12 EMIs, instant approvals, DLD-linked	keyper.com
Urban Company	Flexible payment options for rent & moving support	urbancompany.com
Renty.AI	AI-powered tenant scoring + rent EMI solution	renty.ai
AstroPay Rent	Cross-border friendly, supports international tenants	astropay.com
LetsWork PayLater	Pay office and home rents monthly, no collateral	letswork.io

TIP

When marketing your unit, you can include "EMI-enabled for eligible tenants" to attract more leads without compromising on rental terms.

13.4.4. What's Included in the Rent? Clarify Everything

> Confusion over inclusions leads to disputes.
> Clear terms prevent future headaches, for both sides.

In Dubai's rental market, what's included in the rent can vary widely from one unit to another and even between two tenants in the same building. Ambiguity here is a recipe for disagreement, delayed payments, or sudden complaints during the tenancy. As a landlord, your goal is to eliminate grey zones by clearly outlining, in writing, who pays for what. This not only sets expectations but also strengthens your legal footing should disputes arise. Inclusions should be specified per service, rather than being vaguely implied in conversation or marketing. Ideally, every inclusion or exclusion must appear in the Ejari-registered tenancy contract and be initialled or acknowledged in an annexure.

Let's break down the key cost components and clarify how to handle each one contractually.

1. AC and Chiller Charges – Who Pays for Cooling?

Dubai's climate makes air conditioning a significant utility cost, and tenants will want to know whether it's included.

- **AC Consumption (DX or FCU):** If the unit uses a split-unit AC or ducted system where electricity powers the compressor directly, the cost is typically included in the DEWA bill and is the tenant's responsibility.
- **Chiller Charges (District Cooling):** If the building uses a centralised district cooling provider, such as Empower, Tabreed, or Emicool, chiller fees may be billed separately.

Clarification Needed: Some landlords include chiller costs in rent to make their property more attractive. If so, this must be explicitly mentioned in the lease as: "Chiller charges to be borne by the landlord. Tenant shall not be liable for district cooling bills." Otherwise, default responsibility goes to the tenant, and their cooling account must be registered in their name with the chiller provider.

Best Practice: Attach a screenshot or statement of chiller charges from the previous year to avoid surprises later.

2. DEWA (Dubai Electricity and Water Authority)

By default, DEWA consumption, including electricity, water, and sewerage, is always paid by the tenant unless otherwise agreed.

- The tenant must register the DEWA account in their name and provide the DEWA activation receipt as part of the move-in documentation.
- Landlords typically only cover the DEWA activation fee (AED 110) if it's a developer handover or they want to incentivise a tenant.

Contract Language Example: "Tenant shall register and pay all DEWA charges directly, including electricity, water, and sewerage fees during the tenancy period."

> **INVESTOR INSIGHT**
>
> Don't list "utilities included" unless you plan to cap and cover the bill. Tenants can overconsume if they're not liable for usage.

3. Internet, Wi-Fi & TV Subscriptions

Unless you're marketing your unit as a serviced apartment, it's not standard to include internet or TV in the rent. However, some landlords offer it as a short-term incentive (e.g., free Wi-Fi for the first 3 months). If you're offering it:

- Specify the provider (Du, Etisalat, Virgin).
- List whether it's a prepaid or postpaid plan.
- Mention if the TV subscription (OSN, Netflix) is included or left to the tenant.

Contract Clause: "Landlord shall provide Etisalat Wi-Fi subscription valid until [date]. Thereafter, continuation shall be the tenant's responsibility."

4. Maintenance Responsibility – Who Fixes What?

Maintenance is the most common area of confusion. The golden rule in Dubai is:

- **Tenant:** Responsible for minor repairs and wear-and-tear below a specific limit (usually AED 500).
- **Landlord:** Covers major systems and structural repairs, such as AC compressors, water heaters, plumbing leaks, and electrical faults.

Table 13.10: General Rule of Thumb for Maintenance Responsibilities

Type of Repair	Responsible Party	Consequence / Penalty
Minor maintenance (e.g., light bulb replacement, clogged drains)	Tenant	Tenant bears the full cost of repair.
AC servicing or breakdown (normal wear)	Owner	Potential dispute case at the RDC; landlord liable for repair costs.
Water heater failure	Owner	Potential dispute case at the RDC; landlord liable for repair costs.
Plumbing blockages (unless caused by tenant misuse)	Owner	Potential dispute case at the RDC; landlord liable for repair costs.
Structural repairs (roof, foundation)	Owner	Potential dispute case at the RDC; landlord liable for repair costs
Community rule violations	Tenant	Official fine issued by the Owners Association (OA).
Unauthorised modifications	Tenant	Tenant is liable for all costs to restore the property to its original condition.

Sample Clause: "Tenant shall bear the cost of minor repairs up to AED 500 per occurrence. Landlord is responsible for any single repair exceeding this amount, provided damage is not due to tenant negligence."

Include a Maintenance Annexe: Add an annexure showing recent AC servicing, plumbing inspection, and appliance conditions to avoid debates later.

INVESTOR TIP

Consider a property management contract with a facility services company to handle maintenance calls. This is especially useful if you're overseas.

RERA Perspective on Maintenance

Proactive Approach to Preventing Disputes A clear framework for maintenance is the cornerstone of a healthy landlord-tenant relationship. By establishing rules and procedures from the outset, you can prevent minor issues from escalating into major disputes.

- **Codify Responsibilities in the Lease:** Your tenancy agreement (registered with Ejari) is your primary tool. Use an addendum to explicitly define maintenance terms. This clause should specify a clear financial threshold (e.g., AED 500) separating minor tenant repairs from major landlord responsibilities, protocols for servicing key systems like air conditioning, and an emergency contact with a clear approval process for repairs.
- **Establish a Baseline with a Condition Report:** Before the tenancy begins, conduct a detailed move-in inspection with the tenant. Use a checklist and timestamped photos or video to document the condition of every room, fixture, and appliance. Ensure both you and the tenant sign the report, creating a mutually agreed-upon record.
- **Perform Mid-Term Health Checks:** For longer leases, include a clause allowing for a scheduled inspection (e.g., at six months). This is not about intrusion but about proactive asset protection, allowing you to identify potential issues like hidden leaks or misuse before they become costly.
- **Create a Transparent Digital Trail:** Maintain a shared digital folder (e.g., Google Drive) with all maintenance records, including repair invoices, before-and-after photos, warranties, and technician contacts. This transparency builds trust..

The RDC's General Stance

When disputes are escalated to Dubai's Rental Dispute Centre (RDC) and the contract is unclear, a general precedent is followed:

- **Major Systems:** Responsibility for structural elements and major systems (AC, plumbing, electrical) falls to the landlord.
- **Property Condition:** Tenants must return the property in the condition it was received, allowing for reasonable wear and tear.
- **Ambiguity:** If a specific issue is not addressed in the lease, the responsibility typically defaults to the owner.

LEGAL NOTE

Tenants cannot withhold rent due to maintenance disputes. Even a minor AC breakdown in July can escalate into a tenancy-ending dispute if communication is unclear. Utilise professional leasing agents or property managers to establish standards from the outset. In long-distance arrangements, an AMC with tenant hotline access can serve as a neutral bridge, keeping everyone accountable.

5. Service Charges, OA Fees, and Building Facilities

Service charges (also called OA fees) are paid by the landlord to the developer or building management and are never passed on to the tenant. This covers:

- Building cleaning and security.
- Facility maintenance (gym, pool, lobby).
- Fire and safety systems.
- Pest control.

Do not attempt to recover these fees through rent or add-on invoices. However, if a facility (like the pool) is undergoing maintenance, inform the tenant in writing to avoid complaints.

Contract Line: "Service charges, owners' association fees, and facility levies shall remain the responsibility of the landlord."

6. Parking – How Many Spots?

Most Dubai apartments come with one designated parking space. Villas may include two. But always confirm:

- Is the unit's parking rights registered?
- The parking number, location, and access card details.
- Is additional parking possible (some buildings rent extra spots)? If parking is not included, state that explicitly.

Clause to Add: "Tenant shall have access to parking spot #___. Parking access card to be returned at lease end."

7. Furnishings and Inventory List

A signed inventory list is essential if your unit is furnished or even partially furnished. Include:

- Furniture (bed, sofa, table, chairs).
- Appliances (fridge, oven, washer, microwave).
- Accessories (curtains, rugs, light fixtures).
- Condition notes (e.g., "small stain on left sofa cushion").

Best Practice: Take photos at handover, attach to the lease, and require a signature.

Contract Note: "Tenant acknowledges receipt of the furnished unit as per attached Inventory List signed on [date]."

8. Other Optional Inclusions

- **Gas Cylinders / Central Gas:** Clarify if the tenant needs to refill or if a central supply exists.
- **Cleaning Services:** If included (e.g., weekly maid service), this must be documented with scope and frequency.
- **Garden / Pool Maintenance:** For villas, mention if the landlord or the tenant handles this. Lawn upkeep is typically the tenant's responsibility unless stated otherwise.

Sample Combined Clause: "Tenant shall be responsible for DEWA and chiller charges unless otherwise agreed. The landlord shall cover service charges and maintenance costs exceeding AED 500. The unit includes one parking space, all appliances, and furniture per the attached inventory. The tenant is responsible for setting up the internet and gas. Any additional inclusions are subject to mutual agreement in writing."

13.4.5. Restrictions, Damage Liability & Penalty Clauses - Know the Boundaries Before You Sign

> Clear expectations prevent costly conversations.

While the tenancy contract outlines the rent, duration, and basic responsibilities, many landlords overlook the finer details that often cause disputes, especially those related to property misuse, community violations, or unauthorised modifications. This section explores common limitations and penalty scenarios in Dubai's rental market, enabling you to establish enforceable boundaries from the outset.

It's important to note that the examples and clauses presented here are not exhaustive. Each building, master community, or property type may have its own specific rules; some prohibit pets, others restrict satellite dish installation or disallow certain garden plants due to root system issues. As a landlord, you must align your lease terms with the Owners' Association (OA) guidelines and Developer Community Rules, and ensure these are acknowledged in writing by the tenant.

Now, let's discuss how enforcement works. Most landlords in Dubai collect a refundable security deposit, typically amounting to 5% of annual rent for unfurnished units and 10% for furnished ones. This deposit is held in trust, not spent, and is intended to cover any damages, cleaning, or unpaid dues at the end of the lease. However, deductions can also be made during the tenancy if the tenant causes verifiable damage or triggers a fine through negligence or misconduct.

Here's how you protect yourself:

- Document everything at handover, take photos, list furnishings, and perform a condition inspection.
- Include clear penalty clauses in the tenancy agreement or annexure for items like lost keys, unauthorised pets, or broken appliances.
- Issue written notices for any violations, and keep a record.

Suppose the tenant repeatedly violates terms despite warnings, such as ignoring noise complaints, housing unapproved pets, or damaging fixtures. In that case, you have the right to forfeit the tenancy contract, but only after following the correct legal protocol. In Dubai, early eviction must be initiated through the Rental Dispute Centre (RDC), and you must show proof of warnings and non-compliance. Always seek legal consultation before taking this step. Tenancy forfeiture is a serious action that requires evidence, documented notice, and procedural fairness. But with the right clauses in place, you significantly reduce risk and create a framework that allows you to act when needed.

1. Pets and Animal Restrictions

"Pets are not permitted unless expressly approved in writing by the Landlord and subject to community/ building guidelines. In the event of any fines, complaints, or damage resulting from unauthorised pets, the Tenant shall bear full liability."

Best Practice: Attach the master community rules as an appendix if available (e.g., Dubai Hills HOA guidelines).

2. Smoking Clause (Indoor & Balcony Use)

"Smoking of any kind (including cigarettes, cigars, vapes, or incense burning) is strictly prohibited inside the Premises. Smoking on balconies is permitted only if it does not cause a nuisance to neighbours. Any damage, discolouration, or odour removal required due to smoking shall be rectified at the Tenant's expense."

3. Garden and Landscaping Restrictions (For Villas or Ground Floor Units)

"The Tenant shall not plant or maintain any species prohibited by the Master Developer or Owners' Association (including but not limited to invasive species or deep-rooted trees). The Tenant shall bear any fines or costs resulting from unauthorised landscaping. Irrigation system misuse or tampering is also strictly prohibited."

Add-On Clause: If the landlord provides landscaping services, include: "Garden maintenance shall be performed monthly by the Landlord's designated vendor. Tenant shall ensure access is granted as scheduled."

4. Damage to Fixtures, Fittings, or Appliances

"Tenant shall use all fixtures, fittings, and appliances with due care. Any damage resulting from negligence, misuse, or willful destruction, including but not limited to basins, windows, AC remotes, cabinet hinges, stoves, or light fittings, shall be repaired or replaced by the Tenant at their sole cost. Natural wear and tear is excluded."

5. Loss of Access Cards, Keys, or Parking Remotes

"Tenant is responsible for the safekeeping of all keys, access cards, and parking remotes issued at handover. Any loss or damage will require replacement at the Tenant's cost, including associated programming or deactivation charges."

6. Unauthorised Modifications or Installations

"Tenant shall not make any alterations, additions, or modifications to the Premises without written permission from the Landlord. This includes wall painting, drilling, installing satellite dishes, or smart home systems. Any unauthorised work shall be removed, and the area restored at the Tenant's cost before handover."

Optional: "Tenant may request permission for temporary fixtures (e.g., curtain rods, shelves). Approval may be granted with the condition of full restoration at move-out."

7. Penalty Clause for Breach of Rules or Non-Compliance

"In the event of breach of any clause of this agreement or violation of building/community rules, the Landlord reserves the right to levy a penalty of AED ___ per occurrence, or actual fine amount as invoiced by the authorities, whichever is higher. Repeated non-compliance may lead to early termination of tenancy without compensation."

Best Practice: Set AED 500–AED 1,000 for minor infractions, but state that fines from authorities will be passed through at cost.

Table 13.11: Common Tenant Issues, Responsibilities, and Penalties

This table provides a practical snapshot of common issues that landlords in Dubai may encounter, along with guidance on how responsibility is typically allocated and what penalties or deductions may apply. While not an exhaustive list, it serves as a valuable reference to help you think through the types of scenarios that should be preemptively addressed in your tenancy agreement or annexure. Use it as a prompt to create your own tailored checklist of clauses, based on your unit type, community rules, and risk tolerance.

Category	Responsibility	Penalty (Example)
Pets without permission	Tenant	Fine as per OA + repair damages
Smoking indoors	Tenant	Full cost of cleaning/painting
Broken basin/window due to misuse	Tenant	Full replacement/repair
Noise complaints (verified)	Tenant	OA fine or RERA penalty
Community rule violations	Tenant	AED 500+ or OA fine
Unauthorised modifications	Tenant	Cost of removal + repaint/restoration

13.5. Legal Documentation & Ejari Registration

> Without Ejari, your lease is just a handshake.
> With it, you're protected by law.

Once you've finalised terms and selected your tenant, it's time to make the agreement legally binding. In Dubai, this means preparing a valid tenancy contract and registering it through Ejari, the official rental registration system operated by Dubai Land Department (DLD) and regulated by RERA. Too many first-time landlords rely on informal promises or WhatsApp confirmations. That approach leaves you vulnerable to legal issues, missed payments, or tenant disputes. Ejari registration is not optional; it's what gives your lease legal recognition. Without it, tenants can't activate DEWA, and you can't file disputes with the Rental Dispute Centre.

13.5.1. Drafting the Tenancy Contract

A clear, detailed tenancy contract is the foundation of a secure rental relationship. Whether using the standard Unified Tenancy Contract or a customised lease, your agreement should define financial terms, responsibilities, inclusions, and exit conditions.

Section Details to Include:

- **Parties Involved:** Full names, Emirates ID/passport copies of the landlord and the tenant.
- **Property Details:** Full address, unit number, parking bay (if any), title deed reference.
- **Rent Amount:** Total rent, number of cheques, due dates, and bank account for deposit.
- **Security Deposit:** Typically 5%–10% of annual rent, refundable upon property handover.
- **Maintenance Clause:** Responsibility split: tenant covers minor repairs (≤ AED 500), landlord covers major repairs.
- **Utilities & Services:** Who pays for DEWA, chiller, gas, internet, and TV?
- **Notice Period:** Typically, 90 days for non-renewal.
- **Early Termination:** Penalties and conditions for break clauses.
- **Signature Section:** Both parties must sign with ID verification.

INVESTOR TIP

Always sign two original copies, and initial each page. Attach any annexures such as inventory lists, floor plans, or handover forms.

13.5.2. Collecting the Right Document

Ensure you collect the following necessary documents from the tenant:

- Signed Tenancy Contract
- Passport and Emirates ID copy of the tenant (and spouse/dependants if applicable)
- UAE Residency Visa copy
- Post-dated cheques for rent and security deposit
- Employment/Salary Certificate or Bank Statements (last 3-6 months)
- Previous Landlord Reference (if available)

WARNING

If a unit is jointly owned (e.g., husband and wife), both owners must be listed on the contract and provide ID for Ejari registration.

INVESTOR TIP

Don't skip the paperwork—even when leasing to someone you know. Ejari is your only enforceable proof in the event of a dispute.

13.5.3. Registering the Lease with Ejari

> “ In Dubai, if it’s not registered, it’s not enforceable.

Once the tenancy contract is signed, it must be registered through Ejari to make it legally binding. This registration is mandatory for all new and renewed leases, regardless of property type, and ensures that the lease is recognised by the Dubai Land Department (DLD) under RERA regulations.

What is Ejari? Ejari (Arabic for “My Rent”) is the official lease registration system in Dubai, managed by the DLD. It creates a centralised record of tenancy agreements and protects the rights of both landlords and tenants. Ejari registration is not just a formality; it is essential for:

- Activating DEWA and other utilities in the tenant’s name.
- Filing any rental dispute cases at the Rental Dispute Centre (RDC).
- Obtaining an Ejari certificate for residency visa applications.
- Renewing or cancelling tenancy contracts legally.

Table 13.12: How to Register Ejari - Methods and Fees

Method	Procedure	Fees (Approximate)	
Online via Dubai REST App	The landlord logs in, uploads documents, pays the fee, and the certificate is emailed.	AED 100 (Ejari fee) + AED 10 (Knowledge) + AED 10 (Innovation) =	AED 120
Typing Centre (Offline)	Tenant or landlord visits, submits documents, and gets a certificate on the spot.	AED 120 base + ~AED 95 partner/admin fee + VAT ≈	AED 220–250
Through Broker/ Property Manager	An authorised agent submits online or offline on the landlord’s behalf.	May include additional service charges (commonly	AED 500–1,000)

Ejari Certificate – What You Get: After successful registration, both parties receive via email:

- Unique Ejari Number
- DEWA Premises Number (for utility activation)
- Contract summary, including term dates, rent, parties, and property details. Copy the certificate to your tenant so they can proceed with DEWA, internet, and immigration needs.

INVESTOR PITFALL TO AVOID

"Any agreement not registered in Ejari holds no legal weight." Many landlords rely on WhatsApp agreements or verbal promises. Without Ejari, you can't enforce payment terms, evict non-compliant tenants, or request compensation for damages.

13.6. Lease Renewal and Rent Increase Planning

If you own a property with an existing tenant, you can't raise the rent arbitrarily. The Dubai Land Department (DLD), through RERA, sets strict guidelines for rental increases using the Rental Index as a baseline. This proactive approach to renewal management ensures fair market practices and minimises disputes.

13.6.1. Use the RERA Rental Index

Before increasing rent, check the current average for similar units in your area using the RERA Smart Rental Index (via the Dubai REST app or DLD website).

13.6.2. Rent Increase Thresholds

The amount you're allowed to increase depends on how your current rent compares to the Rental Index:

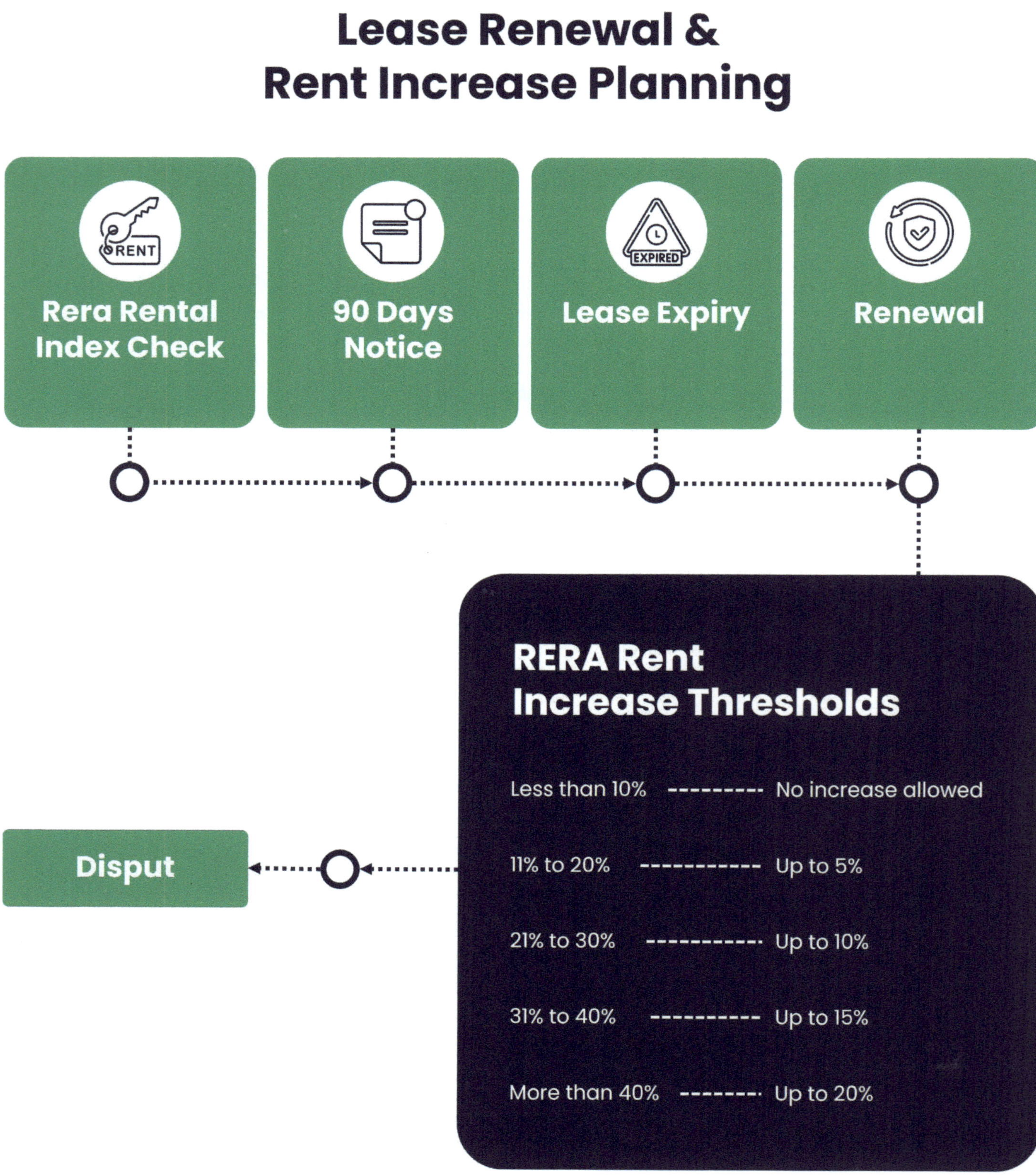

Table 13.12: RERA Rent Increase Thresholds

Difference from the Index Average	Allowed Increase
Less than 10%	No increase allowed
11% to 20%	Up to 5%
21% to 30%	Up to 10%
31% to 40%	Up to 15%
More than 40%	Up to 20%

These percentages apply only if your current rent is below the average by the indicated range.

13.6.3. 90-Day Notice Requirement

To legally increase the rent:

- You must give the tenant at least 90 days' written notice before the lease renewal date.
- The notice must be sent through registered mail, email (if acknowledged), or via the Ejari platform.

PRO TIP FOR LANDLORDS

Proactive Renewal Strategy: Don't just send a notice. Engage with your tenant 3-4 months before the lease expiry to gauge their intent to renew. For good tenants, consider offering a slight discount or covering a minor amenity to secure their renewal and avoid vacancy. This proactive approach minimises vacancy and ensures consistent income.

13.6.4. Disputes and the Rental Dispute Settlement Centre

If a tenant disagrees with the increase, they can file a complaint. The Rental Dispute Settlement Centre (RDSC) will assess your increase based on:

- Rental Index data.
- Property condition and features.
- Comparable listings.

> **PRO TIP FOR LANDLORDS**
>
> Use the Rental Index proactively—plan your increases well in advance, maintain accurate documentation, and ensure transparency. This helps avoid disputes and ensures your income aligns with market value.

13.7. How to Legally Evict a Tenant in Dubai

Vacating a tenant in Dubai isn't as simple as sending a notice—you must follow the legal framework outlined in Dubai Law No. 26 of 2007 and its amendments. Whether you're selling the property or reclaiming it for personal use, specific, strict rules and timelines must be adhered to.

Legal Grounds for Eviction (at Lease Expiry)

You may request to vacate a tenant only at the end of their lease, and only for these four legal reasons:

- You intend to sell the property.
- You or your first-degree relative intends to occupy the property.
- The property needs major renovations or demolition.
- The property is unsafe or uninhabitable.

For reasons 1 and 2, sale or personal use, you must provide a written 12-month eviction notice delivered via a notary public or registered courier. Failing to follow this process may render your eviction invalid, even if justified.

Strategic Tips for Landlords:

- **Plan Ahead:** If you're selling, notify the tenant early and start the 12-month clock even if you haven't listed the unit yet.
- **Document Everything:** Keep receipts of delivery and official notices in case of disputes.
- **Avoid Shortcuts:** Don't pressure tenants with informal notices—any disagreement will default to the Rental Dispute Settlement Centre (RDSC), which favours documented, lawful processes.
- **Negotiate Wisely:** In some cases, offering relocation support or a financial incentive for an early exit may be more effective than waiting 12 months.

PRO TIP

Always align eviction actions with the Ejari-registered lease timeline. You can't reset lease terms informally; Dubai considers the Ejari record as binding.

Initial Steps for Dispute Resolution: If a dispute arises that cannot be resolved amicably, the first official step is usually to open a case via the Dubai REST app or directly with the Rental Dispute Settlement Centre (RDSC). Ensure you have all your Ejari contracts, payment receipts, and communication records organised before initiating a claim.

Chapter Summary

Chapter 13, **"Renting It Right – Long-Term,"** is your essential guide to effectively transforming your property into a consistent, well-managed source of income in Dubai. It asserts that successful long-term renting goes beyond a simple listing, demanding strategic preparation, tenant selection, and adherence to legal frameworks.

The chapter began by highlighting **Pre-Leasing Prep**, guiding you through optimising your property, deciding between furnished or unfurnished strategies, and conducting a crucial formal "Move-In Condition Report" to safeguard against future disputes.

You then explored comprehensive **Listing, Marketing & Tenant Selection** strategies, from choosing between brokers and DIY platforms to creating high-impact listings and screening tenants using a methodical evaluation matrix. A key highlight was the introduction of **Professional Property Management Companies** as a valuable option for hands-off long-term rental management.

The chapter provided deep insights into **Rental Pricing, Payment Terms & Negotiation**, detailing how to leverage the RERA Smart Rental Index for competitive and compliant pricing, utilise flexible cheque structures, and navigate the nuances of rent finance platforms that allow tenants to pay in EMIs. You also learned the critical importance of explicitly clarifying **what's included in the rent** to prevent disputes.

Finally, the chapter armed you with vital knowledge on **Legal Documentation & Ejari Registration** (the cornerstone of enforceable leases), and provided clear guidance on **Lease Renewal and Rent Increase Planning**, ensuring compliance with RERA thresholds and notice periods. You also gained a thorough understanding of **how to Legally Evict a Tenant in Dubai**, including the strict legal grounds and mandatory 12-month notice requirements.

By mastering the principles and practicalities of long-term rental management outlined in this chapter, you are now fully equipped to confidently convert your property into a stable and resilient income-generating asset, maximising its long-term value in Dubai's dynamic market.

Key Takeaways:

- **Prepare Your Property:** Optimise your unit and conduct a formal Move-In Condition Report before leasing.
- **Screen Tenants:** Use a structured approach to select reliable tenants, as a bad tenant can cost more than vacancy.
- **Price Strategically:** Leverage the RERA Rental Index and market comparables for competitive and compliant pricing.
- **Understand Payment Terms:** Navigate cheque structures, rent finance platforms, and clearly define all inclusions in the lease.
- **Ejari is Non-Negotiable:** Register every lease with Ejari for legal enforceability and utility activation.
- **Master Lease Renewals & Evictions:** Adhere to RERA's strict rules for rent increases (90-day notice) and legal eviction (12-month notice, specific grounds).
- **Consider Professional Management:** For hands-off investing, a RERA-licensed property management company can streamline operations and enhance returns.
- **Document Everything:** Maintain records of all agreements, inspections, and communications to prevent disputes.

YOUR JOURNEY
NAVIGATOR

Part 3: Maximising Ownership Value

STEP 02

STEP 01

STEP 03

Recap

You have just completed **Chapter 13: Renting It Right: Long-Term**, where you learned how to prepare your property for leasing, market it effectively, select quality tenants, and manage legal requirements such as Ejari registration. You now understand how to maintain stable occupancy, optimise rent, and protect your property's condition through careful tenant management.

Next Chapter Preview

We now move into **high-yield territory. Chapter 14: Beyond the Lease: Maximising ROI with Short-Term Rentals** explores how to convert your property into a flexible, premium-earning asset. You will see how to operate legally within Dubai's short-term rental regulations, choose the right locations, and furnish and market for maximum revenue.

You Will Learn

- ☑ The performance drivers of Dubai's short-term rental market, including ADR and occupancy rates.
- ☑ Legal requirements and licensing under DTCM regulations.
- ☑ Location selection for short-term rental profitability.
- ☑ How to furnish and equip for guest appeal and ROI.
- ☑ Self-management vs. working with professional holiday home operators.
- ☑ Risk factors, cost structures, and pricing strategies.

Link to Framework

This chapter strengthens the **Value Creation** and **Adaptability** elements of your C.D.R.C. mindset, enabling you to pivot from steady long-term income to dynamic short-term gains when the market supports it. It supports your L.E.A.D. approach by showing how to **Drive Value** through premium nightly rates, **Embrace Calculated Risk** with seasonality in mind, and maintain your **Long Game** by balancing yield with occupancy.

Purpose / Big Picture Link

This is the **yield optimisation stage** of your investment journey. Mastering short-term rentals allows you to unlock higher returns from the same asset while retaining the flexibility to adapt to market cycles, tourism demand, and your own evolving investment strategy.

CHAPTER 14

Beyond the Lease: Maximising ROI with Short-Term Rentals

> Short-term rentals aren't just about maximising income, they're about maintaining agility. In Dubai's dynamic market, flexibility often translates into profit.

When most investors think about rental income, their minds go straight to the traditional 12-month lease. It's predictable, hands-off, and fits neatly into our mental models of property ownership. But if you're only thinking in terms of long-term rentals, you're leaving serious returns on the table.

Over the past few years in Dubai, I've watched a quiet revolution unfold in the short-term rental space. Platforms like Airbnb, Booking.com, and others have not only changed how tourists book their stays but also how investors generate income. What started as a side hustle for a few homeowners has now matured into a fully regulated, highly profitable real estate strategy. I've worked with clients who doubled their annual rental income by converting their units.

However, and this is crucial, short-term rentals are not suitable for everyone. They demand a higher upfront setup, consistent attention to detail, and a more thorough understanding of hospitality than you might expect. This chapter is designed to walk you through what's required, how the returns compare, the licensing rules, and the decision points you'll face. You don't need to become a hotel manager to succeed. But you do need to treat this like a business, with numbers, systems, and structure. If you're ready to go beyond the lease, let's explore how daily and holiday rentals can become a mighty pillar of your investment strategy.

14.1. Dubai's Short-Term Rental Landscape: Trends, Data, and Growth Drivers

A clear understanding of the short-term rental market begins with a close look at both the data and the trends that shape it.

14.1.1. ADR (Average Daily Rate)

Average Daily Rate (ADR) is a core metric in short-term rentals. It calculates the average revenue earned per occupied room or unit per day. This is typically derived by dividing the total revenue (from base rates and cleaning fees, but excluding taxes and platform service fees) by the number of nights the property was booked. This figure is crucial for investors because it directly reflects the earning power of a rental unit on a nightly basis, helping them assess pricing strategies, benchmark against similar properties, and identify seasonal demand trends. A higher ADR typically signals greater profitability, provided occupancy rates are also strong, making it a key indicator for evaluating the potential returns and financial performance of short-term rental investments.

14.1.2. Occupancy Rates

The occupancy rate refers to the percentage of days your property is booked out of the total number of days it's available for rent. In short-term rentals, this is one of the core metrics that determines your earning potential. A consistently high occupancy rate means your unit is in high demand and generating a steady income. However, it's not just about how often your property is booked; it's also about understanding seasonal patterns. Dubai's off-peak season, typically June to September, is marked by extreme heat, leading to a dip in tourism and corporate travel. During these months, demand softens, and many operators adjust pricing, implement discounts, or offer extended stay deals to maintain bookings. Understanding this seasonal rhythm is crucial when planning your investment: it affects not only your income cycle but also your furnishing strategy, marketing efforts, and cash flow buffer planning. Savvy investors use the high season to maximise revenue and the low season to refresh listings, do maintenance, or reposition their offering.

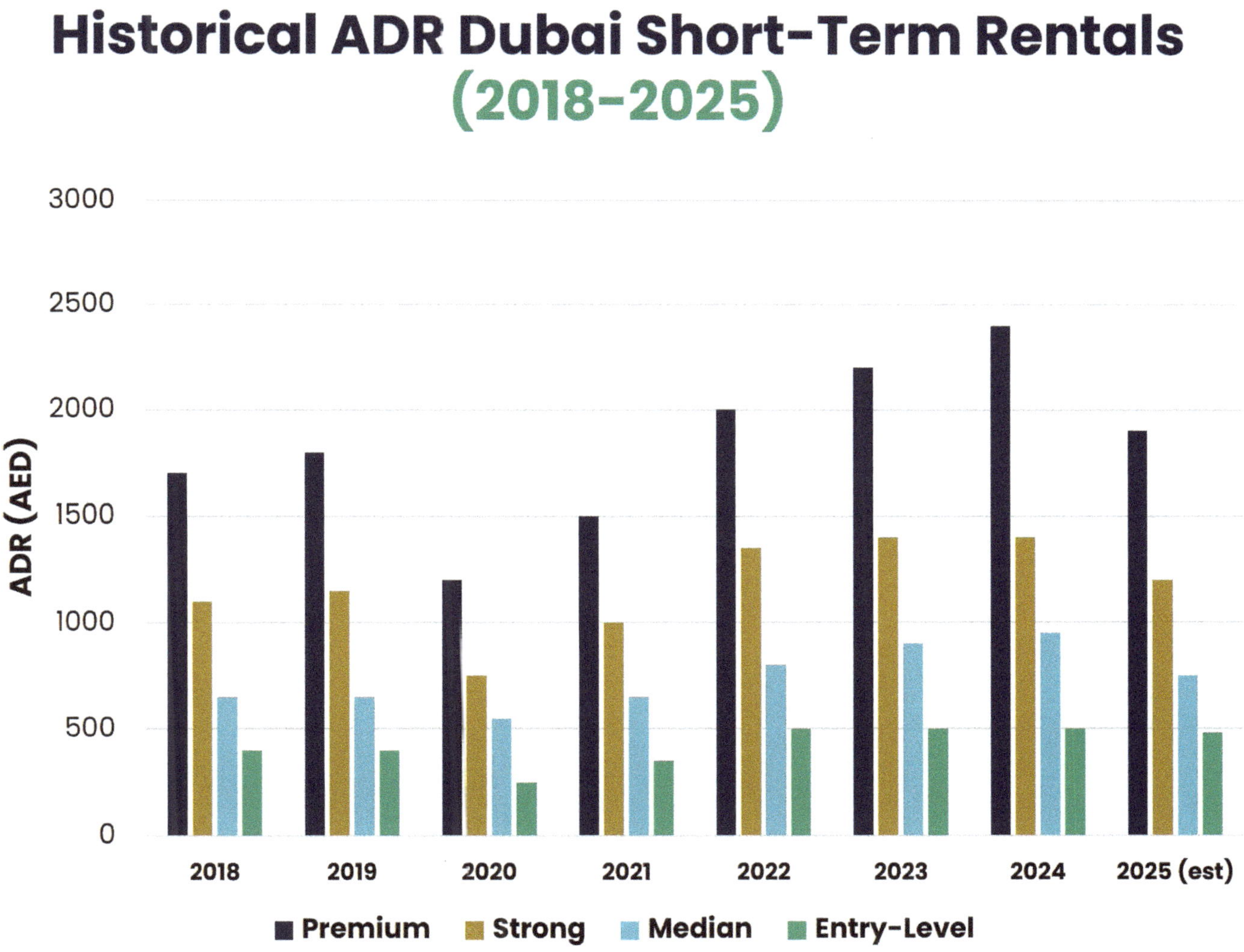

Historical ADR Dubai Short-Term Rentals (2018-2025)

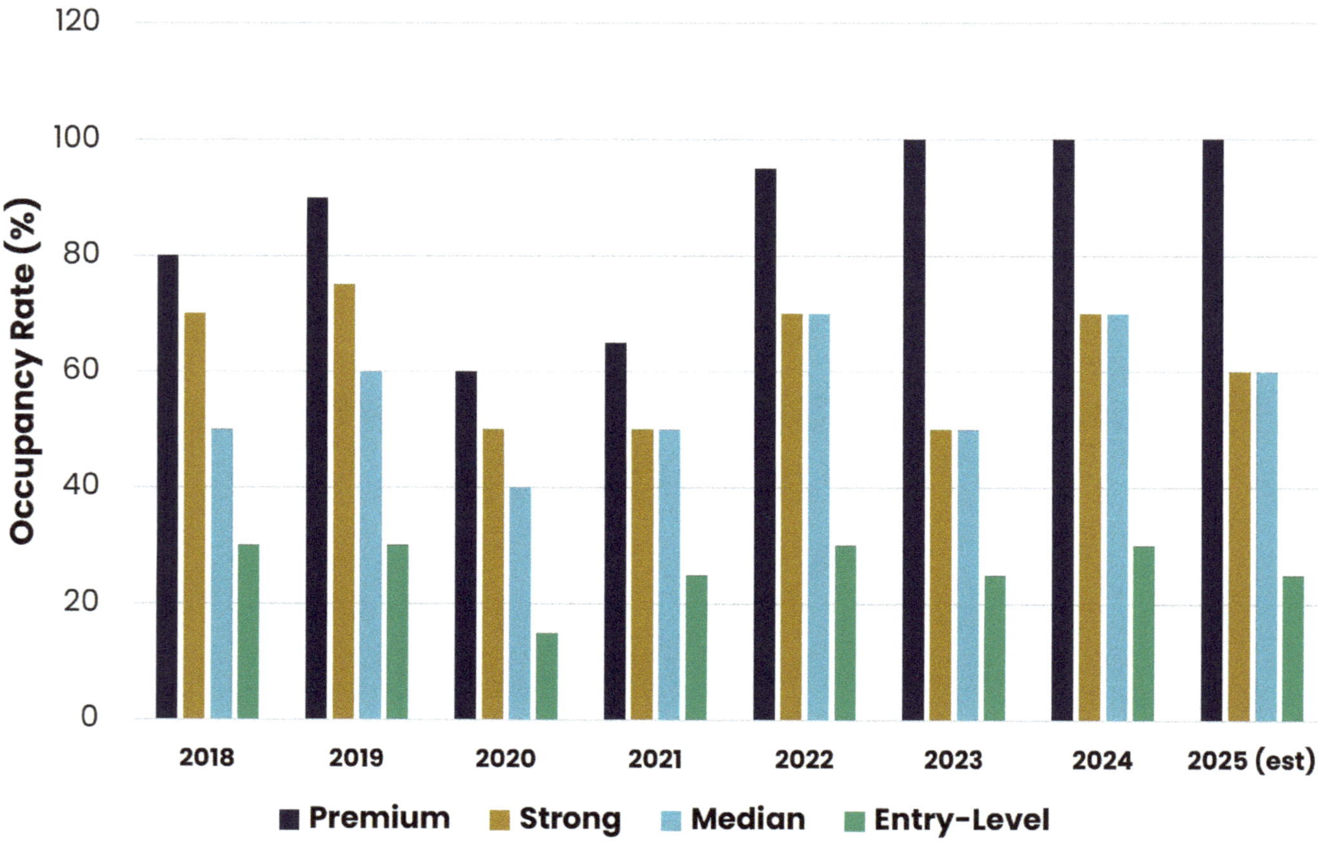

- **Premium (Top 10%):** Consistently highest occupancy, especially in prime locations and during peak season.
- **Strong (Top 25%):** Well-managed, desirable areas, above-market performance.
- **Median:** Typical market property, standard amenities.
- **Entry-Level (Bottom 25%):** Budget, basic, less central. Most affected by market competition and seasonality.

14.1.3. Key Insights: ADR and Occupancy Rates in Dubai Short-Term Rentals (2018–2025)

- **Premium Segments Consistently Outperform:** Premium properties (in the top 10%) have consistently maintained the highest Average Daily Rates (ADR) and occupancy rates throughout the years, even during market downturns.
- **Market Resilience and Recovery:** Both ADR and occupancy rates experienced a sharp decline in 2020 due to the pandemic, with ADRs dropping across all segments and occupancy rates falling to as low as 18% for entry-level properties. The market rebounded strongly in 2021–2022, particularly in premium and high-end segments, driven by Expo 2020 and a surge in tourism. By 2022, premium ADRs reached AED 2,000, and occupancy rates climbed back to 85% or higher.
- **Segmentation Matters:** Strong (top 25%) and median properties also saw significant recovery post-pandemic, but the gap between premium and lower segments widened. In 2025, strong segment ADRs are above AED 1,161, with occupancy rates exceeding 74%. Meanwhile, median properties average AED 731 and have occupancy rates of 49–71%. Entry-level properties (bottom 25%) consistently lag, with ADRs around AED 455 and occupancy rates as low as 23% in 2025, reflecting greater vulnerability to competition and seasonality.
- **Strategic Takeaway:** Premium and strong segment properties offer the best combination of high ADR and occupancy, making them attractive for investors seeking stable, high returns. Median and entry-level properties require careful pricing and marketing strategies to remain competitive, particularly during off-peak periods. Understanding these segmented trends enables more accurate forecasting, risk management, and investment planning in Dubai's dynamic short-term rental market.

14.2. Understanding the Short-Term Rental Model

Short-term rentals are furnished residential properties, usually apartments or villas, leased for periods ranging from one night to six months. Guests are typically tourists, business travellers, digital nomads, or even residents between leases. Unlike traditional long-term rentals, short-term units must be:

- Fully furnished.
- Licensed as a holiday home by DTCM (Dubai Tourism).
- Compliant with hospitality regulations (safety, cleanliness, and guest support). Platforms like Airbnb, Booking.com, and others provide the marketplace for these units.

When you're deciding how to lease your property, it's tempting to assume that long-term is the "safer" route. After all, a 12-month lease feels predictable; the tenant moves in, pays monthly, and there's minimal fuss. But what I've learned, and what many successful investors in Dubai have discovered, is that predictable doesn't always mean profitable.

Short-term rentals flip that script. They're more dynamic, more involved, and yes, more demanding—but they can also generate significantly higher income and give you better control over your assets. On the other hand, long-term leases offer peace of mind, simplicity, and lower hands-on involvement. It isn't just about choosing one over the other—it's about understanding the real trade-offs so you can match the strategy to your goals. Are you seeking passive income with minimal management? Or do you want to maximise yield, even if it means treating your unit more like a micro-hospitality business? Let's break it down side by side.

One of the most under-discussed benefits of holiday rentals is the flexibility of exit. When you lease a unit long-term, it's often locked for 12 months. If you want to sell the property, you must: wait for the lease expiry, sell with a tenant in place (which usually means lower buyer interest), or negotiate a buyout.

With a short-term rental:

- You can block your calendar and show the unit anytime.
- You can sell as vacant possession, increasing the resale value.
- You remain in complete control of the asset. This makes short-term rentals ideal for investors who may flip, upgrade, or cash out early, especially in Dubai's fluid off-plan resale market.

INVESTOR INSIGHT

Vacant vs. Tenanted Sale Premium: Properties sold vacant typically fetch a 5% to 10% higher price in Dubai's secondary market compared to those sold with an existing tenant. That's because end-users and many investors prefer immediate possession and flexibility. A short-term rental strategy gives you an edge; you can sell your unit vacant at market peak without needing eviction notice periods or waiting out tenancy contracts. This agility often translates to faster transactions and higher resale value.

Long-Term Vs. Short-Term Rentals:
A Side-By-Side View

Factor	Long-Term Rental	Short-Term Rental
Income Potential	Moderate Yield, predictable	High yield, variable
Management Effort	Low to moderate	High (requires active guest management)
Vacancy Risk	Lower (Longer Leases)	Higher (seasonal fluctuations)
Upfront costs	Low (Basic repairs, sometimes unfurnished)	High (Furnishing, licensing)
Liquidity / Exit Flex	Low (12-month notice for eviction)	High (can block calendar for sale)
Regulatory	RERA & Ejari (Landlord /tenant disputes)	DTCM (Department of Tourism & Commerce Marketing) & Hospitality Standards

14.3. Legal Requirements and Licensing: Navigating DTCM Rules

When it comes to short-term rentals in Dubai, the rules aren't optional; they're the foundation of a compliant, profitable business. The good news? Dubai's government has embraced holiday rentals as a legitimate asset class. The Department of Tourism and Commerce Marketing (DTCM) has introduced transparent and investor-friendly licensing processes. But that doesn't mean you can list your apartment on Airbnb overnight. You need to register your unit, pay licensing fees, and meet furnishing and operational standards. These steps may seem tedious at first, but they protect your investment, ensuring your unit competes on equal footing with others in the regulated market. And if you're using a holiday home operator, you still carry responsibility, so it's essential to know what they're supposed to handle on your behalf.

In this section, we'll walk you through:

- The types of licenses (individual vs. professional).
- Registration requirements and timelines.
- Ongoing compliance, inspections, and guest documentation.
- Penalties for unlicensed listings. Mastering this process ensures that your holiday rental journey starts on the right foot, with confidence, compliance, and control.

14.3.1. Individual vs. Professional License

In Dubai, all short-term rental activity is regulated by the Department of Tourism and Commerce Marketing (DTCM). To legally list a property on platforms like Airbnb, Booking.com, or Vrbo, you must obtain a holiday home license, either as an individual or through a licensed operator.

Table 14.1: Individual vs. Professional Holiday Home License

License Type	Who's It For	Key Features
Individual License	Property owners managing 1–8 units	You are responsible for compliance, guest check-in, cleaning, and maintenance
Professional License	Operators managing multiple properties	Must register a trade licence; can manage units on behalf of others

INVESTOR TIP

If you want to retain control and manage directly, an individual license is the best option. If you prefer a hands-off approach, work with a DTCM-approved holiday home operator.

14.3.2. License Registration Process

To apply for an individual holiday home license, here's what you'll need:

- **Title Deed or Tenancy Contract:** If you're the owner, submit your title deed. If you're a tenant (subletting with permission), provide the tenancy contract and NOC from the landlord.
- **Emirates ID or Passport Copy:** Required for all applicants (UAE residents and non-residents).
- **Furnished Unit:** You must furnish it to meet the standards listed in the DTCM checklist (e.g., linens, fire extinguisher, safety features).
- **Register on DTCM's Holiday Home Portal:** Upload documents, pay the licensing fee (~AED 1,500 per unit), and complete the classification form.
- **Obtain a Tourism Dirham Certificate:** This enables you to collect and remit the nightly tourism tax (AED 10–15 per night, depending on unit type).
- **Annual Renewal:** The license is valid for one year and must be renewed with updated documents and a new classification.

Table 14.2: Holiday Home License Registration - Step-by-Step

Step / Requirement	Details / Notes
Title Deed or Tenancy Contract	Owners submit title deed; tenants submit tenancy contract + NOC from landlord. Proof of ownership or authorised subletting required.
Emirates ID or Passport Copy	Needed for both UAE residents and non-residents. Valid identification for all applicants.
Unit Classification & Furnishing Standards	Property rated as Standard or Deluxe based on amenities, décor, and location. You must furnish it to meet DTCM standards (e.g., linens, fire extinguisher, safety features).
Register on the DTCM Holiday Home Portal	Upload all documents, pay licensing fee (~AED 1,500 per unit), and complete the classification form. Online process via DET/DTCM portal.
Obtain Tourism Dirham Certificate	Enables collection/remittance of nightly tourism tax (AED 10–15 per night, per unit). Required for legal operation and guest compliance.
Annual Renewal	The license is valid for 1 year; it must be renewed with updated documents and classification. Renewal ensures continued compliance and legality of operation.

- All properties must comply with DTCM/DET health, safety, and furnishing standards.
- Each property/unit requires a separate license and fee.
- Tenants can only register one unit (with landlord approval); owners can register up to eight units without a trade license.

14.3.3. If Using a Holiday Home Operator

A DTCM-approved holiday home company will:

- Hold a professional operator's license.
- Register your unit under their name.
- Handle licensing, documentation, furnishing compliance, and guest relations.
- Charge a management fee (typically 15–25% of gross revenue).
- Often bundle photography, platform listings, guest support, and cleaning. However, remember that the liability still rests with you as the property owner. Ensure the operator provides transparency, monthly statements, and DTCM compliance.

14.3.4. Penalties for Non-Compliance

Operating without a DTCM license or violating the regulations can lead to:

Table 14.3: Penalties for Non-Compliance

Violation	Penalty
Unlicensed short-term rental	AED 5,000–50,000 fine
Failing safety or furnishing standards	Up to AED 10,000
Not collecting/remitting Tourism Dirham	Financial penalty + blacklisting from operating short-term rentals

14.4. Location Matters: Where Short-Term Rentals Work Best in Dubai

When it comes to short-term rentals, location isn't just important; it's everything. Unlike long-term leases, which rely on year-round livability and proximity to workplaces or schools, holiday rentals are driven by convenience, scenic views, tourism demand, and seasonal foot traffic. I've seen two nearly identical apartments, same size, same furnishing, generate drastically different income, simply because one was a 10-minute walk from the metro and next to a mall, while the other wasn't.

Here's what you need to look for when choosing a location for short-term rentals in Dubai:

14.4.1. High-Demand Tourist Zones

These are the areas where you're most likely to attract consistent holiday bookings, especially from tourists, business travellers, and digital nomads:

Table 14.4: High-Demand Tourist Zones for Short-Term Rentals

Area	Why It Works
Dubai Marina	Walkable, near the beach, nightlife, Marina Walk
Downtown Dubai	Burj Khalifa, Dubai Mall and Trade Centre. Key area for Events and Tourism.
Palm Jumeirah	Resort feel, beach access, exclusive
Business Bay	Central business hub, canal views, executive travellers
JBR	Beachfront access, family-friendly, and entertainment
City Walk	Upscale lifestyle, dining, and entertainment

Dubai STR Hotspots:
Where Agility Meets Demand
High-Demand Tourist Zones for Short-Term Rentals
1. Dubai Marina
2. Downtown
3. Palm Jumeirah
4. Business Bay
5. City Walk / Al wasl
Growth Driver Areas for Short-Term Rentals
1. JVC
2. Dubai Hills Estate
3. Arjan / Al Barsha South
4. Dubai South / Emaar South

14.4.2. Growth Driver Areas

These areas may not always attract the top tourist premium, but work well for extended stays, medical tourism, or corporate relocations due to upcoming infrastructure and growth catalysts.

Table 14.5: Growth Driver Areas for Short-Term Rentals

Area	Growth Driver
JVC (Jumeirah Village Circle)	Affordable units, high ROI, easy access to the Expo corridor
Dubai Hills Estate	New malls, parks, upscale developments
Arjan / Al Barsha South	Proximity to the Miracle Garden and the Mall of Emirates
Dubai South / Emaar South	Expo City expansion, future airport hub

14.4.3. Oversupply Warning

Some areas suffer from oversupply, especially where developers have flooded the market with nearly identical units.

Use AirROI or AirDNA to check (AirROI has better Dubai-specific data):

- Number of existing short-term listings.
- Occupancy rates.
- Average daily rates (ADR). You can also check Airbnb and Booking.com for listings in the target community and monitor over time to understand the trends. Areas with high vacancy and low ADRs might appear attractive, but could struggle to stay profitable year-round.

14.5. Furnishing for Success: What's Required and What Adds ROI

In the world of short-term rentals, furnishing isn't optional—it's your product. Unlike long-term tenants who bring their furniture, holiday home guests expect a turn-key, hotel-grade experience. This makes furnishing not just a setup task, but a strategic investment that directly impacts your income.

14.5.1. Minimum Legal Requirements (DTCM Standards)

To legally operate a short-term rental in Dubai, your unit must meet Dubai Tourism's (DTCM) standards for furnishing and amenities. These include:

- Beds, linens, pillows, blackout curtains.
- Sofas and seating in the living area.
- Dining table and chairs.
- Fully equipped kitchen (fridge, stove, microwave, utensils, crockery).
- Wi-Fi and TV.
- Air-conditioning and adequate lighting.
- Wardrobes or clothing storage.
- Safety equipment (fire extinguisher, smoke detector).

TIP

Units are graded by DTCM as "Standard" or "Deluxe" depending on size, furnishing quality, amenities, and building classification. Deluxe properties can charge higher rates but must meet stricter criteria.

14.5.2. Standard vs. Deluxe: How DTCM Classifies Holiday Homes

When you register your property as a holiday home with the DTCM (Dubai Tourism and Commerce Marketing), it must be classified as either Standard or Deluxe. This classification impacts your nightly Tourism Dirham fees and your ability to charge higher rates.

What Defines "Standard" vs. "Deluxe"?

- **Standard Holiday Home:** Must meet the basic furnishing and amenity requirements (e.g., quality furniture, fully equipped kitchen, air-conditioning, safety features). Ideal for mid-range travellers seeking comfort and convenience without the luxury price tag. Dirham fee: AED 10 per room, per night.
- **Deluxe Holiday Home:** Must exceed standard requirements: high-end décor, premium linens, extra amenities (e.g., espresso machine, smart TVs, designer furnishings). Targeted at discerning guests expecting elevated standards. Dirham fee: AED 15 per room, per night.

Property inspectors evaluate your unit based on whether it meets "Standard" comfort levels or exceeds "Deluxe" quality, which then determines your nightly fee and potential rate.

Key Benefits of Classification:

- **Higher Revenue Potential:** A Deluxe rating justifies ~5–15% higher nightly rates and attracts higher-paying guests.
- **Transparent Pricing:** Guests know exactly what to expect, which is essential for building trust and ratings.
- **Compliance & Positioning:** Proper classification ensures compliance with DTCM rules and accurate placement in a competitive segment.

INVESTOR INSIGHT

If you're targeting premium guests and seeking to maximise nightly income, invest in top-tier furnishings and décor. A Deluxe classification often pays for itself in accelerated rate gains.

PRO TIP

Strategic Classification: When furnishing, consider your target nightly rate. If you aim for a premium, ensure your furnishing quality pushes your unit into the 'Deluxe' category to justify higher rates and maximise your ROI.

14.5.3. ROI-Boosting Additions

If you want your listing to stand out and command a premium, consider these enhancements:

Furnishing For Profit – What Adds ROI

Icon	Furnishing Item / Upgrade	ROI Impact
	High-quality linens & towels	Better guest reviews, repeat bookings
	Stylish décor & artwork	Better photos = higher click-through
	Smart TVS & streaming access	Modern guest expectations
	Coffee machine / Kettle / Welcome tray	Hospitality touch = higher ratings
	Work desk / chair	Attracts digital nomads & business travelers
	Full blackout curtains	Essential for guest comfort
	Outdoor furniture (if balcony present)	Expands usable space
	Full-length mirror	Surprisingly high guest priority

INVESTOR TIP

Well-furnished units can justify 10–25% higher nightly rates and significantly boost occupancy. In contrast, a poorly furnished unit, even in a great location, will underperform.

Table 14.6: Approximate Furnishing Cost Breakdown (1BR Unit)

Category	Burget Range (AED)
Furniture (bed, sofa, table, chairs)	10,000–15,000
Appliances & kitchenware	3,000–6,000
Décor, curtains, rugs	2,000–4,000
Electronics (TV, Wi-Fi router)	2,000–3,500
Bedding, linens, extras	1,500–2,500
Total Setup Cost	**AED 18,500–31,000**

14.6. Insurance Essentials for Short-Term Rentals

According to the holiday home permit guidelines, insurance is required by law. Whether you're operating yourself or through an operator, the Department of Economy & Tourism (formerly DTCM) mandates a comprehensive insurance policy covering:

- Guest Injuries & Public Liability – protection in case a guest is hurt or causes damage to others.
- Property & Building Damage – coverage for damage to your unit or the building structure.
- Contents Insurance – protection for furniture, appliances, linens, and decor.

Airbnb Host Protection Is Not Enough: Platforms like Airbnb offer some host protections, but typically don't cover structural damage, content loss, or liability beyond base-level coverage. You're still responsible for complete legal and financial protection.

Investor Insight — Why It Matters:

- **Protect Your Investment:** Furnished holiday homes face high guest turnover, and wear-and-tear cover alone won't protect against everything.
- **Stay Compliant:** No insurance = no holiday home permit. Without it, DTCM can suspend your listing and impose fines.
- **Peace of Mind When Hosting Yourself or via an Operator:** Whether you're hands-on or handing over to a professional, insurance ensures you're covered in emergencies, saving you time, money, and legal trouble.

PRO TIP

Short-Term Rental Security Deposits: For self-managed short-term rentals, guests typically pay a refundable security deposit through the booking platform (e.g., Airbnb's security hold). This is not collected directly by the landlord but is managed by the platform to cover damages. Understand the platform's policy for claims and deductions.

14.7. Managing Short-Term Rentals Yourself: DIY Hosting

If you're the kind of investor who likes control, has an eye for detail, and doesn't mind rolling up your sleeves, managing your holiday home yourself can be both profitable and empowering. You eliminate third-party operator fees and stay directly in touch with your guests and your property, building both income and experience.

But make no mistake, DIY hosting is not passive income. From responding to guest inquiries at odd hours to coordinating check-ins, cleaning, and restocking after every stay, it demands consistent attention. The good news is that Dubai's regulatory environment, along with platforms like Airbnb, Booking.com, and Guesty, makes it easier than ever to self-manage if you're prepared.

In this section, I'll walk you through the practical realities of self-management, from the tools you'll need to common mistakes to avoid. Whether you're trying it out for one unit or planning to scale a personally managed portfolio, this guide will help you approach it like a business, not a side hustle.

14.7.1. What DIY Hosting Means

Managing a short-term rental yourself, what we call DIY hosting, is not just about saving money on management fees; it's also about gaining control over your property. It's a conscious decision to take ownership of the entire guest experience, from the first inquiry to the final review. It means you're not just a property owner, you're also the host, the operations manager, the scheduler of cleaners, and the lead of customer service.

14.7.2. Day-to-Day Realities of DIY Hosting

When you decide to self-manage your short-term rental, you're not just listing a property; you're managing a guest-facing business with moving parts. Here's what your day-to-day or week-to-week responsibilities might look like:

- **Guest Communication:** You'll be responsible for handling all guest inquiries, including pre-booking questions, check-in instructions, issues during the stay, and post-stay reviews. Fast, friendly, and informative communication is key to getting 5-star reviews.
- **Housekeeping and Turnovers:** Between every guest, the unit must be thoroughly cleaned, restocked, and reset. Many DIY hosts build a reliable relationship with a freelance or agency cleaner, but you are still responsible for coordination.
- **Pricing Management:** Regularly adjust nightly rates based on demand, set minimum stay durations, block dates for maintenance or personal use, and monitor competitors in your building or community.
- **Tech Platform Oversight:** Managing listings on Airbnb, Booking.com, or other platforms means regularly updating photos, calendar availability, guest reviews, and compliance settings. Many successful DIY hosts utilise channel managers to synchronise bookings and prevent double bookings.
- **Maintenance and Guest Emergencies:** From broken faucets to A/C issues, you'll be the first call. Even if you outsource the actual repair, coordination is still your responsibility. This also includes preventive maintenance to avoid guest complaints.

14.7.3. Tech Tools for DIY Hosts

Successful DIY hosts treat their units like a micro-business: automated, trackable, and guest-friendly. Here's how to do the same.

- **Channel Managers:** If you're listing your unit on multiple platforms (such as Airbnb, Booking.com, and Vrbo), a channel manager helps synchronise your calendar, pricing, and availability in real-time, preventing double bookings and reducing the need for manual updates.
  - **Popular Tools:** Hostaway, Guesty for Hosts, Lodgify, Smoobu.
  - These platforms also allow you to centralise communication, automate pricing rules, and integrate with cleaning schedules.
- **Cleaning and Turnover Apps:** Coordinating cleaning is one of the most time-sensitive tasks. A missed or delayed turnover can ruin your listing reputation. Apps and shared checklists keep your cleaning crew accountable and ensure consistency.
  - **Examples:** Properly (visual checklists for cleaners), TurnoverBnB (auto-scheduling based on bookings).
- **Automated Guest Communication:** Speed and clarity matter to guests. Automation platforms allow you to send pre-set replies for bookings, check-ins, reminders, and thank-you messages.
  - **Tools to Consider:** Hospitable, Smartbnb, Airbnb's built-in messaging tools.
- **Smart Locks and Entry Systems:** Eliminate the need for physical presence during check-ins. Smart locks or lockboxes enable 24/7 self-check-in, making life easier for both hosts and guests.
  - **Common Options:** Yale or August smart locks, Igloohome or KeyNest lockboxes, integration with Airbnb for code auto-generation.
- Financial Tracking and ROI Management: DIY hosts must track earnings, expenses, and returns for long-term success.
  - **What to Track:** Gross revenue, operating costs (cleaning, supplies, platform fees), occupancy rates and ADR.
  - **Tools:** Excel or Google Sheets, Stessa (rental financial tracking), QuickBooks for rental income categorisation.

14.7.4. When DIY Doesn't Work: Knowing Your Limits

Self-managing your short-term rental can be empowering, but it's not for everyone. At some point, you may realise that the time, energy, or emotional bandwidth required to juggle everything outweighs the savings. Recognising your limits early helps avoid burnout, negative reviews, and costly mistakes.

Red Flags That DIY May Not Be Right for You:

- **You Live Abroad or Travel Frequently:** Even with automation, guests expect quick responses and local problem-solving. Time zone differences and physical distance can delay critical issues, such as maintenance or guest lockouts.
- **You Struggle With Hospitality Demands:** Managing guest expectations is not just about fixing things; it's about creating memorable stays. If you find it draining to deal with complaints, last-minute requests, or feedback, outsourcing may be a more strategic option.
- **Performance is Suffering:** Poor guest reviews are affecting your rating; you're seeing increased wear and tear from delayed maintenance; or you're experiencing personal stress and decreased overall returns.

INVESTOR INSIGHT

"Managing a short-term rental yourself works well, until it doesn't. The smart investor knows when to delegate to protect time, sanity, and guest experience."

14.8. Working with Holiday Home Operators: Pros, Cons, and Fees

When you're ready to take a more hands-off approach or simply want professional-grade service, it's time to consider partnering with a licensed holiday home operator. These are companies authorised by Dubai's Department of Economy and Tourism (DET) to manage short-term rentals on behalf of owners.

As the short-term rental market matures, professional operators have become a vital part of the ecosystem. They handle everything from guest communication to pricing algorithms, professional photography, furnishing, and even 24/7 guest support. For many investors, they offer the ideal middle ground between profitability and peace of mind.

14.8.1. What Holiday Home Operators Do

If you've ever stayed in a professionally managed Airbnb and noticed how seamless everything felt, from check-in to the towels folded just right, you've likely experienced the work of a holiday home operator. In Dubai, short-term rentals are no longer a casual side hustle. They're a regulated business. And if you're not planning to manage every aspect yourself, partnering with a licensed holiday home operator is your gateway into this space.

At their core, holiday home operators act as your property manager, concierge, marketer, and compliance officer, rolled into one. Their job is to keep your unit booked, reviewed well, and maintained, all while ensuring you remain compliant with DTCM regulations.

Here's what a good operator typically handles:

- **Licensing & Registration:** They take care of your unit's annual short-term rental permit through DTCM (Dubai Tourism & Commerce Marketing), including category classification (Standard, Deluxe, etc.), renewals, and fee payments.
- **Listing & Pricing:** They create and optimise listings on Airbnb, Booking.com, and other platforms. Using dynamic pricing tools, they adjust nightly rates based on seasonality, events, and occupancy trends, similar to a hotel.
- **Guest Communication & Support:** From inquiry to checkout, operators handle all guest messages, reviews, emergency support, and even deposit disputes. A 24/7 guest line is standard for reputable operators.
- **Housekeeping & Turnover:** They arrange professional cleaning, linen change, toiletries, and restocking between stays. This is one of the most critical areas for guest satisfaction and 5-star reviews.
- **Maintenance Oversight:** Operators manage minor repairs, routine inspections, and report any significant issues to you with repair quotes. Some even have in-house teams.
- **Revenue & Analytics Reporting:** Monthly statements, performance dashboards, and occupancy trends are shared with you regularly. The best operators provide a live analytics portal or app, so you're never in the dark.

INVESTOR INSIGHT

Holiday home operators are not just service providers; they are your business partners. Choosing the right one can mean the difference between 12% and 5% annual ROI.

14.8.2. How to Select the Right Holiday Home Operator

Choosing the right holiday home operator isn't about finding the cheapest option; it's about finding a partner who will protect your asset, maximise your revenue, and deliver a five-star guest experience consistently. You're handing them the keys, quite literally, to your income stream. Here are some points on choosing, evaluating, and finding the right operator.

1. Experience, Licensing, and Reputation

First, make sure the operator is licensed by Dubai Tourism (DTCM) and has experience managing units in your specific area or building. A well-rated studio in Downtown is not the same as a 3-bedroom townhouse in Damac Hills 2.

Ask:

- Are you licensed for short-term rental management in Dubai?
- How many properties do you currently manage, and where?
- Can you share references or owner testimonials?

2. Services Offered and Technology Tools

Top-tier operators offer a full stack: listing optimisation, dynamic pricing, automated calendar syncing, housekeeping, guest support, and performance analytics.

Look for:

- A live owner dashboard or app showing bookings, revenue, and reviews.
- Integration with major OTAs (Airbnb, Booking.com, Expedia).
- Dynamic pricing algorithms, not just fixed monthly rates.
- 24/7 guest communication and emergency handling.

Ask:

- Do I get real-time access to my unit's performance?
- How do you optimise pricing and adjust for seasonality?

3. Fee Structures and Inclusions

Operator fees can range from 15% to 30% of gross revenue, depending on service scope and location. Some operators include cleaning, linens, and DTCM permit costs; others bill these separately.

Ask:

- Is the cleaning fee passed on to the guest or charged to me?
- What's included in your commission, and what's extra?
- Are maintenance visits, linen changes, and DTCM permits included in the service?

Compare net payout, not just percentage. A less expensive operator that underperforms may result in more missed bookings.

4. Contract Terms and Exit Clauses

Always read the fine print. Some operators lock you in for 12 months with high early termination fees. Others offer more flexible 3- to 6-month options with performance guarantees.

Ask:

- What's the minimum contract period?
- How do I exit if I want to sell or take over management?
- Are there penalties for poor performance or guest complaints?

5. Alignment With Your Goals

Not every operator fits every investor. If your goal is to sell in 12 months, choose someone who understands exit positioning. If your property is high-end, you'll want a brand with a luxury portfolio, not just someone focused on budget travellers.

INVESTOR TIP

Test the operator as a guest. Book one of their listings anonymously. Check the cleanliness, communication, and experience firsthand.

14.9. Costs and Risks: Upfront, Ongoing, and Market Challenges

If you're planning to rent your property as a short-term or holiday home in Dubai, it's easy to get swept up in the excitement of high nightly rates and Instagram-worthy interiors. But before the income rolls in, you need to understand the whole cost structure—both upfront and ongoing. Unlike traditional long-term leasing, short-term rentals operate more like a business than a passive investment. And companies have setup costs, operating expenses, and margin risks. This section also covers the unique risk factors you must prepare for, whether you self-manage or use an operator.

14.9.1. Upfront Costs: The Investment to Get Started

Short-term rental properties must be fully furnished to a livable, often stylish standard, down to linens, cutlery, and Wi-Fi routers. That means your property needs to feel like a home or hotel from day one. These are the significant setup costs you'll likely encounter:

- **Furniture and Appliances:** AED 25,000–60,000 depending on size, furnishing quality, and whether it's a studio or 2-bedroom unit. Essentials include beds, sofas, a dining set, kitchenware, a washing machine, a fridge, and TVs.
- **Interior Styling and Decor:** Aesthetic matters. Adding soft furnishings, artwork, and lighting can enhance your photos and increase your nightly rate. Budget AED 3,000–10,000 for styling.
- **Photography and Listing Setup:** Professional photos, optimised descriptions, and platform setup (Airbnb, Booking.com, etc.) typically cost AED 1,000–2,000 if outsourced.
- **DTCM Holiday Home Permit:** AED 1,520 for individual landlords; varies if you're going through an operator.
- **Initial Deep Cleaning and Stocking: AED 500–800 for comprehensive unit sanitation, including towels, linens, starter toiletries, and** pantry essentials.
- **Insurance:** Holiday home or landlord insurance is strongly recommended. Expect to pay AED 500–1,500 per year, depending on the coverage.

14.9.2. Ongoing Monthly and Per-Booking Expenses

Once your unit is live, operational expenses become a recurring part of your business model. These need to be factored into your ROI calculations:

- **Cleaning and Turnover:** AED 100–250 per guest change, including linens and restocking.
- **Maintenance and Repairs:** A monthly provision for wear and tear, AC servicing, and plumbing issues, estimated at 5–10% of monthly revenue.
- **Platform Fees:** Airbnb takes 3–15% of the booking amount, depending on whether you're a host-only or opt into their full-service platform.
- **Utility Bills (DEWA, Internet, Gas):** AED 300–800 monthly, depending on usage and unit size. Unlike long-term rentals, utilities are typically the responsibility of the landlord or passed through to the guest via charges.
- **Holiday Home Operator Fee (if used):** Typically 15–30% of gross income.
- **Tourism Dirham Fee:** Charged to guests (AED 10–15 per night) but may need to be collected and reported by you or your operator.
- **Annual Permit Renewal and Compliance Costs:** Include annual permit renewal (AED 1,520) and documentation submissions.

CALLOUT

Budget Before You Begin: Too many first-time short-term investors underestimate setup and running costs, only to find themselves frustrated by thin margins or cash flow gaps. Create a detailed cost sheet and conservatively estimate that 25–35% of your gross income will go toward operating expenses.

14.9.3. Risk Factors: Navigating Seasonality, Maintenance, and Management Challenges

Short-term rentals in Dubai can offer lucrative returns, flexibility, and asset control, but they come with a different risk profile compared to traditional long-term leasing. This section walks you through the major risk factors you must prepare for so you can make informed, resilient decisions.

1. Seasonality: The Rollercoaster of Demand

Dubai is a global city with a high influx of tourists, but that doesn't mean demand is consistent throughout the year. The peak season generally runs from October to April, when the weather is ideal, major events (such as Art Dubai, Expo Legacy events, GITEX, and the Dubai Shopping Festival) attract tourists, and global holiday schedules align. The off-peak season, mainly from June to September, sees a significant drop in short-term rental demand due to the intense summer heat and school vacations, both locally and internationally. During these months, investors may:

- See occupancy rates drop.
- Be forced to lower nightly rates.
- Consider longer minimum stays to reduce turnover costs.
- Explore medium-term rentals or temporary offers.

INVESTOR INSIGHT

A successful short-term rental strategy isn't built only on peak rates. It's about effective management during the entire year, including the low season, to ensure consistent profitability.

2. Maintenance and Management Burden

Unlike long-term leasing, where the tenant handles most day-to-day usage, short-term rentals require active operational management. If you're managing yourself, expect to: handle guest communication, check-ins, and check-outs; solve issues on short notice (e.g., power outages, AC failure); and coordinate cleaning and restocking. If you opt for a holiday home operator, their fees will reduce your income, but they handle most of the operational burden. Regardless of the route, the time and attention required must be weighed against your ROI expectations.

INVESTOR MISTAKE TO AVOID

Jumping into short-term rentals expecting passive income is one of the biggest pitfalls. Unless you have systems in place, either personally or via a management partner, expect your "investment" to feel more like a full-time job.

14.10. Investor Strategies: Profit Models, Dynamic Pricing, and Occupancy Management

Once your short-term rental unit is set up, you have the flexibility to optimise your profit and manage your asset strategically.

14.10.1. Profit Models: Which Strategy Fits Your Goals?

Your income strategy determines how you structure your listing, set pricing, and measure success. Here are three standard short-term rental models in Dubai:

Table 14.7: Short-Term Rental Profit Models

Model	Focus	Example
High Occupancy, Lower Rate	Maximise booked nights	AED 200/night × 25 nights = AED 5,000/month
Premium Positioning	Fewer nights, higher nightly rate	AED 500/night × 12 nights = AED 6,000/month
Hybrid Approach	Flexible based on seasonality	Adjusts pricing and minimum stay length throughout the year

The right model depends on your unit's location, furnishing level, and your capacity to manage bookings or optimise listing algorithms.

14.10.2. Dynamic Pricing: Smart Adjustment, Better Yield

Static pricing is a rookie mistake. Top-performing hosts use dynamic pricing tools (e.g., PriceLabs, Beyond, AirDNA) or adjust rates manually based on:

- Event calendars (Expo Legacy, Global Village, Art Dubai).
- Public holidays (Eid, Christmas, Chinese New Year).
- Hotel availability nearby.

> **INVESTOR INSIGHT**
>
> A 2-bedroom unit in JVC that earns AED 95,000/year on a long-term lease can potentially earn over AED 130,000/year on a hybrid short-term strategy, with the correct pricing, positioning, and occupancy discipline.

14.10.3. Occupancy Management: It's Not Just About Being Booked

Don't fall for the trap of chasing 100% occupancy. Your goal is to maximise net profit, not the number of nights booked.

- **High occupancy with low rates** = stress + low ROI
- **Lower occupancy with smart pricing** = optimised revenue

Successful Investors:

- Analyse booking windows (e.g., do you get last-minute vs. early bookings?).
- Adjust minimum night stays to reduce turnover costs.
- Block dates for deep cleaning or owner use.
- Track occupancy vs. competitor benchmarks using tools like AirDNA.

14.11. Short-Term Rental Investor Readiness Checklist

This checklist is designed to help you self-assess whether the short-term rental model aligns with your goals, lifestyle, and investment risk appetite.

14.11.1. Financial Readiness

- Do you have the capital to furnish the property to DTCM standards?
- Can you cover costs during off-peak months if occupancy dips?
- Have you budgeted for ongoing maintenance, cleaning, and guest management?
- Are you prepared to pay the licensing and renewal fees on an annual basis?

14.11.2. Time Commitment

- Do you have time to manage bookings, guest communication, and check-ins?
- If not, are you willing to hire and oversee a holiday home operator?
- Can you commit to regular performance reviews and price optimisation?

14.11.3. Property Suitability

- Is your property located in a high-demand area for tourists or business travellers?
- Does the building allow holiday home use (some do not)?
- Is it easy to access, clean, and maintain?

14.11.4. Mindset and Risk Tolerance

- Are you comfortable with variable income and seasonal fluctuations?
- Can you handle the potential for guest damage or complaints?
- Are you willing to adapt based on data, reviews, and market trends?

Table 14.8: Strategic Considerations for Short-Term Rentals

Item	Why It Matters
Keeping the unit vacant for future resale	Provides agility for exit, especially at market peak.
Potential self-use of the unit	Offers personal benefit alongside investment.
Ability to pause/stop operations	Allows flexibility for personal reasons or market conditions.

INVESTOR INSIGHT

Short-term rentals reward active investors, not passive landlords. If you're willing to treat it like a business, and you choose the correct operator or system, you can outperform most long-term leases. However, if you're looking for a "set it and forget it" income stream, this may not be the model for you.

Chapter Summary

Chapter 14, **"Beyond the Lease – Maximising ROI with Short-Term Rentals,"** asserts that short-term rentals in Dubai have matured into a mainstream investment model with significant upside. It highlights that this strategy demands deliberate planning,from selecting the right location and furnishing to precise licensing, dynamic pricing, and operations.

The chapter began by providing a data-driven overview of Dubai's short-term rental landscape, detailing **ADR (Average Daily Rate)** and **Occupancy Rates** trends and key insights into how premium segments consistently outperform. You learned to distinguish the core differences between **Long-Term vs. Short-Term Rental models**, particularly in terms of income potential, management effort, and crucial exit flexibility.

You then gained a comprehensive understanding of **Legal Requirements and Licensing**, navigating DTCM rules for individual versus professional licenses, the registration process, and potential penalties for non-compliance. The chapter provided strategic guidance on **Location Matters**, identifying high-demand tourist zones and growth areas optimal for short-term rentals.

Crucial sections on **Furnishing for Success** detailed minimum DTCM requirements, the strategic impact of Standard vs. Deluxe classifications, and ROI-boosting additions to make your property stand out. You also learned about essential **Insurance** needs for short-term rentals, understanding that platform protections like Airbnb Host Protection are often not enough.

The chapter explored two primary management approaches: **DIY Hosting** (covering day-to-day realities and tech tools) for hands-on investors, and **Working with Holiday Home Operators** for those seeking professional management. It also broke down the associated **Costs and Risks** (upfront, ongoing, and market challenges like seasonality) for short-term rentals, ensuring a realistic financial outlook. Finally, it armed you with **Investor Strategies** for profit models, dynamic pricing, and occupancy management, and provided a comprehensive **Investor Readiness Checklist**.

By understanding the intricacies of the short-term rental model, you are now equipped to confidently decide if this dynamic strategy aligns with your investment goals, offering a powerful pathway to unlock significantly higher income potential and maintain agility in Dubai's thriving market.

Key Takeaways:

- **High Income Potential:** Short-term rentals can yield 20–50% more net income than long-term leases when managed well.
- **Agility & Exit Flexibility:** STRs offer control over occupancy and allow for selling with vacant possession, providing significant exit advantages.
- **DTCM Licensing is Mandatory:** All short-term rentals must be legally licensed as holiday homes by Dubai Tourism (DTCM).
- **Location & Furnishing are Critical:** High-demand tourist zones and quality, turn-key furnishings directly impact nightly rates and occupancy.
- **Insurance is Essential:** Mandated by law, comprehensive insurance protects against guest injuries, property damage, and content loss, going beyond basic platform protections.
- **Active Management Required:** Whether DIY or outsourced to an operator, STRs are a business that demands consistent attention to guest communication, pricing, and turnovers.
- **Understand Costs & Risks:** Factor in significant upfront (furnishing, licensing) and ongoing operational costs, and manage seasonality and competition risks.

PART 4

Strategic Exits and Advanced Investment Strategies

Turning Assets Into Outcomes
- The Maximisation Phase

You have purchased your property, taken handover, and optimised your returns. Now comes the phase that separates successful investors from those who simply hold assets — knowing **how and when to exit** and exploring advanced strategies that keep your capital working at its highest potential.

Part 4 is the maximisation phase of your investment journey. This is where you translate paper gains into realised profits, recycle capital into new opportunities, and explore innovative, technology-driven approaches to diversify and grow your portfolio.

We begin with **exit strategies** such as selling on the secondary market, pre-handover assignment, refinancing, or rent-then-sell models, and examine the timing, financial planning, and emotional discipline required to execute them well. You will learn to monitor market indicators, calculate your net proceeds, and align your exit moves with both personal and market conditions.

From there, we step into **advanced investment options** such as REITs, fractional ownership, tokenisation, and AI-powered decision-making. These tools can expand your reach beyond traditional property ownership, enabling you to capture opportunities with lower capital outlay, improved liquidity, and enhanced data-driven precision.

Finally, we close with a dedicated chapter on **women in real estate**, recognising the unique challenges and strengths female investors bring to the market. This is not only about inclusion, but about equipping more people to participate confidently in Dubai's growth story.

In this part, you will:

Plan Your Exit
Select and execute the right strategy for your goals and market conditions (**Chapter 15**).

Adopt Advanced Strategies
Leverage REITs, fractional ownership, tokenisation, and AI tools for smarter investing (**Chapter 16**).

Empower More Investors
Understand and apply strategies to support and grow women's participation in Dubai real estate (**Chapter 17**).

By the end of Part 4, you will have a complete roadmap for not only building wealth through Dubai property, but also realising, reinvesting, and expanding it, ensuring your portfolio continues to perform long after your first purchase.

CHAPTER 15

Strategic Exit: Turning Your Investment Into Returns

> Smart investors plan their exit before they enter. Your returns are only real when you unlock them.

When most investors think about rental income, their minds go straight to the traditional 12-month lease. It's predictable, hands-off, and fits neatly into our mental models of property ownership. But if you're only thinking in terms of long-term rentals, you're leaving serious returns on the table.

A successful real estate investment doesn't end when the property is handed over. It ends when the profit is realised, either through a sale, refinance, or income extraction. And this moment of exit isn't something you figure out on the fly. It's a critical part of your strategy from day one.

Too often, investors in Dubai focus all their energy on finding the perfect project, negotiating the right price, or planning for rental yields, while postponing any thoughts about how and when they'll exit. This delay can turn an otherwise profitable investment into a stagnant one, especially in a city where regulatory changes, interest rate fluctuations, and oversupply risks can significantly impact demand within a single quarter.

That's why exit planning is your hidden superpower. It gives you clarity in a market known for its dynamism. Whether your goal is to flip early, hold for income, recycle equity, or walk away with compounded returns, the right exit strategy puts you in control.

In this chapter, you'll learn how to:

- Evaluate four major exit strategies based on liquidity, timing, and ROI.
- Build your own Exit Rulebook with clear ROI, IRR, and holding thresholds.
- Understand legal, emotional, and financial readiness factors.
- Use data tools and market signals to exit before the peak, not after it.
- Avoid emotional bias and anchor your decisions in systemised frameworks.

Let's begin with the most common, and often most misunderstood, exit strategy: the traditional resale.

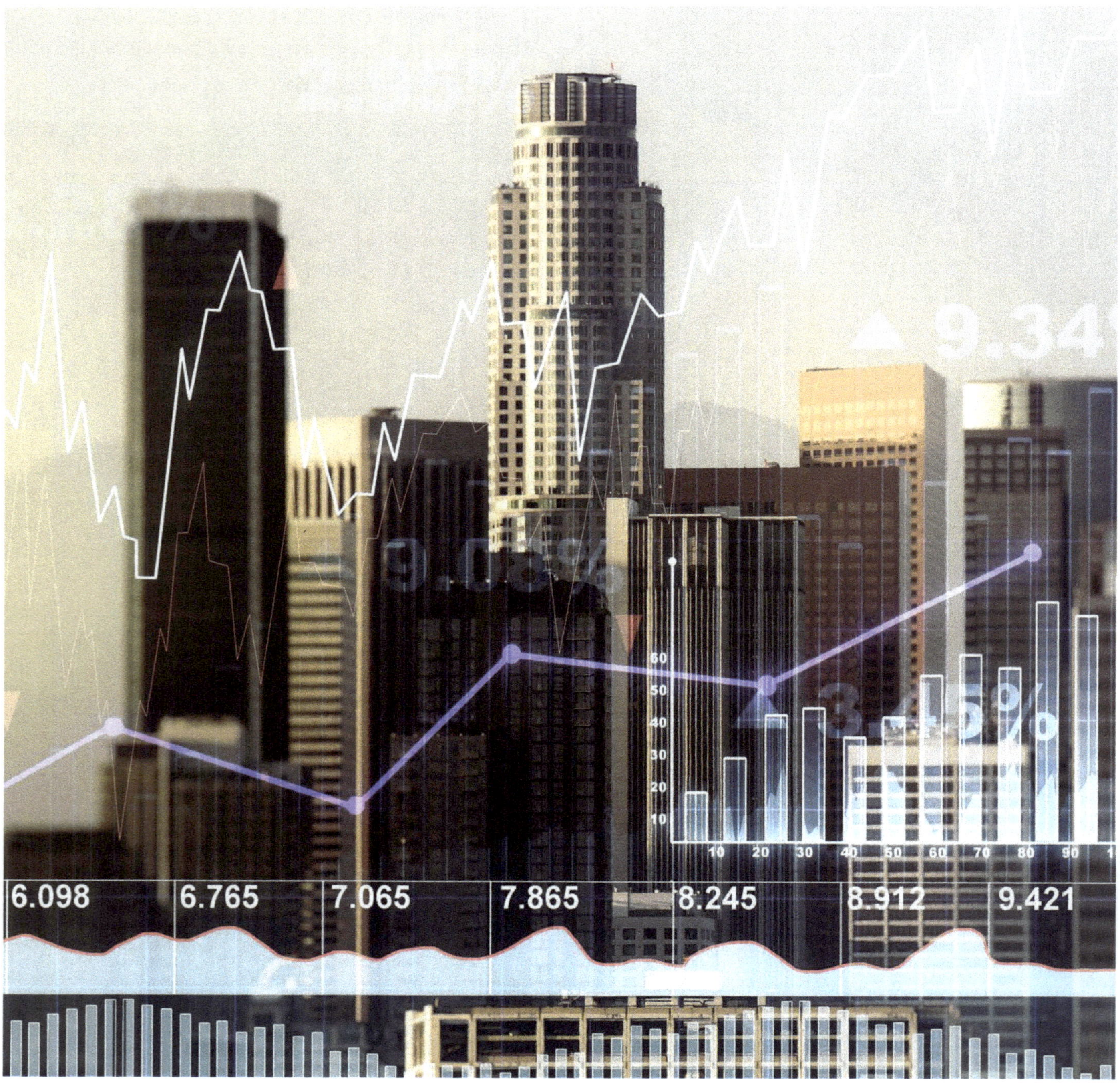

15.1. Exit Option 1: Secondary Market Sale (Traditional Resale)

The Classic Route: Cash Out When the Time is Right

Selling your property on the secondary market, after it's been handed over and registered, is the most straightforward and widely used exit strategy among Dubai investors. It allows you to capitalise on market appreciation, reclaim capital, or reposition your portfolio.

But make no mistake: a successful exit through resale is not simply about listing the property and waiting. It's about strategic timing, legal readiness, and presentation. Investors who approach resale as a planned process, not a reactive move, are the ones who exit profitably.

15.1.1. When to Consider a Secondary Market Exit

You might choose this route when:

- The market is in an upswing, and buyer sentiment is strong.
- You've achieved your target ROI, IRR, or equity multiple.
- You need liquidity for another investment or personal reasons.

Before listing, ensure the following are in place:

Table 15.1: Pre-Listing Checklist for Secondary Market Sale

Item Verified	Why It's Required
Title Deed or Oqood	Legal proof of ownership
Form A (RERA Broker Agreement)	Required to authorise a broker for marketing
Developer NOC	Confirms no outstanding dues and permits transfer
Cleared Service Charges	Mandatory for buyer confidence and DLD clearance
Tenancy Contract & 12-Month Notice	Required to serve legal notice to the tenant if selling to an end-user who needs vacant possession.

15.1.2. Tenant Considerations Before Sale

If your property is rented, Dubai law requires a 12-month legal eviction notice before you can sell the unit as vacant, unless the tenant agrees to vacate voluntarily. That means:

- If you're listing a tenanted property, your buyer pool may shrink (most end-users want vacant units).
- If you want to sell to an end-user, you must issue the eviction notice well in advance and document it via a notary public or registered delivery.
- If the tenant is cooperative, consider offering relocation support or an incentive for early move-out.

Real-World Case Example: ROI from Secondary Market Sale

Scenario: An investor purchased a 1-bedroom unit in Sobha Hartland at its launch in 2021 for AED 1.1 million. He paid 20% upfront (AED 220K). After 18 months, with the market heating up, he listed the unit post-handover and sold it for AED 1.4M.

Result:

- **Gross Profit:** AED 300,000
- **ROI on Cash Invested:** 136% in 18 months (300,000 ÷ 220,000)
- **IRR:** Approximately 79% annualised

This kind of result depends on: entering early, pricing accurately using market comparables, and exiting when buyer activity is peaking.

15.1.3. How to Maximise Your Sale Price

- **Stage the Property:** Fresh paint, minor repairs, deep cleaning, and even light furnishing can boost perceived value.
- **Vacate Before Sale (if possible):** Vacant properties tend to sell better and faster, especially to end-users.
- **Use High-Quality Photos and Floor Plans:** Invest in professional photography and consider including virtual walkthroughs.
- **List with a Motivated, RERA-Certified Broker:** Use Form A and agree on a pricing strategy, not just a listing.
- **Set a Smart Asking Price:** Anchor it using DXBInteract transaction data and Bayut listing trends. Price slightly above your minimum target to leave room for negotiation.

Table 15.2: Key Legal & Cost Considerations for Secondary Sale

Cost Item	Amount / Range
DLD Transfer Fee	4% of the final sale value (paid by the buyer)
Broker Commission	~2% (negotiable; may vary by agency)
Developer NOC Fee	AED 500–5,000 (varies by master developer)
Mortgage Release (if any)	Processing + 0.25% DLD mortgage deregistration fee
Conveyancing (optional)	AED 5,000–10,000

INVESTOR INSIGHT

Timing matters. Exiting too late, even with price growth, can result in longer hold times, tenant complications, or price fatigue.

Table 15.3: When is Secondary Sale the Right Exit?

Trigger	Why It Matters
You've hit your target ROI / IRR	Time to harvest gains
The market shows buy-side momentum	Listing in strong demand maximises price
You're ready to rotate capital	Use funds for higher-growth or de-risked assets
You want to clear your debt portfolio	Exit the mortgage before renewal or rate change

15.2. Exit Option 2: Pre-Handover Resale (Assignment Sale)

Flip Before It's Built: Exit Through Assignment

One of the most lucrative, but often misunderstood, exit strategies in Dubai real estate is the pre-handover resale, commonly referred to as an assignment sale. This allows you, the investor, to sell your off-plan unit before taking actual possession, transferring the Sale and Purchase Agreement (SPA) to a new buyer. This is a preferred strategy for investors seeking high ROI with limited capital exposure and faster churn. However, it requires careful timing, knowledge of developer policies, and awareness of market liquidity..

What Is an Assignment Sale? An assignment sale is when you sell your contractual rights to a property, as outlined in your signed SPA, to another buyer before the property is handed over. You do not receive the title deed, and you do not register an Ejari. Instead, your buyer steps into your shoes, completes the remaining payments, and takes possession. The transaction is executed directly with the developer's approval, and usually requires both parties to sign a tripartite assignment agreement.

Table 15.4: Advantages & Risks of Pre-Handover Resale (Assignment Sale)

Advantages	Risks to Watch
Lower capital outlay (20–40% typically paid)	The developer may restrict resale before certain payment milestones
ROI magnified on a smaller investment base	Market correction can reduce resale value or eliminate margin
No need to register for Ejari or pay service fees	Project delays, changes in the handover timeline, or design specifications
Avoids transfer of physical possession	Assignment buyers often require all documents and developer trust
No long-term maintenance obligations	Buyer pool may be limited—mortgage is harder to obtain for assignment deals.

Real Example: Assignment ROI Breakdown

Scenario: An investor purchased a 2BR unit in Dubai Hills Park Heights at launch in 2022 for AED 1.3 million, with a 60/40 payment plan. He paid 30% (AED 390K) by mid-2024. He sold his SPA for AED 1.65M in Q3 2024.

Your Profit:

- **Profit:** AED 350,000 (AED 1.65M Sale Price - AED 1.3M Original Price)
- **ROI on Cash Invested:** 89.7% in ~2 years (350,000 ÷ 390,000)

This type of result depends on strong market appreciation and knowing developer policies.

Table 15.5: Legal & Financial Notes for Assignment Sale

Item	Typical Value
Assignment Fee (Developer)	AED 2,000–5,000 (varies)
DLD Fee on Resale	4% of the new sale value (paid by the buyer)
Broker Commission (Optional)	~2% or as agreed
Mortgage Allowed Pre-Handover	Most banks won't finance until completion (limiting buyer pool)
Taxation	Capital gains are not taxed, but the buyer pays 4% DLD again (as per current laws)

15.2.1. Understanding Seller-Side Broker Arrangements

When selling an assignment, clarifying the broker's arrangement is crucial:

- **Standard Commission:** The broker earns a percentage (e.g., 2% + VAT) from the seller upon a successful transaction.
- **Net-to-Owner Pricing:** You define a minimum acceptable amount (net to the owner), and the broker keeps any amount above that as commission. This can incentivise aggressive selling, but watch for inflated pricing that deters buyers.
- **Zero Commission (Buyer-Paid):** In some cases, sellers refuse to pay commission and require the broker to collect from the buyer. This limits broker motivation and reach, especially in a competitive market.

INVESTOR INSIGHT

In net-to-owner deals, brokers often add a top-up amount to the seller's price. Whether this is allowed, transparent, or capped should be agreed in writing. Lack of clarity here can cause distrust, or worse, derail deals at the final stage.

15.2.2. Strategic Timing: Integrating Market Signals for Assignment Exit

An assignment exit strategy is highly timing-sensitive. It requires a keen eye on market dynamics. You should cross-reference relevant market signals from **Chapter 4: Market Dynamics: Cycles, Locations, and Investment Timing** before listing your assignment.

Table 15.6: When Is Pre-Handover Resale the Right Move?

Scenario	Recommended Action
Early-stage buyer with substantial equity gains	List assignment now
Weak rental market + strong capital appreciation	Flip instead of hold (if the market favours capital gains over rent)
Need liquidity, but want to avoid ownership hassles	Use the assignment strategy (avoids physical handover responsibilities)
Overheated launch environment with an extended payment plan	Reassess; exit before demand cools

15.3. Exit Option 3: Buy, Rent, and Sell Later

The Hybrid Hold: Earn Now, Exit Later

Some investments are built for both income and appreciation. This strategy, buying a property, renting it out for a period, and then selling it later, lets you extract rental income during the hold while still targeting capital gains down the road. Unlike flipping, this approach plays the long game. It's ideal for investors who are comfortable managing tenants and want to benefit from Dubai's rental yield advantage while keeping the door open for future resale.

Table 15.7: Benefits of Buy, Rent, and Sell Strategy

Advantage	Investor Benefit
Steady rental income	Offsets costs like service charges and mortgage interest
Capital growth over time	Sell when the market has appreciated or your ROI target is met
Flexible hold duration	You're not rushed into selling prematurely
Tax-free gains and income (as of now)	Dubai offers dual-return potential with no capital gains tax
Portfolio leverage	Use future sale proceeds as a down payment for the next asset

15.3.1. Ideal Scenarios for Buy–Rent–Sell

- You've bought in a mid-growth community (e.g., Town Square, JVC, Al Furjan).
- Rental demand is strong and consistent.
- You have mortgage financing and want tenants to help cover the EMI.
- You anticipate the area will appreciate in 3–5 years (e.g., metro extension, school zones).
- You want to scale your portfolio but prefer not to flip every asset.

Example: Strategic Hold and Exit

Case: Investor buys a 2BR in Mudon Views for AED 1.1M in 2022 with 20% down (AED 220K) and finances the rest. Rents it for AED 85,000 per year.

- Annual ROI from Rent: ~7.7% gross
- After 3 years, the property value appreciates to AED 1.35M
- Sale Profit: AED 250K
- Rental Income Earned: AED 255K gross
- Total Value Extracted: AED 505K (before costs)

This strategy doubled the cash return vs. flipping early, and without aggressive risk. You don't have to sacrifice income to earn appreciation. This strategy proves that time in the market, with solid tenants and smart upkeep, can be just as profitable as market timing.

15.3.2. Common Pitfalls to Avoid

Mistake	Consequence
Holding too long without tracking appreciation	Opportunity cost: you miss the market peak
Not issuing a timely 12-month eviction notice	The sale was delayed by an entire lease cycle
Neglecting the property condition	Lower rent and resale value; more negotiation pressure
Failing to plan financing for the next asset	You sell but can't recycle gains quickly enough

Table 15.8: Sell Timing Checklist

Readiness Question	Action
Has your property appreciated by 15–20% since you purchased it?	Start preparing for resale
Is your current tenant nearing the end of their lease?	Issue a 12-month notice if needed
Are you close to loan maturity or a favourable market cycle?	Consider selling before the rate reset
Is nearby inventory increasing rapidly?	Exit before yield compression occurs
Do you need capital for a better opportunity elsewhere?	Plan your liquidity window.

Tactical Tips for Investors:

- Keep lease terms flexible (1-year maximum) to preserve exit agility.
- Maintain the unit well; deep clean, repaint, replace ageing fixtures before sale.
- Communicating clearly with tenants and maintaining respectful relationships improves occupancy rates.
- Use annual rent appraisals to ensure your yield stays optimised.

Table 15.9: When is Buy: Rent: Sell the Right Strategy?

Scenario	Why It Works
You want cash flow plus capital gains	Achieve dual-source ROI
You're in an area with stable rental demand	Income will cover holding costs
You want to hedge against short-term market dips	Rents protect cash flow while waiting to exit
You're building a long-term portfolio	Can recycle equity later for new investments

15.4. Exit Option 4: Refinance or Equity Release

Unlock Capital, Maintain Ownership

In Dubai, where capital appreciation can be significant and rental yields are strong, refinancing or equity release allows you to extract money from a property while maintaining ownership and rental income. It's one of the most underused strategies by individual investors, yet it's standard practice among institutional players.

What Is Refinancing or Equity Release?

- **Refinancing:** Replacing your existing mortgage with a new one, usually to get better terms, a longer tenure, or to unlock cash based on your property's appreciated value.
- **Equity Release:** Borrowing against the increased value of a property that is fully paid or partially paid. In both cases, you're turning equity into liquid capital without selling the property.

Table 15.10: Why Use Refinance/Equity Release as an Exit Strategy?

Advantage	Investor Benefit
Maintain rental income	You still own the property, and the monthly cash flow continues
Access lump sum capital	Can be reinvested into new assets or other opportunities
No disruption to tenants	No notice or eviction required
Avoid market timing risks	You don't need to guess when to sell, just refinance when the value rises
Tax-free capital (as of now in the UAE)	Released equity is not considered taxable income

INVESTOR INSIGHT

Smart investors don't sell good assets; they leverage them." You've done the hard work, picked the right property, held through the early years, and managed it well. If its value has grown, why rush to sell? Refinancing buys you flexibility while keeping your asset.

15.4.1. Ideal Scenarios for Refinance/Equity Release

- Your property is already tenanted, generating stable rental income.
- Market values have risen by 15–25% since your purchase.
- You want to reinvest in a new project or expand your portfolio.
- Your current mortgage is nearing the end of the term, and you wish to extend it.
- You want to consolidate debts or free up cash for life events (education, business, etc.).

Example: Equity Release in Action

Case: Investor bought a 1BR in Downtown Dubai for AED 1.5M, 80% financed at purchase; now 5 years into the mortgage. Current property valuation: AED 2.1M. Outstanding loan: AED 900K.

Available Equity: Bank allows refinance at 75% Loan-to-Value (LTV) > 0.75 x 2.1M = AED 1.575M. New mortgage replaces old one (AED 900K), and releases AED 675K cash. Property continues generating rent while the owner reinvests the money into a new launch.

Table 15.11: Refinance vs. Equity Release: What's the Difference?

Feature	Refinance (with cash-out)	Equity Release (on wholly-owned property)
You already have a mortgage	Yes	No (property is owned outright)
The process involves	Replacing the loan	A new loan is placed against the property
Purpose	Better terms, plus unlock cash	Pure capital access without sale
Ownership remains unchanged	Yes	Yes
Income from rent continues	Yes	Yes

Table 15.12: Fees and Documentation to Expect for Refinancing

Cost Item	Approximate Fee
Property Valuation	AED 2,500 – 3,500
Mortgage Processing Fee	~1% of the loan amount
DLD Mortgage Registration Fee	0.25% of mortgage value
Bank NOC Fee	AED 500 – 1,000 (varies by bank)
Life Insurance (linked to mortgage)	Varies based on age, loan amount

NOTE

Always compare multiple banks. Terms and rates can differ significantly across institutions and depending on your profile (salary, nationality, residency).

15.4.2. When to Avoid or Delay Refinancing

Situation	Risk / Reason to Wait
Interest rates are unusually high	You may pay more in interest over the long term
Rental income is not covering the loan instalments	Risk of negative cash flow
You plan to sell within the next 6–12 months	Refinancing may add costs without enough time to recover them
Your credit score or financials have recently weakened	You may not get favourable terms

15.4.3. Market Timing for Refinancing: Use Inflection Indicators

This strategy depends heavily on timing your refinance after property appreciation, but before prices plateau or interest rates rise. Use the market insights gained from **Chapter 4: Market Dynamics: Cycles, Locations, and Investment Timing** to time your refinance smartly. This means monitoring trends in transaction volume, mortgage uptake, and overall market sentiment for signals that favour unlocking equity.

Table 15.13: Refinance vs. Sell Property

Question	Sell the Property	Refinance Instead
Do you need a lump sum of cash?	Yes	Yes
Do you want to continue the rental income?	You lose it	You keep it
Are you emotionally ready to exit?	Yes	Not necessarily
Is the market favourable for resale?	Then, consider selling	Or consider partial monetisation
Want to expand your portfolio using equity?	You'll need to re-qualify	Easier leverage for new investments

FINAL WORD

Don't Sell a Winner Just to Raise Cash. Selling isn't the only way to move forward. If you've selected a good asset in a desirable area, let it continue to work for you. Refinance smartly, release capital, and redeploy it into your next winning move.

Four Strategic Exit Options

Your Roadmap To Returns

	Secondary Market Sale	Pre-Handover Resale (Assignment)	Buy, Rent, and Sell Later	Refinance or Equity Release
Why Choose It	Cash out on appreciation Liquidity for new investments Straightforward resale process	Lower capital outlay High ROI potential No long-term obligations	Rental income + capital gains Flexible hold period Dual return potential	Maintain ownership & rent Unlock lump sum cash Avoid market timing risks
Key Considerations	Tenant eviction notice needed Market timing crucial Broker / legal fees apply	Developer restrictions Limited buyer pool Market correction risk	Must manage tenants Risk of holding too long Eviction delays affect sale	Higher interest rates risk Loan fees & insurance Negative cash flow risk

15.5. Choosing the Right Exit Strategy

Match Your Method to Your Money Goals

By now, you've explored the four primary ways to exit a Dubai real estate investment: sell on the secondary market, flip via assignment before handover, rent and sell later, or refinance to unlock equity without selling. But how do you choose the right one for your situation?

Ask yourself these questions before selecting your path:

Table 15.14: Questions to Ask Before Selecting Your Exit Path

Factor	Why It Matters
What return am I aiming for: ROI, IRR, or equity multiple?	Helps define your exit trigger
Do I want income now or capital later?	Income = Rent-and-Hold; Capital = Sale or Refinance
Am I looking to exit fully, or recycle funds into a new deal?	Clarifies whether to sell or refinance
Is my asset ready, off-plan, or recently handed over?	Determines the feasibility of each option
How long am I willing to hold?	Your time horizon shapes the strategies that fit your lifestyle and liquidity needs.

Your answers create your Investor Profile, which helps narrow down your choices.

Table 15.15: Compare Exit Routes: Strategy Matrix

Your Situation	Recommended Strategy
"I want quick returns with lower upfront capital."	Pre-Handover Assignment (Section 15.2)
"I want to build cash flow now, then sell when prices rise."	Rent, Then Sell (Section 15.3)
"I need cash now, but I still like the asset."	Refinance / Equity Release (Section 15.4)
"I'm ready to cash out fully and move on."	Secondary Market Sale (Section 15.1)

Investor Case Study: Picking the Right Path

Case: Let's say you bought a 2BR apartment in Arjan off-plan for AED 950,000, and you've now paid 30% (AED 285,000). Project handover is 14 months away. The market has appreciated, and similar units are now selling for AED 1.2M on assignment.

You have 3 options:

- **Sell via Assignment Now:** ROI = (1.2M - 950K)/285K ≈ 87.7% return on cash. Fast, no rental income, no ownership.
- **Hold to Handover, Then Rent + Sell:** Delay returns, but collect 6–8% annual yield before selling at a higher price later.
- **Hold, Take Handover, Then Refinance:** If the value exceeds AED 1.3M, you can refinance at 75% LTV and extract ~700K in cash, while still retaining the asset.

What's best? If you're risk-averse and want liquidity, option 1 is the ideal choice. If you want passive income plus long-term upside, option 2 is the winner. If you want to scale your portfolio without selling, option 3 is most strategic.

15.6. Don't Skip This Step: Forecast Your Net Proceeds

Before making any final exit decision, always forecast your net proceeds. This means subtracting all anticipated exit costs from your expected sale price to arrive at your actual net profit. Overlooking these costs can significantly erode your actual returns.

Key Exit-Related Costs to Factor In:

- Agency Commission: ~2% (seller amount is negotiated at onset).
- Developer NOC Fee: AED 500–5,000.
- Mortgage Settlement Charges: Bank-specific (plus valuation, registration fees).
- Conveyancing / Legal Support: AED 5,000–10,000 (optional, but advised).

PRO TIP

Always subtract your actual total cost from the expected sale price to arrive at net ROI. Use your Chapter 5 models to include all holding and exit costs.

15.7. Monitoring the Market: Exit When It Makes Sense

> The best exits happen when preparation meets timing, not when desperation meets the market.

You've held the property. You've collected the rent. Maybe you've even exceeded your original ROI target. But how do you know when it's time to move from "holding" to "harvesting"? This section is about learning to read the room, specifically, Dubai's real estate room. Unlike emotional investing or instinct-led exits, we focus here on exit-specific inflection points that tell you: "It's time to act."

> Markets whisper before they shout. If you're listening closely, you'll know when it's time to move.

15.7.1. Exit Indicators vs. Entry Indicators: What's the Difference?

In **Chapter 4: Market Dynamics: Cycles, Locations, and Investment Timing**, you learned how to spot early signs of recovery and growth, like transaction momentum or mortgage uptake, that help you enter before the wave builds. Here, we flip the lens. Now you'll learn to track signs of saturation, overheating, or shifting demand, so you can time your sale, assignment, or refinance before the wave crests or cracks.

Entry indicators are about identifying the "start of something", exit indicators are about recognising the "end of advantage."

Table 15.16: Key Exit-Specific Market Signals to Watch

We'll focus on inflexion points that signal potential market peaks or declining ROI, specifically for exit.

Indicator	What to Watch For	What It Signals
Yield Compression	Falling rental yields while property prices stay flat or rise	Signals reduced holding value, time to sell or reallocate capital.
Surge in Off-Plan Launches Nearby	Multiple new launches in your community with 8–10 year payment plans	Oversupply risk in 12–18 months, consider exiting while resale inventory is low.
Drop in Transaction Volume or Mortgage Approvals	Slowing sales or financing activity (via DLD Cube or CB UAE)	Indicates weakening buyer demand; act before liquidity shrinks.
Longer Days on Market	Your type of unit is sitting longer unsold or unrented	Signals soft pricing and buyer hesitation, adjust price or prep for exit.
Stagnant Rents + Rising Service Costs	Flat rents combined with rising CA charges or inflation	Your net yield is dropping; consider shifting to a better-yielding asset.
Infrastructure Project Completion	The Metro, school, or park is now operational	Your price bump is likely peaking; consider exiting before post-hype stagnation.

PRO TIP

If you've hit your IRR or equity multiple target, or if rental yield is below 4.5% and new launches are aggressive nearby, it's time to ask: "Is this capital better deployed elsewhere?"

15.8. Emotional Discipline & Exit Triggers

> Don't rise to your goals, fall into your systems.
> **Investor Principle**

We've already covered the what and when of exiting: secondary sales, flips, refinancing, and how to interpret inflection indicators to time the market. But strategy alone doesn't ensure action. Many investors fail at the final step, execution, because they let emotion cloud rational decisions.

This section is not about data. It's about you, your ability to stay disciplined when the market, your peers, or even your gut says, "Wait a little longer" or "Sell now before it crashes." Without a pre-set decision framework, investors often miss significant exits or act too soon, reducing hard-earned returns.

Final Word: Exit Smart, Not Last. Whether it's fear, greed, overconfidence, or inertia, emotion shows up strongest when it's time to sell. Here's how these mindsets can sabotage exit performance:

Table 15.17: Emotional Biases and Their Impact on Exit Performance

Emotion	How It Shows Up	Impact
Fear	"What if the market tanks?"	Panic selling below fair value
Greed	"Let me wait for another 10% gain"	Missed peak, decline begins
Overconfidence	"I always know the right timing"	Ignoring signals, holding too long
Inertia	"It's too much hassle to sell"	Opportunity cost, stagnant capital

15.8.1. Set Your Exit Rulebook

Smart investors create an **Exit Rulebook** with predefined, objective triggers. This isn't a theoretical number; it's your benchmark for when "enough is enough."

Example Triggers to Define:

- Target ROI or IRR (e.g., 20% ROI, 10% IRR).
- Target Equity Multiple (e.g., 2.0x).
- Minimum Acceptable Sale Price (after fees).
- Maximum Holding Period (e.g., 5 years).

15.8.2. Identify Market-Based Exit Triggers

Some market conditions should override personal preference. If any of these occur, your system should signal it's time to review or act:

Table 15.18: Market Signal Exit Implications

Market Signal	Exit Implication
Yields drop below 4.5% in your area	Consider reallocating to better income zones.
Off-plan launches double in 12 months nearby	Area entering oversupply; sell beforehand, before the handover glut hits.
Rental income no longer covers financing	Price appreciation may slow; assess refinancing or sale.
Mortgage rates rise >200bps from the purchase date	Cash flow erosion; reconsider holding.
End-user sentiment weakens (per broker feedback)	Liquidity risk: exit while buyers still transact.

Reference **Chapter 4: Market Dynamics: Cycles, Locations, and Investment Timing** for more on how to read these inflection indicators and translate them into actionable signals.

15.8.3. Recap: Exit Readiness Self-Audit

Table 15.19: Exit Readiness Self-Audit Checklist

Check
Title deed or Oqood in order
Service charges are fully paid
Tenant served 12-month notice (if needed)
The property is well-presented and maintained
ROI model updated in the last 6 months
Emotionally prepared to act

INVESTOR REMINDER

"Real estate returns are made by strategy, not sentiment. The moment you ignore your plan, your emotions start running the investment." Pre-set logic always beats emotional delay.

Emotional Biases & Their Impact On Exit Performance

Emotion	How It Shows Up	Impact	Objective Trigger
Fear	What if the market tanks?	Panic selling below fair value	Target ROI
Greed	Let me wait for another 10% gain	Missed peak, decline begins	Max Holding Period
Over-confidence	I always know the right timing	Ignoring signals, holding too long	Profit Target
Inertia	It's too much hassle to sell	Opportunity cost, stagnant capital	Stressful Conditions

Chapter Summary

Chapter 15, **"Strategic Exit: Turning Your Investment Into Returns,"** is your essential guide to ensuring your real estate investments in Dubai culminate in realised profits. It fundamentally asserts that a successful investment doesn't end with acquisition; it concludes when profits are strategically unlocked, emphasising that exit planning is a core part of your strategy from day one.

The chapter began by outlining the four primary **Exit Options**: Traditional Secondary Market Sale, Pre-Handover Resale (Assignment Sale), Buy, Rent, and Sell Later, and Refinance or Equity Release. For each, you gained a clear understanding of its process, advantages, risks, and ideal scenarios, including critical considerations like tenant rights and legal costs.

You learned the importance of **Forecasting Your Net Proceeds** by factoring in all potential exit costs, ensuring your final returns are realistic. Crucially, the chapter armed you with strategies for **monitoring the Market for Exit Signals**, differentiating between entry and exit indicators, and providing specific signals to watch for, such as yield compression, surge in new launches, or drops in transaction volume.

Finally, a key focus was placed on **Emotional Discipline & Exit Triggers**. You learned how common emotions like fear, greed, and overconfidence can derail exit performance, and how to combat them by setting up a clear **Exit Rulebook** with predefined, objective triggers (e.g., target ROI/IRR, maximum holding period, market-based signals).

By mastering these strategic exit pathways, monitoring market signals, and cultivating emotional discipline, you empower yourself to navigate Dubai's dynamic real estate landscape, ensuring your hard-earned profits are not just theoretical but truly realised and available for your next strategic move.

Key Takeaways:

- **Plan Your Exit Before Entry:** The exit strategy influences your initial acquisition decisions.
- **Four Primary Exit Routes:** Understand the mechanics, pros, and cons of Secondary Sale, Assignment Sale, Buy-Rent-Sell, and Refinance/Equity Release.
- **Forecast Net Proceeds:** Always account for all fees and costs to determine your actual profit.
- **Monitor Exit Signals:** Actively track market indicators (referencing Chapter 4) to identify optimal times to sell, refinance, or hold.
- **Segment Cycles Matter for Exit:** Different micro-markets will reach their peak or correction at different times.
- **Combat Emotional Bias:** Set predefined, objective exit triggers (your "Exit Rulebook") to avoid allowing fear or greed to dictate your decisions.
- **Documentation is Key:** Maintain records for a smooth and legally sound exit process.

YOUR JOURNEY
NAVIGATOR

Part 4: Strategic Exits and Advanced Investment Strategies

Recap

You have just completed **Chapter 15: Strategic Exit: Turning Your Investment Into Returns**, where you explored the full range of exit options including secondary market sales, pre-handover assignments, refinancing, and rent-then-sell models. You learned how to assess timing using market indicators, calculate net proceeds, and apply emotional discipline to ensure profitable, well-planned exits. This chapter gave you the tools to transform unrealised gains into actual capital, ready for redeployment into new opportunities.

Next Chapter Preview

We now move into the advanced strategies stage. **Chapter 16: Smart Real Estate – From REITs to AI-Powered Investing** introduces innovative, technology-driven approaches that expand your investment capabilities beyond direct property ownership. You will see how to leverage REITs, fractional ownership, tokenisation, and AI to diversify your portfolio, enhance returns, and increase liquidity.

You Will Learn

- ☑ How REITs work and how to invest in them in Dubai and globally.
- ☑ The potential of fractional ownership platforms and real estate tokenisation.
- ☑ How AI can improve deal sourcing, underwriting, and rental yield optimisation.
- ☑ The challenges, ethics, and human factors in technology-driven investing.

Link to Framework

This chapter strengthens your C.D.R.C. mindset by reinforcing adaptability and openness to new tools, while supporting your L.E.A.D. approach by introducing strategies that drive value, embrace calculated risks, and extend your long-term market engagement.

Purpose / Big Picture Link

This is the advanced diversification stage of your journey. Understanding and applying these strategies ensures your portfolio is resilient, future-proof, and able to capture opportunities that go beyond traditional buy-and-hold models.

CHAPTER 16

Smart Real Estate – From REITs to AI-Powered Investing

> The best investment on Earth is Earth, but you don't always have to own the land beneath your feet.

The rules of real estate are changing and fast. For decades, the only way to participate in property was to buy it. You needed capital, a loan, a title deed, and usually some local knowledge. But today, you can invest in real estate across continents with the tap of an app, fractionalise ownership into tokens, automate pricing and renovation plans with AI, and earn passive income from properties you've never even seen. Welcome to the era of smart real estate.

This chapter is about these new frontiers. You and I are no longer limited to thinking in brick-and-mortar terms. Whether you're a hands-on investor or someone looking to diversify your portfolio with minimal effort, the tools now available, such as REITs, tokenised real estate, fractional ownership platforms, and AI-driven analytics, are transforming the landscape. They offer unprecedented access, liquidity, and efficiency, democratising real estate investment and opening new avenues for wealth creation in Dubai's dynamic market.

16.1. What Are REITs and Why Do They Matter

When most investors think of real estate, they picture a property they can see, touch, and walk through. But in today's investment landscape, you don't need to be a landlord or even own a single unit to participate in the returns of real estate. That's where REITs come in.

A Real Estate Investment Trust (REIT) is a company that owns, operates, or finances income-producing properties. Instead of buying a flat or a villa, you purchase shares in a trust that holds dozens, or even hundreds, of assets: malls, warehouses, offices, hotels, or rental communities. The best part? You earn dividends from the rental income without worrying about maintenance, tenant issues, or market timing.

Think of it as the stock market's version of real estate. You can buy and sell REITs on exchanges, diversify across asset classes and geographies, and gain liquidity that traditional property investment doesn't offer. In a market like Dubai, where real estate cycles can be pronounced, REITs provide a lower-risk entry point and a convenient way to gain exposure without deep operational involvement.

16.1.1. How They Make Money & What You Earn

REITs generate income primarily through the rents collected from their properties. They are legally required to distribute a significant portion of their taxable income (typically 90% or more) to shareholders annually in the form of dividends. This makes them attractive for income-focused investors.

- **Equity REITs:** These own and operate income-generating properties, such as apartments, offices, shopping malls, and hotels. They make money primarily through rental income, and you earn dividends from rents and potential capital gains from rising property values.
  - **Example:** Emirates REIT (Dubai) owns educational buildings, offices, and retail properties and pays dividends based on rental yield.
- **Mortgage REITs (mREITs):** These provide financing for income-producing real estate by purchasing or originating mortgages and mortgage-backed securities. They generate income from the interest on these investments.
- **Hybrid REITs:** These combine both equity and mortgage strategies, holding both physical property and financial instruments. They make money from a blend of rental income and interest payments, offering balanced returns.

16.1.2. Public vs. Private REITs

- **Public REITs:** These are listed on stock exchanges (e.g., Nasdaq, DFM) and can be bought and sold like any stock. They offer high liquidity.
- **Private REITs:** These are sold through brokers and are not listed on exchanges. They may have lock-in periods or high minimum investment thresholds, offering less liquidity but sometimes higher yields.
- **Public Non-Listed REITs (PNLRs):** These sit in between, not traded on exchanges but offering some liquidity and typically lower minimums than private REITs.

16.2. How to Invest in REITs – UAE and Global Access Platforms

REITs are one of the most accessible ways to invest in real estate, especially if you prefer liquidity, diversification, and minimal day-to-day management. In this section, we'll look at how you can invest in REITs from Dubai, and what platforms and products are available both locally and globally.

16.2.1. Investing in REITs in the UAE

Several prominent REITs operate within the UAE, offering investors direct exposure to the local property market.

- **Emirates REIT:** Launched in 2010, Emirates REIT is the UAE's first Sharia-compliant REIT and is listed on Nasdaq Dubai. Its portfolio includes education, office, and retail properties across Dubai, including GEMS schools and office buildings in DIFC. The DFSA regulates it.
- **ENBD REIT:** Managed by Emirates NBD Asset Management and also listed on Nasdaq Dubai, ENBD REIT focuses on commercial and residential properties in Dubai, aiming for stable income and capital appreciation.
- **YASREIT (National Bonds REIT):** YASREIT is a Sharia-compliant, fractional real estate investment vehicle offered via the National Bonds platform. It allows small-ticket investors to access rental-income assets in the UAE, with investment starting from AED 500. The Central Bank of the UAE regulates it.
- **Rasmala Long Income Fund:** A private real estate fund operated by Rasmala Investment Bank, targeting long-lease commercial and logistics assets in the GCC and the UK. It is not publicly listed and typically caters to high-net-worth investors.
- **Dubai Residential REIT:** Launched in 2025 via IPO and managed by Dubai Holding, this is the largest residential REIT in the GCC. It manages a portfolio of over 35,000 housing units and offers a target yield of approximately 7.7% with semi-annual payouts.

Access Methods: You can invest in most of these REITs via local brokers licensed with Nasdaq Dubai or the Dubai Financial Market (DFM). Some UAE banks also offer brokerage services or platforms, such as Sarwa.

Tax Considerations for UAE Residents: There is no capital gains tax or dividend tax in the UAE for individuals investing in REITs. This means the income you earn from REIT dividends and any profit from selling your shares is generally tax-free at the individual level.

16.3. Fractional Ownership Platforms in Dubai – Real Estate for the Rest of Us

Not every investor starts with millions. And not every smart deal needs full ownership. Fractional ownership is quickly becoming one of the most exciting entry points into Dubai real estate, particularly for those seeking to diversify with smaller capital or explore the market before making a larger investment.

In simple terms, fractional ownership allows you to co-own a share of a property, much like holding equity in a company. You receive a portion of the rental income, and your share grows in value if the property appreciates. It's not a timeshare; you own a legal share, often through a Special Purpose Vehicle (SPV), and you're entitled to your share of income and capital appreciation. Over the past few years, Dubai has witnessed the emergence of multiple regulated platforms that have made this model more accessible, transparent, and increasingly profitable.

16.3.1. How It Works & Top Players

Each platform typically purchases carefully selected income-producing properties, often luxury apartments or villas in prime locations. These properties are then divided into hundreds or thousands of shares, which investors can buy. The platform then manages the property, collects rent, handles maintenance, and distributes net income to the shareholders proportionate to their ownership.

Here are the top players you should know:

- **Stake (GetStake):** A DFSA-regulated platform based in DIFC, Stake is one of the most prominent names in the region. Investors can start from AED 500, choosing from a portfolio of income-producing properties in Dubai and Saudi Arabia. Stake distributes monthly rental income and offers biannual "exit windows" for liquidity.
- **Maisour:** Also regulated by DFSA and now owned by Meteora Developers, Maisour focuses on high-quality Dubai rentals. Investors can participate from as little as AED 500. The platform combines real estate and tech to offer hands-off ownership with long-term value creation.
- **SmartCrowd:** As one of MENA's earliest DFSA-licensed real estate crowdfunding platforms, SmartCrowd offers access to curated rental assets with a low entry threshold. Investors receive their share of rental income, with options for resale depending on platform liquidity.
- **PRYPCO Blocks:** A tech-driven platform offering AED 2,000 entry into Dubai's rental market.
- **Baytukum:** Focused on micro-investing, Baytukum aims to democratise real estate ownership for first-time investors. The platform is still in its early stages of development, but it offers access to select Dubai rental units.
- **HomeCubes:** An emerging proptech startup that blends tokenisation with fractional ownership, HomeCubes is targeting younger, tech-savvy investors seeking automated solutions. It is anticipated that the company will integrate blockchain-based transparency into its operations.
- **Analah:** A diversified investment platform offering fractional real estate and private equity access starting from AED 500. It is DFSA-regulated and based in DIFC, with plans to expand secondary market trading.
- **InvestDubai (SmartCrowd-powered):** InvestDubai integrates crowdfunding infrastructure powered by SmartCrowd, offering a government-linked gateway for investing in real estate-backed securities.

16.3.2. What You Need to Know Before Investing in Fractional Real Estate Platforms

The Upside – Why Investors Love It

- **Low Barrier to Entry:** With minimums as low as AED 500–2,000, you can get exposure to Dubai real estate without the usual down payment, mortgage, or registration costs.
- **Diversification with Small Capital:** Instead of putting AED 1 million into one apartment, you can split that amount across 10–20 properties, balancing areas, asset classes, and tenant types.
- **Fully Managed Experience:** Most platforms handle tenanting, maintenance, compliance, and distributions. You receive rental income directly into your wallet, without having to field calls about broken faucets.
- **Regulated Environment:** Top platforms are licensed under the Dubai Financial Services Authority (DFSA) in the DIFC. This brings greater transparency, robust legal frameworks, and enhanced investor safeguards.
- **Monthly or Quarterly Rental Returns:** Unlike traditional ownership, which pays annually, these platforms often distribute income monthly, providing a cash flow that can be reinvested.

The Downside – Risks and Limitations

- **Exit Windows May Be Restricted:** Liquidity is not guaranteed. Some platforms offer only one to two exit windows per year, and resale markets are still in development.
- **Management & Platform Fees:** You'll typically pay 10–15% in fees (platform, SPV, legal, property management, etc.), which eat into your returns.
- **Variable Occupancy and Rental Income:** Returns are based on the actual rent collected. If the unit stays vacant, your income drops. Some platforms offer vacancy buffers, but many don't.
- **Capital Appreciation is Not Realised Until Exit:** While platforms may claim an expected IRR (e.g., 6–10%), appreciation only materialises if the property is sold at a higher price. And that's not always in your control.

Exit Options – How You Can Cash Out

Most platforms provide one or more of the following exit routes:

Table 16.1: Fractional Ownership Exit Methods

Exit Method	Description	Liquidity	Notes
Platform Exit Window	Scheduled biannual or annual buyback/sale events	Moderate	Often priced via valuation or peer bids
Secondary Marketplace	List your shares for resale to other users on the platform's marketplace	Variable	Liquidity depends on demand and platform rules

Most platforms advertise Net IRRs (Internal Rate of Return) of 6% to 10%, combining rental yield and projected capital appreciation. Here's how it breaks down:

Table 16.2: Fractional Platform IRR Components

Component	Range	Description
Rental Yield (Net)	4% – 7%	After fees and vacancies
Capital Appreciation	0% – 5%	Realised only on the property sale
Platform Fees	-1% to -2% annually	Reduces net income
Exit Costs	1% – 3%	Legal, admin, or exit charges

Reality Check:

- Properties in prime areas with firm tenant profiles tend to deliver more stable returns.
- You may not get rich overnight, but it can be an excellent stepping stone to build capital or reinvest cash flow.
- Vacancy, tenant default, market price stagnation, or forced exits at lower-than-expected values can impact final returns.

What to Watch Out For

- **Are the properties overvalued at purchase?** Always ask for the original valuation and the third-party appraisal.
- **Who controls the exit decision?** Do you, as a shareholder, vote? Or is the platform in charge?
- **What are the SPV rules?** Do you have limited liability? Can you see the financials?
- **Is there a track record of successful exits?** Platforms with no exits may be new, or they may be avoiding brutal realities.
- **What happens in a market downturn?** Many investors wrongly assume platforms will bail them out.

16.4. Real Estate Tokenisation – Fractional Ownership, Blockchain-Backed

Fractional ownership made it possible for regular investors to purchase a small stake in a property, such as owning one-tenth of a share in a rental apartment. But with tokenisation, this idea has been upgraded using modern digital tools. Instead of paperwork or company shares, your ownership is recorded as digital tokens on a secure online system called blockchain. In Dubai, these tokens are now fully linked to the official property records, so owning a token means you legally own a part of the real estate. The benefit? It's faster, more transparent, and easier to track or sell. You can clearly see your share, trust that it's recorded correctly, and in the future, even sell your tokens to other investors. In short, tokenisation is the next step in fractional ownership, enabling global accessibility.

This means investors can now purchase tokenised shares of fundamental Dubai properties from as little as AED 2,000, with their ownership recorded both on blockchain and within the official Dubai registry.

16.4.1. The Technology Behind Tokenisation – How It Works

Tokenisation is not just a buzzword; it's a technical infrastructure that is transforming how real estate assets are issued, owned, and transferred. In Dubai, the process of tokenising real estate is now officially recognised and regulated, offering investors a secure bridge between physical property and digital ownership.

At the core of Dubai's real estate tokenisation lies the XRP Ledger (XRPL) – a public, decentralised blockchain developed by Ripple. Unlike traditional blockchains, which are primarily used for cryptocurrencies, the XRPL was chosen by the Dubai Land Department (DLD) for its speed, energy efficiency, and built-in tokenisation capabilities. This ledger allows real estate tokens to be "minted", meaning that a digital token is created to represent a legally recognised share of a specific physical property.

What makes Dubai's model unique is its integration with the government registry. Each tokenised share of a property is not just a piece of code on a blockchain; it is also linked to an official title deed in the DLD system. This dual recognition ensures that when you purchase a token, your ownership is both blockchain-verified and legally enforceable.

Here's how the system works step by step:

- **Asset Tokenisation:** A registered property is fractionalised into digital tokens, with each token representing a defined percentage of the real asset (e.g., 0.1% of a villa).
- **On-Chain Minting via XRPL:** These tokens are minted on the XRP Ledger. XRPL enables low-cost, real-time, and highly transparent issuance and tracking of these tokens. Once minted, tokens can be held in digital wallets or traded via licensed platforms.
- **Ownership and Title Linkage:** Through platforms like Prypco Mint and Ctrl Alt, every token is mapped to the Dubai Land Department's title records. This ensures compliance, security, and direct recognition of ownership by the authorities.
- **AED-Based Transactions:** Unlike tokenisation models elsewhere that require cryptocurrency, Dubai's ecosystem supports transactions in AED, ensuring ease of use and avoiding volatility risks associated with crypto markets.
- **Custody and Licensing:** Token issuance is conducted through licensed custodians, under the oversight of the VARA (Virtual Assets Regulatory Authority) and in accordance with Central Bank guidelines. This adds institutional trust to the entire framework.

16.4.2. Why Tokenisation Matters – Key Benefits for Investors

- Low Entry Point: Tokenisation democratises real estate access; anyone can become a fractional property owner for the price of a smartphone.
- Liquidity and Flexibility: Unlike traditional property ownership, tokenised assets can be traded on regulated secondary markets (planned rollout), making real estate more liquid.
- Regulatory Protection: Because Dubai's tokenisation program is approved by the DLD and overseen by VARA and the Central Bank, it offers a legal backbone most global crypto-based tokenisations lack.
- No Need for Crypto Exposure: Investors can pay and be paid in AED. This removes volatility and onboarding challenges.
- Streamlined Ownership Process: No need for complex SPV setups or joint title deeds; ownership is clear, digitised, and individually registered.

"Tokenisation is doing to real estate what the internet did to media—removing friction, lowering entry barriers, and unlocking access."

16.4.3. Tokenisation in Numbers – Current Value & Future Outlook

Tokenised real estate is no longer theoretical; it's already reshaping how property is owned and traded.

Dubai Snapshot

- In May 2025, Dubai recorded AED 66.8 billion in property deals.
- An estimated AED 1.5 billion (~2.2%) came from tokenised transactions.
- The Dubai Land Department aims to scale tokenised deals to AED 60 billion annually (~7% of total volume) by 2033.

Global Projections

- Current global tokenised real estate volume: USD 100–300 billion.
- **Forecasts suggest:**
  - USD 3–4 trillion by 2030–2035 (ScienceSoft, Deloitte).
  - Up to USD 16 trillion (Boston Consulting Group) under optimistic scenarios.

INVESTOR INSIGHT

Tokenisation transforms real estate into a liquid, divisible, and accessible asset class. But what sets Dubai apart is that it's doing it within a regulated, fiat-linked, and title-synced framework, making the technology not just futuristic, but functionally safe and investable today.

16.4.4. How to Buy and Sell Real Estate Tokens in Dubai

Tokenised real estate lets you buy small shares of a property, like owning pieces of a building, without needing to purchase the whole unit. This is now fully legal and regulated in Dubai through platforms like PRYPCO Mint and Eqarat.com, with official support from the Dubai Land Department (DLD).

How to Buy Tokens

- **Choose a Platform:** Sign up with a licensed tokenisation platform (like PRYPCO Mint). You'll need a valid Emirates ID and basic KYC (know-your-customer) verification.
- **Select a Property:** Browse available tokenised properties. These are usually residential buildings or apartments divided into digital shares. Prices can start as low as AED 2,000.
- **Pay in AED:** You don't need crypto. Payment is made in dirhams (AED) directly through the platform.
- **Receive Your Tokens:** Once payment is processed, your share of ownership is issued to you in the form of blockchain tokens. These tokens are legally linked to the property title with DLD.

How to Sell Tokens

- **Use the Platform's Marketplace:** Most platforms include a secondary trading section where you can list your tokens for resale. You set your price and quantity.
- **Wait for a Buyer:** Other users on the platform can view your listing and buy your tokens. The platform securely handles the transfer of ownership and payment.
- **Get Paid in AED:** Once the sale is completed, the funds are transferred to your registered bank account in dirhams.

Key Things to Know about Tokenised Real Estate:

- You control when to sell, no long lock-ins.
- Fees are small (usually 1–2%).
- Liquidity depends on demand; popular properties sell faster.
- Your tokens represent real, legal ownership of Dubai property, registered with the government.

16.4.5. How Rental Income and Expenses Work in Tokenised Real Estate

When a tokenised property is rented out, the net rental income (after deducting service charges, maintenance, and management fees) is distributed to token holders in proportion to their ownership. This is usually done monthly or quarterly, depending on the platform.

But what happens when the property is vacant? Even if there's no rental income, ongoing expenses like service charges, repairs, and platform management fees still apply. Most platforms handle this by:

- Deducting from a reserve fund, if available.
- Advancing the cost and recovering it later from your future income or sale proceeds.
- In some cases, they may ask you to top up your balance if the vacancy lasts too long.

So while tokenised real estate offers passive income, investors should always factor in vacancy risk and ongoing costs to manage expectations and ensure sustainability.

Example: You own 1% of a tokenised unit. Annual service charges are AED 10,000. That's AED 100 owed by you.

- If the property is rented, your AED 100 is deducted from your rental income.
- If the property is vacant, the AED 100 may be:
    - Deducted from future rent.
    - Taken from a reserve fund.
    - Requested as a top-up, depending on the platform terms.

16.5. AI in Real Estate – Smarter Decisions, Better Outcomes

In the era of ChatGPT and ubiquitous AI, it's no surprise that real estate is beginning to benefit in powerful ways, especially for investors. The same technologies that help us automate emails, summarise documents, or analyse trends in seconds are now being applied to property markets, opening a new level of insight and efficiency.

For real estate investors, AI isn't just a buzzword; it's a practical tool. It helps us evaluate neighbourhoods faster, predict market shifts with more precision, optimise short-term rental pricing, and even scan through legal documents or financial models in minutes. It reduces guesswork, speeds up decision-making, and allows us to operate with the kind of clarity that used to take teams of analysts. Whether you're scouting for your next unit in Dubai, running a short-term rental, or deciding when to exit a project, AI tools today can transform your entire investment process, from market research to portfolio management. Here's how leading investors are leveraging AI, with the most relevant tools and real-world applications.

16.5.1. Market Analysis & Deal Sourcing

AI platforms now scan vast databases of listings, transaction records, and market trends to surface undervalued or high-potential opportunities in seconds. These systems can identify patterns and anomalies that would take humans days to uncover, giving investors a decisive edge.

Key Tools:

- **DXBInteract:** Dubai-focused platform offering real-time transaction analytics and area trend insights.
- **Mashvisor / Propwire:** Global tools using AI to rank and score deals based on yield, occupancy, and price trends.
- **Kyna AI:** Uses 100+ data points to match investors with Dubai's top 1% properties, providing ROI projections and market timing insights.
- **pX (Dubai):** AI-powered MLS and investment intelligence platform, unifying fragmented data for instant deal analysis.
- **Custom Alerts:** Integrate ChatGPT, Zapier, and Google Sheets to automate personalised market alerts based on your specific investment criteria.

16.5.2. AI for Underwriting & Financial Modelling

AI can significantly enhance the precision and speed of financial analysis for real estate investments.

- **AI Financial Modellers:** Instantly generate stabilised income statements, Discounted Cash Flows (DCFs), and yield capitalisation models from property data, no coding or Excel expertise needed.
- **ChatGPT & Document Extraction:** Upload a property brochure or financials and have AI extract key numbers, calculate breakeven points, and run ROI scenarios tailored to Dubai's market.
- **Bayut TruEstimate™:** AI-powered property valuation tool for the UAE, providing instant, data-driven appraisals.

16.5.3. Short-Term Rental Optimisation

AI has revolutionised short-term rental management, especially in dynamic markets like Dubai. Intelligent pricing engines and automation platforms now optimise nightly rates, occupancy, and guest experience in real time.

Key Tools:

- **PriceLabs, BeyondPricing, AirDNA Smart Rates:** AI-driven pricing tools that adjust rates based on seasonality, events, and local supply, boosting revenue by 15–40% and saving hours of manual work.
- **RentalReady, Hostex, Boom:** All-in-one property management systems with AI features for automated guest communication, task management, and reporting.

16.5.4. Legal & Compliance Automation

AI is increasingly being applied to streamline legal due diligence and ensure compliance in real estate transactions.

- **Spellbook, LawGeex, and Ironclad:** AI platforms that review, draft, and compare real estate contracts, highlighting unusual clauses and compliance risks.
- **ListedKit, Kolena:** Upload SPAs, MOUs, or lease agreements and let AI extract critical terms, deadlines, and red flags, streamlining due diligence and transaction workflows.
- **Custom LLMs (e.g., GPT-4):** Can summarise, compare, and analyse legal documents before sending them to a lawyer, reducing review time and minimising errors.

16.5.5. Custom Workflow Automation

AI and no-code automation tools are now central to efficient real estate operations. They handle everything from lead tracking and investor communications to document generation and reporting.

Key Tools:

- **Make.com, Zapier:** Automate document creation, lead follow-ups, and report delivery by connecting property portals, CRMs, and email platforms.
- **Whimsical, Notion AI:** Generate property pitch decks, market snapshots, and investment memos with AI-driven content and design.

16.5.6. New AI Tools in Dubai Real Estate

Dubai's real estate sector is rapidly adopting AI, with several new and specialised platforms emerging beyond the most widely known names. Here are notable AI-driven platforms and tools shaping the Dubai property market, each offering unique features for investors, agents, and property managers:

Key Tools:

- **Prop-AI:** Automates property search, valuation, and investment analysis for buyers and professionals using real-time data and predictive AI.
- **Unique Properties & AIR:** AI-native brokerage platform providing real-time insights, predictive analytics, and automation to boost agent efficiency and client transparency.
- **AnySqft:** AI-driven platform for buying, selling, renting, and investing, featuring personalised property recommendations and predictive analytics.
- **Refty.ai:** Property intelligence tool for brokers and investors, identifying high-yield properties, providing owner data, and automating research.
- **Realiste:** AI platform delivering market data, property analysis, and investment recommendations using predictive models.

INVESTOR INSIGHT

The edge isn't just in using AI; it's in integrating it into your daily decision-making process. Investors who build systems powered by AI tools can scale faster, reduce errors, and focus their energy on strategy rather than spreadsheets.

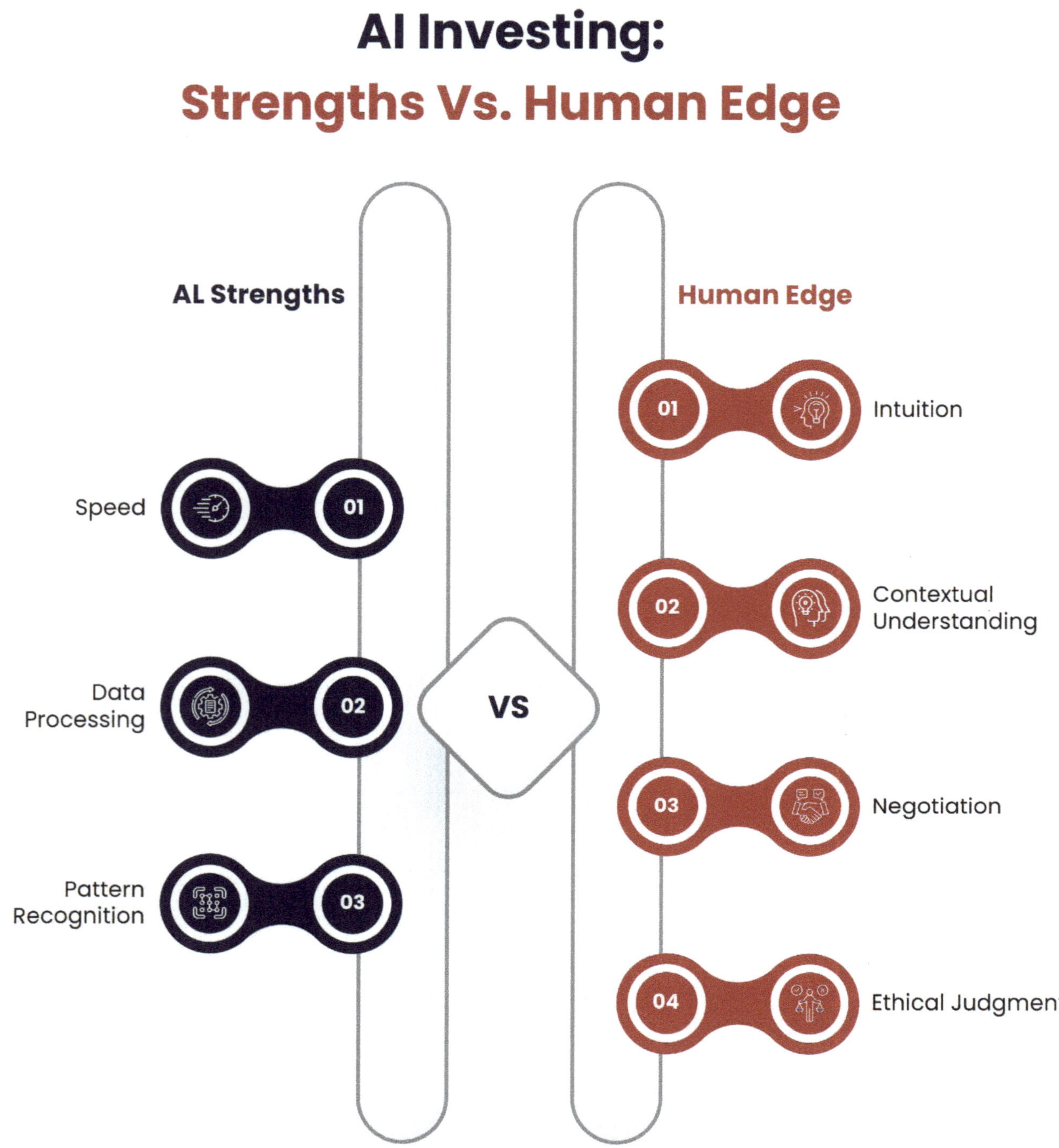
AI Investing:
Strengths Vs. Human Edge
AL Strengths
Human Edge
Speed
01
Data
Processing
02
Pattern
Recognition
03
VS
01
Intuition
02
Contextual
Understanding
03
Negotiation
04
Ethical Judgment

16.6. Challenges, Ethics, and the Human Edge in AI Investing

AI might feel like magic, but it's not without flaws, limits, and responsibilities. As investors, we need to be aware of where AI adds value, where it can mislead, and why human judgment still matters.

16.6.1. Challenges and Limitations

- **Garbage In, Garbage Out:** AI is only as good as the data it's trained on. If the underlying property data is outdated, biased, or incomplete (which is often the case in emerging markets), predictions can be off.
- **Overfitting to Trends:** Some AI models may over-weight recent price spikes or short-term anomalies, leading to unrealistic forecasts or missed risks.
- **Regulatory Blind Spots:** AI tools may flag a building as high-yield without considering critical factors like specific community rules, short-term rental prohibitions, or pending legal disputes.

16.6.2. Ethical Use of AI

As AI becomes more powerful, investors and platform developers alike need to ask:

- Is the AI model transparent and fair?
- Are specific neighbourhoods or user profiles being unintentionally excluded or overrepresented?
- Is personal data being used responsibly and with consent? In a market like Dubai, where regulatory compliance is crucial, the ethical use of AI will be the differentiator, not just a buzzword.

16.6.3. Why Human Insight Still Wins

- **Intuition Matters:** No AI can replace your lived experience, your ability to ask the right questions, or your understanding of relationships and timing.
- **AI Lacks Context:** An algorithm might not be aware that a new metro line has just been approved, or that a developer is struggling with handovers. You do.
- **Negotiation is Human:** The deal-closing process, price negotiation, seller psychology, and off-market leads are still very much a human game.

INVESTOR INSIGHT

AI is a tool like a compass. It helps you navigate, but you decide the destination.

Market Analysis & Deal Sourcing

AI platforms analyze listings, transactions and trends

Underwriting & Financial Modelling

AI expedites financial analysis and risk assessment

Short-Term Rental Optimisation

AI optimizes pricing and occupancy rates

Legal & Compliance Automation

AI streamlines contract review and compliance

Chapter Summary

Chapter 16, **"Smart Real Estate – From REITs to AI-Powered Investing,"** marks a pivotal shift, asserting that real estate investing is no longer just about bricks, deeds, and down payments. We've entered an era where technology, data, and digital innovation are reshaping the very foundation of property ownership and access to investment.

This chapter explored how modern investors can diversify and amplify returns using:

- **REITs** for passive, dividend-generating exposure to large property portfolios.
- **Fractional Ownership Platforms** (like Stake and Maisour) for curated, bite-sized entry into income-producing properties with low barriers.
- **Tokenisation** to access fractional shares of high-value assets on blockchain, offering enhanced liquidity and transparency within a regulated, AED-linked framework.
- **AI Tools** for more innovative deal sourcing, underwriting, short-term rental optimisation, legal compliance automation, and overall decision-making efficiency.

The chapter highlighted that smart real estate is not about blindly chasing every trend; it's about understanding the tools that genuinely align with your strategy, risk tolerance, and long-term goals. In a market like Dubai, these innovations offer unprecedented access, liquidity, and transparency, but also demand a nuanced understanding of their benefits and limitations.

Key Takeaways:

- **REITs for Passive Exposure:** Invest in professionally managed property portfolios for dividends and diversification without direct management.
- **Fractional Ownership for Accessibility:** Co-own property shares with lower capital outlays, ideal for diversification, but understand liquidity limitations.
- **Tokenisation for Transparency & Liquidity:** Leverage blockchain-backed ownership for secure, divisible, and potentially more liquid real estate investments in AED.
- **AI for Smarter Decisions:** Utilise AI tools for market analysis, financial modelling, rental optimisation, and legal due diligence to gain a decisive edge.
- **Balance Innovation with Caution:** While embracing new models, always vet platforms, understand exit processes, and review fees and legal enforceability. Human insight remains crucial for context and negotiation.

Action Plan:

Here's a practical action plan to begin integrating smart real estate tools into your investing:

- **Explore REITs:** Try investing in a REIT via your bank or brokerage.
- **Research Fractional Platforms:** Open an account on a platform like Stake; research PRYPCO Mint or similar DLD-approved tokenised property platforms.
- **Set Up a Tracking Dashboard:** Use tools like DXBInteract, Google Sheets, or AI chatbots to track market trends, transaction data, or your own portfolio's ROI.
- **Attend a Demo or Webinar:** Most new platforms offer investor walkthroughs; watch a few to understand the backend and support they offer.
- **Balance Innovation with Caution:** Embrace new models, but always vet the platform, understand the exit process, and carefully review the fine print regarding fees, insurance, and legal enforceability.

YOUR JOURNEY
NAVIGATOR

Part 4: Strategic Exits and Advanced Investment Strategies

Recap

You have just completed **Chapter 16: Smart Real Estate – From REITs to AI-Powered Investing**, where you explored advanced strategies to diversify your portfolio and leverage technology. You learned about REITs, fractional ownership, tokenisation, and AI-driven tools, gaining insights into how these innovations can expand your reach, optimise operations, and enhance returns while reducing reliance on traditional property ownership..

Next Chapter Preview

We now move to **Chapter 17: Women and Real Estate – Investing with Confidence**, authored by Hajra Jaafar. Drawing on 15 years of experience building and managing a diverse Dubai property portfolio, Hajra brings a personal and practical perspective to empowering women in real estate. She combines real stories with actionable strategies to help women overcome common barriers, structure their investments for safety and control, and tap into supportive networks and mentorship opportunities..

You Will Learn

- ☑ Why women are uniquely positioned to excel in real estate investing.
- ☑ Common challenges women face and strategies to overcome them.
- ☑ Legal and structural approaches for safeguarding ownership and legacy.
- ☑ Real-life case studies from women investors in Dubai.
- ☑ How to find platforms, mentorship, and community support.

Link to Framework

This chapter deepens the value creation and long-game elements of your C.D.R.C. mindset by highlighting inclusivity and long-term resilience. It strengthens your L.E.A.D. approach by providing adaptable strategies that can be applied by women at any stage of their investment journey.

Purpose / Big Picture Link

This is the empowerment stage of your investment journey. By integrating mindset, market knowledge, and tailored strategies, you will see how real estate can be a powerful vehicle for financial independence and legacy building, particularly for women ready to invest with confidence.

CHAPTER 17

Women and Real Estate – Investing with Confidence

> The future is female. And in real estate, that future is about building security, freedom, and legacy on your terms.

Welcome to a special section of this book, a dedicated conversation for women navigating the exciting world of real estate. While the entire book equips you with the knowledge to succeed as an investor, this chapter affirms that your unique strengths as a woman are not just relevant, but they are powerful assets. From financial independence to building a secure legacy, real estate offers a tangible path to empowerment. This chapter explores why women are excelling in Dubai's property market, the specific challenges you might encounter, and the resources available to help you invest with unwavering confidence.

Introduction:

My name is Hajra Jaafar, and I'm a passionate advocate for empowering women in real estate investment. I've seen firsthand how owning property can transform lives, offer financial independence, and secure a lasting legacy. For years, I've worked closely with clients, helping them navigate market complexities and build portfolios that reflect their unique goals and values. This bonus chapter is dedicated to you, whether you're an aspiring or seasoned female investor. It's my firm belief that when women invest, they not only grow their wealth but also positively impact their families, communities, and the broader economy. Let's tap into your full potential in Dubai's dynamic real estate landscape, together.

17.1. Why Women Make Excellent Real Estate Investors

In a market often perceived as male-dominated, women are not just participating; they are leading, shaping, and transforming the landscape. The numbers speak for themselves: in 2024, women invested over AED 118 billion in Dubai property, making up 34% of all investors. This isn't just a trend; it's a testament to inherent strengths that align perfectly with successful real estate investing.

Women often possess distinct qualities that make them exceptional investors:

- **Long-Term Strategic Vision:** Research suggests women tend to adopt a longer-term perspective in investment, aligning perfectly with real estate's nature as a generational wealth-building tool. They are less prone to short-term speculation, prioritising stable growth and consistent returns that compound over time.
- **Meticulous Due Diligence:** Women are often noted for their thoroughness and attention to detail during research and verification processes. This diligent, comprehensive approach leads to more informed decisions, reduces risks, and uncovers opportunities others might miss.
- **Calculated Risk-Taking:** While often perceived as risk-averse, this translates into a disciplined and analytical approach to evaluating opportunities. It's not about avoiding all risk, but about making calculated, informed choices that protect capital while achieving desired returns, focusing on sustainable growth over speculative gains.
- **Focus on Stability and Legacy:** Many women invest with a strong focus on financial security for their families, creating a stable income, and building a lasting legacy that can be passed down through generations. This often leads to investments in well-established, resilient communities.
- **Community and Lifestyle Focus:** There's a growing inclination among female investors to consider properties that align with quality of life, community engagement, and wellness-focused amenities. This often leads to investments in areas with strong, sustainable demand and higher long-term appeal for end-users.

INVESTOR INSIGHT

Your unique strengths as a woman, whether it's your long-term vision for family security, your attention to detail, or your innate ability to build community, are not just personal traits; they are powerful investment advantages in Dubai's real estate market.

17.2. Common Challenges Women Face: How to Overcome Them

While Dubai has actively fostered an inclusive environment, women investors may still encounter specific challenges. Recognising these is the first step to overcoming them, ensuring your investment journey is as smooth and empowering as possible.

- **Navigating Legal Complexities:** Property laws, particularly concerning inheritance or asset protection across borders, can appear daunting.
  - **Solution:** Dubai has made significant strides in this area. Recent legal reforms (Federal Decree-Law No. 41 of 2022) now allow non-Muslims to register Wills in the UAE to ensure asset distribution according to their wishes, independent of traditional Sharia law applications for succession. Always engage with qualified real estate lawyers for contract reviews and proactive estate planning (as discussed in Chapter 10).
- **Access to Information & Trusted Advisors:** Despite growing transparency, finding unbiased information or a trusted advisor can be a hurdle.
  - **Solution:** Leverage established DLD initiatives and reputable platforms (as covered in Chapters 7 & 16) and actively seek out women-specific networks and mentorship programmes.
- **Overcoming Societal/Cultural Biases:** While increasingly rare in Dubai's progressive environment, some women may still face subtle biases or expectations regarding financial decision-making.
  - **Solution:** The increasing visibility of successful women in Dubai real estate is actively breaking these stereotypes. Focus on your data-driven approach and trust your research. Your informed decisions are your most powerful argument.
- **Confidence Gap:** Sometimes, even with knowledge, a self-perceived "confidence gap" can lead to hesitation in making significant investment decisions.
  - **Solution:** Education, mentorship, and actively connecting with other women investors can boost confidence. Attend workshops, engage in forums, and celebrate every successful transaction; each step builds your internal conviction and empowers you.

INVESTOR INSIGHT

Dubai has rewritten the rules to empower you. Grasp the legal autonomy you have, proactively seek legal counsel, and leverage the growing ecosystem of support. Your confidence will grow with every informed step you take.

17.3. Structuring for Safety, Control, and Legacy

For women, especially those managing family wealth or building a personal portfolio, the choice of legal structure can be a powerful tool for enhanced safety, control, and clear legacy planning. Beyond individual ownership, consider options that provide robust asset protection.

- **Company Ownership (SPVs):** As discussed in Chapter 10, Special Purpose Vehicles (SPVs) can be highly effective for segregating personal and investment assets, offering a layer of liability protection and streamlining future transfers. This allows for greater control over your real estate holdings.
- **Trusts and Foundations:** These sophisticated structures (also covered in Chapter 10) provide the highest level of asset protection and privacy. They ensure seamless, private wealth transfer across generations, bypassing potentially lengthy probate processes and aligning perfectly with legacy goals.

INVESTOR INSIGHT

Structuring your investments strategically isn't just for tax benefits; it's about peace of mind. It ensures your assets are protected, managed as you intend, and provides a clear path for your legacy, regardless of future circumstances.

17.4. Real Stories, Real Confidence

The narrative of women in Dubai real estate is being actively rewritten by trailblazers and savvy investors. From financial independence to building a secure legacy, women are demonstrating exceptional leadership and financial acumen. These are not just statistics; they are real stories of women who have embraced the opportunity and found success:

- **A young mother from Sweden** who started with a single 1-bedroom apartment in JVC, managing it as a holiday home while navigating motherhood. Her attention to guest reviews and cost management allowed her to scale to three units, providing significant passive income to support her family.
- **A doctor from India** who, after years of practice, strategically invested in two commercial office units in Business Bay. Her thorough due diligence on tenant financials and a long-term vision for Dubai's economic growth ensured stable rental yields, outperforming many of her equity investments.
- **A businesswoman from Saudi Arabia** diversified her regional portfolio by acquiring a luxury villa in Dubai Hills Estate. Her focus on asset appreciation and a family-centric community choice not only provided a beautiful second home but also secured a significant asset for her children's future inheritance, protected by Dubai's clear property laws.

These are but a few examples. From leading broker Fatima Al Kobaisi, who guides high-net-worth clients and Gen Z investors, to pioneering entrepreneurs like Lynne Akkawi in property management and Mahwussh Alam in short-term rentals, women are demonstrating exceptional leadership and financial acumen. Look around you, the landscape is changing. Women are not just investing; they are leading.

17.5. Platforms & Mentorship for Women

You are not alone in this journey. Dubai actively supports your success by fostering a robust ecosystem of platforms and mentorship opportunities specifically designed for women in real estate. These resources provide invaluable knowledge, networking, and direct support to help you thrive.

- **DLD's Real Estate Empowerment Programme:** This initiative by the Dubai Land Department (DLD) has attracted over 1,000 women into the sector, offering tailored training and advisory support.
- **"She Pioneers" Initiative:** A groundbreaking partnership (including Samana Developers and DLD) aimed at increasing female leadership and participation in the sector through mentorship programs, networking opportunities, and specialised training.
- **Property Finder's "SheForShe" Mentorship Program:** Designed to promote and nurture the next generation of female real estate leaders, offering one-on-one mentoring sessions with accomplished professionals.
- **Dubai Business Women Council (DBWC):** Provides valuable resources, connections, and support to empower women entrepreneurs and professionals in various sectors, including real estate.
- **Legal Literacy Campaigns:** The DLD and Dubai Women Establishment (DWE) conduct periodic legal literacy campaigns and workshops focused on asset protection and property law for women.

INVESTOR INSIGHT

Leverage these platforms. Join community groups and property forums to stay informed about local issues, connect with like-minded investors, and learn from experienced professionals. Networking is a powerful tool for gaining market insights and identifying opportunities.

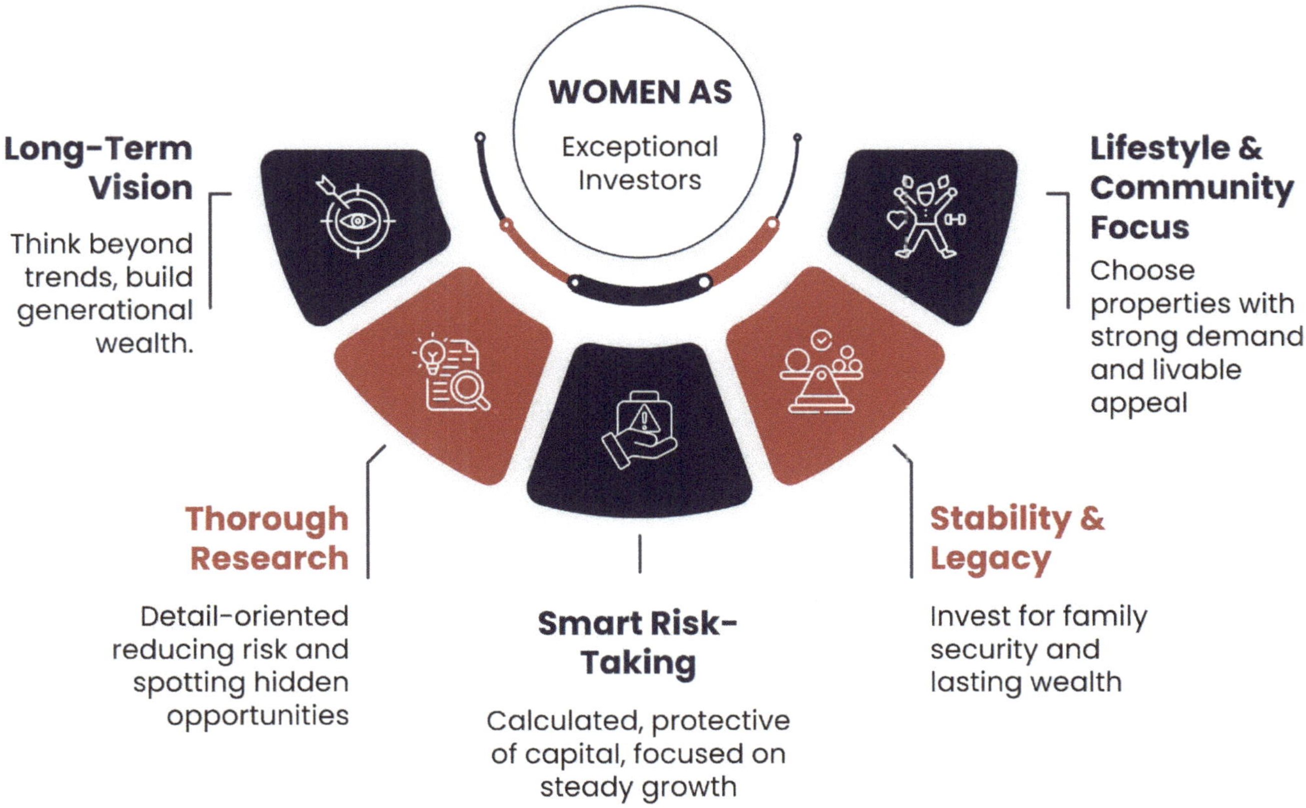
WOMEN AS
Exceptional Investors
Long-Term Vision
Think beyond trends, build generational wealth.
Lifestyle & Community Focus
Choose properties with strong demand and livable appeal
Thorough Research
Detail-oriented reducing risk and spotting hidden opportunities
Smart Risk-Taking
Calculated, protective of capital, focused on steady growth
Stability & Legacy
Invest for family security and lasting wealth

17.6. Why Dubai Is the Right Place for Women to Begin Their Investment Journey

Dubai isn't just welcoming you; it's actively building a future designed for your success. The emirate stands out globally as an exceptionally supportive environment for women to invest in real estate, owing to a unique confluence of factors:

- **Legal Protections & 100% Ownership:** Dubai provides robust legal protections for female property owners, ensuring they have equal ownership rights. Women can own property outright, in their name, without needing male consent or a co-sign, unlike some other jurisdictions.
- **No Taxes:** The absence of property tax, capital gains tax, and personal income tax on rental earnings means every dirham you earn is genuinely yours, directly enhancing your financial independence.
- **High Rental Yield:** Dubai's property market consistently offers attractive rental yields, even for smaller units, providing a strong pathway to passive income and financial security.
- **Safety & Stability:** Dubai consistently ranks among the safest cities globally, offering an unparalleled sense of personal security. This allows women to move, visit, and invest without fear, focusing purely on their financial goals.
- **Government-Backed Empowerment:** Beyond policies, the DLD and various government initiatives actively seek to empower women in real estate, offering investment incentives, advisory services, flexible financing, and promoting women's representation in leadership roles.
- **Developer Responsiveness:** Developers are increasingly designing properties with amenities and features (e.g., sustainability ratings, wellness-focused communities) that align with priorities often expressed by female investors: long-term security, community engagement, and future-ready design.
- **Residency & Quality of Life:** Flexible visa options and world-class infrastructure contribute to an appealing lifestyle that attracts international female investors seeking long-term stability and quality of life.

Summary Table

Why Dubai Works For Women Investors

Icon	Long-Term Rental	Short-Term Rental
	100% ownership allowed	No male consent or co-sign needed
	No Taxes	Every dirham you earn is yours
	High rental yield	Even small units generate consistent cash flow
	Safety	Move, visit, and invest without fear
	Legal protection (Wills)	Use Wills, SPVs, and contracts to your advantage (referencing Chapter 10)
	Access to financing	Mortgage options available for women, including non-residents
	Investment education	Growing courses, coaching, and women's groups actively provide support
	Government initiatives	DLD-backed programs empower women's participation & leadership[
	Developer responsiveness	Designing properties aligned with women's preferences (wellness, community)

17.7. Bonus Tips

- Work with female real estate advisors or agencies who understand your perspective.
- Join community groups and property forums to stay informed about local issues and developments.
- Schedule site visits at different times of day to assess the vibe and safety.

Chapter Summary

Chapter 17, **"Women and Real Estate – Investing with Confidence,"** is a powerful affirmation that women are not just participants but pivotal leaders in Dubai's dynamic real estate landscape. It celebrates the unique strengths women bring to investment, including a long-term strategic vision, due diligence, and a focus on security and legacy.

The chapter began with **Hajra Jaafar's introduction,** setting an inspiring tone and highlighting the life-changing power of real estate for women. It then delved into **Why Women Make Excellent Real Estate Investors**, highlighting their inherent strengths in strategic thinking and a focus on long-term value.

The chapter addressed **Common Challenges** women may face, such as navigating legal complexities, and highlighted how Dubai's progressive legal reforms and proactive engagement with professional legal counsel empower them to overcome these. It emphasised the importance of strategic structuring (using SPVs or trusts, as discussed in Chapter 10) for enhanced safety, control, and seamless legacy planning.

A significant focus was placed on **Real Stories, Real Confidence**, providing anecdotal examples of women investors succeeding in Dubai, and the robust ecosystem of **Platforms & Mentorship for Women**, detailing specific DLD initiatives like the Real Estate Empowerment Programme and "She Pioneers," alongside industry-led programs. This underscores the active support available for women to build confidence and networks.

The chapter then articulated **Why Dubai Is the Right Place for Women to Begin Their Investment Journey,** citing its unparalleled legal protections (100% ownership, independent financial control), tax advantages, exceptional safety, high rental yields, and the government's strategic commitment to empowering women in the economy and leadership roles.

By embracing their inherent strengths, leveraging comprehensive legal and financial knowledge, and utilising the extensive support networks available, women investors in Dubai are uniquely positioned to build substantial wealth, economic freedom, and lasting legacies on their own terms.

Key Takeaways:

- **Inherent Strengths:** Women's long-term vision, due diligence, and focus on security are powerful investment advantages.
- **Legal Empowerment:** Dubai's legal reforms (e.g., Wills Law) provide women with significant autonomy over property ownership and inheritance.
- **Strategic Structuring:** Utilise SPVs and trusts for enhanced asset protection, control, and streamlined legacy planning.
- **Leverage Support Networks:** Engage with DLD initiatives, mentorship programs, and women-specific real estate communities for knowledge and support.
- **Dubai's Unique Advantage:** The city offers unparalleled safety, tax benefits, high yields, and a government actively promoting women's success in real estate.
- **Build Your Legacy:** Real estate offers a tangible path to financial independence, security, and wealth creation for future generations.

Final Thought: Property investment is more than just numbers; it's about building security, freedom, and legacy. As women continue to rise as influential decision-makers, Dubai offers a dynamic and supportive environment in which to establish roots and grow wealth. When women invest, it changes more than just bank balances; it changes narratives, families, and futures. Dubai offers the infrastructure, opportunities, and safety to make your first move. The only thing missing is your decision to start. Start with one unit. One goal. One belief: You belong in the room.

YOUR JOURNEY
NAVIGATOR

Completion of Your Investment Journey

Recap

You have reached the end of **License to Deal**, having travelled through every stage of the Dubai real estate investment journey, from building the mindset of a confident investor in Part 1, to executing safe and strategic purchases in Part 2, to maximising ownership value in Part 3, and finally, mastering strategic exits and advanced strategies in Part 4.

You began by learning **how to think** like an investor, grounding every decision in the C.D.R.C. pillars and L.E.A.D. approach. You understood **why** Dubai presents exceptional opportunities, explored **where** to look at both macro and micro levels, learned **when** to act by reading market cycles, and mastered **how** to analyse deals with precision.

You then moved into **execution**, gaining a step-by-step understanding of buying processes, due diligence, legal frameworks, taxation, and handover. In ownership, you explored strategies to protect, manage, and grow your assets, whether through long-term leasing, short-term rentals, or operational enhancements. Finally, you mastered **exit planning** and advanced investment tools, including AI, tokenisation, and REITs, before closing with Hajra Jaafar's empowering guide to women investors in Dubai.

Where Are You Now

You now have the complete roadmap to navigate Dubai's real estate market with clarity, confidence, and control. The tools, checklists, and frameworks in this book are designed to be revisited often, adapting with you as market conditions change and your personal goals evolve.

Your Next Steps

- ☑ Revisit your SMART goals regularly to ensure they align with your current resources and ambitions.
- ☑ Keep your research systems active, tracking market data and opportunity zones.
- ☑ Maintain your network of trusted agents, developers, and advisors to support execution and scaling.
- ☑ Review your exit strategies annually to ensure they remain aligned with market conditions and personal timelines.

Final Word

Real estate investing is not a one-time event; it is a continuous journey of learning, adapting, and acting with purpose. You now have the knowledge to think like an investor, act like a professional, and grow like a strategist.

Your license to deal is not just a title, it is your permission to engage with the Dubai property market from a position of strength. The opportunities are here. The decision, as always, is yours.

Master Bibliography

Research Note

This book is based on a combination of **first-hand market experience in Dubai** and c**omparative analysis with global real estate investment principles.**

The UAE-specific data, laws, and processes are current as of **July 2025**, and the strategic frameworks draw from both l**ocal insights and international best practices.**

The global references listed below were consulted not for direct market data, but for **conceptual alignment** — adapting proven investment models, analytical tools, and strategic thinking to the **unique legal, economic, and cultural environment** of Dubai's real estate market.

Government & Regulatory Bodies

- **Al Etihad Credit Bureau** – Official source for credit scores and financial history in the UAE.
- **Central Bank of the UAE (CBUAE)** – Mortgage lending data, official economic statistics, and interest rate guidance.
- **Dubai Land Department (DLD)** – Primary government authority for all property transactions, registration, and regulation.
- **Real Estate Regulatory Agency (RERA)** – Regulatory arm of the DLD, overseeing brokers, developers, escrow, and tenancy laws.
- **Trakheesi System** – DLD platform for verifying broker licences and issuing listing permits.

- **Oqood System** – Provisional property register for off-plan real estate under the DLD.
- **Ejari System** – Official tenancy contract registration system under the DLD.
- **Mollak Platform** – DLD-regulated system for Owners Association (OA) registration and service charge management.
- **Dubai Municipality** – Issuer of Building Completion Certificates (BCC) and enforcer of the Al Sa'fat Green Building Code.
- **Virtual Asset Regulatory Authority (VARA)** – Regulator for virtual asset activities in Dubai.
- **Dubai International Financial Centre (DIFC) Authority** – Economic data and regulatory oversight for platforms like Stake and SmartCrowd.
- **Department of Economic Development (DED)** – Dubai – Licensing and zoning compliance authority for commercial properties.
- **Dubai Courts** – Real Estate Dispute Resolution Centre – Mediation and dispute processes.
- **UAE Federal Laws & Dubai Decrees** – Property ownership, inheritance, and registration regulations.
- **Master Developer NOC Requirements** – Approval processes from Emaar, Nakheel, and other master developers before transfers.

Market Data & Transaction Platforms

- **DXBInteract.com** – Real-time market data platform tracking and analysing DLD transaction data.
- **Bayut.com & PropertyFinder.ae** – Leading property portals with price indexes, listing data, Days on Market, and rental trends.
- **Property Monitor** – Platform providing real-time property valuations and comparable sales data.
- **AirDNA, AirROI, Mashvisor** – Short-term rental performance and yield analytics.
- **Kyna AI, Propwire** – AI-driven market intelligence tools.

Market Research & Consultancy Reports

- **CBRE** – Global real estate consultancy providing Dubai market reports and sector analysis.
- **Knight Frank** – Global property consultancy with in-depth Dubai market reports.
- **Savills** – International real estate services provider with research on Dubai's property market.
- **JLL (Jones Lang LaSalle)** – Leading global real estate firm producing Dubai market insights.
- **UBS Global Real Estate Bubble Index 2024** – Assessment of market risk and valuations.

Developers & Project Case Studies

- **Emaar Properties PJSC** – Case studies and payment plan examples (e.g., Dubai Creek Harbour).
- **Nakheel PJSC** – Master developer guidelines, project NOCs.
- **Damac Properties** – Payment plan and project marketing examples.
- **Sobha Realty** – Quality benchmark case studies.
- **Ellington Properties** – Design and brand positioning references.
- **Reportage Properties LLC** – Case study on Taormina Village pricing and discounts.
- **Meteora Developers** – Case study on Vivanti post-handover payment plans.
- **Other Developers** – As cited in examples for JVC, Meydan, and Liwan.

Other References

- **"License to Deal" Course and Content** – Original educational framework forming the basis of the book.
- **Hajra Jaafar** – Author of the bonus chapter on women in real estate investment.

International Real Estate & Investment Books Referenced for Conceptual Alignment

(Adapted to Dubai context for market analysis, due diligence processes, financial modelling, and portfolio strategy)

1. **Brandon Turner** – *The Book on Rental Property Investing: How to Create Wealth and Passive Income Through Smart Buy & Hold Real Estate Investing* – BiggerPockets Publishing, 2015.
2. **Ken McElroy** – *The ABCs of Real Estate Investing: The Secrets of Finding Hidden Profits Most Investors Miss* – RDA Press, 2004.
3. **Gary Keller, Dave Jenks, and Jay Papasan** – *The Millionaire Real Estate Investor* – McGraw-Hill, 2005.
4. **Than Merrill** – *The Real Estate Wholesaling Bible: The Fastest, Easiest Way to Get Started in Real Estate Investing* – Wiley, 2014.
5. **William J. Poorvu** – *The Real Estate Game: The Intelligent Guide to Decisionmaking and Investment* – Free Press, 1999.
6. **Frank Gallinelli** – *What Every Real Estate Investor Needs to Know About Cash Flow... And 36 Other Key Financial Measures* – McGraw-Hill, 2008.
7. **Don R. Campbell** – *Real Estate Investing in Canada: Creating Wealth with the ACRE System* – Wiley, 2012.
8. **David Lindahl** – *Multi-Family Millions: How Anyone Can Reposition Apartments for Big Profits* – Wiley, 2008.
9. **Dolf de Roos** – *Real Estate Riches: How to Become Rich Using Your Banker's Money* – Wiley, 2004.
10. **John T. Reed** – *How to Buy Real Estate for at Least 20% Below Market Value* – Self-published, 2002.

Combined Glossary & Index

A

- **ADGM (Abu Dhabi Global Market):** An international financial free zone with its own legal framework, including a registry for non-Muslim wills. See Chapter 10.
- **ADR (Average Daily Rate):** A key metric in short-term rentals that calculates the average revenue earned per booked night. See Chapter 14.
- **AI (Artificial Intelligence):** The use of technology to automate market analysis, deal sourcing, and financial modeling, providing a strategic edge to investors. See Chapter 16.
- **Al Maktoum International Airport (DWC):** A mega-project in Dubai South planned to become the world's largest airport, driving development and demand in surrounding areas. See Chapter 3.
- **Al Sa'fat Green Building Code:** A mandatory green building rating system for all new construction in Dubai, which impacts a property's long-term value and operational costs. See Chapter 3.

- **Al Etihad Credit Bureau:** The official source for credit scores and financial history for residents in the UAE, used by banks to assess mortgage eligibility. See Chapter 8.
- **AMC (Annual Maintenance Contracts):** A professional service agreement for the regular upkeep and repair of a property's systems, like AC and plumbing. See Chapter 12.
- **Appreciation, capital:** The increase in a property's market value over time. See Chapter 5, Chapter 15.
- **Arjan:** An emerging residential and commercial zone in Dubai known for its growth potential and mid-market properties. See Chapter 3.
- **Assignment sales:** The process of reselling an off-plan property before it has been handed over, transferring the original purchase agreement to a new buyer. See Chapter 8, Chapter 15.

B

- **BCC (Building Completion Certificate):** A crucial document issued by the Dubai Municipality that certifies a building is complete and compliant with regulations, necessary for the handover process. See Chapter 11.
- **Blockchain:** A decentralized digital ledger used for creating and securing digital records, the core technology behind tokenization. See Chapter 16.
- **Brokers:** Real estate professionals licensed by RERA to represent buyers or sellers in a transaction. See Chapter 8.
- **Business Bay:** A core commercial and residential zone known for its high-density, mixed-use properties and proximity to Downtown Dubai. See Chapter 3.

C

- **Capital gains tax:** A tax on the profit from selling an asset. Dubai has no personal capital gains tax. See Chapter 10.
- **C.D.R.C. mindset:** The core mental framework of a successful investor: Clarity, Discipline, Resilience, and Curiosity. See Chapter 1.
- **Chiller systems:** Centralized air conditioning systems used in many Dubai buildings, which can be billed separately (chiller-paid) or included in service charges (chiller-free). See Chapter 12.
- **Co-ownership:** A legal structure where two or more individuals hold title to the same property. See Chapter 10.
- **Commercial property:** A non-residential real estate asset, including offices, retail shops, warehouses, and plots. See Chapter 6.
- **Community management:** The company or Owners Association (OA) responsible for the day-to-day operations and upkeep of shared areas in a building or community. See Chapter 12.
- **Confluence of signals:** The strategic practice of confirming a market trend by observing multiple, reinforcing indicators from different data sources simultaneously. See Chapter 4.
- **Conveyancers:** Legal professionals who specialize in managing the transactional process of property sales and transfers. See Chapter 8.

- **Core Zones:** Established, mature, high-demand areas in Dubai with strong liquidity, stability, and prestige. See Chapter 3.
- **Corporate Tax:** A 9% tax on net profits exceeding AED 375,000 for businesses in the UAE, including SPVs used for investment. See Chapter 10.

D

- **D33 Economic Agenda:** Dubai's strategic plan to double its economy by 2033, targeting growth in key sectors like finance, trade, and tourism. See Chapter 3.
- **Developers:** Companies that build and sell real estate projects. They must be licensed by RERA. See Chapter 8, Chapter 9.
- **DIFC (Dubai International Financial Centre):** A key financial free zone and a hub for global finance, also home to a popular Wills Service Centre for non-Muslims. See Chapter 3, Chapter 10.
- **DLD (Dubai Land Department): T**he primary government authority overseeing all property transactions and a central source for official data. See Chapter 2.
- **DLD Project Tracker:** A DLD online tool for monitoring the construction progress of off-plan projects. See Chapter 9.
- **DOM (Days on Market):** A key indicator of market liquidity that measures how long a property has been listed for sale or rent. See Chapter 4, Chapter 7.
- **Dubai 2040 Urban Master Plan:** A two-decade strategy for urban development focused on livability, sustainability, and quality of life. See Chapter 3.
- **Dubai Internet City:** A free zone and technology hub that drives commercial and residential demand in surrounding areas. See Chapter 3.
- **Dubai Marina:** A core waterfront community known for its high-end apartments, strong rental demand, and vibrant lifestyle. See Chapter 3.
- **Dubai Metro:** The city's urban rail system, which consistently drives property value and rental premiums in adjacent communities. See Chapter 3.
- **Dubai South:** A future-facing zone surrounding Al Maktoum International Airport, positioned as a hub for logistics, aviation, and mid-tier residential growth. See Chapter 3.
- **Due diligence:** The meticulous process of verifying all aspects of a property and a transaction to mitigate risk and ensure a sound investment. See Chapter 7, Chapter 9.

E

- **Ejari:** The official digital system for registering tenancy contracts in Dubai, making them legally enforceable. See Chapter 13.
- **Emirates NBD:** A prominent UAE bank that offers both conventional and Islamic finance options, including for non-residents. See Chapter 8.
- **Emerging Zones:** Areas in active development with significant upside potential, often targeted by growth-focused investors. See Chapter 3.

- **Estate planning:** The process of arranging for the transfer of assets after death, which in Dubai requires a registered Will. See Chapter 10.
- **E.O.I. (Expression of Interest):** A non-binding deposit paid to a developer to secure early access to an off-plan project. See Chapter 8.
- **Escrow accounts:** DLD-monitored bank accounts where off-plan payments are held and released to the developer only upon verified construction milestones. See Chapter 9.
- **Eviction, legal grounds:** The specific, RERA-mandated reasons for which a landlord can legally ask a tenant to vacate a property. See Chapter 13.
- **Exit strategies:** The planned method for realizing a profit from an investment, including sale, refinance, or assignment. See Chapter 15.

F

- **Financing, mortgage:** The process of borrowing funds from a bank to purchase a property. See Chapter 8.
- **First-Time Buyer Program:** A DLD initiative offering incentives like fee waivers and tailored mortgage packages to eligible residents. See Chapter 8.
- **Flip strategy:** An investment approach focused on buying a property (often off-plan) and quickly reselling it for a profit. See Chapter 7, Chapter 15.
- **Forecasting, financial:** The use of models and data to project future returns, cash flows, and profitability. See Chapter 5.
- **Fractional ownership:** An investment model where multiple individuals co-own a single property, often facilitated by a digital platform. See Chapter 16.
- **Freehold ownership:** The permanent and complete ownership of a property and the land it sits on, with no time limit. See Chapter 6, Chapter 10.

G

- **Golden Visa:** A long-term residency visa for investors, entrepreneurs. and professionals in the UAE. See Chapter 2.
- **Governance, UAE:** The political structure of the United Arab Emirates, which combines a federal government with local autonomy for each emirate. See Chapter 2.
- **Gross Yield:** A quick measure of a property's income potential based on annual rent before deducting any expenses. See Chapter 5.

H

- **Hajra Jaafar:** The author of the bonus chapter on women in real estate, an expert investor and coach.
- **Handover:** The final physical and administrative process of taking possession of a property after purchase. See Chapter 11.

- **Hessa Street:** A major west-east corridor in Dubai that serves as a lifeline for many mid-market and suburban communities. See Chapter 7.
- **Hybrid strategy:** An investment approach that combines different models, such as holding for long-term rent and selling for capital appreciation. See Chapter 5, Chapter 15.

I

- **Index, RERA Rental:** An official reference tool for average rental prices in Dubai, used by landlords to set rent and justify increases. See Chapter 13.
- **Inflection indicators:** Data signals that hint at a transition in the market cycle, guiding strategic entry and exit timing. See Chapter 4.
- **Inheritance:** The process of transferring assets after death, which requires a registered Will for non-Muslims in Dubai. See Chapter 10.
- **Insurance, property:** A policy that protects a property against damage (building insurance) and a landlord against liability (landlord insurance). See Chapter 12.
- **IRR (Internal Rate of Return):** A time-sensitive financial metric that measures the annualized return of an investment with multiple cash flows over time. See Chapter 5, Chapter 7.
- **Islamic mortgages:** Sharia-compliant financing options that avoid interest-based loans. See Chapter 8.

J

- **JAFZA (Jebel Ali Free Zone):** A logistics and trade free zone that serves as a major driver of commercial and industrial real estate demand. See Chapter 3.
- **Jumeirah Village Circle (JVC):** A popular mid-market community in Dubai known for its affordability and rental yields. See Chapter 6.
- **Joint ownership:** A legal structure where two or more individuals hold title to the same property. See Chapter 10.

K

- **Keys, handover:** The final, symbolic act of gaining physical possession and control of a property. See Chapter 11.

L

- **L.E.A.D. mindset:** The advanced principles of an expert investor: Long Game, Embrace Calculated Risk, Adapt & Learn, Drive Value. See Chapter 1.
- **Lagging indicators:** Data signals that confirm a trend that has already passed, such as inventory accumulation or stagnant prices. See Chapter 4.
- **Land banking:** The long-term strategy of buying and holding undeveloped land with the expectation of future price appreciation. See Chapter 6.

- **Leasehold ownership:** A form of ownership that grants the right to use a property for a fixed period (e.g., 30-99 years), not in perpetuity. See Chapter 6, Chapter 10.
- **Legal structures:** The different ways a property can be legally held, such as individual ownership, joint ownership, or a corporate entity. See Chapter 10.
- **Liquidity:** The ease and speed with which an asset can be converted into cash. See Chapter 4, Chapter 6.
- **Location, research:** The process of evaluating a property's geographic position from both a macro (city-wide) and micro (community-specific) perspective. See Chapter 7.
- **LTV (Loan-to-Value):** The ratio of the loan amount to the property's appraised value, a key metric for mortgage eligibility. See Chapter 8.

M

- **Maintenance, property:** The ongoing upkeep and repair of a unit. Responsibilities are typically split between the owner and the tenant. See Chapter 12, Chapter 13.
- **Market cycles:** The recurring pattern of expansion and contraction that real estate markets follow over time. See Chapter 4.
- **Mollak:** The DLD-regulated system for Owners Association (OA) registration and service charge management. See Chapter 12.
- **Mortgage pre-approval:** A conditional commitment from a bank to lend a specific amount of money, which defines a buyer's budget. See Chapter 8.
- **Mortgage life insurance:** A mandatory policy for mortgaged properties that repays the loan in case of the borrower's death or disability. See Chapter 12.

N

- **Net Yield:** The actual return on a rental property after all operating expenses have been deducted. See Chapter 5.
- **NOC (No Objection Certificate):** A document from a master developer or Owners Association (OA) that confirms there are no outstanding dues and approves a sale. See Chapter 8.
- **Non-residents:** Individuals who do not hold a UAE residency visa. They can purchase property but may have different mortgage terms and LTVs. See Chapter 8.
- **NOI (Net Operating Income):** The income a property generates after all operating expenses, but before debt payments and taxes. See Chapter 5.

O

- **Off-plan property:** A property that is purchased before its construction is complete, directly from the developer. See Chapter 7, Chapter 8.
- **Oqood:** The official DLD certificate of ownership for off-plan properties before the final Title Deed is issued. See Chapter 8.
- **Ownership structures:** The different legal frameworks for holding property, including individual, joint, SPV, and trust. See Chapter 10.
- **Owners Association (OA):** A legal entity that manages the common areas and services of a jointly owned property or community. See Chapter 12.

P

- **Palm Jebel Ali:** An ambitious new coastal mega-project that will significantly expand Dubai's waterfront. See Chapter 3.
- **Palm Jumeirah:** An iconic, man-made island community known for ultra-luxury villas and high-end apartments. See Chapter 3.
- **Part 1:** The book section focused on Defining the Opportunity.
- **Part 2:** The book section focused on Executing the Opportunity.
- **Part 3:** The book section focused on Maximising Returns.
- **Part 4:** The book section focused on Advanced Strategies and Leadership.
- **Payment plans:** Staggered payment schedules offered by developers for off-plan properties, which can be construction-linked or date-based. See Chapter 8.
- **Penalties, rental:** Clauses in a tenancy contract that define fines for late payments, damages, or violations of community rules. See Chapter 13.
- **Peripheral Zones:** Areas on the urban edge with high-risk, long-horizon potential, dependent on future infrastructure and policy. See Chapter 3.
- **POA (Power of Attorney):** A legal document that authorises one person to act on behalf of another. See Chapter 10.
- **Pre-approval, mortgage:** See Mortgage pre-approval.
- **Pre-handover resale:** See Assignment sales.
- **Price per square foot:** A standard metric used to normalise and compare the value of properties of different sizes. See Chapter 5.

R

- **RAK (Ras Al Khaimah):** A neighboring emirate to Dubai, home to the upcoming Wynn Casino mega-project. See Chapter 3.
- **RERA (Real Estate Regulatory Agency):** The regulatory arm of the DLD, overseeing brokers, developers, and tenancy laws. See Chapter 2.

- **REITs (Real Estate Investment Trusts):** A company that owns and operates income-producing properties, allowing investors to buy shares and earn dividends without direct ownership. See Chapter 16.
- **Rental Index, RERA:** An official reference tool for average rental prices in Dubai, used by landlords to set rent and justify increases. See Chapter 13.
- **Rental income:** The money earned from leasing a property. In Dubai, personal rental income is not subject to income tax. See Chapter 5.
- **Research, due diligence:** See Due diligence.
- **ROI (Return on Investment):** A financial metric that measures the total profit relative to the total capital invested in a deal. See Chapter 5.

S

- **Safety:** A key value proposition of Dubai, encompassing personal, economic, and lifestyle safety. See Chapter 2.
- **Secondary market:** The market for properties that have already been built and handed over. See Chapter 7, Chapter 8.
- **Security deposit:** A refundable amount paid by a tenant to a landlord to cover potential damages or unpaid bills. See Chapter 13.
- **Sharia law:** A legal system based on Islamic principles. In the UAE, it can apply to inheritance for non-Muslims without a registered Will. See Chapter 10.
- **Short-term rentals:** An investment strategy where a property is leased for periods shorter than a year (e.g., as a holiday home). See Chapter 14.
- **SMART goals:** A framework for setting investment goals that are Specific, Measurable, Achievable, Relevant, and Time-Bound. See Chapter 1.
- **Snagging inspection:** The process of identifying defects or unfinished work in a property before handover. See Chapter 11.
- **SPA (Sales and Purchase Agreement):** The binding legal contract between a buyer and a developer for an off-plan property. See Chapter 8.
- **Special Power of Attorney (SPA):** A POA that grants specific, limited authority for a single task or transaction. See Chapter 10.
- **SPVs (Special Purpose Vehicles):** A corporate entity established solely for the purpose of holding assets, often used for asset protection and tax efficiency. See Chapter 10.
- **Strata properties:** The legal system of individual ownership within a jointly owned building, such as an apartment tower.
- **Sustainability:** A central theme in Dubai's urban planning, influencing property value and appeal through certifications and eco-friendly infrastructure. See Chapter 3.

T

- **Taxation, Dubai:** The tax environment in Dubai, which is favourable to investors with no property, capital gains, or personal income tax on rentals. See Chapter 10.
- **Tenancy contracts:** Legal agreements between a landlord and a tenant. They must be registered with Ejari to be enforceable. See Chapter 13.
- **Tenants, screening:** The methodical process of vetting potential tenants to ensure they are reliable and financially stable. See Chapter 13.
- **Time horizon:** The length of time an investor plans to hold a property, which is a key factor in strategic decision-making. See Chapter 1.
- **Title deed:** The official legal document from the DLD that proves full ownership of a property. See Chapter 8, Chapter 11.
- **Tokenisation:** The process of converting real estate ownership rights into digital tokens on a blockchain, enabling fractional ownership and increased liquidity. See Chapter 16.
- **Tourism Dirham Fee:** A per-night fee charged to guests staying in licensed holiday homes in Dubai. See Chapter 10, Chapter 14.
- **Trusts:** A legal arrangement where a trustee holds and manages assets for a beneficiary, often used for estate planning and asset protection. See Chapter 10.

U

- **Usufruct:** A legal right to use and benefit from a property for a fixed period without owning the land. See Chapter 6, Chapter 10.
- **Utilities, DEWA:** The official provider of electricity and water in Dubai. Setting up the account is a mandatory step after handover. See Chapter 11.

V

- **VAT (Value Added Tax):** A 5% tax in the UAE that applies to commercial property transactions and new residential properties. See Chapter 10.
- **Villas, luxury:** High-end residential properties that offer space, privacy, and long-term appreciation, often in master-planned communities. See Chapter 6.
- **Visas, Golden:** See Golden Visa.

W

- **Warehouses:** Commercial properties used for logistics, trade, and industrial purposes, which often offer high rental yields. See Chapter 6.
- **Wills:** Legal documents that specify how assets should be distributed after death. A UAE-registered Will is crucial for non-Muslims. See Chapter 10.
- **Wynn Casino:** A major tourism project in Ras Al Khaimah that will have a synergistic impact on Dubai's hospitality market. See Chapter 3.